Published 2007 by the Parish of St Mary and St Michael,
Commercial Road, London E1 0AA
in association with Terry Marsh Publishing

ISBN 978-0-9549999-2-6

British Library Cataloguing – in – production data
A catalogue record for this book is available from the British Library
Printed and bound in Britain by Biddles Ltd

A HISTORY
OF
ST MARY & ST MICHAEL'S
PARISH
Commercial Road
East London

Including the history of Virginia St Chapel
and the formation of
St Patrick's Parish, Wapping

FOREWORD

I send my warmest congratulations, prayers and good wishes to the Priests and People of the Parish of St. Mary and St. Michael as you celebrate together the 150th anniversary of the building of your church.

Such an historic occasion is, in the first place, a time when we give thanks for those who " ... have gone before us marked with the sign of faith". Their faith, vision and courage are the foundations on which this parish is built. The 150th anniversary also invites us to celebrate the life of the parish today, with the many challenges that face the Church in a society very different to that of previous generations. So we are invited to look to the future with *Gaudium et Spes* - the Joy and Hope spoken of by Vatican II. The mission of every parish is sustained by the gathering of people of all ages united in faith. Together they hear God's Word proclaimed in situations both old and new. They celebrate the sacraments which bring them into communion with God and with each other. This task has been fulfilled magnificently by the parish of St. Mary and St. Michael over many generations.

What better prayer can I offer for you on this anniversary than that of St. Paul to the Christian church at Colossus? So I ask" ... that you may be filled with the knowledge of his will in all spiritual wisdom and understanding, to lead a life worthy of the Lord, fully pleasing to him, bearing fruit in every good work and increasing in the knowledge of God". (Col: 1 :9-10). May God bless you all on this important occasion.

+Cormac Cardinal Murphy-O'Connor
Archbishop ofWestminster

Introduction

By Cornelius George Donovan
(known as Con Donovan)

Whilst attending the funeral of my father's youngest sister who had passed away at the age of 101, the last of that particular Donovan generation, sitting in the Roman Catholic Church of St. Mary & St. Michael it occurred to me just how much this church had contributed to a very large part of my life.

During the service my wife Kath turned to me and said that we really should come back here and renew our wedding vows to mark our forthcoming 50th wedding anniversary. This comment made me further reflect on just how much the Church in general, and this parish church in particular, had influenced my way of life. I had been brought up in a deeply religious Catholic household with strong Christian beliefs. The influence of our Parish Priest and the Catholic community formed a very, very large part of my upbringing. From my childhood at the Catholic schools and the after-school youth clubs, I have nothing but fond memories. I remember as a boy racing home from school because I couldn't get to the youth clubs quickly enough. We had terrific schoolteachers, nuns and youth club leaders alike and I am sure their influence has contributed in many ways to the business success that I have since enjoyed.

I met Kathleen Marriott at a Catholic dance and two years later we got married. I wasn't the only one of my friends who met and married a girl from the congregation. When Kath and I got married, we moved out of the parish, but coming back after all those many years had great poignancy for both of us.

After my aunt's funeral I met Father Jim Mulligan, St Mary and St Michael's current Parish Priest, and some time later, after the ceremony to renew our wedding vows, I invited him along to a family celebration lunch. I found Father Jim an affable man with a strong interest in sport and we recounted many highs and lows in the careers of East End sporting heroes. At the end of the lunch I asked Father Jim if there was anything I could do to help the parish. He said he'd been looking for financial sponsorship for a book on the history of St Mary and St Michael's parish. I offered my assistance and suggested that a longtime family friend, Stepney-born Terry Marsh, the former undefeated world light-welterweight boxing champion, who had a publishing company and who'd recently had an autobiography published, might help. Shortly after this myself, Father Jim and Terry got together in the boardroom of my company. I would look after the financial side, Fr Jim would take responsibility for the production and editing and Terry would take care of typesetting, layout and design. The project was born.

It's now 150 years since the construction of the Church of St Mary and St Michael – the 'Cathedral of the East End'. It gives me enormous pride to be in a position to sponsor this book and help commemorate this wonderful anniversary.

Con Donovan
December 2007

Special thanks to…

This is in effect Jean Maynard's book. Jean has been indefatigeable in her researches and has accumulated a priceless treasure trove of local and national history – particularly ecclesiastical history.

There many others to thank – Con Donovan for his magnificent generosity in sponsoring the book, Terry Marsh, the Sisters of Mercy, the parish 150th Anniversary Commemorations Planning Committee and all who have shown such enthusiasm that this valuable Church and London East End history should be committed to record.

Fr Jim Mulligan
December 2007

SS. MARY AND MICHAEL'S CHURCH.
8th. DECEMBER 1856

St Dunstan's Stepney

During the Middle Ages almost all Tower Hamlets was served by one parish church, St Dunstan's. Two chapels of ease were opened in the fourteenth century: St Mary's Bow, and another St Mary's near the City which gave its name to the surrounding village – Whitechapel. The Tower Hamlets still *were* hamlets, dotted in between farmers' fields and pastures, extensive marshy areas, and common land. Mile End Green, which stretched from Whitechapel to Mile End, and from Stepney High Street all the way to the village of Bethnal Green, was used for sports and leisure activities, and also for military exercises: it provided a very convenient drill ground for London's citizens' militia or Trained Bands. Wealthy and important people built houses along the borders of Mile End Green. Sir Henry Colet, head of the Mercers' Company which was (and still is) the most prestigious of the London trade guilds, lived just west of St Dunstan's. He was Lord Mayor of London in 1486 and 1495, and owned considerable property around Stepney.

A number of the Rectors of St Dunstan's were distinguished men: John Colet, son of the aforementioned Henry, was an internationally famous scholar, and later became Dean of St Paul's. His friend Thomas More wrote to him extolling the rural delights of Stepney, to try to persuade him to spend more time in his parish, instead of paying a substitute or "vicar" to do the work. As the only surviving child of a family of 22, Dean John inherited all his father's property in Stepney. In his will he bequeathed it for the support of St Paul's School, and entrusted it to the care of the Mercer's Company.

John Colet, Rector of St Dunstan's Stepney, became Dean of St Paul's

Because it was not held by a religious body, this estate escaped the confiscation which befell so many other charitable trusts at the Reformation. Colet had not lived to face the issues raised by Henry VIII's decision to break with the Pope in order to marry Anne Boleyn, but Thomas More was imprisoned in the Tower of London for refusing to agree that the King could be Head of the Church. During a visit from his daughter Margaret, in May 1535, More watched from his cell window as three distinguished Carthusian priors were led out, to be executed at Tyburn (Marble Arch) for a similar refusal, and said, "Lo, does thou not see, Meg, that these blessed fathers be now as cheerfully going to their deaths as bridegrooms to their marriage?" Another fellow-prisoner, the Bishop of Rochester John Fisher, was beheaded on Tower Hill in June, and More's own turn came in July. Less than a year later Anne Boleyn herself was discarded and sent to the block, but still nobody was allowed to question the King's right to decree what we should believe about God. No actual evidence was required for someone to be found guilty of treason: it could be done by Act of Attainder, whereby Parliament simply passed a law declaring that the charges were true. This was the procedure adopted in the case of two intransigently Catholic noblemen imprisoned in the Tower in 1539: they were beheaded on Tower Hill on 9th July that year. Adrian Fortescue happened to be Anne Boleyn's cousin. Both he and Thomas Dingley were Knights of Malta, and the Order has always regarded them as martyrs. Cardinal Pole, who had infuriated Henry by writing a book in defence of the Unity of the Catholic Church, was living safely overseas in Rome, but Henry got his revenge by seizing his mother Margaret Pole, Countess of Salisbury: she was beheaded inside the Tower in May 1541.

Cardinal Pole

Under Elizabeth I a number of priests and lay Catholics were brought to the Tower to be tortured, to try to make them confess to imaginary plots against the state – though their executions usually took place elsewhere, most often at Tyburn. Later it was made a High Treason for a Catholic priest simply to be present in England, while to help a priest, or be reconciled (converted) to Catholicism, also carried the death penalty. When England was threatened by the Spanish Armada in 1588, Tower Hamlets erupted with patriotic fervour. The Trained Bands staged a pageant on Mile End Green to raise morale: a fort was erected, and a mock battle staged in which the "Spaniards" were crushingly defeated.

Once the real danger was past, the government took a decision to stage a series of much grimmer propaganda exercises: public executions of Catholics. None of the victims had had anything to do with the attempted invasion, but the carrying out of the death sentences at that point in time would link them with it in people's minds, and convey the implication that all who shared their faith were dangerous fifth columnists. In the first show trial, held on 26th August, six priests and eight laypeople were condemned to death.

Stepney Martyrs

Henry Webley, a layman from Gloucester, was arrested in 1586 on board a ship in Chichester harbour, and despatched to London where he spent the next two years imprisoned in the Marshalsea. Fr William Dean, from Linton in Craven, Yorkshire, had been captured twice before in London and banished, then arrested again in March 1588. The case against Fr Dean and his fellow clergy was clearcut: they had trained for the priesthood across the Channel, been ordained and entered England illegally, and were sentenced to the penalty for treason which was to be hanged, drawn and quartered – though "by the Queen's mercy" the more gruesome elements (being disembowelled while still alive) were to be remitted on this occasion. Henry Webley was found guilty of giving assistance to Fr Dean. He was offered a pardon on the usual condition that he would conform to the Church of England, but refused. On 28th August Dean and Webley, together with a second priest named William Gunter, were brought to Mile End in a cart. Fr Dean "was beginning to speak of the cause for which he and his companions were condemned to die, but his mouth was stopped by some that were in the cart, in such a violent manner, that they were like to have prevented the hangman of his wages." Once Dean and Webley were dead, Fr Gunter was taken on to Shoreditch, and hanged there. Afterwards a guard was set on all the scaffolds to ensure against people taking relics of the martyrs. Other executions went ahead at Tyburn, and various sites in and around London.

A second wave of executions began a month later. Fr John Hewett, from York, had like Fr Dean been arrested twice before and banished. On being banished the second time he had crossed over to the Netherlands, been re-arrested *there* by the Earl of Leicester, and sent *back* to England as a prisoner charged with plotting to murder the Earl. After the Earl's death he was put on trial for illegal entry into England as a priest ordained overseas! That was blatantly unfair, and he said so, but was found guilty anyway and sentenced to be hanged, drawn and quartered. On 5th October he was brought to Mile End Green, and then left standing there in the cart, while someone sped back to enquire whether the full process of quartering was actually to be carried out in his case. The Queen replied that simple hanging would do. Meanwhile, Hewett passed the time arguing with the Protestant ministers who were urging him to recant – and thereby acknowledge that he really had committed an offence against the state. According to the Catholic account, he held his own very well. On being told, when the messenger at last returned, that the Queen had given leave for him to be spared the quartering, he commented, "the less is my merit." To the Protestant ministers, who were still hoping for a last-minute conversion, he declared: "I have done nothing but as a Roman Catholic priest ought to do by the direction of our most Holy Father the Pope, being head of the church … and in this Roman Catholic religion I will die and willingly shed my blood."

The Stepney Martyrs plaque in St Mary and St Michael's Church

The Stepney Martyrs Chapel in St Mary and St Michael's church.

Philip Howard, Earl of Arundel, was a prisoner in the Tower at the time of the Armada, but he was tried and condemned to death for allegedly praying for its success: Elizabeth could not bring herself to sign his death warrant, but he died in the Tower, forbidden even to see his beloved wife and children because of his refusal to attend Anglican services. After the discovery of the Gunpowder Plot on 5th November 1605, four Jesuits were arrested and accused of complicity with Guy Fawkes: one of them, the lay brother Nicholas Owen, was savagely tortured in the Tower to make him reveal the secrets of the ingenious hiding places he'd built in Catholic houses across the country, but he would not speak, and died under torture. The last of the English Martyrs was William Howard, grandson of Philip Howard: one of a large number of people falsely condemned of plotting against Charles II, on the evidence of the unsavoury Titus Oates, he was beheaded on Tower Hill in December 1680. After the accession of William of Orange, Protestant Nonconformist groups such as the Congregationalist Stepney Meeting (formed in 1644) were permitted to worship legally, but the laws against Catholics remained on the statute books. The death penalty as

Philip Howard
Earl of Arundel

such was never again invoked, but under a new statute a convicted priest was to be imprisoned for life (which, given the state of the gaols, was equivalent to a death sentence), with £100 reward to the informer.

Virginia Street Chapel

A significant proportion of the immigrant textile workers who settled in and around Spitalfields during the seventeenth century were from Ireland, or from Catholic areas in continental Europe, and Irish migrants were also being drawn into the riverside hamlets by the job opportunities along the waterfront. Their presence was flagged up from time to time because of the government's continuing interest in harassing recusants, ie religious believers, especially Catholics, who refused on conscientious grounds to attend Anglican services as required by law.

Richard Challoner

During the eighteenth century more and more Irish Catholics came to live in Tower Hamlets. By 1758, when the saintly Richard Challoner became Vicar Apostolic of the London District (which covered the whole of South East England), governmental and social attitudes were growing more tolerant. Nevertheless the Penal Laws remained on the statute books, and it wasn't easy for Catholics to practise their faith. Those in London could worship legally in the chapels attached to the embassies of certain Catholic countries, or – provided they knew the ropes – illegally, in a handful of scattered clandestine chapels and Mass centres. "W.Y.", writing in 1823, recorded some of the stories handed down within the Catholic community about the situation in Tower Hamlets in Challoner's time:

the Catholics of the neighbourhood were accustomed to assemble on Sundays and holidays, at a house in Branch-place, Cable-street; and obtained admittance by producing tickets, which were occasionally changed to prevent the intrusion of spies. Here the divine mysteries were offered up, and in this house the holy sacraments were administered to the faithful. A public house, the Windmill, in Rosemary-lane, was also converted into a house of prayer, and here Catholics met and assisted at the holy sacrifice of the mass, unsuspected by the pursuivant or by the informer. We now come to the Catholic chapel in Virginia Street. Strange as it may appear, this chapel owes its origin in great measure to the project of a Portuguese Jew, named Emanuel; this man represented himself to doctor Challoner, and to the embassador from the court of Portugal, as a Catholic priest, and by means of papers which he had surreptitiously obtained, passed for a considerable time unsuspected; through his exertions the chapel was erected and placed under the protection of the king of Portugal, whose arms were fixed over the principal entrance, and it assumed the name of the Portuguese hospital. Emanuel was afterwards discovered to be an impostor, he was consequently driven from the chapel, and some years afterwards died in the poor-house of Whitechapel, in a state of wretchedness and abject poverty.

The story about Emanuel sounds far-fetched, and another theory has it that the chapel was started as part of a hospital for Catholic sailors. Its date of origin is not precisely known: Johanna Harting, in her book about London's oldest Catholic missions, gave the date as 1762 but didn't explain her reasons. However the first priest was appointed by Challoner, and he was Fr James Webb.

Today, Virginia Street is just a very short turning off the south side of the Highway, but originally it ran north-south all the way to Wapping High Street. The side of the chapel ran along Virginia Street, but the entrance was at the end nearest the river, in King's Head Alley from which led off a warren of tiny courts – a useful route to take if you wanted to shake off a pursuer. A doorkeeper scrutinised everyone who came in, and when everyone was inside the door was locked. Another man kept watch in the street outside, and after a few moments rapped on the door to indicate that there were no suspicious characters hanging around, so Mass could begin.

Fr Webb on trial

Anti-Catholic feeling was stirred up from time to time for all sorts of reasons, and died down as soon as the public found something more important to worry about. But during one such agitation in 1765, a handful of low-lifes latched on to the money to be made out of convicting Catholic priests under King William's law. William Payne, nicknamed the "Protestant Carpenter", unleashed a reign of terror. All over London clandestine chapels were raided and shut down, and a large number of priests were arrested, though most of them got off. The recommended strategy was for the priest to refuse to make a statement, and so throw the onus of proof on the prosecution: even if everyone knew perfectly well that he was a priest, it wasn't easy to prove it in court. But Fr John Baptist Maloney, who admitted his priesthood in writing; was found guilty and sentenced to life: the sentence was mandatory so that the judge had no choice in the matter, and the Sheriff of Surrey, as required by law, handed over £100 reward to Payne. Subsequently Payne engineered the arrest of James Webb, and the Virginia Street priest spent seventeen months in Newgate.

Meanwhile the newspapers carried on whipping up public hysteria, and calling for something to be done about the threat to national security posed by the growing numbers of Catholics. Eventually the Anglican bishops, who knew very well that there'd been no dramatic increase in Catholic numbers, decided to conduct a survey so as to prove it, and shut up the troublemakers: letters went out during the summer of 1767 to their clergy throughout the country, asking them to count the number of "Papists or reputed Papists" in their parish. They were *not* asked to give names, but only to provide breakdowns by gender, age and occupation, and give a rough idea how long the people had been resident in the parish. Catholics apparently made no difficulties about co-operating with the survey, and the returns are considered to be fairly accurate.

426 were counted in Wapping, 381 in St George's in the East, and 326 in St Paul's Shadwell. The Rector of St Dunstan's listed only 82 for Stepney, but said there were 80 others "who refuse to give an account of themselves". The vast majority of the men were put down simply as labourers, while most of the women were lumped in with them as "wives", or said to be scratching a living at trades like oyster-selling. Only a small number were described as sailors; sailmakers; or specialist dock workers such as coal heavers, lightermen or lumpers. St Mary's, Whitechapel, which counted 60 Catholics overall, had a few "sugarhouse men" and weavers, and 14 of the Stepney Catholics were weavers, but the majority of East London's Catholic weavers naturally lived in Spitalfields or Shoreditch. St George's seems to have had the largest number of well-settled married Catholic couples, drawing a living from a small business or skilled trade – also an elderly schoolmaster and his wife, though it was illegal for Catholics to teach schools. Shopkeeper households usually dealt in food, or else were chandlers – which meant they sold a bit of everything: these were low-capital, rapid-turnover enterprises. Wapping's 18 Catholic bakers, all unmarried, will have been live-in journeymen. Women on their own typically worked as washerwomen, mantua makers or milliners; one was a midwife. Only 29 Catholics were listed for Limehouse, and 33 for Poplar and Blackwall – among them a very old man reputed to be a priest. Some people were known to have lived in East London for 30-40 years, others to have moved in only a few weeks previously. But apart from a handful of children, none of them were locally born.

Fr Webb was brought to trial on Saturday morning 25th June 1768, at the Court of King's Bench Westminster, before William Lord Mansfield. Various witnesses were called, including the chapel doorkeeper from Virginia Street, who determinedly avoided giving any information the prosecution could make use of. W. Y. describes him as "a tall formal figure; a man peculiarly neat and clean in his dress and person: his appearance attracted the attention of the learned judge, who enquired of him his name; *Tyte, my Lord,* was the answer: *An appropriate name,* rejoined his Lordship, *for a very tight man you are.* This incident the old man related to me himself many years after, with a great deal of glee." Mansfield's handling of the case was unashamedly biased, as he was determined to get Fr Webb acquitted. He highlighted the point that Payne was only in it for the money, rubbished his evidence, and instructed the jury not to bring in a guilty verdict if they had the slightest doubt. Webb walked free – one of the last ever to be imprisoned in England for his priesthood. Fr Maloney remained in prison for several years, but his sentence was then quietly commuted to banishment, and he was allowed to emigrate to America.

Lord William Mansfield

In 1773 an 84-year lease was taken out on the Virginia Street chapel in the name of "James Talbot, Esq., gentleman" (Challoner's coadjutor bishop), the document implying that the building was already in use as a chapel. £46 10s a year in rent had to be paid to the Wakerbarth family, which owned the freehold, for the chapel and the adjoining house where the priests lived. Baptismal and marriage registers began to be kept from 1773, after Fr Michael Coen had replaced Webb as priest in charge.

The Gordon Riots

In a first, fairly modest, effort to dismantle the Penal Laws, the government passed a Catholic Relief Act in 1778. Only after it had received the Royal Assent did the Protestant Association, headed by Lord George Gordon, begin to orchestrate popular feeling against it. On Friday 2nd June 1780 a crowd marching to Westminster, to present a petition demanding repeal of the Relief Act, got out of hand and attacked the Archbishop of York, Lord Mansfield and other pro-tolerance Members of Parliament. The chapels belonging to the Bavarian and Sardinian Embassies were burned down, and Bp Challoner, at nearly 90 years old, had to go into hiding. On Sunday the mob gathered in Moorfields, where they burned the Catholic chapels, and looted and destroyed a great many private Catholic dwellings. On Monday, while the rioting continued in Moorfields, another body of rioters headed farther east.

The Irishmen of Wapping had already spoken with their priest about the situation, offering to defend the chapel, and Fr Coen had gone in the morning to see the Home Secretary, and propose that the offer be accepted. He could assemble 3,000 men. However the Minister discouraged the idea, promising that troops would be sent to Virginia Street, and asked that the priests use their influence to prevent the Irish from fighting the rioters. Coen and his two assistants, Frs Thomas Walsh and Michael Copps, spent the next few hours going round the streets, visiting every pub known to have an Irish clientele, and persuading their people to go home and stay there quietly. A military detachment duly arrived to stand guard, but the mob entered the street from the other end, and the first the soldiers knew about it was seeing the furniture come flying out of the windows of the priests' house. Even then, they took no action because they had no orders to do so, and just stood there while the rioters took the chapel apart. Nevertheless the Irish obeyed their pastors, and did not come out to fight. Fr Copps had remained at the chapel until the last minute, and he had to run for it: he escaped by jumping over a wide ditch, whereupon the mob ceased pursuing him.

On Tuesday the violence turned against the authorities: the prisoners in Newgate were released and the prison destroyed, and the houses of many eminent Protestants burned down, including that of Lord Mansfield. King George III insisted on action, and by Thursday things were quieting down, with large numbers of rioters under arrest. The Protestant Association began desperately trying to disassociate itself from the riots, and even had the cheek to accuse the Catholics of burning down their own chapels. Trials of those rank and file rioters unlucky enough to be caught were conducted with amazing promptness, and 68 death sentences handed down, but no one believed that the real ring leaders had been picked up.

Lord Gordon was put on trial before Lord Mansfield, but found Not Guilty: however much he might be thought morally responsible for the violence, he had not incited it and done his best to discourage it. He was later convicted for libelling Queen Marie Antoinette, converted to Judaism while in prison, and died of gaol fever in 1793. According to W. Y. one of the Wapping rioters, who had fractured his leg demolishing the gallery of the Virginia Street chapel,

was not prosecuted, but became a cripple, and lived during many years an object of commiseration and compassion to those very persons, whose destruction he had aimed at, who practising the divine precept, forgave their enemies, and returned good from evil.

Gordon Riots from the painting by Seymour Lucas, R.A.

The Chapel Rebuilt

Government compensation was paid for the destruction not only of the private property which had been destroyed, but also for the places of worship – even though their legal status was still doubtful, at best. The compensation wasn't sufficient to defray the full cost of reconstruction, but the Catholics knew it would be unwise to draw attention to themselves by complaining. The work of putting the chapels back into commission went ahead while Bp Talbot, who became Vicar Apostolic on Challoner's death, sent an appeal to Spain for additional financial assistance. London at that time had just seven permanent public Mass centres: four embassy chapels of Catholic countries, which enjoyed diplomatic immunity and were funded by their ambassadors, and three other chapels in Moorfields, Bermondsey and Wapping, for which the Vicar Apostolic was responsible. The money from Spain took a few years to be got together and sent, so Talbot wrote again confirming that it was still needed. He added that once the building expenses had been settled:

> *we shall still require money for the support of the priests, and there are many things that must be supplied for the chapels which require the collection of large alms annually from the rich residents. But one of these chapels, which is situated in the sailors'*

part of the city, and is frequented by sailors from every nation, has hardly any, I will not say rich, but even people who are able to give anything except from their necessaries. I mention this, so that if any further alms could be obtained, they should be.

Bishop John Douglass

Bp Talbot died in 1790 and John Douglass was appointed to the London District. On 24th June 1791, thanks to the second Catholic Relief Act, it became legal once again to celebrate Mass in England provided the chapel and the priest were registered, and a month later Fr Coen completed the necessary formalities:

These are to certify that there is a Roman Catholic chapel dedicated to Sts Mary and Michael situate in Kings Head Alley Virginia Street in the Parish of St John Wapping County of Middlesex and I do hereby require you to record the same at the present Quarter Sessions for the said County of Middlesex agreeable to the Act of Parliament made and passed in the 31st year of the Reign of his present Majesty King George the 3rd entitled an Act to Relieve upon condition and 'under restrictions' the persons therein described "from certain penalties and disabilities to which 'papists or persons professing the popish religion are by law subject'. Witness my hand this 22nd day of July 1791. Michael Edward Coen Clerk. To H Selby Esq Clerk of the Peace for the County of Middlesex.

Poor and unpretending

For fear of the Penal Laws, most of the assets of the Vicars Apostolic had been held in France, and the Catholic Church in England was left poorer than ever when they all vanished in the French Revolution. None of the Catholic chapels, school-chapels and Mass centres in England counted as parishes under Canon Law: they were usually referred to as missions, and they led a precarious existence. No illustrations or detailed descriptions of the Virginia Street chapel have been handed down, beyond the comment that it was "poor and unpretending" – and this must refer to *after* the turn of the century, when it was rebuilt larger than before, and with a larger gallery. In its final form it was oblong, roughly 100 ft x 50 ft, with a semicircular apse at the end opposite the main door, and additional doors on either side.

The chapel's financial and practical affairs were managed by a lay committee, drawn from the elite of the congregation who were its main financial backers. It was not the custom to take up collections during or after a service, unless it was a special appeal service, and had been announced as such beforehand. Instead, worshippers paid an entrance tariff – the amount depending on the type of service, and where they wanted to sit. The best seats were in the tribune, beside the altar, and the next best in front of the altar, separated by a barrier from the space behind, and known as the enclosure. The less opulent, and the servants of the rich, went up into the galleries and sat on plain benches without backs. The space behind the enclosure, known as the body of the church, was for the poor. It might or might not have seats, but even if you had to stand throughout Mass, you still had to pay to come in – though you'd probably only be charged 1d or 2d. The entrance tariff was a very important part of each chapel's finances.

It was only natural in a port area that many of the people who came to the chapel for baptisms or weddings were only passing through London. On 18th April 1800 Fr Coen solemnised a marriage between James Wiseman, scion of an Irish merchant family normally resident in Spain, and Xaviera Strange from Co Kilkenny. The couple remained in England for another year, during which a son was born to them, but their second son, Nicholas, was born in Seville in 1802. Two years later James died suddenly, the widowed Xaviera returned to Ireland with her children, and a large part of Nicholas' childhood was spent in boarding school at Ushaw. He later became Rector of the English College in Rome.

Pastoral responsibility for Spitalfields and Mile End lay with St Mary Moorfields, while Bow was served by a chapel which had been operating in Stratford since 1789. The three priests at Virginia Street – Frs Coen, James Delaney and John Serjeant – looked after the whole area south of the Whitechapel-Mile End-Bow Road, and also the south-east part of the City. By 1805 the total Catholic population of the riverside districts was already being estimated at 7-8,000, and London's port and ship-handling functions, which had always been important, and generated so many employment opportunities, were in the process of being vastly expanded by the excavation of the docks.

Trouble broke out at Virginia Street when the priests tried to bring in liturgical changes: they wanted organ music, and High Mass, but the lay

Committee wouldn't agree. Bp Douglass recorded in his diary in August 1808:

Much disturbance at Virginia street chapel between the Committee & chaplains of the said chapel, concerning the repairs, alterations of the chapel, & the music introduced into the choir. The same being inflamed, & at last breaking into an absolute fall out, chaplains against the Committee, I assisted at the Committee held on the 25th Inst, & reconciled both Parties. Those, who had used intemperate language at former meetings, arose, & begged pardon publicly for the same and for the offence they had given &c &c. Peace and harmony were restored. May discord never more enter among them!

Shortly after this incident:

Mr Berger, a German having acquired a large fortune by success in business, made a present of more than twelve hundred pounds to Virginia street in gratitude to Alm. God for granting to him that success, & by this money the alterations in the chapel were made, & an Organ & High Mass &c were introduced.

Mass was never celebrated after midday, but most chapels had an afternoon service – usually a catechetical instruction, with Sung Vespers. It became fashionable at some of the central London chapels with well-to-do congregations, like St Mary Moorfields, to hold a weeknight service in Lent: Compline, with a sermon and Benediction, and early in 1809 some of the St Mary and St Michael's people, without a word to the clergy team, signed a petition to Bp Douglass asking that a similar service be introduced at Virginia Street. He was naturally delighted, and instructed Fr Coen to comply. Quite upset, the three priests sat down and composed a joint letter, arguing that it would mean pointless extra work for the priests, because only a handful would turn up, and the people who'd promoted the petition certainly had no intention of coming. Hardly anyone bothered to come to the existing Sunday afternoon service except the schoolchildren, for whom it was compulsory, and a few other children. Given that St Mary and St Michael's was "the most numerous and most widely extended of all the congregations in this Metropolis", they really didn't have the time – especially as they'd have to write a sermon specially.

Catholics in East London were overwhelmingly of Irish extraction, but other nationalities were represented – especially Germans. In 1808 a Swiss priest, John Becker, was appointed as a German chaplain attached to Virginia Street, and in the following year it was arranged for the Germans to have a chapel of their own, St Boniface's, located in the City. Irish numbers continued to grow steadily, boosted from the 1820s onwards by the introduction of cheap steamer passages across the Irish Sea.

Origins of the Wapping Catholic Schools

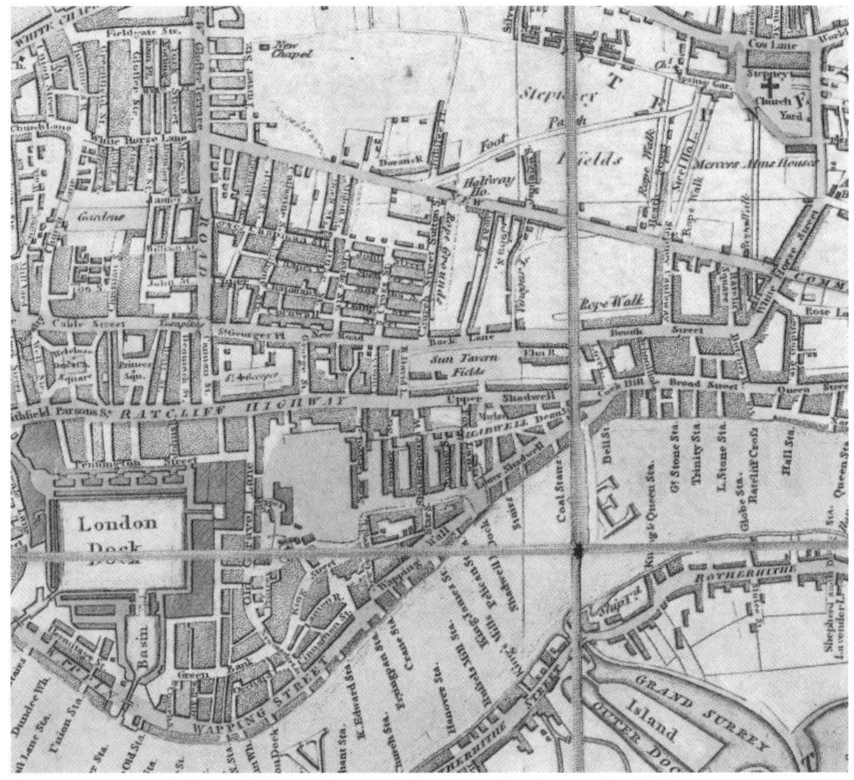

Map of Wapping and Stepney in the early 1800s

A little group of Catholic tradesmen used to meet after work in a public house near Bunhill Road, where they prayed together the Office of the Dead, took up a collection and discussed plans for charitable projects, and then "forgot the labours of the day in a pint of porter and a pipe". One of them was Peter Lyons, a screwmaker who became the "father" (senior member) of the Blacksmiths' Company. Though he lived in Tooley Street, Bermondsey, he was a member of the Virginia Street Chapel Committee, and in 1778 he helped start a school in Wapping "in which about thirty poor Irish boys might be educated." When he died in 1789, he bequeathed £1,000 in 3% stock towards the support of the Wapping Charity School. It was managed by a committee made up of anyone able and willing to donate money, and generally take an interest. Student numbers were at first necessarily small: the schoolmaster was in charge of an all-age class in which he was expected to tutor each child individually, while the rest got on with work he'd set them. But from the early years of the nineteenth century, charity schools across the country adopted the monitorial method, whereby older children taught the younger ones: in this way a single teacher could educate a hundred or more children. From 1808, therefore, the school committee was keen to expand, and take advantage of the economies of scale offered by the monitorial method. The existing building wasn't big enough, so one of the committee members, Mr Nowlan, erected a structure 32 ft long in a yard in Dock Street which belonged to his father, and the school rented it for the next five years at £25 a year.

The McCarthy brothers, who were coal importers with business premises in Wellclose Square, were members of the school committee, and generous benefactors: Daniel McCarthy gave £100 in 3% bonds to the school in 1808. A £50 legacy from Mrs Brown, already invested in 4% stock, was sold and reinvested at 3% – a thoroughly sensible decision, because 3% stock was safer.

A major financial burden on underfunded schools was the time-honoured practice of providing free clothes for the children – partly as an inducement to get them to classes, and also because they were ashamed to attend without something decent to wear. Each boy was supposed to be provided with velveteen trousers, a shirt and cloth jacket, a pair of shoes and stockings, and a cap: the colour was decreed to be grey, and the cost of the ensemble in 1814 came to £1 8s per boy. Mr O'Leary, another committee member, undertook to provide the clothes himself – though one wonders how long he could keep that up for, especially as the numbers increased. In 1813 the school moved again when the committee signed a seven-year lease on a house in Chapman Street belonging to the treasurer, Edward Ryan, for which they paid £30 a year.

The East London Catholic Institution

Fr Coen died in 1810, and was buried on 20th October in the churchyard of St George's in the East. Catholics still had no burial grounds of their own in the London area, so had to use Anglican churchyards: the Anglican burial service was conducted at the graveside, and Catholic prayers were usually not allowed. Fr Delaney started a girls' school, either before or just after he succeeded as senior chaplain on Fr Coen's death. (The eldest priest in a mission, or the one who'd been there longest, ranked as senior chaplain and might be paid a little extra, but he didn't exercise much authority over the other priests, who were very free to do their own thing.) Though founded with help from the boys' school subscribers, the girls' school occupied rented premises on a different site, and a separate ladies' committee was established to run it. Space at the Chapman Street premises was still quite limited, so the committee in 1814 resolved to maintain the roll at a maximum of 55, but demand was growing and the limit was quickly exceeded. The boys' school was reckoned capable of holding 80, and the girls' school 36 – but only at a very tight squeeze. The teachers' salaries were very low even by the standards of the time, so it's not surprising the committee had staffing problems, and quite rapid turnover. The schoolmistress was paid half as much as the boys' master.

Bishop William Poynter

In 1815 Fr Delaney went off to try his vocation as a Trappist (it didn't work out), Fr Serjeant returned to his native Lancashire for health reasons, and Fr Thomas Dobson was left all alone. William Poynter, Douglass' successor as Vicar Apostolic, puzzled over how to fill the gaps given his very limited number of priests, but on 15th July wrote to Fr Richard Horrabin, another Lancashire man. Horrabin moved in to Virginia Street on 21st July. In November the chapel's account books were handed over to Fr Dobson by Mr Marlow Sidney, a paint dealer who lived at Star and Garter Yard, Ratcliffe Highway (the Highway), and was a prominent lay leader in the local Catholic community. The third priest on the team, recently-ordained John Rolfe, didn't stay long, because Poynter needed him to teach at the seminary. When he was moved in January 1816 the congregation got up a petition, and a 50-strong delegation, to the Vicar Apostolic to get him back. Poynter stood firm, but did his best to help them understand how crucial it was to build up the seminary, in order to resolve the priest shortage.

From the time of Fr Horrabin's arrival a whole lot of new things started to happen. Most importantly for the future of St Mary and St Michael's, the idea came up of constructing a much larger building. By tradition the coalwhippers' work assignments were organised, and their wages paid over, in public houses. For this reason it was the custom to hold meetings on Sundays in the pubs, in order to take up collections for the upkeep of the chapel and maintenance of the clergy. During one of these meetings, on 7th December 1815, the first collection was taken up towards the costs of a new church. From then on the pub meetings regularly included donations for the building fund, though the money took a *very* long time to accumulate.

Fr Horrabin was cautiously supportive of plans to set up a British Union School in Shadwell, to educate Catholic and Protestant children together, with funding mainly from wealthy Protestants. Fr Dobson, too, immediately expressed interest by sending a donation, but Bp Poynter was chary of the scheme, since it would involve joint reading of the Bible. It had to, because the Bible was always read in schools, and was often the only textbook available. There were always strong objections to Catholic children being made to read from the King James I version, especially without appropriate explanations. A possible solution, which had proved workable in Ireland, was for Catholics and Protestants to agree on certain portions of scripture, which were sufficiently uncontentious, to be used in the school. However around that time a number of schools were being set up in various parts of London, specifically for Catholic or Jewish children, which turned out to be fronts for proselytisation. Was this British Union initiative in good faith?

Called in 1816 before a Select Committee appointed by Parliament "to inquire into the education of the lower orders in the metropolis" Fr Horrabin explained that a committee had been set up to agree on scripture portions, and various other issues. He reckoned there were up to a thousand Catholic children in his district not going to school at all, and the Catholic schools could take a hundred at most. After a lot of hard work, taking and analysing everyone's evidence, the Select Committee presented a report recommending state support for education, but nothing was actually done for many more years. Meanwhile discussions with the British Union people progressed well, and the Virginia Street clergy happily recommended their school to local Catholic parents. No proselytising agenda emerged, requests from priests for Catholic children to be sent for catechism classes were always respected, and they were always marched to Mass on holy days of obligation. (For many of them, it was the first time they'd ever been to Mass.)

Nevertheless Fr Horrabin, like other Catholic leaders, regarded these undenominational schools as a temporary stopgap: it would be far, far better to educate Catholic children in a fully Catholic ambience. To do this, the

Catholic school system would need to be greatly expanded, and accordingly he launched a colourful fundraising appeal, aimed at the better-off among the general public, and playing shamelessly on their fears of hooliganism:

In a quarter of the town where youthful depravity lamentably prevails, a very great proportion of the children are unavoidably left to receive their first impressions from street companions, who are often both wicked themselves, and artful in perverting others. Owing to this the bands of infant depredators on the public have alarmingly encreased; and it is undoubted that many youthful criminals have pined in a prison, or perished on the scaffold, who by a good education might have been made pious Christians and respectable members of society. It must be acknowledged too that many of the parents contribute to the ruin of their children, by exhibiting before them lives of the lowest depravity.

This first argument could work as well with Protestants as with Catholics (and it did), but a second argument was directed specifically at his co-religionists. Deliberately, Fr Horrabin said nothing about the amicable arrangement with the managers of the British Union School. Instead:

the pious Catholic ought to be informed that in the Eastern division of London there are numerous Protestant and dissenting schools, which hold out to Catholic parents the lure of education and clothing for their children, if they will give them to be educated in sectarian principles, and attend sectarian places of worship.

To widen the schools' regular supporter base, a new-style fundraising body was launched: the East London Catholic Institution. Like similar charitable bodies in other parts of the city, it set out to attract subscriptions and donations by holding grand annual dinners, with big name guests, speeches about how much sweetness and light the schools were spreading in the slums, and at a certain point the children (newly clothed and scrupulously washed) paraded in for inspection. Tickets for such functions were extremely expensive (15s – £1 10s), and the well-heeled guests were also expected to give generously to the collection at the end. Both men and women attended charity dinners, but they did *not* sit down together to eat – that would have been considered shocking, and the women were segregated upstairs in the gallery. The East London Institution's inaugural dinner was held at the City of London Tavern in October 1816, and at quite short notice Prince Augustus Frederick, Duke of Sussex, agreed to chair it.

One of the younger sons of King George III, Prince Augustus' life had been blighted by his father's obsession with controlling every aspect of his children's existence. Blocked like all his brothers from taking up any sort of career or useful work, and from marrying the woman he loved, throughout the later part of his life he threw himself into fundraising work in support of a wide range of charitable causes – especially the sort likely to get up his royal father's nose. At a time when it was still being argued that no education should be permitted unless conducted under the auspices of the Established Church, Sussex happily bestowed his benevolent presence on Anglican, Dissenting, Catholic and Jewish schools alike. The fact that he enjoyed his food and drink suited the fundraising methods of the period, which revolved so much round the big charity dinners, but he was a major asset at them not only for his prestige, but also for his convivial good humour which often persuaded the other banqueters to donate far more than they had intended. Thanks to his kindness, the Institution was given the best possible kick-start. Top priorities for the East London Institution were to obtain larger premises both for the Wapping schools, and for another boys' school recently started in Poplar. Joseph Daniel, a new young assistant priest who arrived at Virginia Street around the beginning of 1817, eagerly took over responsibility for the outreach to Poplar, and spent a year building up a Catholic community there. But in January 1818 he contracted typhus and died. Typhus, which is passed on by infected lice, was an occupational hazard of priests attending sick calls in slum dwellings. The following Friday his body was brought into the chapel at Virginia Street

where a solemn dirge was performed for the repose of his soul, at which a numerous Clergy and crowded congregation assisted, who, after divine service, attended him to St. George's in the East, where he was buried in the same grave with the Rev. Mr Coen, formerly of the same chapel. After the minister had finished the burial service, the Rev. Mr. Horrabin repeated, in an audible voice, the Ps. Miserere, and the Prayer Absolve quaesumus, in which he was joined by the surrounding Catholics.- The deep impression made by the loss of this young and amiable pastor, was visible in the mournful appearance of an immense and sorrowing multitude (including Protestants) who followed him to the grave, justly regarding him as a glorious victim to the most dangerous, but perhaps the most holy of the pastoral duties.

Before the year was out the Poplar school-chapel became an independent mission, and started its own separate fundraising body. In 1820 the lease ran out on the Chapman Street premises, but a new building was acquired at No 14 Red Lion Street: the Freemason's Hall of the Dundee Lodge, established by Scottish tradesmen. The freehold was purchased by Bp Poynter on 25th March 1821 for £200. The two-storey building was "about 64 ft. in length by 25 in width", and only needed a little alteration to provide accommodation for 250 boys and 150 girls, and living quarters for the teachers. Over the next three years, according to W. Y., the Wapping schools "through the beneficence of charitable individuals, gradually increased" so that by 1823 *nearly four hundred Catholic children are educated in these establishments, and sixty boys with forty girls are annually clothed. Some of the most illustrious names now grace the list of subscribers to these schools, and, among others, that of the first lord of the treasury is seen with peculiar satisfaction.*

Lord John Russell was indeed a subscriber to the Institution, as was the Anglican Bishop of Norwich, well-known for his liberal views. The Institution's patron was the Vicar Apostolic of the London District, its president was the Duke of Norfolk, and other Catholic aristocrats served as vice-presidents. (All these positions were honorary – the local school committee did all the real work.) Besides its annual dinners, the East London Catholic Institution organised steamer cruises up the Thames, though one excursion ended tragically when a tripper, Mr Fox, fell through the paddle wheel housing and was killed. According to the committee's report many of the children – the unlucky ones who hadn't received clothes that year – had to come to school ragged and barefoot, even in winter.

Meanwhile, Fr Horrabin was throwing himself into a whole range of educational initiatives for the benefit of the Church generally, attracting support from enthusiastic Catholics all over London. Funds were desperately needed for training priests, so Virginia Street started a London Mission Fund which, within a year, raised over £250, mostly from people paying tiny subscriptions of just 1d or 2d a week: it was handed over to Bp Poynter to sponsor three seminarians. Any effort to make available inexpensive, and sound, Catholic reading material had Fr Horrabin's sympathy. In collaboration with Marlow Sidney, he brought out a cheap edition of the New Testament, with abbreviated Catholic notes, to be sold in the East End for 6d. When a London Catholic Library was started, in 1822, Horrabin happily agreed to serve as President, and he was also one of the Trustees, along with Bp Poynter and Marlow Sidney. James Luddy, Librarian and Secretary, was headmaster of the Red Lion Street school. Some of the committee members were City businessmen, some East Londoners: George Gibson was an auctioneer in Ratcliffe Highway, and James Creamer an anchor smith in Wapping High Street. William Lescher, a partner in the starchmaking company Joseph Lescher and Sons, of Thomas Street, Whitechapel, was involved with the East London Catholic Institution, as was Thomas Rolph who also acted as surgeon to the school.

The Charitable Sisters

The Society of Charitable Sisters was a women's lay association, founded in 1814 and run from the home of its president, *Mrs* Marlow Sidney, in Star and

Garter Yard. Members could be either single or married, were drawn from all over London, and worked mainly on the eastern edge of the City, both north and south of the river. Mrs Sidney and her Council of four other women officers met every Tuesday morning, from 10.00 am to 1.00 pm, to discuss and plan their work, and the meeting was open to any other members who chose to be present. Their main purpose was to help "lying-in women" – that is, mothers-to-be at the end of their pregnancies, while they had their babies and recovered from the birth – by provision of clothes and linen, and sometimes a small sum of money to buy food. Many poor women lived so hand-to-mouth that childbirth was a terrifying prospect, because they would be unable to work for at least a few days, at the same time as incurring extra expenses.

Funds were raised through subscriptions and donations (mostly from local people subscribing small sums on a regular basis), charity sermons preached by sympathetic priests, and an annual boat trip down the Thames – and the Sisters were proud to be able to point out that some of their supporters were Protestants. They also collected second-hand clothing (which may have needed repairs or alteration), and sewed articles of clothing themselves for distribution: one way in which some of them spent their time at the Tuesday morning meeting was to sit sewing. By the mid-1820s they were distributing thousands of articles of clothing each year, and keen to obtain permanent premises of their own where the clothing could be stored.

The success of the clothing work led the Sisters on logically to helping poor schools, because of the tradition of clothing schoolchildren. Catholic Sunday Schools were beginning to be set up, and one of the earliest was started in East London by the Charitable Sisters in 1816: soon they had fifty girls learning their catechism. Sunday Schools targeted children who were in full-time work Monday – Saturday, seeking to get them off the streets on their only free day, and give them some education which usually included a large component of religious instruction, but also reading and writing. Soon several Catholic Sunday Schools were operating in various locations in East London, one of them using the boys' schoolroom at the British Union School. The Virginia Street Chapel Sunday School Committee was strong enough to provide support to other missions: it helped the East Lane Chapel in Bermondsey rent premises in which to set up its very first day school.

The Charitable Sisters went through a crisis in 1827, when Mrs Sidney dropped out. A Mr and Mrs Dinmore took over, and the headquarters was moved to their stationery shop in City Road. But income went down, and the school activities had to be given up in order to concentrate all efforts on the women in childbirth. The Society kept going into the 1850s, but eventually disappeared.

Catholic Emancipation

Daniel O'Connell

Adult Catholic men were entitled to vote, provided they could meet the property qualification (which excluded the vast majority of the population), but not sit in Parliament. To campaign for an end to this discrimination, a Catholic Association was formed in Ireland. Membership was £1 a year, which restricted it to the better-off, but the barrister Daniel O'Connell had a brilliant idea, and declared that anyone who paid a penny a month could become an *Associate* member. This meant virtually everyone in Ireland could participate, and monthly pennies from vast numbers of people quickly mounted up to thousands of pounds: the proceeds came to be known as the "Catholic Rent".

Recognising O'Connell's celebrity status, the East London Catholic Institution invited him to chair the 1825 annual dinner. Their treasurer, Stephen Philips of 27 Arbour Square, objected and wrote a letter to the *Courier* protesting the decision to invite such a controversial figure: this caused a row, and he was made to hand over the books to someone else. 300 wealthy guests attended the dinner, at the Freemason's Tavern, Great Queen Street, and O'Connell proposed a toast to the Duke of Sussex. The collection was higher than usual by at least half as much again: slightly over £300 was raised, including £21 sent down by the ladies in the gallery. St Mary and St Michael's actively backed O'Connell's campaign: the schoolroom was made available on Sunday evenings for collection of the Catholic Rent, and in February 1826 a well-attended meeting took place there "to take into consideration the propriety of Petitioning Parliament for the abrogation of the Penal Laws, which affect conscience." Fr Horrabin chaired, and a series of resolutions were proposed and seconded by Fr Foley, William Lescher, James Luddy, Thomas Rolph, James Creamer, Joseph Delany, John Rosson, Joseph Daly, George Platt and Dennis Hyde. O'Connell was invited to chair the dinner again in 1827, but couldn't make it, so the Institution had to settle for the Duke of Norfolk.

At last, in 1829, the law was changed to allow Catholics to sit in Parliament. Daniel O'Connell duly took his seat in the House of Commons as elected member for Co Clare, and the Catholic peers were able to resume theirs in the Lords. Next, O'Connell began a campaign for Repeal of the 1800 Union of Great Britain and Ireland, which had taken away Ireland's own independent parliament, but this campaign met with determined resistance from the British Government.

Hard-working clergy

Fleet Prison

Many years previously, Fr Dobson had agreed to act as executor and trustee in some money matter, though it had nothing particularly to do with him. Unfortunately this got him entangled in a lawsuit in Chancery, and a writ was issued against him. Towards the end of 1834, he was arrested in the vestry at St Mary and St Michael's, immediately after Mass, and taken to the Fleet prison. From the moment the prison gates closed behind him, he became deeply depressed. His friends visited frequently, and brought him everything they could think of to make him comfortable, while an eminent lawyer made representations to the Lord Chancellor on his behalf, trying to get him released on compassionate grounds. Nevertheless he was convinced he would never get out of the debtor's prison alive, and he couldn't bring himself to eat or sleep properly. Within two months he was skeletally thin. The only thing he made an effort to keep up was praying the Divine Office. The last rites were administered on 17th February 1835, he became unconscious on 24th and died on 25th.

According to the *Catholic Magazine and Review*:

> *On the following Monday a solemn dirge was celebrated for his repose at Virginia Street chapel, which was attended by many of his brother clergyman and by a numerous congregation, and on the same day he was buried as he had directed, at St George's in the East, in the same grave with his predecessors, the Rev. Mr. Coen and the late Rev. Mr. Daniel. A crowd, consisting of some thousands, followed him to his grave. Out of respect to his memory several of the shops were closed, and the many sobs that were heard and the tears that were shed, proclaimed how deep was the impression that in him the poor had lost a kind friend, society a cherished ornament, and religion a pious and zealous pastor. R.I.P.*

Dobson's bed was bequeathed to his faithful housekeeper, and 80 years later an old man named O'Brien, the housekeeper's grandson, was still keeping it as a "sacred treasure" in his house in Joseph Street.

The Virginia Street entry in the Catholic Directory for 1835 shows one Mass each weekday morning at 10.00, three on feastdays, and four on Sundays at 8.00, 9.00, 10.00 and 11.00, with a "discourse after the Gospel at High Mass", and Vespers at 3.00 pm. Additionally the three priests had

daily to attend the London Hospital, Mile-end-road, the receptacle of all accidents in the docks, wharfs, and ships from Blackwall to London Bridge, as well as fifteen workhouses; the chief of which are St George's in the East, Wapping, Shadwell, Ratcliffe, Stepney-green, Aldgate, Crutched-friars, Barking, St. Dunstan's, and St Olave's.

The lowest unit of local government in England was the (Anglican) parish, and a whole range of local responsibilities still came under the parish Vestry. Rates levied on the better-off residents were supposed to support the parish's own poor, and administration of this money, which was the only safety-net for the destitute, was the responsibility of the parish's Board of Guardians. Under the New Poor Law of 1834, parishes were being encouraged to join together into "Unions" in order to save on administrative overheads, so most of the small workhouses would gradually be phased out, to be replaced with larger, more efficient and much stricter workhouses, and huge residential "barrack schools" for pauper children. Although the tie between local government bodies and the Church of England remained (and could lead to complications), the duties of both Vestries and Boards of Guardians were mainly of a secular nature, and you didn't have to be an Anglican to vote, or sit on them.

The Virginia Street clergy were also "the spiritual directors of the East London Catholic Charity Schools", but the practical responsibility for keeping the schools going lay entirely with the lay committee. The "Gentlemen of the Committee", of whose "activity and perseverance" Fr Horrabin was highly appreciative, currently included Andrew Loughnan, a merchant with an office in Coleman Street in the City; George Gibson, and William Lescher. Lescher had prospered sufficiently to move his family out to the suburbs, but he remained very committed to the promotion of Catholic education in East London. The endowment funds grew more substantial, though they always had to be supplemented by subscriptions and other fundraising activities. In 1833 the Institution received a very substantial legacy under the will of Richard Neale, a wealthy shipowner resident at No 2, Cannon Street Road: over £10,000 in consols. Some years later it shared in another large bequest by Charles Jacob Wilkinson to all the Catholic schools in East London.

Edmund Rice

The Irish Christian Brothers, founded by wealthy ex-businessman Blessed Edmund Rice, were engaged in 1826 to teach the boys at St Patrick's Charity Schools, Soho. Previously, the school had quite a bad reputation, and the new regime was seen as a vast improvement. In October 1837, therefore, Fr Horrabin wrote to ask if the Brothers would take over his own boys' school. He agreed to pay two teaching religious 50 guineas a year each, and provide accommodation, and sent £15 over to Ireland for travel expenses. The Brothers were installed in Wapping before the end of the year. A description of the Red Lion Street School at this time was recorded by Edward Timmons, a pupil who later became a Brother himself. There were two large schoolrooms, for girls on the lower floor and boys upstairs, each with about 250 children. Both the Brothers worked in the upper schoolroom, which had a window at both ends and a large skylight in the flat roof. There was no playground as such, but the boys were allowed up on the roof for "quiet recreation". Despite the school committee's harping on rags and bare feet, as Timmins recalled it the boys were not really poor, as their docker fathers were usually in work, and there were very few who didn't have shoes. (Now that literacy was becoming an asset in the job market, the better-off working-class families made sure to get their children into the limited number of school places available.) On Sundays and holy days of obligation the children assembled at the school and marched to Virginia Street, about a mile away, to attend Mass, and they also attended the Sunday afternoon service. "The Brothers were received into the District with much respect" wrote Timmins.

It was a novelty to see anyone in a religious dress... We assembled at the [Brothers'] house in Bedford Square for instruction for First Communion about 5 p.m. for several weeks. I was particularly interested and pleased with my visit to a religious house. To see a domestic chapel was a rarity in those days, as was also a good Catholic school.'

Since 1833, grant money had been made available by the government for schools run under the auspices of the National (Anglican) and British (Nonconformist) School Societies, and later for those of certain other

Protestant bodies, but not for Catholic schools. The Hon Charles Langdale, one of the first English Catholic MPs, was determined to challenge the continuing religious discrimination, and at his urging a Catholic Institute was established in London in the summer of 1838, for the defence of the Catholic faith and "the protection of the poorer classes of Catholics in the enjoyment of their religious principles and practices". This was a national-level, upper-class initiative, with a membership subscription of 6d a month, well out of the reach the "poorer classes" it aimed to help. Nevertheless, some months later the Catholics of Wapping held a meeting at the George Tavern, and a resolution was

Moved by Mr. Scipio Clint and seconded by Mr. Dennis Murphy, 'That the Catholic Institute of Great Britain, having for its professed objects these desirable and philanthropic ends, and having received the sanction and patronage of the Vicars Apostolic, and the approbation and co-operation of many of the Clergy, together with our Nobility and Gentry, it is desirable to establish an Auxiliary Society in this district, to carry out the benevolent designs of the Institute, to be called The Virginia Street Auxiliary Catholic Institute.

Fr Horrabin was elected President; Fr James Foley and Fr Doyle Vice-Presidents; the Treasurer was Richard Swift and the Secretary William Keens; and a committee of ten was formed with power to co-opt additional members. By the end of the year the total received from subscriptions came to £22 18s 3d. This included £9 1s 6d handed in immediately at the meeting. Collectors had to be sent round to chase after most of the other subscriptions, and as this was quite a time-consuming job, they were paid 10% commission. But the subscription level necessarily limited recruitment, and the enthusiasm of those who did sign up quite quickly petered out.

I am an Irishman!

In 1839 Fr Horrabin was transferred to St Mary Moorfields, leaving Virginia Street under the care of his assistant and good friend Fr Foley, but he returned in 1841. On Friday 8th October the Christian Brothers marched their boys from the school to the chapel, bringing them in immediately after Mass, whereupon a boy named Joseph Daly delivered a fulsome address hailing the return of Fr Horrabin. He added a word of welcome to a newly-arrived curate, Fr John Moore. A little later the same day the priests returned the visit by walking over to inspect the school, where "as soon as they entered they were again cheered with all that vehemence so truly characteristic of the Irish." Recent alterations meant that fifty additional children could now be accommodated.

St Mary Moorfields

John Moore's parents were Irish, from Athlone, though he was probably brought up in England. Accepted by the London District as a candidate for the priesthood, he was sent to France to train at the Sulpician seminary of Issy, Paris, and was there in July 1830 when the unpopular Bourbon dynasty, restored after the defeat of Napoleon, was overthrown in a three-day uprising during which about 500 civilians were killed in Paris. Revolutions in France usually threw up anti-clerical manifestations, and some of the revolutionaries built a scaffold outside the seminary, saying they were going to execute all the inmates. At the crucial moment Moore forced his way to the front and cried out: "It was the Irish that won the battle of Fontenay for you Frenchmen, and I am an Irishman!" The leader acknowledged the point and asked what he wanted, "I want the lives of my fellow students and those who teach us." After some discussion the revolutionaries agreed, on condition that the seminarians march through the streets carrying the red flag and singing the Marseillaise. Conservative French seminarians might well have had a problem with that, but Moore didn't, and the others followed his lead. As the story suggests, Fr Moore was always ready for the dramatic gesture, with an amazing flair for getting people on his side, and getting them organised. He was passionately interested in new ideas, and startlingly unconventional. From Paris he'd gone on to Rome in 1836, and studied at the English College under Dr Wiseman. But in his pastoral approach, he seems to have been influenced less by Roman practice than by approaches which had been shown to work in the British Isles – in particular an outstanding contemporary success story in Ireland: the temperance campaigns of the Capuchin Fr Theobald Mathew. As much to his own surprise as anyone else's, huge numbers had flocked to him in Cork to take the pledge of total abstinence from alcoholic beverages, and within just a few years millions of Irish people had declared themselves teetotallers, while government figures showed that the consumption of spirits in Ireland had been cut by half. Fr Mathew,

Apostle of Temperance, was seen as a miracle worker. A Metropolitan Roman Catholic Total Abstinence Association was founded in London by a Quaker, John Giles, who lived in Mile End. Fr Moore set to work with a will, and over the next few years persuaded 800 Wapping Catholics to become total abstainers.

The means to the end

Similarly open to new ideas, though his background and training were different, was Fr William Kelly. Dr Griffiths had sent a priest over to Maynooth, Ireland's national seminary, to try to recruit some prospective priests for London. He arrived to find "some five Bishops from various parts of the Catholic world soliciting students for their respective dioceses. They succeeded, but not one could be found to volunteer for England." At this point the Dean buttonholed Kelly in the corridor and said, 'What a pity none of the students will volunteer for London. For God's sake, do volunteer! There are a sufficient number of priests for Ireland, but hardly any to look after your fellow countrymen in London."' Kelly agreed, and five other students followed his lead. He was ordained in England in September 1839, and sent "on the Mission to Hammersmith".

During his first week there, Fr Kelly went to the workhouse to give instruction to the Catholic children – just as he would have expected to do in Ireland. To his amazement, he wasn't allowed to see them, and he discovered that all children in Poor Law institutions were being routinely brought up as Anglicans. This was *not* official government policy. Politicians and civil servants at central government level, though always chary of upsetting the "No Popery" lobby, were usually quite enlightened and tolerant. But parish-level decision-makers and petty office-holders could be extraordinarily bigoted. Their deeply-entrenched religious prejudices went along with an attitude of smug contempt for unskilled working-class people, who were seen as parasites on the better-off, with no right to be treated with even minimal human dignity. Fr Kelly obtained authorisation from the Poor Law Board to instruct the children, but the Guardians quickly arranged for them to be moved to other institutions, out of his reach. Such behaviour was among the grievances which the Catholic Institute was seeking to address, so as soon as the Institute was started Fr Kelly got involved, and went to all the meetings. Along with Fr Thomas Sisk, senior priest at the mission in Chelsea, he launched a campaign about the Poor Law issue:

We held most enthusiastic meetings. We certainly excited attention, for Lord John Russell sent for the Vicar Apostolic on this subject. The Vicar convened all the clergy of the vicariate the following day at S. Patrick's, Soho-square; whereas, he had in reality, to send for two only – myself and Father Sisk. He forbade any future meetings to be held, because Lord Russell told the Vicar that the following week it would be arranged to admit Catholic schools to a participation in the national grant. I whispered to an English priest sitting next me: 'God help that poor, good man! How little he knows about the world.' Did Lord Russell keep his promise?" Not a bit of it.

Meanwhile Fr Kelly was proving tremendously popular with his congregation in Hammersmith, but during his early years as a priest he suffered several illnesses, probably due to picking up infections to which he'd not previously been exposed.

Sent on the mission in 1839, with the skeleton of many branches of knowledge in my head, I had resolved to master between times each one of them. But as to entering the brick and mortar line, I had no more notion of such a thing than of becoming Emperor of China. There is an old saying, 'Man proposes but God disposes;' and so it came to pass in my case. After some eight or nine months of missionary life, I was ordered under medical advice to leave London and go on vacation to a certain place for the benefit of my health. Now, it so happened that in that locality there was a learned and pious Priest in delicate health, of whom I had read and heard much. By him I was kindly received; but whilst sojourning in that locality the local Church seemed to me almost extinct; and it was then and there came over your humble servant an indescribable impression, as clear and distinct as if spoken by a living voice, to this effect: Suppose you were ten times more learned than the Priest of this place, and instead of enlarging the Kingdom of Christ, allowed it to become extinct, how could you expect eternal life? The change was immediate. I saw as clear as noon-day, schools and churches were the means to the end; and so I have been engaged in them ever since.

The Hammersmith mission was one of the oldest in the London area, being based in the convent chapel of the Institute of the Blessed Virgin Mary, which was established in 1669. The problem, Fr Kelly realised, was that it was *still* using the convent chapel. Not only was it failing to reach out adequately to the much-increased and rapidly spreading population it was now supposed to serve, but more people were actually turning up for Mass than there was space available. As Griffiths was chary about proposals for enlarging the existing premises, Fr Kelly obtained land in Fulham to build an additional church there.

A Piece of Freehold Land

It was never easy to fundraise for a church until a site had been secured, so high time for St Mary and St Michael's to acquire land on which to build.

Erecting a new chapel near the old one was not even considered: the congregation were said to be ashamed of their chapel being so deep in the docks area, where it had become "literally isolated and buried in obscurity." Fortunately a plot became available in a newly developing area, much more salubrious and respectable than Wapping.

Commercial Road after the completion of the London and Blackwall Railway in 1840

Before the docks were excavated, the main east-west roads through the riverside hamlets had been Cable Street and the Ratcliffe Highway, but they were too narrow and crooked to handle the increasingly heavy and valuable dock traffic. So a brash new route was carved through: Commercial Road, branching purposefully into the East and West India Dock Roads. The Commercial Road Act set up a body of Trustees to construct it (it was completed in 1810) and thereafter to control, maintain and pave it, and keep it clean and well-lit, charging tolls to cover the expense. Contemporary writers described the road as "fine and beautiful". Blocks of granite were laid along the south side in 1829-30 to form a well-surfaced stoneway, along which the heaviest wagons coming from the docks could be drawn with ease: westbound traffic using the stoneway paid a special extra toll, and the north side of the road was reserved for westbound traffic *not* paying the extra; there was a centre lane for eastbound traffic. Parallel with the road ran the London and Blackwall Railway. The Commercial Road Trustees had opposed its construction for fear of competition, but despite their objections it was opened in 1840. Most of the road was already lined with housing, but a large field alongside a ropewalk remained undeveloped.

In 1842, therefore, "a piece of freehold land was purchased in the Commercial-road East for the intended new church of St. Mary and St. Michael by the Rev. Messrs. Foley and Horrabin." The price was £3,000, of which £2,000 had to be paid immediately, and the balance within 12 months or else it would incur interest at 5%. Fr Horrabin paid over £500 which he had in hand. Another £1,500 was reportedly donated by the Vicar Apostolic, Thomas Griffiths. However a study some years later, of records then held at

St Mary and St Michael's, suggested that this £1,500 was in fact money collected by the congregation over the years, and deposited with the bishop's predecessors for safe-keeping.

Fr Horrabin had been at Virginia Street continually since 1815, except for the short break at Moorfields, and he was now 60. He estimated the Catholic population of his district at "21,000 persons, who, with very few exceptions, are of the working and humbler classes." To pay off the £1,000, and proceed with the building work, he looked first to

> *our own poor, but generous and devoted flock, for alacrity of aid and assistance, in a cause sacred to God – sacred to the faith of their fathers. In the second place, to our brethren whom Divine Providence has more abundantly furnished with the means of doing good we stretch out the hand of earnest and confident supplication.*

The Holy Guild

On 8th December 1842, at a meeting held under a railway arch behind the new church site, Fr Moore launched the Holy Guild of St Joseph and Mary. Its purposes were to encourage mutual charity (undefined, so difficult for anyone to disagree with), and zealous Catholic observance (very precisely defined, by the clergy); on a practical level it would function as a friendly society, providing insurance against sickness and funeral expenses. On Tuesday 31st January 1843, at a crowded meeting in a hall in Cable Street, the Guild elected its first officers. Only enrolled brothers were allowed to vote (the sisters weren't) and they all voted unanimously for the candidates proposed by Fr Moore. J J Hedley was to be Warden, responsible for organising festivals, funerals, processions and meetings; the three Mortuary Officers were W Reeves, J Dwyer and J Toohy; S Johnson was Bursar, and the Council members were Messrs D Murphy, L Cronin, Muldary, Joseph Daly and Thomas Delahunte. Mr A Creamer would act as Moore's secretary. Next the newly-enrolled brothers and sisters ceremonially presented their chaplain with a de-luxe version of the Guild uniform: a velvet green cloak edged with ermine, and a gold cross and chain.

The inauguration ceremony was performed on Thursday 2nd February, Feast of the Purification, at Virginia Street chapel. Tickets were on sale to interested spectators, to raise money for what Moore called "the sacred deposit" (a financial reserve, in case there should be a sudden run on benefits before enough subscriptions had been paid in). Seats in the tribune ranged from 2s 6d in the front to 1s at the back; entrance to the side galleries was 1s and to the body of the chapel 6d. In their uniforms – green cloaks with white linen collars for the men, and for the women green dresses and white-edged green sashes, straw bonnets and long white veils – and carrying candles, the Guild members came forward two by two (two men or two women together) to kneel down in front of Fr Moore and repeat the words: "I devoutly place myself under the patronage of St Joseph and our Blessed Lady, and promise that I will faithfully observe the rules of this holy Guild." Moore then invested each member with a little gold shield, saying "I invest thee, dear brother (or sister), with the shield of this holy Guild. God bless you and give you grace to fulfil the duties of your brotherhood (or sisterhood)." The ceremony ended with Te Deum and Benediction. Adult members paid 1s a month, or 3d a week, and received free medical care when sick, plus 10s a week while unable to work, or (if the illness proved fatal) £8 for a decent burial. Children could become members if 1d a week was paid for them, and were entitled to medical care and burial. (Child mortality rates were such that it was routine to enrol children in burial societies.) Mass was said once a month by the chaplain for every member, a special Mass for anyone who was sick, and three Masses if they died.

The case of an old woman interviewed at her home off Rosemary Lane (Royal Mint Street) in 1850, by the journalist Henry Mayhew, shows how remarkably effective the Guild could be in offering spiritual and social redemption even to the very poor, and raising them literally out of the gutter. Mayhew calls her "Old Norah", which may or may not have been her real name. "Her shawl was fastened over her large frilled cap. She had a little 'button' of a nose, with the nostrils entering her face like bullet holes. She wore over her gown an old pilot coat, well-stained with fish slime, and her petticoats being short, she had very much the appearance of a Dutch fisherman or stage smuggler." The walls were covered in saints' pictures, and a rosary sat in a tumbler on the window sill. Nine years previously Fr Moore

> *'the father' of the district – 'the Blissed Lady guard him!' – had found her late at night, rolling in the gutter, and the boys pelting her with orange-peel and mud. She was drunk – 'the Lorrud pass by her' – and when she came to, she found herself in the chapel, lying before the sanctuary, 'under the shadow of the holy cross'. Watching over her was the 'good father', trying to bring back her consciousness. He spoke to her of her wickedness, and before she left she took the pledge of temperance. From that time she prospered, and the 1s 6d the 'father' gave her 'had God's blissin' in it', for she became the best dressed woman in the court, and in less than three years had £15 in the savings' bank, 'the father – Heaven cherish him' – keeping her book for her, as he did for other poor people. She also joined 'the Association of the Blissed Lady', (and bought herself the dress of the order 'a beautiful grane vilvit, which she had now, and which same cost her 30s.'), and then she was secure against want in her old age and sickness.*

The good times for Old Norah came to an end when her brother was discharged from the army and came to live with her. He persuaded her to start drinking again, got her savings off her and spent them all. Now, however, she was looking to Fr Moore to get her back on the straight and narrow once again "and with his help and God's blessing, she would prosper once again."

The Wapping Boys

The Catholic Institute always attracted an impressive turnout once a year at its big Annual Meeting in London, held during the season, when the Catholic elite from all over the country were in town. Well-dressed men crowded onto the floor space, while their womenfolk packed the galleries, to hear the big-name speakers. In 1842 they had the thrill of seeing the flower of the old English Catholic aristocracy and gentry sharing a platform with Daniel O'Connell. But O'Connell was openly critical of the Institute's strategy, which was failing to establish roots in the Catholic community at large. He plugged his own idea of the Catholic Rent:

Widen your base. Diminish the sum that has to be paid by members. That is what we have done in Ireland. Let every man pay a shilling. You have about a million Catholics in England, and at one shilling a head that would produce £50,000. And how much is this? Why, it is one farthing a week (hear, hear) – one penny a month – one shilling a year – with four weeks discount. (Cheers and laughter.)

Fr Moore responded eagerly, pledging to enrol 3,000 members in the Virginia Street Auxiliary at the penny a month rate. At the Auxiliary's next Annual Meeting, in June 1843, 1,500 people crowded into the hall, and an equal number stood outside – many of them were also members of the Holy Guild. The 3,000 target had been met, and the priest distributed prizes to the over fifty dedicated men and women who collected in the subscriptions – without expecting any recompense, since the commissions had been scrapped: one of them, a man named Davis, wasn't even a Catholic. From an embarrassing failure, the Auxiliary had been transformed into the Institute's most resounding success story, though the national Institute itself – as was openly acknowledged during the meeting – was in a bad way, with subscriptions falling off through most of the country. At the national Annual Meeting in the Freemason's Hall the following week, several speakers referred appreciatively to the Virginia Street example, and Fr Moore was loudly cheered when he got up to speak:

Ladies and gentleman, I hold in my hand, a document whereof an Irishman, a

Catholic priest, an apostolic missioner in England, might well be vain. It is a document containing the names of the zealous, the indefatigable collectors of the Catholic Institute, I will not say of Great Britain, but of Great Wapping. (Roars of laughter, and much cheering.)... I am proud my faithful Wapping Boys are here to attest, to prove their unswerving loyalty to honour, to religion, and to country... I do not feel justified in trespassing further on your indulgence, it is past dinner time in Wapping (loud laughter); and it is nearly dinner hour at the west end. (Renewed laughter.)

On Trinity Sunday, the usual day for chapel building appeals, sermons were preached at Virginia Street by guest speakers both morning and evening, in aid of the collection for the new church. A brick wall, costing £800, had been built round the site, and part was to be set aside part for a burial ground, as a means of bringing in some income. The cemetery was consecrated by Bp Griffiths on 24th July 1843. The Holy Guild marched in at full strength – 200 brothers and 200 sisters with banners flying, led by a processional cross and Fr Moore in his green robes – and drew up in a square round the cemetery. The service lasted two hours. The 600 people actually in the cemetery, watching, had been charged 1s entrance money, but thousands more enjoyed the spectacle for free, perched on top of the walls, or looking on from the windows and rooftops of the houses round about. The first burial, that of a Timothy O'Connor, took place on 30th July.

The Apostle of Temperance

Fr Matthew was touring England that summer, and he arrived in London on Friday 28th July. Placards went up to say that beginning on Monday, he would be administering the pledge on the space of ground opposite the George Inn in Commercial Road (the church site). The Virginia Street Catholic Total Abstainers and the Holy Guild, led by Fr Moore, processed out to meet him on the way and escorted him back. A platform had been erected, and a refreshment tent to sell non-alcoholic drinks and sandwiches. Shortly before the procession reached the spot, the platform collapsed, but no one was hurt. The meeting began with Frs Horrabin, Foley and Moore, the Protestant temperance leader Earl Stanhope, and other dignitaries standing with Fr Mathew on the platform, and an audience of about 4,000. Fr Moore was the first to kneel down to take the pledge, followed by most of the Guild members. Next Lord Stanhope spoke for an hour before himself kneeling to take the pledge. These people were alreadyteetotallers, but they were keen to renew their pledge from Fr Mathew in person, and it was also a way of setting a good example to the crowds.

Throughout the day speeches were interspersed by hymns from the boys' choir of the German Chapel, and by batches of people coming forward to take the pledge. Some of the speeches were pre-arranged, but anyone who volunteered to address the meeting, and appeared to be in good faith, might be invited onto the platform.

Fr Mathew at Commercial Road

Fr Mathew never made long speeches himself, as he needed to conserve his voice for administering the pledge. Visiting temperance delegations usually brought with them an address to Fr Mathew, composed in advance by one of their members (in high-flown language), and proudly declaimed on their behalf. Many of those taking the pledge were Anglicans or Nonconformists, and so were many of the speakers. Numbers increased until the crowd was estimated at 30,000, and vendors did a roaring trade in ginger beer, biscuits, and ribbons for the temperance medals which Father Mathew was giving out. At 8.00 pm the Capuchin returned to his hotel. Next morning's meeting began at 10.30 am; at first there weren't as many people present as on the first day, but before long there were reckoned to be at least 40,000, while the numbers on Wednesday were even higher.

Fr Moore delivered a lengthy speech on the Wednesday. He began by dealing as tactfully as he could with the fact that Frs Horrabin and Foley had *not* taken the pledge, and were somewhat nervous of the absolutism of the movement:

Father Horrabin, who is to me what Paul was to Timothy, recommended me to take a little wine for the good of my stomach, but Father Mathew says that I must not take any at all. (Laughter and cheers.) So, for the first time in my life, I believe, I must put aside St. Paul for the moment and obey Father Mathew; and, I can safely say, that Father Horrabin is quite delighted with our distinguished visitor.

However as Fr Moore continued speaking, he got more and more carried away:

There are 21,000 Catholics in this neighbourhood, and why do they not come to be enrolled in the Total Abstinence ranks? Father MATHEW: We have already, my friend, 10,000 of them, and if they all come together what shall we do for the remainder of the week? (Laughter and cheers.) The Rev. Mr. MOORE (in continuation): there are 100,000 inhabitants in the Tower Hamlets, and, I trust, they will not let such an opportunity as the present one pass. It is said that the English people can do everything that man can do. Their industry and ingenuity are unparalleled. Look to yonder railway (the Blackwall one) and ask if our grandfathers could have supposed that such a singular mode of travelling could ever be devised? And yet that railway is only a fraction, as it were, of what has been accomplished by British genius. The English can now travel hundreds of miles without horses, and cannot they live without intoxicating drinks? (Laughter and cheering).) They have made short roads to almost every part of their island, and why cannot they make short roads to Heaven, by laying down Total Abstinence as the foundation of a virtuous life.

Frs Horrabin and Foley recognised the good intentions behind the teetotal campaign, and avoided open disapproval, but privately they were sceptical. It was still the practice to pay wages to dockworkers and other unskilled labourers in pubs, and the landlords often had a stranglehold over job opportunities, so that non-drinkers could not obtain work. Fr Foley also pointed out how difficult it was to obtain a drink of water: "It is all very well for in-door workers, but as for the out-door workers they must get some drink, and I'll not believe that they can do without going into the public-house, until I see pumps sunk at every corner between London Bridge and the Regent's Canal." Even at home, most people couldn't just turn on a tap, and away from home it was difficult to get a non-alcoholic drink of any sort. Where tea or coffee were available, they were more expensive than beer, and soft drinks and bottled water hadn't been invented.

Fr Kelly had launched a teetotal group in Hammersmith, but it wasn't very successful, and he was now having second thoughts. Fr Mathew's rallies left him even more perturbed. Many of the speakers were making out that wine was evil in itself, and this was clearly contrary to the teaching of the New

Testament. He also felt that Fr Mathew was "making it a sin" for anyone to break their pledge. Though unfair on Fr Mathew, this probably was what a lot of his hearers did think he was saying: whether the misunderstanding really mattered all that much was something about which Catholic leaders could, and would, sincerely disagree Fr Mathew chose to be laid back about it: when Fr Kelly tried to remonstrate with him, he only remarked calmly "that the Irish don't understand what they are talking about, and if some of them do their faith is too strong to be undermined."

On Thursday throughout the day the rain "fell in torrents, but still Fr Mathew continued his labours, and never left the platform." The *Illustrated London News* (which sent a reporter each day to take sketches and notes) estimated that despite the rain there were 40,000 present. The piper of a Highland battalion, after taking the pledge, brought out his bagpipes and "insisted on playing martial airs to the great amusement of Fr Mathew and the irritation of the dripping crowd who resented the delay thus caused."

Americans who were present pressed Fr Mathew to visit their own country. The eminent writer Thomas Carlyle had accidentally wandered into one of Fr Mathew's meetings in Liverpool, been so impressed that he wrote about it to his wife Jane Welsh Carlyle. Hearing he was in London, Mrs Carlyle determined to go to hear him at Commercial Road, and wrote a glowing description afterwards to her husband, concluding: "I could not speak for excitement all the way home. When I went to bed I could not sleep. The pale faces I had seen haunted me, and Father Mathew's smile."

A temperance festival was organised on the Sunday, and the following day the campaign left Commercial Road and moved to South London. But towards the end of the month Fr Mathew worked his way back towards the East End, speaking in Bermondsey, Stratford and Hackney, and then at Rosemary Lane – famous for its dense Irish settlement, appalling slums, and disreputable Rag Fair (second hand clothes market). Notices went up: "All labourers from the wharfs, Billingsgate, the docks, and its neighbourhood, are invited to attend, particularly soldiers from the Tower, and sailors from the shipping and the steamers." The piece of open ground selected was the site of a ruined brewery, capable of holding 8-9,000 people. Fr Moore was the first main speaker:

This is a glorious and magnificent day for the boys and girls of Rosemary-lane; this is a meeting which will soon make all the tatters of Rag-fair disappear, and all the secondhand stall-keepers in the lane turn bankrupts, or rather it will set them up in a more respectable line. Shreds and patches will be exchanged for coats of fine Saxony, coarse stuff gowns for mousselines de laine if you please; the bonnets to be worn for the future will be of the best Dunstable kind, the stockings of the best web, and the women's frills of the best Brussels lace. (Laughter, and great cheering from the ladies.)

The district was then much more Irish than Jewish, but it was noted that two of those who took the pledge were "of the Hebrew persuasion". The meeting went on till 8.30 pm, and ended with three cheers for Queen Victoria and Prince Albert, and for Inspector Donegan of the local police, who had been one of the first to take the pledge that day.

On the first Sunday in September Father Mathew preached at 11.00 High Mass in Virginia Street "in aid of the funds for the erection of the new church of SS. Mary and Michael, Commercial-road East." Next he proceeded, once again, to the church site. The platform this time was decorated with green boughs and the words of the pledge in Irish: *"Geallaim, le cabhair Dé, gan aon sort ólacháin mheisceamhail a dhéanamh arís go brath".* During the day over 2,000 more people took the pledge, including the schoolchildren from Red Lion Street.

The Virginia Street chapel's finances were still very dependent on whip rounds and "clergy nights" at certain of the local pubs. Paddy Vernon, born in Ratcliffe and baptised by Fr Foley, recalled that the Half Moon and Seven Stars, kept by Mrs Kearns, was one (Donohue the blind piper used to play there). Mrs Dowling's establishment, the Phoenix at Ratcliffe Cross, had a meeting nearly every Sunday night: "Songs, dances and homely addresses at times enlivened the evening, and a 'friendly lead' for the Rector and his buildings ended the night." All that was about to change.

A couple of months after Fr Matthew's departure, Fr Moore assembled a huge crowd of teetotallers at Virginia Street on a Sunday evening, half inside the chapel, and the rest filling the street and lanes outside. After making a speech, he invited everyone to come forward in turn to lay a money gift before the altar. Other speakers affirmed the importance of collective fundraising for the support of the mission, but deplored "the humiliating necessity hitherto imposed on our loved and venerated pastors of having recourse to public-house meetings, on the Lord's day, or *at all*, for the support of the mission in this locality …" and pledged those gathered to find an alternative method. However a resolution proposed by Fr Foley, and unanimously accepted along with the rest, declared that there was not the least intention to hurt the feelings of the local publicans, praised them for their efforts in assisting the mission, and invited them to continue to add "the strength of their aid to this meritorious and Catholic work." The collection amounted to over £37, mostly contributed at short notice by the very poor: four gold sovereigns had been handed in, but most of the amount was made up of pennies, contributed by people who couldn't afford more.

By December the Eastern Total Abstinence Society had divided the district up among Temperance Wardens. The wardens systematically collected money from the members in their district, and reported any member who broke his pledge, or joined a secret society. The Society fundraised on a regular basis for the Catholic schools, and for building their own Temperance Hall to provide somewhere for members to relax after work without having to go to the pub. Every meeting ended with three cheers for Fr Mathew and Queen Victoria.

The Investiture of the Liberator

On the afternoon of St Patrick's Day 17th March 1844, which happened to be a Sunday, thousands of Irish people were to be seen lining the streets around the Virginia Street chapel. Cheers went up when, around 3.30, a handsome carriage drawn by four grey horses arrived, and Daniel O'Connell stepped out. While he was treated to dinner, the chapel was decorated with artificial flowers, wreaths of shamrock were placed on the altar, and 300 members of the Holy Guild assembled inside wearing their uniforms. At 7.00 O'Connell was escorted in by Fr Foley and Fr Moore. Everyone prayed Vespers, then O'Connell went to kneel on the altar steps. Fr Moore "placed across his shoulders a magnificent silk green cloak, lined with white silk, and trimmed with rich ermine. He also presented him with a solid gold cross, and placed on his head a Genoa velvet cap."

Afterwards the Guild members, still in their uniforms, processed their honoured new Brother to the schools in Shadwell where 5-6,000 people had gathered. Constantly interrupted by cheering, Fr Moore read an address to O'Connell, who made a speech in reply:

He had been an agitator all his life, not only for the Catholic Church, but in every class, of freedom of caste and colour. (Hear.) He preferred the Catholic Church, because he thought it preached the Word of truth and God, and he could assure the meeting that the day was fast coming when England would be Catholic again. (Loud cheers.) Ireland, happy Ireland, had always proved her fidelity, and he was rejoiced in becoming one of the guild on that day (St Patrick's), an anniversary of a day so dear to the heart of every Irishman.

Whether or not it showed, O'Connell must have been under tremendous strain that day. His series of "monster meetings" in Ireland, calling for Repeal, were supposed to have culminated in October 1843 with the biggest one of all, at Clontarf, but the British government called his bluff by banning the event. Although he obeyed the ruling, he was then put on trial charged with conspiracy, and in February 1844 – the month before his appearance at Virginia Street – a guilty verdict had been returned. In May that year he was sent to prison at the age of 69. He was very well treated while there, and released in early September when the judgement was reversed on appeal to the House of Lords. But the experience visibly aged him.

The Investiture of Daniel O'Connell the Liberator

Persecuted childhood

As well as a difference of opinion about teetotalism, it was rumoured that a difference of opinion existed between Frs Horrabin and Foley on the one hand, and Fr Moore on the other, over pastoral priorities: *they* wanted to get the new church built, whereas *he* thought it far more urgent to expand the school accommodation. The word in the district was that Fr Moore had resolved 'not to contribute a single stone to the material edifice (the church), until living temples to the Holy Ghost shall have been raised in the hearts of these little ones, infinitely more precious in the sight of God."' Moore did his best firmly to squash the rumour, without seeking to deny that there was some truth in it. Since the Red Lion Street premises couldn't accommodate all the Catholic children, he began establishing additional schools in rented premises. Some of them didn't last very long, but gradually a stable pattern emerged, with a pair of schools – a boys' and a girls' school, run separately but in tandem – in each of three different parts of the St Mary and St Michael's district: one in Red Lion Street; one near Rosemary Lane; and one in Shadwell, within easy distance of the church site in Commercial Road. According to a survey conducted by the Catholic Institute around 1845, these three pairs of schools were between them educating 500 boys and 480 girls, out of a total of 2,500 Catholic school-age children believed to be living in the parish.

The girls' school at the Rosemary Lane end of the district was using the meeting hall of a local temperance group. It adjoined a Nonconformist chapel in Princes Square (Swedenborg Gardens) and had originally been built (with the help of a government grant) to accommodate the chapel's school, which had subsequently closed down. The teetotallers were paying the chapel £20 a year in rent, and Moore was making a contribution towards this. But on Monday 28th July 1845, the children arrived to find the doors locked. The schoolmaster went to inform Fr Moore that they were being refused admittance, and that the school furniture and all the equipment was locked inside. The chapel trustees had decided they weren't going to have Catholic teaching in their school building, even if they themselves had no use for it. Neither the temperance committee, nor John Giles, were prepared to help Moore, and the Schools Inspector admitted that under the prevailing system, the government had no control over the school buildings it helped pay for. The negotiations dragged on fruitlessly for several weeks. A few of the children were squeezed into the other two Catholic schools, but the majority were left to roam the streets. On 31st August Fr Moore, together with Fr Horrabin, held a public meeting at the Virginia Street chapel. Fr Moore related the story of the correspondence, and an interview he'd had with one the trustees in which, he reported:

I gathered some rather interesting information respecting the views of the gentleman on the subject of Catholic education and the value of the Bible. On my asking him why he objected to the Catholic catechism being taught as a school book (for in that consisted the 'promotion of the Catholic faith'), he said it was contrary to the Bible. In what part was it contrary? 'I don't exactly know as I have not read it.' I remarked that it was an excellent mode of judging of Catholic doctrine. 'Well,' said he, 'it is enough for me that you do not teach the Bible.' We do not teach the Bible, I replied, as a school-book, because we have too much respect even for the material letter, and would not have it thumbed, inked, torn, and eventually sent to the butter-shop. 'Oh!' replied he, 'as for that matter, the more Bibles are destroyed or sent to the butter-shop the better it is for trade.

The shocking story was taken up by the newspapers: it was reported in *The Times*, the *Morning Chronicle*, *Morning Advertiser* and *Dispatch*, in the Home Rule press in Ireland, and even further afield. The Hon Edward Petre, a socially-committed Catholic aristocrat who was one of the vice-presidents of the East London Catholic Institution, read a version of it in translation in a German newspaper, and cut short a holiday on the Rhine to rush back and see if there was anything he could do to help. Another meeting was held in the schoolroom at Love Lane, Shadwell, with the Hon Edward as one of the speakers: he declared that "the whole Continent was ringing with execration of the barbarous deed" and "called emphatically on the aristocracy of England to stamp their eternal abhorrence on sectarian bigotry, by coming forward at once and without delay to the rescue of persecuted childhood." Despite these animadversions, and the press coverage, the trustees in Princes Square remained intransigent.

Fr Foley was ill, and Fr Moore (or so he told Daniel O'Connell) was having to do most of the work of the mission that summer. Nevertheless he was authorized to take leave of absence, to go on a fundraising tour round both England and Ireland. O'Connell sent £5 and promised to help bring in other donors, saying "It is a cause of real charity – the instruction of the Irish poor in your district of London." Over the next few years the expelled school continued to operate, though its position remained precarious. Fr Moore moved it into a railway arch, where it flourished for a year and the roll went up to 240. But at the beginning of August 1846 it had to leave in a hurry "in consequence of a seizure made on the adjoining premises for arrears of taxes made by the occupying tenant. Fortunately the school furniture escaped." An arrangement to take a loft on the top floor of a former sugar factory in the Highway fell through because the tenants on the first floor – the Seamen and Soldiers' Evangelical Friend Society – objected. Nevertheless the school was somehow saved, and moved back to Princes Square.

Meanwhile, Fr Moore set about moving the Shadwell schools into a proper, permanent building in Johnson Street, round the corner from the church site on Commercial Road. A site was leased, and an impressive design in the perpendicular gothic style commissioned from William Wilkinson Wardell. Born into an Anglican family in Poplar in 1823, and received into the Catholic Church at the age of 20, Wardell was already showing tremendous promise as an architect. Fundraising continued while construction got under way, and the name selected for the new school was St Patrick and St Austin.

The Ancient Faith

Fr Foley died in February 1846, aged only 53. Out of respect, all the shops were shut along the route taken by the cortège from Virginia Street to the Commercial Road cemetery, 20,000 people lined the streets and all the traffic was brought to a halt. The death of his friend broke Fr Horrabin's heart, and he never fully recovered. When Daniel O'Connell died the following year, heartbroken by the catastrophic famine which was depopulating Ireland after successive failures of the potato harvest, Fr Moore celebrated a Mass for the repose of his soul every day for a week. Most of the Brothers and Sisters of the Guild would have found it difficult to attend weekday Masses, because they were working long hours, but they all came on Sunday and "devoutly and reverently received the Holy Communion in behalf of their departed Brother, friend and benefactor." Moore wrote to the *Tablet*

> *We only regret that an opportunity is not afforded us of testifying more publicly, and in a more solemn manner, our tender attachment to, and undying veneration for, the Father of his country, and the invincible defender of the Ancient Faith.*

Fr Ignatius Spencer

Before the 1850s parish missions were rare in London, because no one was readily available to give them. Most diocesan priests were far too busy, and the few nascent communities of specialist mission priests were working mainly in other parts of the country. Luigi Gentili, the celebrated Rosminian preacher, hated having to give missions in London because of the small size of most of the chapels: he liked to operate in a much larger space. But in February 1847 the Passionist superior, Blessed Dominic Barberi, came to give a mission in Poplar. In March he was back, accompanied by Fr Ignatius Spencer (an upper-class convert, from the family which was to produce Princess Diana) and Fr Vincent Grotti, for a mission in Virginia Street.

The Passionists were prepared to manage as best they could with the little old

Blessed Dominic Barberi

chapel, but St Mary and St Michael's had never had a mission before, and it was very difficult to get people to turn up to the services. So they took the mission out into the streets. It was very risky to wear religious dress in public: priests in England didn't even wear clerical collars, but dressed like laypeople to avoid attention, and they were addressed as "Mr", not "Fr". Yet Blessed Dominic and his companions went out in their habits, their sandals and their conspicuous Sacred Heart badges, carrying crucifixes, and began preaching in the open air. However the actual preaching took place not in the main streets or squares, but in "courts", crowded little cul-de-sacs deep in the slums. There was no reason for anyone who didn't live in a court, or have business with someone there, to venture inside, and court-dwellers didn't welcome strangers: in the worst courts any intruder risked being robbed and beaten up, and there were courts considered so dangerous that the police didn't dare go in alone. Many East End courts were populated almost exclusively by Irish Catholics, and in those courts the Catholic clergy were absolutely safe, even if nobody else was. The missioners took it in turns preaching, and people would gather around down below, crowd to the windows in the surrounding houses, and even climb up on the roofs to hear and see what was going on.

By the end of the mission Blessed Dominic's evident holiness had made a deep impression, and the people wanted to keep him in Wapping. A crowd assembled to try to persuade him to stay, and when he eventually got into a cab, they followed the cab all the way to the station, five miles away. After this first Passionist experiment in open air preaching in Wapping, the idea of court missions caught on, and was tried out in slum areas in other parts of London. Cardinal Wiseman was to take part in some of them, and was bowled over by the simple-hearted devotion of the poor Irish people. However the court missions were never considered an end in themselves: the goal, usually, was to get people into the nearest church, where a more conventional evangelistic service would direct them into the confessional. Some people began arguing that court missions, and networks of small low-cost centres, rather than large ornate central churches, were the best way to evangelise the poor, and maximise the limited resources available to the Church. However in a confidential report to Rome, in June 1847, Gentili stressed the urgency of opening large churches at three locations – Virginia Street, Chelsea, and St George's Southwark: "If we had these three great churches, the other priests would begin to be ashamed of their wretched chapels, and this example would be followed." The reason he'd picked those places was because he knew there were plans afoot to build large churches in each of them.

During the 1840s St Mary and St Michael's, in line with other London chapels, gave up the impossible struggle to try to induce adults to attend the Sunday afternoon catechism service, and moved towards holding a separate service of Vespers and Benediction for them, later in the evening. Initially this was at 5.00 with a "catechetical instruction", but eventually 7.00 was settled on as the best time, and the talk was billed as a sermon. Once properly established, this evening service came to be very well attended.

Pounds shillings and pence

The projected new church in Fulham was coming along nicely, and Bp Griffiths laid the foundation stone in June 1847. Construction continued without a hitch, but also without Fr Kelly, because in late July he was abruptly transferred to Virginia Street. Shocked at his sudden removal, 2,000 Hammersmith parishioners got up a petition to Bp Griffiths, but were informed that he was too ill to give an immediate reply. To their acute embarrassment (as they'd been pressing for an answer) his illness proved terminal, and he died on 12th August. He was succeeded by Nicholas Wiseman, but Wiseman's appointment was as *Pro*-Vicar Apostolic – the "Pro" meaning that it was temporary, pending a definitive decision from Rome.

Fr Kelly strove to be philosophical about his transfer, and concentrate on making the best of things in his new posting. All the priests were living in Virginia Street, but he was not quite fully recovered from a bout of "Irish famine fever" (typhus) contracted in the course of his duties in Hammersmith, and like most Victorians, he had a bit of a fetish about the health-giving properties of fresh air. So he insisted on moving to Arbour Square: "The walk to Virginia-street in the clear bracing air of early morning soon restored me to health." He soon got to know the parishioners well, and learned all sorts of things about the district. In January 1848, after much heartsearching, he penned a letter to Bp Wiseman, to warn him about the school building which Moore had under construction in Johnson Street. The land belonged to the Mercers, but was leased to the Gas Company which had sub-leased it to Moore. The duration of the lease was 64 years only, and a condition was that the building should be more or less finished by the end of 1847 – in fact it was nowhere near completion. If it ever did get finished, recurrent costs would be high because they would include both ground rent, and the interest on the money owed to the builders. Fr Kelly was worried that once the more astute of the local laypeople had worked out the economics of the school, donations would dry up, and Fr Moore might end up in the bankruptcy court:

In conclusion I beg to assure your Lordship that I have written the above with no motive except that of the kindest feeling towards the Revd Mr Moore and the good of religion. If Mr Moore saw the necessity of explaining this matter to your Lordship I feel sure he would do so, but in this money matter of pounds shillings and pence he appears to me hoping against every principle by which men judge of these things.

Poland had been wiped off the map of Europe, its territories occupied and divided up between Prussia, Austria and Russia, and large numbers of Poles from the educated classes and nobility became political exiles in other European countries and in the Americas. Those in London were even worse off in terms of spiritual provision than the Irish immigrants: they had among them a very distinguished priest, the Rev Dr Krainski MA, but no chapel. On 23rd September 1847, in the aftermath of a failed nationalist uprising in Poland, they gathered at Virginia Street for a Requiem Mass for two of their nationalist heroes, Professor Michał Wiszniewski of the Jagiellonian University, and another revolutionary named Kapuscinski, who had both been executed on the last day of July. Krainski "pronounced an eloquent funeral discourse in the Polish language on the occasion." It would be many more years before the London Poles acquired a church of their own.

Charles Langdale had lobbied tirelessly to obtain a share in government assistance for Catholic schools, and towards the end of 1847 this was at last achieved. The Catholic Institute was wound up, but Langdale became Chairman of a new body, the Catholic Poor School Committee (CPSC), which emerged out of the ruins of the Institute, and took a leading role in Catholic educational affairs from then on. Other socially-concerned upper-class Catholics involved with the CPSC were the Hon Edward Petre (though he died suddenly soon after it was set up) and Lord Edward Howard, younger son of the 13th Duke of Norfolk.

Of the three church projects which had so excited Gentili, St George's was opened the following year, but the Chelsea project collapsed when Fr Sisk left to become a monk. As for the plans at Commercial Road, they were making very slow progress. The debt of £1,000 on the land, plus legal expenses, had been paid off, but the actual building was still no more than a twinkle in Fr Horrabin's eye. Beyond talking in vague terms of a church with accommodation for 4,000, he was doing nothing to move the project forward. During a cholera outbreak which raged in London 1848-49, Fr Kelly "penetrated into every nook and corner of the Virginia-street district" visiting the sick and dying. In the process he grew increasingly convinced that building small chapels and schools "in fetid lanes and alleys" was wrong on health grounds, if nothing else. Walking along Commercial Road he often passed the empty church site, and one Sunday he sat down on an impulse and wrote a letter to Wiseman, offering to take responsibility for erecting "a noble building on it". But next morning during Mass he suddenly remembered this letter and, given his abiding horror of "bricks and mortar", lost his nerve: as soon as he got back to Arbour Square he looked for it, found to his relief that the servant had forgotten to post it, and tore it up. Two months later he was transferred to Portsea.

Our Lady of Loreto

On a Saturday afternoon in September 1849 "about half a score" of Fr Moore's "right hearty 'Wapping Boys" set up a marquee at the church site in Commercial Road, inside the cemetery walls. "At the South end" he wrote,

> *stands an altar of rude materials, but ornamented with a handsome antependium, designed and executed by a worthy member of the new flock, Mr. Alfred Sprague, a man consummate in the knowledge of ancient Catholic Art, but too incorrigibly modest, I fear, to raise himself to the pinnacle of fame or fortune.*

The following Sunday evening, at six o'clock, the

> *novel chapel... was solemnly opened with the recital of the Rosary of Our blessed Lady, the chanting of the beautiful Litany of Loretto, the delivery of an appropriate discourse, the devotions concluding with the prayers for night, in which the whole congregation devoutly joined.*

Part of the space under the tent was provided with benches, and four Masses were celebrated there on Sunday 9th September. Fr Moore had been going round all the missions he knew, begging for liturgical equipment: the altar stone and vestments were supplied by Bermondsey, and everything else borrowed from Virginia Street. The big old St Mary and St Michael's district was to be divided. Fr Horrabin would remain in charge of the eastern half, with the Virginia Street Chapel and the Red Lion Street Schools, but the western half would become a new mission: this new mission would go ahead with building the new church on the Commercial Road site, and when it was finished, it would be named Our Lady of Loretto. Until the division was formalised, the priests of the district would continue to work as a team, with half based at Commercial Road and half at Virginia Street, and an agreed informal division between the two halves of the district for purposes of sick calls and visiting. Each half was reckoned to have about 12,000 Catholics.

The Johnson Street building wasn't quite ready, so the prospective headteachers, Mr Falbey and Mrs Conn, set up a temporary school on the church site, by. Paddy Vernon, who'd briefly attended several of Moore's other schools, was one of the pupils there, though he remembered more about Mrs Conn's use of the cane than her lessons. At the opening of the new schools, in early December, a reception for about a hundred of the wealthier supporters was held in the upper schoolroom, which was to serve as the girls' school: "a large, handsome room, reminding one of the superb banqueting halls of the olden time". Charles Langdale was in the chair, with Bp Wiseman seated on his right. Everyone drank "Success to the Schools", after which the children were brought in "boys and girls – in numbers that quickly filled every hitherto unoccupied space in the room, and presenting, from their innocent, happy countenances, and their cleanly and comfortable appearance, an interesting sight." A collection held for the schools' furnishing and equipping amounted to £146. To this, Fr Moore announced, could be added another £20 raised by the Wapping Boys, and £12 by the Ratcliffe Boys. Knowing that he would impress his hearers most effectively not by flattering them for their generosity, but by stressing the far more sacrificial contributions of the local poor, he

gave several touching instances of the sums collected for him by certain individuals, whom he named: amongst others, that of one Bridget White, an apple woman, who, though occupied for seventeen hours a day at her apple-stall, was enabled in the course of twelve months to present him with £15. towards the erection of this edifice; of a poor man, a coal-whipper, who was disabled, who in eighteen months collected £38.; of another, a female, who, though her husband was out of employ and they were supperless, insisted on giving her last penny for the cause, with the remark that God would bless their mite by providing work for her husband. The next day the husband found employment, and is now one of the most comfortably-situated working men of the district. These instances were received with loud cheers.

Langdale proposed "The Health of the Protestant Friends of the Institution", and this was responded to politely by one of the Protestant supporters present. On Christmas Eve 1849, as Fr Moore described it:

the tent was struck, and the altar transferred to the newly-built schools of St Patrick and St Austin, in Johnson Street, the lower, or boys' schoolroom having been hastily fitted up for the occasion. Midnight Mass was here chanted in a corner of the old Stepney parish, where, since the days of the good and benevolent Dean Colet, the anniversary of our Saviour's birth had not been commemorated in the ancient Catholic fashion.

The building was still not really finished, and Fr Moore was later to recall "its naked, cold and cheerless walls and rafters singularly contrasting with the warm flame of devotion that animated the assembled adorers." 3-400 could be accommodated at each Mass.

Fr Kelly's intimations of disaster had so far not come to pass: the building was roofed and usable, and Fr Moore's dodgy lease had not been overturned. On St Patrick's Day, 1850, the Lord Mayor of Dublin came in his official robes for a ceremonial visit, at which the designs for the new church were passed round. Fr Moore was in fine form. He said he'd told the Vicar Apostolic that he didn't have a farthing to build the church with, but God was with him, and six months' trial was all he needed. The building they were in had cost £3,000, and apart from a donation of £50 from the Vicar Apostolic, the whole amount had been raised by the people themselves. Amid loud cheers and "waving of hats and handkerchiefs" Moore declared that the new church would be opened and consecrated in three years. The Mayor asked everyone who agreed to raise their hands, and everyone's hand went up. After further rousing speeches, Fr Moore announced that he'd just received a cheque for £5 from Charles Langdale. The meeting ended with a collection which raised "a very handsome sum".

In June, however, an anxious letter arrived from Bp Wiseman. Fr Moore had innocently let him know that he was using the Johnson Street building for political meetings: that was to stop forthwith, so long as the building was in use as a chapel, and the Blessed Sacrament was reserved there. The Pro-Vicar Apostolic also wished to see Fr Moore's full, detailed accounts. He was aware of his congregation's enthusiasm, but enthusiasm wouldn't last: in the long run people would only be persuaded to give committed financial support if the facts and figures showed that the project was solid. He concluded his letter: "The failure of the mission would be to me a grievous disappointment."

Restoration of the Hierarchy

Cardinal Nicholas Wiseman first Archbishop of Westminster

By Papal decree in 1850, the old makeshift arrangement of vicariates apostolic came to an end, England and Wales were divided into 12 dioceses, and Wiseman was appointed the first Archbishop of Westminster. The old London District was divided into two: he continued to administer Southwark for another year, but in June 1851 it was given a bishop of its own: Thomas Grant. Both dioceses were considerably larger than they are today: Southwark covered the whole area south of the Thames, including the Isle of Wight and the Channel Isles, while Westminster still included the whole of Essex as well as Hertfordshire. The biggest and most impressive church in London was St George's, which naturally went to Southwark. There was no money to build a cathedral for Westminster, and St Mary Moorfields had to serve as pro-cathedral. The plight of the Wapping and Stepney Catholics wasn't unusual – everywhere in London it was the same story: making do with inadequate buildings. The old system – unavoidable in Penal Times – of setting up lay committees with legal control over church property was being phased out, because it caused far too much aggravation, and all real power came to be vested in the priests. But for those facing the need to construct new buildings, their crown really was a crown of thorns, a back-breaking burden of gnawing anxiety and sleepless nights. It was a common joke among the clergy that a priest who set out to erect a church should order his coffin at the same time – and although they all laughed about it, it wasn't really funny.

Coal Whippers

The economic position of one very important section of the St Mary and St Michael's parishioners – "That large and influential body of men, called coal whippers" – who until recently could have expected to earn over £2 a week, had deteriorated badly. A group interviewed by Henry Mayhew in Wapping explained that an Act of Parliament setting up a proper registry office had broken the stranglehold of the pub landlords over them, but with around 2,000 coalwhippers on the books there wasn't enough work to go round: they could expect to get work only five days out of eight in winter, and three days out of eight in summer. Because of all the days they spent sitting idle at the depot, their take-home pay averaged only around 14s a week. Ballast-heavers, who worked by night to shovel gravel into the ships as ballast for the return journey, were still being shamefully ripped off by the publicans and other middlemen: Mayhew reckoned they earned on average 10s a week, but took home only 5s, or even 2s 6d, so their wives and children went hungry. In 1840 there had been 170 ballast-heavers, but "the men assembled declared that their numbers had more nearly trebled than doubled since then. Within the last two or three years many new hands had got to work, on account of the distress in Ireland." Some of the riverside workers were certainly heavy drinkers, but a significant number either were total abstainers, or said they would very much like to be. Visiting one non-drinking dockworker's family, Mayhew saw "a print of Father Moore the teetotaler" on the wall.

Irish street-seller

The number of Irish street-sellers in London had doubled since the Potato Famine: there were now thought to be over 10,000, including children. Mostly they peddled fruit and nuts, turning over tiny amounts of stock for halfpennies and farthings. Older Irish women specialised in hawking cheap damaged fruit: "they make, I was told, from 4d.to 1s. a day the year round, or perhaps 7d. or 8d. a day, Sunday included. They are all Roman Catholics, and resort to the street-sale after mass... Two of their best pitches are on Saffron-hill and in Petticoat-lane." Other Irish immigrants worked as tailors or shoe-makers in the East End "sweatshops" – tiny factories, often occupying a single room which doubled as living quarters, and using casual, low-paid labour to mass-produce goods on the cheap – or as unskilled labourers in the building trade and on the docks. All this work was casual and seasonal, and the workers could be laid off at any time.

Visiting Rosemary Lane, the part of St Mary and St Michael's district which was most thickly populated with very poor Irish people, Mayhew explored the labyrinth of courts and alleys which branched off the Lane itself, noting the barefoot children and the shockingly "bonnetless girls". ("Respectable" young women could only go out swaddled in coats, hats and gloves, however hot the weather.)

Some of the alleys were so narrow that neighbours could chat from windows on opposite sides, and whole families lived in one room, or perhaps two, with beds, chairs and tables crowded in. Yet inside they were surprisingly neat, with sanded floors and "showy-coloured prints of saints and martyrs" covering the walls. The doors were mostly left open, and nobody seemed to mind if he strolled in for a closer look.

Street-sellers, whether Irish or English, were usually illiterate, but the increasing number of Catholic schools was encouraging Irish parents to want their own children to have some education. Mayhew was impressed by the chastity of the Irish women and girls, and the low incidence of cohabitation outside marriage. He accompanied a Catholic priest on his rounds, and witnessed the high esteem in which he was held. The Irish were not great beer drinkers, but when they did drink they were more likely to go for spirits, on which they got drunk very quickly. On the other hand they were twice as likely as the English to be teetotallers "– teetotallers too, who, having taken the pledge, under the sanction of their priests, and looking upon it as a religious obligation, keep it rigidly." They were very generous about lending money, and also very honest about repayment. Whiprounds and raffles were held for anyone who fell sick, or for funeral expenses.

The Catholic community in Tower Hamlets was, taken overall, very poor, with many individual members extremely poor. But a growing number were managing to improve their position in a modest way. Some of the docker families had secured permanent jobs, or become superintendents, and these positions were passed down from father to son. Others saved up and invested their money, usually in houses which they rented out, or small shops. According to Mayhew:

> *Money is also advanced to the deserving Irish through the agency of the Roman Catholic priests, who are the medium through whom charitable persons of their own faith exercise good offices. Money, too, there is no doubt, is often advanced out of the priest's own pocket.*

Finally, among the regular Massgoers at St Mary and St Michael's were some highly successful business men, and also a few professionals such as doctors and customs officers, coming usually from a middle-class, educated background back in Ireland. A significant proportion of parishioners were therefore at least sufficiently well-off to have to pay poor rates, which in turn entitled them to vote in local government elections – and perhaps consider standing for election themselves. We can identify two of the more prosperous families from this period. John Michael Calnan was born in London around 1807, and his wife Sarah (ten years younger than he) was also London-born. Calnan ran a successful building and decorating business, and was elected to the Vestry of St George's in the East in 1855. The Calnans lived just off Commercial Road on the corner of Star Street, a very short walk from the Oratory of Loretto. Francis and Norah Scannell were immigrants from

Ireland who'd come to settle in Ratcliffe around 1848, when they were both in their late 20s and already had a small daughter, Kate, born in London. They found that "Virginia-street Chapel had a congregation respectable and numerous … and the usual business was going on of a well-attended church by a congregation likely to leave some traces of good behind them in proportion to their numbers." Francis did very well for himself as a cooper, not a journeyman, but an employer with his own workshop in Broad Street.

The 1851 Census

St Mary's Cable Street

St George's in the East had been established at a time when the space between it and St Dunstan's was mostly open fields, so the traditional parish boundary didn't follow the streetplan: it doglegged northwards to take in the George Tavern, back across Commercial Road to run south-eastwards, diagonally across the church site where the new Catholic church was to be built, then turned roughly due east and meandered along to Hardinge Street, where it reached the boundary with the hamlet of Ratcliffe. The big old Anglican parishes, while remaining the Civil Parishes for all purposes of local government, were gradually subdivided for religious purposes into smaller districts, each with its own church and vicar. All round the church site on Commercial Road, new Anglican churches went up. Directly to the north St Thomas' Arbour Square, a cheaply built shoebox, was completed in 1838. To the west, Christchurch Watney Street was opened in 1841. Most of the church site lay in an L-shaped district to the east and south of Christchurch's, for which St Mary's Cable Street was built 1849-50. It was paid for by Lord Haddo, eldest son of Lord Aberdeen, and named as a tribute to his wife: willing to pay a bit extra for a good looking church, he told the architect to add a tower and spire, and he also provided an endowment of £3,200.

The 1851 Census shows Fr Horrabin living at No 5, Virginia Street, with his assistants Frs David Toomey and James Foley (*another* James Foley, very young and newly ordained) living at No 6, and his housekeeper, 59-year-old Harriet Creamer (James Creamer's widow) living with her daughter at No 7. Fr Toomey had been ordained in 1849, when in his late 30s, and he'd previously worked at Spitalfields, in the exciting task of pioneering the new mission which was to become St Anne's: he had excellent leadership qualities, and was thoroughly reliable. He was also Irish-speaking, and since about a third of the East End Catholics spoke Gaelic more readily than English, and down in Wapping a lot of people couldn't understand English at all, this was a precious asset. Fr Moore, and his assistant Fr John Gallagher, were living at the Johnson Street school, camping uncomfortably in side-rooms.

As part of the national Census that year, an enumeration was made of how many people actually attended church services of any denomination, on a selected Sunday, and also a survey of the amount of accommodation available at each place of worship. The returns filled in by Fr Horrabin for Virginia Street show that the old chapel had just 15 free sittings, 700 "other sittings", and standing room for 350. Attendance at the 8.00 Mass was 600; at 9.00 500; and at each of the next two Masses 1,000. 450 attended the evening service. Fr Moore stated that the "Oratory of Loretto" in Johnson Street had 360 sittings (he didn't indicate whether he considered them to be "free" or "other"), and standing room for another 150; total attendance in the morning, taking all four Masses together, was 1,000, and at the evening service 500. Total Mass attendance for the two chapels came to 4,100. These figures are not precise: neither priest had not done a proper count, only looked round and made a rough estimate. Since we know there was an entrance tariff, it's doubtful that even the standing room in either location was actually free, but clearly almost all the seating at Virginia Street was reserved for the better-off. It's also clear that neither venue was anything like full at the earlier Masses. Nevertheless it's likely that some of the Masses really were packed out. Charles Fay, as a child, was often put up into the organ loft at Virginia Street for lack of room, and he recalled both the side doors being left open, so people outside could participate: he'd seen them kneeling on the pavement at the consecration.

The returns of the Church Census, revealing for the first time how many people in England, across all denominations, were *not* attending church, sparked off a further wave of church construction by both Anglicans and Nonconformists. Only the Catholics lagged behind, because they lacked the resources to build. In the long term this may have been a blessing in disguise, because a lot of the new Protestant churches were redundant from the start: just because churches were there didn't mean people were going to go to them, and many had to function half empty. But in the short term, Catholic provision really was woefully inadequate.

U-turn

Fr Moore was still confident that the mission of Our Lady of Loreto had a glorious future ahead. A number of new guilds and other religious associations were thriving, about 400 children were attending classes during the day, and a highly successful ragged school, being run by volunteers in the evenings and at weekends, was putting some of the local Protestant ragged schools out of business. Nevertheless, despite the glowing impression Moore had given on the occasion of the Lord Mayor of Dublin's visit, the Johnson Street school-chapel was *not* paid for: there was a large debt owing, and Fr Moore himself wasn't altogether clear what the liabilities amounted to. The process of dividing the old Virginia Street district was therefore halted, and put into reverse. Halfway through 1851, Fr Horrabin's congregation in Wapping established a committee and began fundraising very hard for the new church on Commercial Road: by the end of the year the foundations of the new church had been completed and paid for. At the beginning of February 1852 Fr Moore abruptly announced to the Johnson Street people that he was leaving; he'd been transferred to Stratford. Protests immediately broke out, but he insisted he had to be obedient to his bishop.

Fr Horrabin resumed overall charge of the whole of the big old St Mary and St Michael's district, which now had two Mass centres – the one in Virginia Street, and the Johnson Street school-chapel – about a mile apart. A middle-aged, very experienced priest named Henry Philips was brought in to look after Johnson Street, and help the congregation over the difficult months which lay ahead. For a while it looked as though the school-chapel would have to be put up for sale – in which case it would be eagerly snapped up by one of the Protestant groups. But it would be impossible to go back to managing with just the old chapel – and in any case Virginia Street was under threat: the lease still had a few years to run, but once it expired it would not be renewed, because the land was being purchased by a dock company, to expand the docks. A whole lot of money collected for the new church was therefore used instead to rescue Johnson Street

A meeting was then held at Johnson Street for the people who normally attended Mass there, and five men were elected to form a committee: M O'Grady, J Dennan, William Flinn, Mr Grace and Mr Conway. Thus both congregations had a committee, and their fundraising efforts were henceforth combined. People from both chapels must have joined together for a confirmation at Virginia Street in March, which involved 523 candidates, children and adults – the largest number at one time ever in London up to then.

A design for a church of cathedral-like proportions was commissioned from William Wilkinson Wardell. It was to have a tower at the front along Commercial Road, with a spire soaring up to a height of 250 ft and forming a conspicuous landmark. At the back would be a spacious presbytery, linked to the church by sacristies, and at the front (where the temporary school had stood) a tiny lodge for a caretaker.

**William Wilkinson Wardell ...
Architect of St Mary and St Michael's**

Tenders went out, the lowest – £14,674 – was selected, and Fr Horrabin signed a contract. The builders were John and Edward Bird of Hammersmith, and the foreman in charge of the site at Commercial Road was a Mr Tindall. The "Our Lady of Loretto" name was dropped into the discard pile of history: the new church would be the continuation on a different site of the Virginia Street Chapel, keeping the old name St Mary and St Michael's.

Cardinal Wiseman came in May to lay the foundation stone, but the event did *not* go with a swing. Although a temporary altar had been set up, plans to celebrate Mass had to be cancelled because of a high wind, and "The attendance of London Catholics ... was far from being satisfactory, considering the day being a holiday and the beauty of the weather." (That was a pity, because such events were attended mainly by wealthy outsiders who would have donated money to the cause.) As the Cardinal was feeling unwell, he couldn't even stay to the reception. The building work continued, and the walls went up to a height of about 8 ft, but then the momentum was lost: "The collections gradually fell off, and the builders removed all their scaffolding. Hope disappeared from the congregation, and depression and despair took its place."

Shall we despair? God forbid

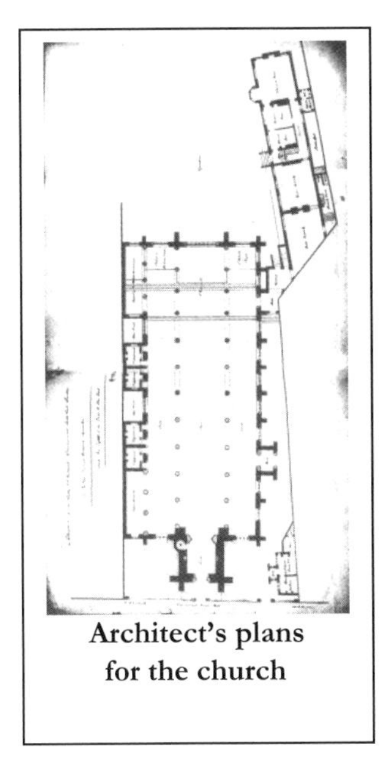

Architect's plans for the church

The idea of bringing Fr Kelly back to St Mary and St Michael's had been raised on several occasions. Morale in the parish was very low, and many parishioners didn't think the mess could ever be sorted out, but quite a lot of them had developed an idea that *Kelly*, and nobody else, would be able to sort it out and get the new church built. Wiseman agreed, and his Vicar General Dr Robert Whitty travelled down to Portsmouth on several occasions to discuss the proposal.

However Fr Kelly was enjoying life in Portsea: by the usual (low) standards of Catholic missions it had quite a good income, the workload was reasonable, and the sea air was – he firmly believed – keeping him in good health. "I often calculated the pros and cons, but the worldly motive was triumphant." One night, however,

> *I awoke in a terrible state of confusion, as if someone had been lecturing me whilst I was between asleep and awake – saying to me – 'This place is too comfortable for you. Much more is expected of you yet. Remember what is said in the gospel to the rich man who had made himself comfortable. "Thou fool, this night do they require thy soul of thee." Get away and build the Church for those poor people in Virginia-street district...' I tried to sleep again, but in vain; and I may say that for one whole week sleep fled from me; and in bed I rolled about like a ship in a storm, but sleep would not come. But the above sentence kept rushing backwards and forwards, upwards and downwards, ringing in my ears, so I had to give in.*

Since Portsea was now in Southwark Diocese, the move involved negotiations with Bp Grant, and Fr Henry Phillips was transferred to Portsea as replacement. Fr Horrabin was to remain at Virginia Street as "honorary chaplain", but Fr Kelly would actually be in charge. On 18th October 1853 he arrived back in London, and on the evening of that

> *cold cheerless day, I found myself in the Commercial-road, East, viewing what might have been the ruins of some large buildings destroyed by an earthquake. There were the foundations of an immense building, with some low stunted pieces of walls standing here*

and there upon them. Not a bit of scaffolding was to be seen in any direction. The builders, as I learned subsequently, had a claim of £500 upon this seeming wreck... My predecessor had paid them all he had in hand shortly before my arrival, so he had not even sixpence to hand over to me to meet so large a balance.

Moving in to Johnson Street did nothing to lift his spirits:

the smoke nearly pecked my eyes out, and I had to sleep in a small room off the school where no fire could be lit by night or by day, and where in the morning the counterpane was as wet as if soaked in a bucket of water.

Nevertheless he quickly put together the facts and figures, composed a brief rehearsal of the saga since the collections for the new church began, and got an appeal printed up, dated November 1853, and issued in the name of himself and the whole clergy team – himself, Frs Horrabin, Toomey and Foley, and the new curate Fr Daniel Santry:

They have a large, and in many respects a praiseworthy congregation, but the scanty income which they derive from the better off amongst the poor, is no sooner received than it is expended on a much poorer class of our people, who are struck down by famine, fever, and cholera. What is to be done? Shall we despair? God forbid. 'If God be for us, who is against us?'

Poor Fr Horrabin fell quite seriously ill, with suspected cholera, and although he survived he retired from the active ministry, and went to live in Houndsditch. Only Frs Toomey and Foley were left from the old team, wondering if the new boss really would be able to turn the situation round. "The case" wrote Fr Kelly,

was a very sad one. I knew it beforehand, and this is precisely the reason why I could not help accepting the fate of sinking or swimming with so many thousands of helpless people... the agreeable report of the feeling of the congregation, brought to me by some of the collectors, was, that Father Kelly might induce the builders to erect the scaffolding again, but not one of the present generation would see the church built, nor indeed anyone before the scaffold poles grew into large trees.

Though he knew all about the problems with the stalled church project, Kelly was under the impression that there was no pressing difficulty about the schools. The district currently had three sets of schools located in Red Lion Street, Johnson Street, and Princes Square where 500 boys and girls were enrolled. But during his first week in charge, he had to appear at the County Court to try to fight an eviction order against the Princes Square schools: he lost. "Such work as this I never expected. The children were ejected." Johnson Street, he discovered, was still burdened with debts. They included some transactions by Fr Moore which took Fr Kelly a while to track down – and when he did, he promptly received a demand for several years' arrears of interest. At one point Fr Moore himself was arrested, and briefly imprisoned. Even the Red Lion Street building turned out to be in a very poor state structurally, and liable to eat up large amounts of money for repairs.

Still reeling from the shock, Fr Kelly examined the accounts for the two chapels: "I studied the matter over and over, and found to my amazement both chapels were insolvent, in other words, the expenditure exceeded the income. I found myself, therefore, under the painful necessity of reducing the expenditure, already only moderate, but I also reduced the price of the sittings; and these two measures made the accounts square." By a neat piece of lateral thinking, he reduced the charges for attending Mass, and thereby increased the takings, because immediately far more people began to attend. Clearly a great deal of the space in the two chapels had previously been going to waste. As well as squaring the accounts, Fr Kelly managed to provide temporary accommodation for the schoolchildren ejected from Princes Square.

We find time for everything

The most important question facing him was whether to go ahead with the original idea of building a really large church on Commercial Road. Having decided yes, he stuck to his decision despite mounting criticism. Dr Whitty became convinced that it would be better to build two or three smaller centres in different parts of the district, to divide it up into more manageably-sized parishes, and a number of other priests heartily agreed with him. As Fr Kelly complained

> *To some it seemed like insanity to attempt to continue the building of the church, and so, Job's comforters gathered around, and earnestly urged me to pull up the foundations, and with the brick and stone erect a shanty here and a few others in different parts of the parish."*

He had a duty to provide adequate accommodation for the thousands of potential Massgoers in the St Mary and St Michael's district. Building one very large church would do the job far more easily and cheaply than building two or three – besides the waste of pulling up the foundations, and the expense and difficulty of having to acquire additional sites. Even if the big church idea *was* a mistake, it was too late to start saying so now:

We find the building in the position already described, and we must endeavour to finish it.

Father William Kelly

While the work proceeded, Fr Kelly said goodbye to his uncomfortable room off the school-chapel, and moved into lodgings at No 22 Colet Place, one of a row of terraced houses on Commercial Road, a little way along from the church site. Fr Foley joined him at Colet Place, and the other three priests found lodgings in Ratcliffe. They all regarded the old chapel house in Virginia

Street as unhealthy for anyone to have to live full-time, but the curates took turns to sleep there, and at the Johnson Street school, so as to be readily available in case of sick calls. Fr Kelly made a point of visiting both Mass centres every Sunday. They each had four Sunday Masses at 8.00, 9.00, 10.00 and 11.00, and an evening service.

The usual arrangement was that the Ratcliffe curates did the Masses at Virginia Street, but one of them also did a Mass at Johnson Street. At first the arrangement didn't work very well: quite often the curate wasn't notified (or didn't get the message), so people would turn up at Johnson Street for Mass, and there'd be no priest and no Mass. On one occasion when this happened the junior curate, Fr Edmund Pennington, got the blame (he had no idea why), and was summoned by Dr John Maguire, Wiseman's other Vicar General, to be bawled out. He explained calmly that it wasn't his fault, so Dr Maguire tried to nail him on another issue:

'Now,' he continued, 'you are a young man, and I am told you play at cards.' 'Quite so, Doctor, but I hope you do not mean to say that it is wrong.' 'I will not enter into that question,' was his reply, 'but I want to know (he was very emphatic) where you find the time?' 'We are so clever down East,' I said, 'that we find time for everything.' Scored again!

London's sewage went straight into the Thames, from which the city's drinking water was drawn. Sanitation laws were beginning to be passed, but very slowly: the mechanisms of disease transmission were not properly understood, and reformers had to battle against tremendous opposition from vested interests. One reform which did go through fairly quickly was the prohibition of burials in the built-up areas of London, and the Catholic cemetery at the church site on Commercial Road was accordingly closed on 1st May 1854.

The cholera epidemic which Fr Kelly mentioned in his appeal was still raging. There was no effective cure, though people developed all sorts of trial-and-error techniques, a few of which may have provided some alleviation of the symptoms. The Ratcliffe priests used "a mixture prepared by Mr. Hewitt," a Catholic chemist in Well Street, Wellclose Square, and made a point of carrying some around with them. A priest was likely to arrive at a poor family's home several hours before a doctor could be got hold of, and Fr Santry reckoned Hewitt's medicine could save the patient's life if it was administered early enough. But the Johnson Street priests either didn't know about it, or didn't share Fr Santry's touching belief in its efficacy. "In the year 1854," wrote Fr Kelly, *there arrived at my lodgings in Johnson-street, Commercial Road, East, without any application on my part, from Mr. Waterton, a gallon of cholera mixture, with a note of instruction how to administer it to cholera patients, and from Lord Edward Howard, five gallons of real French brandy. Myself and assistant priest tried the cholera mixture, first of all, but it was a failure, except in one case. It may have been an excellent remedy, but the conditions required could only have been complied with in a hospital. We sent the cholera mixture overboard and tried the brandy, and saved, as we believe, many lives. Take one case out of many. I enter a room and find a man twisting about like a serpent through excessive pain. There is not a spark of fire in the grate. Everything has been pawned, and there is not sufficient bedclothes to warm him, and there is not an ounce of coal to put into the grate. The man is as cold as a stone. What is to be done? Firstly all the Church requires, and then the brandy. To know the quantity to be administered a priest ought to be a good judge of the pulse. Some cases one meets are beyond recovery, but, even then, a little brandy seems to comfort them.*

Around this time a chemist in King David Lane set to work to produce a cure for malaria. William Henry Perkin was not a retail pharmacist like Hewitt, but a young student working in his home laboratory, and the reason he was focusing on malaria – rather than on cholera, or any of the other diseases which plagued East London – was that it was one of the few conditions for which there was already a known cure: quinine. However quinine was in desperately short supply, so Perkin was trying to synthesise it, though without success. Instead he accidentally discovered the first aniline dye: mauveine, which he went on to develop commercially and make his fortune. But Perkin's discovery did more than transform the fashion world, as it led on to a great many other useful applications, including pharmaceutical ones.

Counting sheep

Rent for the Virginia Street chapel was now being paid to the London Dock Company, which had completed the purchase of the property. In one of many letters to the Catholic papers, appealing for donations, Fr Kelly wrote: "They are very anxious to get us out even now, and would willingly pay us compensation, but we have no place to go to. It is absolutely certain that we must give up possession in June, 1857, *i.e.*, in less than three years from this date." He had managed to pay off some outstanding debts, and now had just £300 in hand to restart work on the church. According to his calculations the total required was £10,176 14s.

The builder will not lay a stone for us unless we are able, according to our contract, to pay him seventy-five per cent, as he goes on, and at the conclusion, before opening the church, the remaining twenty-five per cent… On the faith of what we (I mean this congregation) may be able to do with the assistance derived from the charitable, the builder has consented to resume the works next August, but will, of course, again stop the moment we are unable to pay him. This congregation, though very poor, is numerous; we purpose, therefore, laying a tax upon ourselves for three years, heavier and more general than anything hitherto attempted.

Fr Kelly concluded his letter with a list of items which he stressed were not included in the previous calculations, but which were nevertheless badly needed, and were the sort of things that wealthy individuals might like to donate: vestments ("we are wretchedly off in that respect"), three altars, benches, a organ, stained glass windows, and a baptismal font.

Up to this point figures given for total numbers of Catholics in the district had been guesstimates. The figures quoted by the clergy team had shown a steady upward progression throughout the first half of the nineteenth century – with, interestingly, not the slightest hint of an upward blip at the time of the Potato Famine – and around 1850 had reached 24,000. Fr Kelly suspected the real figure was probably less than 20,000, but he'd heard estimates as high as 32,000. During a CPSC meeting, when all sorts of figures were being wildly bandied around, it occurred to him to carry out a census and find out for sure. So off he went, "large book in hand, and pen and ink in waistcoat pocket."

He did the whole survey himself. It wasn't just a question of going door to door along the street – he had to go into most of the houses and work room to room, because each room might accommodate a different household. Whenever people identified themselves as Catholics, he put a series of questions to them, and signed them up for financial contributions. Then, as soon as he'd finished each section, he drew up a list and assigned a collector to go round once a month and collect the money. The census

was commenced on the 8th of July 1854 and continued to the 22nd of December1854, with the exception of three weeks spent in preparing children for their first Communion … Three weeks in 1855 brought the Census to a close. The time daily employed in making the Census ranged from 4½ to 9 hours, but as I did not go out every Saturday, being obliged to see to the preparation of the Collectors Books for the Sunday it may be stated, free from exaggeration, that for six days out of seven every week, five hours daily during a period of five months and fourteen days, were spent in this work of Census making, going personally from house to house & penetrating from cellar to garret.

During all this time, wrote Fr Kelly in a later reminiscence, *the Asiatic cholera raged violently, so that frequently a family I had been speaking to would send after me because one of its members, four or five minutes after I left, had been attacked by the cholera. I used to go back directly and hear the confession and give absolution, and then send for one of my assistant priests to administer the other Sacraments of the Catholic Church.*

His findings were:

Number of persons, children included, contained in the Census Books, 15,566, discovered by Collectors about 200 more, say 234 more from various causes escaped our notice, total 16,000. No of children from 1 day to 4 years inclusively 2030, from 4 to 6 years inclusively 912 from 6 to 7 exclusively 86, total number of children under 7 years of age 3028. From 7 to 11 inclusively 1963 from 11 to 14 inclusively 257, total from 7 to 14 inclusively 2220, total number of children from 1 day to 14 years inclusively 5,248. At Catholic Schools 1060. At Protestant Schools 93. No of Protestant wives 38 Do of Husbands 70. No of Baptisms from July 2 1854 to July 2 1855 1,153.

The previous estimates of 20,000 or more had been quoted in good faith: they were based on an extrapolation from the baptism figures, which at St Mary and St Michael's ran at around a thousand a year. However, as Fr Kelly explained to Wiseman, a lot of children baptised at St Mary and St Michael's were not brought up in any sense as Catholics – not even as non-practising ones. Many were the products of mixed marriages, and in some cases neither parent was a Catholic: they were brought for baptism by another relative, or a friend of the family.

Non-Catholic parents were often willing to let a child be baptised Catholic, especially if it was thought unlikely to live. Finally, a high proportion of the children ended up in Poor Law institutions, where they were brought up as Anglicans – or rather, in what Fr Kelly called the "Workhouse Religion".

The Catholic Working Classes do not get their fair share

Catholic leaders were constantly whingeing about how generously Protestants gave to religious causes, and wanted to know why the Catholics didn't. Fr Kelly reckoned he'd discovered part of the answer to that one. Catholics contributed to the poor rates like everyone else, but were being systematically discriminated against when it came to claiming benefits.

I have to observe, that there are some six millions of money raised annually in this Country for the support of the Poor. This is a bank upon which the Working Classes fall back in cases of distress arising from sackings and other causes. But owing to the intense bigotry in this Country, the Catholic Working Classes do not get their fair share out of this Bank; when they apply for any portion of this money contributed by Catholics as well as Protestants. They are generally told in the most insulting way to go to their Priests. They seldom meet with sympathy from any member of the various boards of Guardians; the Relieving Officer is frequently a ribald bully and the Parish Doctor, when they can get one, ridicules the faith of the Catholic mother during the throes of childbirth.

The parish which was required by the Poor Law to support you, if you were destitute, was usually the one where you were born – even if you hadn't lived there for years. This meant that Irish immigrants who applied for relief could be shipped straight to Ireland. If they happened to want to return to Ireland, and couldn't afford the fare, it was a useful way of getting free transport. But a great many immigrants had come over precisely because the situation in their home area was completely hopeless, and the last thing they wanted was to be dumped back there.

The fear of deportation was therefore a major deterrent to applying for poor relief. Recently there'd been a change in the law: an Act of Parliament in 1846 laid down that applicants who had been resident for five years could not be removed to their original parish, but had a right to relief where they lived now. After some hesitation, it was generally agreed that this Act applied to the Irish-born. But many poor Irish didn't know the law well enough, or had no way to prove residence for the requisite time period, and Poor Law officials were only too happy to take advantage of their vulnerability:

The threat of being sent back to Ireland, even where they have legal rights to relief but no friend to vindicate it for them, sends the poor applicant back broken hearted among his or her friends. The consequence of all this is that the Catholic Working Classes, have a heavy burden thrown upon them in relieving their poorer brethren, whilst this duty is taken off the shoulders of the Protestant Working Classes, by falling back in cases of distress, upon the rates levied on Catholics and Protestants alike.

Fr Kelly's observation is borne out by evidence given to a Parliamentary Select Committee in 1854: a relieving officer stated: "Sometimes I beat off Irish applicants for a good while... they have universally a great dread of being sent back to Ireland... All that we want is not to see them again."

Sogarth Aroon

Making the census had been a fascinating experience, and Fr Kelly wished afterwards that he'd kept a proper diary. Many of the people couldn't speak English, and he couldn't speak Irish, but he kept hearing the phrase "sogarth aroon", and he knew it meant: "beloved priest".

I found a large class of single men and women, of married men and old men, who had not entered a church for ten, fifteen, twenty, thirty and forty years. The largest number of those were born in London, and many of them had been to the Catholic schools when children. In many cases, the people born and brought up in Ireland tried to prevent me entering the rooms of those above referred to, saying I was sure to be insulted by them, for they had heard them often swear at the Priests and ridicule them. I used to say to my protectors, Well, well, you don't understand those stray sheep of mine, but they will hear and understand 'Sogarth Aroon.' I entered every room and was received joyfully, and those who had not spoken to a Priest for years not only promised to mend their ways, but also to subscribe to the new church. Several Protestants wished for instruction. Indeed, I may say I gave a short Mission in every Catholic dwelling, and when objectionable pictures and other things of that kind were exposed to view, I expressed a wish for their removal.

I occasionally met in the streets and lanes, men made furious by drink, surrounded by dozens of women, men and boys, endeavouring to take them home, but to no purpose. Whenever I came in view, the words Sogarth, Sogarth, were heard aloud, and surely enough, Sogarth walked in amongst the crowd, took such men by the hands, and walked them home as tame as lambs. Six hours daily up stairs and down stairs and talking all the time is a work that will fatigue any constitution. During those five months I received neither incivility nor insult from any person except an Irish Orangeman, whose daughter was a Catholic.

Fr Kelly asked parents whether children were attending school – and if so, was it a Catholic or a Protestant one. Since he knew they'd tell him what they thought he wanted to hear, he planned to double-check by getting the teachers in the schools to keep registers. But it proved very difficult to persuade them to do it: keeping registers was an unheard of innovation, and teachers were always delightfully vague about how many children they were actually educating. The Christian Brothers were particularly resistant. Fr Kelly did ascertain that many children *couldn't* go to school, because they were busy trying to earn their own living:.

it is a fact that hundreds of the children of this district are like the birds of the air, depending on each days labour for their sustenance, from the age of seven years and upwards labouring after one fashion or another from early morn, to late at night.

There were all sorts of ways children could earn money, by doing odd jobs, or selling things on the streets: the smallest and poorest children sold watercress. Large numbers of children disappeared from London every year in late summer, having gone off with their families to the countryside to work for farmers getting in the harvest. Whenever there really wasn't any work available, these children might turn up in school again for a few days or weeks, but it was unusual for any child to be seen after the age of 11.

Something Fr Kelly made a special note of for future action was the 300 Catholics whom he identified as "unfortunate women" – that is, working as prostitutes. Very few were locally born, most coming from maritime cities in Ireland: "Dublin, Cork, Belfast, Limerick, Galway, &c., &c." He kept in touch with them, trying to persuade them to take the big step of breaking with their miserable way of life, and eventually contacted the Mother Superior of the Good Shepherd Sisters at Hammersmith to enquire how many "unfortunates" could be offered a refuge in their "penitents' home". "She desired to know how many he would be likely to send." He told her "he thought about sixty. But as she only had room for one, he sent her one, and there the matter ended."

Despite frustrations of that sort, Fr Kelly felt the visitation exercise had been thoroughly worthwhile, and he resolved thereafter to repeat it every few years. His having taken the trouble to establish the facts on the ground made an excellent impression on some people, among them an Hon Mr Browne whom he had never met before, but who got in touch and pledged to pay a regular subscription of *£10 a week* towards the church building fund. Birds, the builders, also became far more confident, and willing to get on with the job and trust that the instalments would be paid as they fell due – though Mr Bird used to drop in from time to time for long conversations with Fr Kelly, during which he would ask some *very* searching questions. Fr Kelly didn't resent the contractor's importunities: under the circumstances he thought he was being very generous and understanding.

A high-flying young priest named Herbert Vaughan, ordained in Rome in October 1854, was wondering whether to accept at teaching post at the diocesan seminary, as Cardinal Wiseman wanted him to, or go "on the mission" (ie into parish work). He never did have a normal parish appointment, but he must have thought it would be good for him to gain *some* experience of pastoral work in one of the poorer London missions.

He therefore arranged to spend some time at St Mary and St Michael's, going the rounds of parish visiting like any other young curate. It was not a formal assignment, and no record has survived to show when he came, or how long he stayed. He may only have been there for a few weeks – perhaps covering for a curate who was away on holiday, or ill. However there's no question that he *was* there: he referred to it on numerous occasions in later life, saying how important the experience had been for him.

One long continual wail and lament

A three-week mission was given by the Redemptorists to the St Mary and St Michael's Catholics in January 1855. Ten priests divided their efforts between the two separate chapels, and – as was often the case with these very early missions – the impact was dramatic. By the end of the first week, both venues were packed each night two hours before the services were due to start. 28 adult converts were received into the Church during the mission itself, and many others were enrolled to be given courses of instruction afterwards. Although all ten Redemptorists were available for hearing confessions

> *from an early hour in the morning until late at night... their number was insufficient to meet the wants of the crowds, who pressed forward with anxiety to the confessionals, so that on the very morning of the departure of the missionaries, numbers were obliged to quit the confessionals unheard.*

11,000 received Communion, including 400 children making First Communions. Because the space in each chapel was so small, the final farewell sermon at Virginia Street on the last Sunday was delivered in shifts: to an all-women congregation in the afternoon and an all-men congregation in the evening. Two hours later a working man, still tearful with emotion, remarked to Fr Kelly:

> *I did not wonder at the women sobbing and crying in the afternoon; but at seven this evening, when there was not even one woman in the chapel, and it was crowded to suffocation, the whole of the men, young and old, borne along, as it were on a resistless tide, burst forth into one long continual wail and lament during, but more particularly towards the end of the fathers farewell address.*

To his account of the mission Fr Kelly added:

> *'Blessed be God for ever!' During the mission a piece of timber running in and supporting the centre of one hundred square feet of the gallery broke in two, yet, though the gallery was crowded to almost suffocation, every one escaped unhurt.*

No sooner was the mission over than he issued an invitation to the Redemptorists to come back and give a "renewal" (a follow-up mini-mission) as soon as the new church was opened. Though it was unquestionably a highly successful event, and he was genuinely satisfied with the outcome, he was secretly convinced that although "The good Fathers went away delighted, for they believe all the success was theirs," much of the credit was properly due to the spadework he had put in during his parish census.

Winter was always a difficult time. In extreme conditions, when ice on the river prevented ships from docking, thousands of dockers were thrown out of work at a time when not much was doing in the building trade either. Because the unemployed labourers then crowded into other marginal occupations like street selling, the distress spread through a huge proportion of the poor population. During January and February 1855, the situation became so bad that riots broke out in the East End. Fr Santry put out an appeal for humanitarian assistance:

Some thousands of our people derive their whole support from the daily shilling or half crown earned in the docks; but the last three or four weeks these thousands have been idle and starving, in consequence of adverse easterly winter winds preventing ships coming to London. Thus it is that the deepest, direst distress pervades our poor amid this awful inclement season... The small offerings of our poor boxes are gone – our own scanty purses are empty in their relief, and still the cry in our ears is, bread, bread. To give them this I ask charity, not for the helpless widow and fatherless child, of whom the cholera has left us but too many, but I ask it for the strong man of toil and labour, who, when he has his honest, hard-earned shilling, never grudges his penny to the poor, the Priest, or God's Church.

Early in March Fr Santry wrote again, to thank those who had sent donations, and state that the need was still there:

The 'dockmen', the 'ballast-men', the 'coal-whippers,' of whom the majority are honest, hard-working Irish Catholics, composing our congregation, are all begging from the public, and the distress among those of large families is appalling.

The river had frozen over completely: it was unnavigable all the way from Richmond to below London Bridge, the worse blockage since 1814. The workhouses distributed outdoor relief, and a number of charitable funds were set up, but there still was never enough to relieve all the suffering. It was noted, however, that many of the coalwhippers and other manual workers volunteered to assist the police in the protecting the property of the shopkeepers. Fortunately, a thaw set in before the end of February.

Mutiny on all sides

Unfortunately for Fr Kelly, Fr Toomey left in 1855 to take charge of St Joseph's, Bunhill Row. Donations had somehow kept coming in, and the chances of the new church being ready by the time the lease on Virginia

Street expired were looking up. However although young Fr Foley was shaping up well, serious problems developed with some of the other curates, with the Christian Brothers, and with the lay schoolteachers.

Fr Kelly had obtained some small building grants from the CPSC – £30 in 1853, and £80 more in 1854. For the children ejected from Princes Square he leased a former Methodist chapel in Pell Street, and adapted it into two large schoolrooms with space for 700 children. He also significantly reduced the debt on Johnson Street. For both these schools rent had to be paid each year: ground rent of £30 on Johnson Street, and £50 for Pell Street. The schools' endowment funds did cover part of the expenses, but Fr Kelly was trying to work out a deal whereby the endowments could be used to release money for the new church, thereby tying up the income for a considerable period of time. The East London Catholic Institution continued in existence, but fundraising dinners had gone out of fashion, and subscriptions were declining. The only other money coming in regularly was the traditional school pence: one penny a week per child. The answer to the schools' financial problems, Fr Kelly believed, was to put them under government inspection to make them eligible for state support. Besides capitation (so much per child per year), he would be able to apply for assistance with building work, and with obtaining textbooks and equipment. He should also be able to obtain stipends for pupil teachers. Pupil teachers were boys or girls of 13, apprenticed to work full-time as auxiliary teachers, learn on the job, and eventually earn their qualification; they were much better value than child monitors, and the government was willing to cover the full cost of deploying them. As well as government funding, Fr Kelly wanted to explore the feasibility of charging the children more than a penny a week. Unfortunately the Christian Brothers would have nothing to do with his proposals. This led to a row, exacerbated and brought to crisis point by the Brothers' refusal to co-ordinate their school holidays with all the other St Mary and St Michael's schools, or even notify Fr Kelly of their plans. Almost every year, Red Lion Street Boys' would close down early, and as soon as word spread round the district's juvenile bush telegraph, the other schools started to fall apart. While requesting intervention from the congregation's Superior General in Dublin, Fr Kelly tried to work round the Brothers by bringing the other schools' holidays into line with theirs, but met with open defiance. One Monday morning in July, after he'd announced at all the Sunday Masses that the holidays were over, and the schools were to re-open, he "found the Brothers School locked and several boys waiting in the passage. Those amongst them who were at Mass yesterday, told me that after the 9 oclock Mass Brother Corbett told them not to go to School today nor during the week." It was the last straw: Fr Kelly sacked the Brothers forthwith, and replaced them with a certificated lay teacher. When William Lescher heard, he "heartily approved", though the school's other lay trustee, Mr Hewitt, was quite upset and tried unsuccessfully to get the decision reversed.

Confirmation and First Communion were usually conferred on the same day, or fairly close in time, and the usual age was 12. Fr Kelly was anxious to ensure that the children received both sacraments, and he certainly didn't have time to prepare them himself, on top of everything else. But the schoolteachers, and also the assistant priests, didn't want to do it, and argued that they, too, were far too busy. It was true that each week, two curates had to be constantly on duty for sick calls, and the priests also had to spend massive amounts of time hearing confessions. But there was also an issue about Fr Kelly wanting the children to receive their full sacramental initiation before they left school, when – according to the prevailing norms – they were not considered strictly old enough, and his staff probably thought it pointless to try to instruct them. However he knew that if he deferred it, they'd vanish, and he'd never get hold of them again.

Since the Brothers had gone, Fr Kelly's main headache was the headmistress of the Red Lion Street Girls' School. Mrs Mary Catherine Worsp, wife of a Protestant sea captain, had been in charge of the school for about six or eight years, had six girl pupil teachers working under her on government stipends, and was earning overtime for tutoring them. Yet whenever he dropped into the school, she wasn't there. Her pupil teachers always had an excuse for her, but he had his doubts about them too: he'd put several of them in charge of other schools in his district, and they'd proved totally useless. Moreover he had a suspicion that Fr Santry, when he was supposed to be catechising the schoolgirls, spent his visits there chatting to the teachers, wasting his own time, theirs and the children's.

As it turned out, Fr Santry was nursing a number of grievances. He had money problems, and felt the pay of an assistant priest in a poor mission wasn't enough to live on. He'd also been very friendly with the Christian Brothers, and now they were gone had formed an alliance with Mrs Worsp, and was egging her on to defy him. Without warning, Fr Santry and another curate made a complaint to Dr Maguire about the First Communion policy at St Mary and St Michael's. They alleged that Fr Kelly was admitting children as young as seven, who'd never been instructed or even been to confession, and that their behaviour in church was shocking: one girl had spat out the host. Fr Kelly wrote frantically to Cardinal Wiseman, explaining the dilemma he'd been in, and insisting he'd taken all possible measures to police the First

Communion celebrations, to minimize irreverence and scandal, and avert sacrilege. Deeply hurt, he promised in future to stick religiously to the minimum age rule, though reiterating that he did not think it pastorally appropriate.

Discovering that the Catholic School Inspector, Thomas Marshall, was colluding with Mrs Worsp in helping the pupil teachers cheat in their exams, to cover up the fact that she wasn't teaching them properly, Fr Kelly demanded her resignation, but agreed not to expose the situation publicly. It was a delicate situation: the parents of the pupil teachers had been running up bills in the local shops in anticipation of their daughters' stipends, and if the government discovered the truth, those stipends would not be paid.

Long experience had taught Fr Kelly always to avoid making unnecessary enemies, and he was quite terrified of the trouble Mrs Worsp could cause if she chose to kick up a fuss: "She is a woman of strong nerve and equal therein to any act of desperation." On top of all the infighting with his curates and schoolteachers, Fr Kelly picked an all-out row with the local Catholic teetotallers. Since Moore's departure, John Giles had resumed overall leadership, and they'd come to focus on teetotalism to the exclusion of anything else. They were constantly organising teetotal social events, but not coming to Mass. As Fr Kelly told it, "Teetotalism was like the abridgement of the Christian religion." Although the group no longer felt the need for any hands-on priestly involvement, it was still Catholic enough for his determined condemnation to break it up – and he did: "I smashed the whole affair to atoms".

Fr Kelly could see that drink caused untold misery in a great many families: it was a major cause of domestic violence, an all too common reason why children went to bed hungry. He didn't drink himself, because alcohol gave him a headache, and for his flock he was very keen on promoting temperance, in terms of moderate drinking habits, or voluntary abstention for those who believed abstention was the best course for them personally. Every time there was a parish mission, he hoped to see a harvest of men converted from sozzled drunks to respectably suited and booted Massgoers. On the other hand, doctors at the time seriously believed alcohol could be medically beneficial, and Kelly's own experiences during the cholera epidemics had convinced him they were right. But perhaps his main reason for disliking teetotalism was his firm conviction that for most people, the absolutism was counterproductive: anyone who had taken the teetotal pledge only had to break it once, and their overwhelming sense of guilt would drive them into alcoholic excess. He'd known doctrinaire teetotallers who ended up drinking themselves to death.

So much protest was aroused by the closing down of the temperance group that Fr Kelly agreed to give it another try, and let a group use the premises of one of the schools, making sure that either he or one of his assistant priests was always present at the Sunday evening meetings. He painstakingly drew up a set of rules, to make it into a friendly society. However the members still insisted on having Protestant speakers, who were readily available, and had an established repertoire which was entertaining and made them laugh. Fr Kelly grew increasingly uncomfortable, regarding a lot of what was said as blasphemous, and after a while he stepped in once again and suppressed the group.

Deadline approaching

The church was originally designed to have a spire

By September 1855 the tower of St Mary and St Michael's was already up to 40 ft. But time was running out: if the new church wasn't ready by the time the lease expired, the congregation would be homeless, and Fr Kelly still needed £5,000 to complete the building. By the end of August 1856 he had resolved that, to save time and money, the spire would have to be wait till later. Meanwhile, a truncated tower was temporarily levelled off and roofed over at a height of 60 ft, high enough to incorporate a large window for light. He had just paid the builder £200 and had "not now one farthing of balance in hand for the next monthly instalment". He wasn't planning to have stained glass windows – except that it would be nice to have just one for the Blessed Sacrament Chapel.

Within another month, he became determined to push on even faster and have the new church opened before the end of 1856. Since the Dock

Company had blocked off the main access route to Virginia Street, the stretch by the chapel had become "an universal resort for prostitutes and sailors at night, so much so that the man in charge of living in the house, has sometimes to throw water upon them from his window to make them move off from his sight." Provisionally, the opening date was fixed for 8th December, the Feast of the Immaculate Conception.

At the beginning of October Fr Kelly told Birds to get the presbytery finished, so he could move in and no longer have to live in lodgings and pay rent. He then prepared to sink all his personal assets – money, some property in Hammersmith, and some stock – into the church building fund, and at the same time to make arrangements for a loan of £3,000 from a wealthy sympathizer, secured by two life insurance policies, one for Fr Kelly and one for Fr Foley who was now his senior assistant priest. Although the church would open with a huge burden of debt, Fr Kelly explained to the parishioners that the property could never be mortgaged or seized, or used for any other purpose than as a church. This was because Fr Horrabin, shortly before he retired, had had the title deeds enrolled in Chancery. Fr Kelly was hopeful of persuading Wiseman to agree to consecrate the church on the day it opened, but this the Cardinal was not prepared to do. Churches were not supposed to be consecrated until they were fully paid for.

One afternoon Fr Kelly returned to Commercial Road to find that a problem had suddenly arisen while he was out: the Surveyor of the Commercial Road Trust had stopped the builders from beginning work on the caretaker's lodge. There was a regulation about how far back buildings had to be from the road, and the lodge was too close: it needed to be 3 ft further back – but that would leave insufficient space between it and the entrance to the church. Fortunately Wardell was at the site at the time, and he immediately sent off a formal letter to the Board of Trustees to ask if they'd make an exception. Failing that, he'd have to modify the design of the lodge.

Missionary Rector

The terms "parish" and "parishioner" were coming into use among Catholics, as their religious life settled into a more stable pattern – though none of the churches or chapels in England were, strictly speaking, parishes according to Canon Law, and their location and staffing could be changed at any time by the bishops, in order to adapt to new circumstances. Just twelve favoured churches in Westminster Diocese had been chosen to bear a special status, with the priests in charge of them being named "Missionary Rectors" (which was understood to give them permanent tenure). Thus on 21st October 1856,

Cardinal Wiseman placed his signature at the foot of a ceremonially worded letter to Fr Kelly:

> *as we consider it expedient to increase the number of such churches, we have resolved, with the consent of our Chapter, to include in this same number the Church of the most Holy Mary and Blessed Michael in St. George's-in-the-East ... We therefore by these presents declare and decree that this newly-built Church of the Most Holy Virgin and Blessed Michael be now raised to a rank similar to that of the twelve already agreed upon, and bear henceforward the same title; and in testimony of our appreciation of his exalted merits, his untiring zeal, assiduity and energy in the building of the said church, we appoint our beloved priest in Christ William Kelly to the same, and bestow upon and invest him with the title of Missionary Rector, together with all the honours, titles to pre-eminence, and privileges which thereunto belong.*

Fr Kelly needed Missionary Rector status to convince Birds that he wouldn't just disappear from the scene once the church was opened, leaving them to wonder how their bills were going to be paid. To the same end he obtained an undertaking from Cardinal Wiseman, confidential but backed up by a written document, not to divide the Virginia Street mission district for at least ten years. Even very tiny per capita contributions, if paid on a regular basis by the huge number of Catholics served by that district, should ensure that the money would slowly but steadily mount up to the required total.

At last the big day arrived, and the church was opened as planned on 8th December 1856. 26-year-old William Potter, who went on to have his own undertaker's business in King David Lane, was among those who helped move furnishings and old records over from the doomed chapel. The old high altar was not brought over, but stored in the school basement at Red Lion Street. Potter also attended the actual first Mass at the new church, which was celebrated by Fr Horrabin at 6.00 am. Cardinal Wiseman came for the formal opening Mass, which began at 11.00 am and went on until nearly 2.00 pm: this included him preaching for a full hour. Afterwards he and two hundred guests went to breakfast in the schoolrooms of the mission. Fr Horrabin was far too old and frail to have sat through the long ceremony, but a cheer went up when he walked in during the reception. At the final sermon by the Bishop of Northampton, after Compline, the building was

> *thronged to excess by the working classes, who, after the labours of the day, had hastened to offer up their thanksgivings to Almighty God for enabling them to witness the realisation of their hopes in the erection of this sacred edifice, for which both Priests and people have for so many years strenuously laboured.*

This splendid church

According to a contemporary description by Hodges in the *Weekly Register*,

> *the great feature which strikes the spectator on entering the vast edifice is the open, spacious sanctuary, and the great elevation of the altar; every part of the ceremonies can be distinctly witnessed from every portion of the church.*

The original high altar had three panels showing the Annunciation, the Crucifixion, and St Michael slaying the archangel. At either side of the entrance to the chancel stood two large statues by T Phyffers, Our Lady of the Immaculate Conception and St Patrick. From the viewpoint of the person in the pew there was a side-chapel to the right of the sanctuary for St Patrick, a matching one for the Blessed Virgin on the left, and another in the far left corner for the Blessed Sacrament. Four confessionals were built into the left-hand wall of the nave, and another recess in the same wall accommodated an organ. Along both walls there were carved and coloured panels showing the Stations of the Cross. Total seating accommodation was 2,500, though Hodges reckoned that if extra chairs were put out an additional 1,000 could be seated.

Five Sunday Masses, at 7.00, 8.00, 9.00, 10.00 and 11.00, replaced the eight previously held in the two centres, but more people could be accommodated at those five Masses in the new church than before at eight. Immediately, Fr Kelly launched a new policy on seat charges. Seats (benches and chairs) at the first four Sunday Masses, in any part of the church cost 1d each, with free standing room available for 300-400; at the 11.00 High Mass all seats would be 2d. This "first come, first served" policy was revolutionary. Most churches charged higher prices for at least some of their seats, partly as a money-spinner, and partly to accommodate the expectation of Massgoers that class distinctions be respected. But Fr Kelly firmly disagreed with class distinctions in church, and he knew that the conventional system had a negative impact on Mass attendance: it led to seats being left empty, working men feeling insulted and leaving the Church, and families with social pretensions but no money giving up going to Mass rather than sit among the poor. Above all, he declared:

> *I would be despised for all time to come, as the money to build this church had mainly come from the sweat of the working man's brows.*

Although an unsightly wooden hoarding still surrounded the new-built church, and the approach to the entrance was unpaved and muddy, attendance was definitely higher than before. Fr Kelly knew that, because the income was up, by four or five pounds each Sunday. Once again, by reducing the charges for attending Mass, he had not only encouraged attendance, but also increased the takings. On 30th December he sent a letter to the Catholic newspapers to thank everyone who'd helped and wish them (belatedly) a happy Christmas. He declared that the Mass attendance had doubled, and because the new church's beauty beat the local gin palaces hollow, people preferred attending church. He looked forward to evangelising and drawing in the whole of the East End:

> *This church is situated almost in the centre of these Tower Hamlets, which include more than half a million of London's population. It will, as time rolls on, speak gently, quietly, and it may be soothingly, to many aching hearts outside its communion...*

To Cardinal Wiseman he wrote:

> *This splendid church has in the eyes of our protestant neighbours raised this poor congregation at least fifty years in social position and consideration. And under God's blessing will in time do quietly yet really mighty things not only for the present congregation but for many outside it at present.*

A sixth Mass was added later on, and Fr Kelly often used to declare proudly that the new building could accommodate 50,000 people. What he meant was that – provided you accepted that "in such a congregation not more than one-fourth can go to Mass on Sundays" – the ones who did come could all fit in if spread over six Masses! The presbytery always had at least two live-in domestic servants: a housekeeper, who was usually an older woman, and one or more young housemaids. The first housekeeper, Barbara Fitzgerald, had already been looking after Fr Kelly and his colleagues at Colet Place. The old cemetery was made into a private garden for the priests. Three of Barbara's brothers – Patrick, Mortimer, and Garrett – were buried there: they'd all died within three months of each other in late 1849, so were probably cholera victims. An Irish couple, Timothy and Mary Sullivan, moved into the lodge and lived there for many years, looking after the church. Sign boards were erected at the front, close to the road, so whatever was going on in the parish could easily be publicised.

In Lent 1857 the Redemptorists came to conduct a prolonged mission in the new church. It was led by the Clapham superior, Fr Robert Aston Coffin, who had been a follower of Newman and one of the Oxford converts, and focused specially on the young people. Afterwards, Fr Kelly wrote that the mission had surpassed his expectations.

To see a church the size of this filled every night, and well attended in the morning, for three weeks, is a fact of no ordinary occurrence… The closing sermon last Sunday was at seven p.m. Our own congregation, and some of our Protestant neighbours, began to move in about half-past four. This was a lucky hit, for about seven times as many people came from other parts of London as would have filled St. Paul's Cathedral, but in St. Mary and St. Michael's they could not find one inch of standing room… The Very Rev. Rector, Father Coffin, was not only willing, in his closing sermon, to bless, but did actually bless, everyone present, and everything belonging to each except sin and the humble writer of this letter. From the latter he said he hoped for a blessing which I forgot to give. I now supply the deficiency by saying, Ex toto corde. May God bless Father Coffin and his coadjutors who worked at St. Mary and St. Michael's.

Fr Coffin went on to become Bishop of Southwark.

The Final Bill

The final bill for St Mary and St Michael's was over twice Fr Kelly's original estimate: £21,236 4s 8d. (This figure was only for what had been done since the work was re-started in 1854: if the payments made previously are added on, the full cost was nearly £30,000.) Most of the money had of course gone to the builder: £18,724 7s 11d. The architect's fees came to £1,060 12s 6d. While the work was ongoing, very large amounts had been raised by the congregation and donated by outsiders, and so far £13,613 2s 11d of the bill had been paid off, leaving £7,623 12 9d still to go. However, Fr Kelly explained, the payments already made to Birds included the £3,000 loan, which would eventually have to be paid off. So the total outstanding was £10,623 12s 9d. To have raised half the cost of the building in the few years between Fr Kelly's taking over the mission, and the opening of the church, was a remarkable achievement. No exceptionally wealthy benefactor had come forward, and Cardinal Wiseman had been able to give very little financial help. Many years later Herbert Vaughan, when he became Cardinal, dropped a possible clue in his 1894 Pastoral Letter for the Trinity Sunday church building fund collection:

Some years ago when a splendid church was rising in the midst of a great working population, and the collectors were busy week by week among the poor, it was a nobleman, the Hon. Mr. Browne, of the Kenmare family, who not only sent secretly thousands of pounds, but with equal zeal and self-denial, contributed £50 a fortnight while the work was going on.

Fr Kelly had made a few trips to France and Belgium, ostensibly to study the practicalities of maintaining large churches – but no doubt he took his begging bowl along.

Donations from the wider Catholic public, in England and beyond, had undoubtedly been crucial in getting the church built, because there was no way the local Catholics could have collected quite enough money within a reasonable timeframe. A tidy sum will have been made selling tickets for the opening ceremony, and from donations handed in on that occasion. Nevertheless, Fr Kelly always awarded the bulk of the credit for raising the money for St Mary and St Michael's to the parishioners. He adopted this position from the time the church was opened, and as the years passed it would become even more true than it was then – because unfortunately, appeals for a building were never so popular once all the excitement of the opening was over, and it had been in use for a while: outsiders quickly lost interest, and it was the local community which had to slog away to pay off the debt. Fr Kelly had done his sums beforehand, and calculated that the weekly income of St Mary and St Michael's, besides providing enough for running expenses, was sufficient to cover interest at 5% on the £3,000 loan, plus the annual life insurance premiums. Paying off that loan, therefore, could wait. But during the first year or so after the church opened, while everyone was still happy and excited, fundraising must be pushed as energetically as possible. Unless a big dent was made in the £7,623 12 9d still owed to the builders, the architect and so on, before that too began to incur interest, servicing the debt might be unmanageable.

Canon O'Neal, who was always very supportive of Fr Kelly, launched a scheme to pull in large numbers of wealthy outsiders, each committing to pay relatively modest sums on a regular basis, but it wasn't very successful. Meanwhile the parishioners agreed to "tax" themselves through regular, intensive, sacrificial giving over another three-year period.

To start with, the collections were bringing in £17 a week, which was very good going. But, as Fr Kelly was informed by "the oldest and best-informed" of his congregation, the district was undergoing a particularly bad, and prolonged, economic recession. A large number of Catholics had emigrated "and a still larger number would have done so could they but have procured the necessary means." In 1858 he was able to confirm that the income was still covering the liabilities, but only just, and he noted: "the baptisms are not now so numerous as they were then. Old inhabitants have told me that they never remember the labour market so depressed and unsteady as during the last four or five years; and the squalid poverty and comparative comfort of this congregation are regulated by this fickle standard; but, God be praised, they have done wonders in their poverty …"

Despite the recession, Fr Kelly had no choice but to organise a third three-year round of intensive collections.

The Workhouse Religion

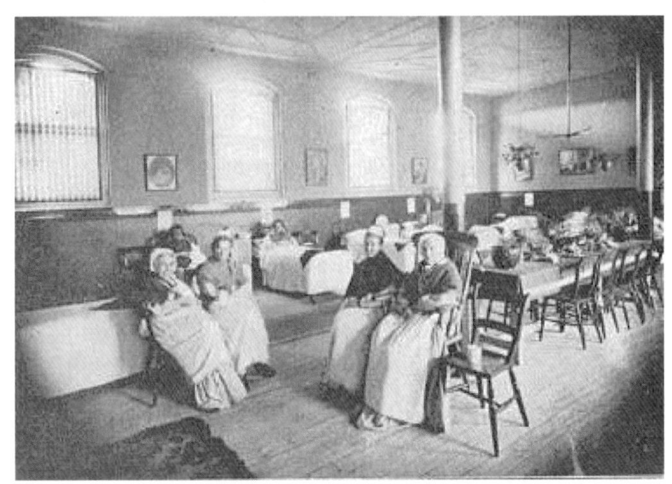

Whitechapel Workhouse

Although the Civil Parishes and Unions in the East End covered quite large areas, Fr Kelly's district was larger still, so for anything to do with local government, or the administration of the Poor Law, he had to deal with more than one set of officials. To the north, Poor Law responsibility lay with Stepney Union, which covered the hamlets of Limehouse, Mile End Old Town, Ratcliffe, Shadwell and Wapping, to the south with St George's in the East, and to the west with Whitechapel Union. Whitechapel placed its pauper children in a residential school at Forest Gate, St George's had one at Plashet, and Stepney's was in Limehouse. In 1854 a girl of 15 came to Fr Kelly of her own accord, to be prepared for First Communion. She'd been brought up as a Catholic, but taken into the workhouse at the age of ten

and though she knew the Catholic prayers, she was compelled to learn the Protestant and live so in all respects. About the age of 13, she was confirmed in the Protestant Church of St Georges in the East with many others from the workhouse about fifty others as far as she could recollect like herself, were of Catholic parents.

The Poor Law authorities had recently placed her in a job, and as soon as she was free to do so she'd come to see Fr Kelly. But as far as all the others were concerned, she "did not know of any of them who returned to the Catholic Church when free from the authority of the workhouse."

As ratepayers of St George's, Fr Kelly and Fr Foley both used to receive official invitations to attend the annual examination (a sort of open day) at the Plashet school, and see the children show off their prowess at reading and writing, and how well they'd memorised the Anglican catechism. Their first visit was on 31st August 1855. They were treated with great courtesy, and the officials clearly had no idea that they were extremely upset by what they'd seen:

Total number of children in the School at present 400 boys and girls. It struck me, nearly half these were Catholic. Mr Foley knew that a Mrs Conway with her four or five children, one or two of whom he brought to their first communion, was there.

Mr Conway had been an upholsterer, and at one time modestly successful. In contrast to so many hapless children in the parish's elementary schools, his two girls had been "educated at a private school, and brought up respectably": they were well taught and devout, "Indeed, they used to be monthly communicants." But their father's business failed, he abandoned his family and fled to Australia and "the mother was obliged to go into the House". Fr Kelly knew a Catholic woman who'd been employed at the Forest Gate school, but quietly resigned the job (which she badly needed) when she realised she'd be expected to prepare children whom she knew to be Catholics for confirmation in the Church of England. It wasn't only in the case of children whose parents weren't around, or had abandoned them, that the Guardians expected to turn them into little Anglicans. In a garret in Whitechapel, interviewed a widow named Johns. She and her children worked day and night sewing sacks, which Mrs Johns delivered after dark because she had nothing decent to wear. She explained that she'd actually applied to enter Whitechapel Workhouse, and have her children sent to Forest Gate, but first

'she had one of the Marist fathers to draw up for her a written request to the Guardians to have her children instructed in the Catholic faith – that she no sooner handed the note in person to the Guardians than one of them, a Mr. Craven, sugar-baker, exclaimed, "Oh. The infernal priest;" she interposed at once and said it was not a fit expression to be employed of the minister of any religion, at which Mr. Craven, sugar-baker and Guardian, flew into a passion, and ordered herself to be turned out of the Workhouse, and her children out of the Industrial School – and it was done accordingly.'

Sisters of Mercy

The new church at least made it possible to organise systematic catechesis of children still living at home with their families. All the schoolchildren were expected to attend the 9.00 Mass, accompanied by their teachers: they took up half the church – girls in the nave, and boys in the side-aisles. At the 3.00 catechism class, when they had the church to themselves, attendance was "fourfold what it used to be," and "When they sing in tune with the organ, the effect is very fine." A middle-aged woman had been engaged at 10s a week as a catechist, available in the church to give instruction to children who didn't attend school, and to adults if needed.

Problems nevertheless continued with the schools. The master of one of the boys' schools had contracted an irregular marriage, and when threatened with the sack he tried to sue Fr Kelly for £70 worth of commission payments for his services collecting money for the new church. Fortunately his action had failed, or else some of the other collectors would have demanded commission. The only bright spot in the situation was that Mr Guilmartin, recently appointed headmaster of Red Lion Street, had stuck by Fr Kelly and been a real help. But it seemed impossible to find reliable staff for the girls' schools. Finally the government suddenly condemned the Red Lion Street building: no more grants could be paid till it was put right. The school committee's own trustees commissioned a survey which confirmed that two of the outer walls were on the verge of collapse, and plans had to be drawn up for rebuilding.

All the worry and overwork made Fr Kelly quite ill, and he decided to go home to Ireland for a holiday. Despite his exhaustion, it occurred to him that he might find an opportunity to do a useful bit of business while he was there. St Mary and St Michael's had been trying to acquire a convent of teaching nuns since Fr Horrabin's time. But nuns were a very valuable commodity, and there wasn't an unlimited supply: to attract them to settle in his parish, a priest might have to go round begging very hard, and he would usually need to offer some sort of financial package. Fr Kelly had been advised to apply to the Sisters of Mercy, founded in Dublin by Catherine McAuley. Whereas many religious congregations were centrally organised, each Convent of Mercy was independent under the spiritual jurisdiction of the local bishop, and responsible for its own decision-making and financing, and its own recruitment and training. Fr Kelly had intended to postpone the question for another four years, till his finances were in better order, yet the schools situation was getting desperate, so although it was a long shot, before he set off he made sure to obtain

> *the necessary Ecclesiastical authority to bring back with me a community of Sisters of Mercy, should I succeed in finding any willing to come to London, though I had*

no notion at the time where I was to meet with such a community.

When he went to the Convent of Mercy in Tullamore, and begged for Sisters, the local priest promptly imposed a veto, on the grounds that not enough Sisters were currently available for the needs of his own parish. But Fr Kelly would not take no for an answer. Remaining in Tullamore, he offered Mass on three successive days in honour of the most Holy Trinity "that spiritual help might be found for his flock." He didn't only pray: he continued to talk earnestly to the people he needed to convince, stressing the huge needs of his flock: "He painted a vivid picture of the huge numbers of their own Irish people huddled together in the slums of the east end of London, their children deprived of any chance of education or religious instruction…" His persistence wore down the opposition, and the Bishop of Meath resolved that while no woman should be *sent* on foundation to Commercial Road, anyone who freely volunteered would be allowed to go. He laid down one condition: the Superior of Tullamore, Mother Mary Angela Gilsenan must accompany the expedition and remain in London for two months to see the new community properly established.

On 1st March 1859, Fr Kelly left Ireland accompanied by Mother Angela and seven volunteers: professed Sisters Evangelist Daly and Gertrude Dunn; Sisters Patrick Gray and Teresa Ryan who were still novices; Annie McDonald who had just completed her postulancy; and two further postulants named Brigid (or Eliza) Gallagher, and Catherine Greenan. An eyewitness account was sent to the *Tablet* from someone who had seen them set sail from Kingstown in the *Le Wellen* "on the most beautiful blue bay of waters the eye could behold"; this correspondent pointed with pride to the fact that in the twenty years of its existence Tullamore had already founded three daughter-houses in Ireland, and now "I trust, the most auspicious of all – that of St. Mary and St. Michael's Commercial-road East, London."

On 2nd March two parishioners, Mr Crawley and Mr Calnan, set off from

Wapping in a horse and cart to fetch the party from Euston. It was "a cold and dreary morning", and as the Sisters approached Commercial Road "the raucous shouting, the squalor and the noise on the streets, together with glimpses here and there of sickly birds in little cages, feebly chirping in the small-paned windows of the full high buildings, were not exactly inviting." A terraced house was waiting for them, about five minutes' walk from the church, and an anonymous benefactor of the parish had promised to pay the rent for the next three years – which he did. Barbara Fitzgerald had sat up all night waiting to welcome the Sisters.

The convent address was initially No 1, Mercer's Place, but when the street numbering was rationalised some years later, it became No 535 Commercial Road. Cardinal Wiseman visited almost immediately, to welcome the Sisters and give his blessing, and present the new convent with an altar stone. "The Sisters of Mercy took possession of the poor schools this week," wrote Fr Kelly, "and have had in the three schools nine hundred children – nine hundred girls, not merely on the books, but actually in the schools." (Such attendance levels were extraordinary, and it wouldn't last, but to start with the children must have been agog to see what real live nuns looked like.)

Each morning the nuns set off in pairs to walk to their schools, some going to Johnson Street, others making the longer hike to Wapping or Pell Street. They were in charge of the girls' schools from the time they arrived, each team managing up to 300 girls in a single large schoolroom. At the end of March two Sisters, Patrick Gray being one, were assigned to the infant school in Wapping. Sr Patrick used to tell a few stories to show how naïve she'd been then. Once she left her basket on a window sill to chase after a truant child, and when she came back she found a coster's donkey eating her lunch. Next day, instead of a lunch basket, she took 2d, but met a poor man on the way who she thought looked like St Joseph, so gave him the money – however the dreadful language with which the beggar abused her for not giving him 6d, convinced her that "he had no connection with the Saints". Bridget Gallagher, though only a postulant, was 27 and already held a teaching certificate, but she was probably the only one with a formal qualification. So Fr Kelly sent "four or five Nuns" to the Holy Child Sisters' training college at St Leonards to sit the examination. They passed, but to his chagrin they "were refused their certificates of merit on the charge of copying." He did not believe "his" Sisters had been cheating: he reckoned the School Inspector, Marshall, had it in for them. As far as he was concerned, he judged the nuns by what he saw of their performance in the schools, and he gave them top marks. Annie McDonald, "beautifully and tastefully attired in a dress of white satin", was formally received as a novice on Sunday 8th May 1859, becoming Sr Scholastica. The ceremony was held in St Mary and St Michael's immediately after High Mass, presided over by Cardinal Wiseman. It had been advertised on the signboards in front of the church for a fortnight beforehand, and admittance was fixed at 2d, in order to bring in as many spectators as possible, and counter the silly stories that were circulating about convents being sinister places, where hapless girls were systematically tortured. Sure enough, the church was full:

Some 2,500 persons were present, many of whom were Protestants from the neighbourhood, who behaved with the greatest respect, and seemed exceedingly attentive; it must have been plain to them that there was no anxiety to make the convent a prison from which there is no escape, as everything was conducted in the most open manner.

Life and work in East London proved so overwhelming for Sr Gertrude that she changed her mind and returned to Ireland after only a few months. But Mother Angela also changed her mind: instead of returning to Tullamore, she stayed on as Mother Superior of Commercial Road. Fresh recruits began to arrive, and the Sisters started a small fee-paying school at their convent. There was a great demand in Tower Hamlets for relatively inexpensive private day schools, for the daughters of small businessmen, customs officers and senior clerks. The social status of nuns, and their usually having received a good education themselves, gave their convent schools a cachet which made them very attractive, even to non-Catholic parents. Among the first pupils were the Scannell's daughters Kate, Ann and Alice. Girls learned "the various branches of English literature", "a thorough knowledge of modern languages", and a lot of singing. By the time they were put through their paces at the first annual examination in August 1860 there were four classes, each with a pious label – the top class was "Our Lady of Mercy's", and the infants were "the Holy Angels.

The Commercial Road house needed quite a lot of adaptation, both to make it fit for purpose as a convent, and to provide suitable space for the convent school: the cost came to £300, which Fr Kelly had to pay. What bothered him was not the expense as such, but the fact that it came at such a difficult time: if he could only have deferred bringing the nuns over for a few more years, the cost would have been more manageable. But he recognised that if he'd left it any longer, he might not have been able to get them at all.

I did succeed in finding the community I was in search of, but only by a hairs breadth venture; for the community I took to London, had left the convent at Tullamore only a few days before a Colonial bishop arrived at Tullamore seeking in vain for nuns.

That dreadful and very Irish religion

When Fr Kelly returned from Ireland bringing with him the Sisters of Mercy, he found lots of letters sitting on his table waiting for him. Among them were several from an actuary named Edward Ryley, urging him to take up the Workhouse Question. Fr Kelly wrote back saying no: his mission was insolvent, and he *must* devote all his time and energy to fundraising. Post within London was so quick in those days it was almost as good as e-mail: several notes could travel back and forth the same day. Ryley replied: "Come to my office in the City; my sister has given me ten pounds for you." When Fr Kelly arrived, Ryley had some letters to show him

> *from the then head of the Poor Law Board; he was an old friend of his. All that was required was that the Catholics should kick up a jolly row, and if they showed themselves in earnest, the Catholic children in the workhouses should be brought up in their own religion.*

An eager new ally presented himself: the energetic Fr James McQuoin, in charge of the mission at Stratford. The Poor Law schools in Plashet and Forest Gate, where so many St Mary and St Michael's children ended up, were both in his district. "I know there are scores of children in these two establishments who ought to be Catholics," wrote Fr McQuoin

> *and I also know that the only positive religion they learn there is to hate and to dread the Catholic Church… every difficulty is put in the way of discovering the Catholic children, and the children themselves are at times closely examined as to their personal wish to be instructed by the priest. I have this very month past failed with three cases of children, who were all orphans, and who, although they asked the master to see the priest, yet did not manage, under the rather formidable cross-questioning of a Solemn Board of Guardians, to convey a perfectly clear expression of their wish to be put under my instruction.*

Even if children managed to clear all the hurdles to get themselves acknowledged as Catholics by the Board

> *they see a priest for one hour every week. No going to Mass ... no going to Confession or Communion, and a very marked public opinion in the school against them for belonging to that dreadful and very Irish religion called Roman Catholic.*

Fr Kelly couldn't resist the call to "kick up a jolly row". He set to work to mobilise his parishioners: they might be working class, but they paid their share of taxes and the poor rate! In March 1859 a well-attended meeting of ratepayers at Johnson Street School passed a series of resolutions, calling on

Poor Law administrators to respect the religious rights of Catholic paupers, and a committee was set up, comprising "Rev. W. Kelly, Drs. Mahony, Hewett, and Lynch, Messrs. W. Flynn, Scannell, O'Brien, Carroll, Gallagher, Calnan, Rearden, Driscoll, and White", to present the resolutions to "the Boards of Guardians of the different parishes and unions in which St. Mary and St. Michael is situated… and in default of obtaining satisfaction to apply to the Poor Law Board." The assistant priests were also involved in the campaign, and doing whatever they could to support it: Fr Bartholomew Fallon got particularly fired up about it.

The committee met twice a week on Monday and Thursday evenings to formulate plans and discuss progress, and on 15th April a deputation of six ratepayers had an hour's meeting with the Guardians of St George's in the East, and delivered a Memorandum setting out the parishioners' demands. The committee felt this first meeting had gone well, and the secretary was instructed to write to the Stepney Guardians to arrange a suitable time to call on *them.* However the courteous reception of the deputation by St George's didn't translate into concrete action, and the Stepney and Whitechapel Unions refused even to meet the deputations. The Poor Law Inspector, a central government official, strenuously backed up the Catholics, but the Guardians coolly ignored him too. Commercial Road's action was nevertheless hailed by Fr McQuoin:

> *The Rev. Father Kelly (even with his thousand other duties) has taken a bold initiative and given the example to both clergy and people what they should do, and what I fervently trust they will do, in all the towns of Great Britain. He has begun by teaching the people their duty and their power, and then he has banded the rate-payers into an organised body that will know how to urge with courage their claims for a fair distribution of their own hard-earned money before the boards and commissioners and even before the throne itself.*

And Fr McQuoin added a little story to remind everyone of what it all meant in human terms. One Sunday a poor widow, probably from St Mary and St Michael's, had come 12 miles on foot to visit her two little girls, but wasn't allowed to see them because she hadn't brought the proper authorisation from the Guardians:

> *The poor creature called on me, foot-sore and broken-hearted, and was partially consoled for her fatigue and disappointment by hearing from me of their courage and firmness in proclaiming themselves Roman Catholics, whereas, before I visited them, they were hardly even aware of being Catholics at all.*

Oh mother, I am forgetting all my prayers

Fr Kelly believed there were altogether about 500 Catholic children in the Limehouse, Plashet and Forest Gate Poor Law schools schools, but there was no easy way of finding out for sure. Working largely on the evidence of Irish surnames, he and Fr McQuoin drew up provisional lists of children who seemed likely to be from Catholic backgrounds, and then checked up their baptismal records. In June 1859 Fr Kelly published a list of definites, with the dates on which the priests had applied for each child to be properly registered as a Catholic. These applications were mostly being ignored: out of 43 children in the Limehouse school for which applications had been made, only eight were allowed to see a priest

and numerous complaints reach us of the efforts of the relieving officer to browbeat and terrify the relations of these children, as also the altered and hostile feelings of the paid underlings of the establishment towards the children so applied for. One boy said to his grandmother a week ago, 'Oh, mother, I am forgetting all my prayers. I now only recollect "Our Father!" and "Hail, Mary!"; and since Mr.--- asked me if I were a Catholic, and I said I was, he looks so cross and vexed at me that I am afraid for my life. I dare not refuse to learn their prayers.'

On 25th November 1859 a meeting of Catholic clergy was held at Commercial Road. This led to an all-London committee of priests being set up, and the clergy of Westminster and Southwark were officially requested to co-operate in compiling full documentation on all Catholic children in Poor Law institutions, and all cases of refusal by the Guardians to permit Catholic instruction, or of removal of the children to another institution to avoid honouring permission once obtained. A parallel committee of Catholic peers and MPs was established to pursue the issue in Parliament. Fr Kelly made a point of attending the lay committee as well as the clergy one, and when deputations met with the Prime Minister, or the head of the Poor Law Board, he usually accompanied them – though he left all the talking to the lay representatives.

A test case was brought against the Stepney Guardians in respect of two orphans in Limehouse Industrial School, James and Catherine Cole, aged nine and six respectively. Both their parents, parishioners of St Mary's and St Michael's, "were not only Catholics all their lives, but died after having received all the rites of their Church", and before she died their mother had put in an application for them to be brought up as Catholics. The case was fought up to the Court of Queen's Bench before the Guardians agreed to allow a priest to see the children. But although the law eventually came down on the Catholic side, the long delay involved in the litigation meant that the Guardians won because "when the priest did see them he could make no hand of these children, and they have, like hundreds of others, ever since been brought up Protestants."

The Poor Law officials could point to such an outcome as evidence that the Catholic leaders were being totally unreasonable, and that the children themselves – given a choice – actually preferred to be Protestants, or simply didn't care either way. But Fr Kelly asked how anyone could be so naïve as to imagine that

Children long under Protestant instruction, ridiculed, buffeted, and mauled by their Protestant pauper playmates, and enlightened, it may be, by the sneers of the schoolmaster and mistress, and repeated examination in the Protestant Catechism by the Protestant minister on the beauties of the Established Church and the horrors of Popery

would "still have remained such Catholic martyrs and theologians" as to hold steadfast to their Catholic (and Irish) identity.

The Irish Brigade

The Popes had traditionally ruled over the whole of central Italy, while the rest of the peninsula was made up of a patchwork of small states, but a process now began which was to result in the unification of the country. While a conventional war was fought in the north, the nationalist revolutionary Giuseppe Garibaldi waged a remarkably successful guerrilla campaign to "liberate" Sicily and the south, and then invaded the Papal States. Majority public opinion in Britain went completely overboard in support of Garibaldi: because he was anti-Catholic, he was seen in absurdly glamourised terms as a sort of Protestant superhero, sent by God to resolve all Italy's problems, and make it overnight into an efficient, modern country. During the first half of 1860, collections were held for the Pope throughout Westminster Archdiocese: Commercial Road's contribution was a handsome £55 6s 0d. Meanwhile, in Ireland, thousands of volunteers came forward to defend the Pope. They had to travel via London, and Fr Pennington was given the job of organising their embarkation: they had to be put on ships going from London Docks to Rotterdam, from where they would make their way via overland to Trieste, and then make another sea crossing to Ancona in the Papal States. Under the passport system at the time, you could apply for a passport, pay the fee of one shilling, and ask for permission for 500 other people to travel with you. When a civil servant asked why so many of Queen Victoria's subjects were so keen to travel to Italy, Fr Pennington returned a glib answer, playing on people's unrealistic expectations of what Italian unification would achieve:

You must understand, sir, that since the existence of a Kingdom of Italy began there is a most wonderful amount of enterprise created; where formerly everything was so slow and stagnant railways are being constructed in all directions, and these men, having little or no occupation at home, want to earn a living abroad.

Pope Pius IX

Unfortunately the arrangements in the Papal States for looking after the men, once they arrived, left a lot to be desired – partly no doubt because the authorities were so hard-pressed, and also because Italians were used to a much lower standard of living. Some of the volunteers couldn't stick it: "500 stalwart Limerick men" whom Fr Pennington had seen off came back after just six weeks, with

a terrible account of the want of common necessaries for themselves and others! It so happened that on the day of their return I was away from the presbytery. The whole of the five hundred remained squatted around the Church of SS. Mary and Michael's, Commercial Road, awaiting my return. But after remaining some time they took their departure without seeing me. On the next morning the Rector, Rev. William Kelly, said in a somewhat severe tone, 'Look here, young man, I am not going to have my church turned into a bivouac for soldiers.'

St Patrick's Irish Brigade, under Major Myles O'Reilly, fought at Perugia, Spoleto and Castelfidardo, taking heavy casualties, and finally at Ancona where, in September 1860, they surrendered along with the rest of the papal forces. As prisoners they were not well treated, and had a very hard time of it. The cause for which they had fought was hopelessly lost, though the city of Rome was to remain for a little while longer under the Pope's sovereignty, protected by a French garrison. Mass was offered at St Mary and St Michael's on 1st October 1860 for all the Irishmen "who had lately laid down their lives in Italy in defence of the legitimate rights of Pius IX."

Laus Deo Semper

Four years after the opening of St Mary and St Michael's church, it narrowly escaped disaster. On the morning of Sunday 2nd September, 1860, a fire broke out next door in the old three-storey wooden building of Messrs Frost and Sons, one of the largest rope factories in England. At 8.35, the sacristan rushed into Fr Kelly's confessional with the news.

That evening he sat down and wrote a detailed account of what had happened:

When I came into my house I found the corridors on the north-west side of the house intensely hot and suffocating; a lurid glare of unearthly light dazzled the eyes, and the crackling of glass stunned the ears. The men of my congregation behaved nobly. Rushing into the house, they seemed determined to be grilled alive rather than the buildings should perish. Coats off and water fetched in every kind of vessel to cool the windows and keep the corridors from igniting. The women, who ran into the garden frantically screaming, were ordered back into the Church to beseech the Almighty to save the building from the devouring element.

The wind blew from the north west, and consequently wafted the heat and flame towards the house, Church, and sacristies, and as the fire seemed every moment to increase in intensity, the men, though working hard, were losing ground, and the supply of water was nearly exhausted. At this time the fire suddenly doubled its force, and shot its huge forked tongues seventy or eighty feet up into the heavens – the wind beat them towards the house, and at that moment all seemed lost. It was then that one who was present and who felt much, exclaimed from the bottom of his heart, 'Oh God! Holy Mary, save from destruction your own Church, House, and Sacristies!' At that instant the tops of the vast columns of liquid fire were turned away from the house, and in about a minute afterwards some fifty yards of the burning mass fell down. And the one that was present said with deep felt gratitude, 'Deo gratias.' Though we did not then know it, the crisis was over.

The dwelling house, opposite the Church and adjoining the engine house, still burned fiercely, and the slates on the north-western side of the Church seemed to assume that hue which they usually have under the action of great heat. Some members of the congregation rushed off to the Captain of the firemen to request him to direct one of the engines on to the roof of the Church. He refused. I went to him myself, and he told me he could not spare even one hose. In a moment I saw that he perfectly understood his duty. All his efforts were directed to save the engine house, in which he succeeded; and this building was the nearest of all to our Church, and some six feet from the porch of our Church, and between it and the engine house there was a large quantity of coal and other combustible matter. At a quarter to ten a.m. all danger had passed away, though the firemen still continue, now close to midnight, to throw water on the smouldering ruins.

A Protestant gentleman told one of our congregation to-day that he viewed from his window the conflagration and direction of the wind for a long time, and that he looked on our buildings as doomed, but at the critical moment the wind veered round, and that Providence alone had thus saved the buildings. I need not say that we had as many 'Te Deums' to-day as we could introduce into the services. Laus Deo Semper."

London in the 1800s: Destitute mother and child

> *Wretched houses with broken windows patched with rags and paper; every room let out to a different family, and in many instances to two or even three fruit and 'sweetstuff' manufacturers in the cellars, barbers and red herring vendors in the front parlours, cobblers in the back; a bird~fancier in the first floor, three families on the second, starvation in the attics, Irishmen in the passage, a 'musician' in the front kitchen, a charwoman and five hungry children in the back one, filth everywhere a gutter before the houses, and a drain behind clothes drying, and slops emptying from the windows; ... men and women, in every variety of scanty and dirty apparel, lounging, scolding, drinking, smoking, squabbling, fighting, and swearing.*
>
> **Charles Dickens, Sketches by Boz**

During the severe winter of 1860-61, when the docks and the building trade closed down, and everyone was thrown out of work, John Hollingshead, a reporter on *The Morning Post*, toured the streets on either side of Commercial Road and wrote descriptive accounts of the wretched state of the housing, and how desperately people were struggling to get by. On one of his trips he accompanied Rev George M'Gill of Christ Church, Watney Street, on a tour of his parish which covered a rough rectangle along the south side of Commercial Road, between Cannon Street Road and Sutton Street: 43 acres, housing 13,300 people. Star Street, where many St Mary and Michael's parishioners must have lived, was no more than a narrow lane, its entrance "half blocked up with fruit stalls, crossing-sweepers and loiterers", and the roadway "black and muddy, half filled with small pools of inky water". Overcrowding was rife: a four-room house would hold four families, one to a room, each with up to eight children, each paying 1s 9d in rent. In one room the father of the family had just died, and his body lay stretched out on the bed covered in a borrowed sheet. Walking along with M'Gill, the reporter met "poor thin women, in scanty dresses, representing every variety of dirt and poverty." Their husbands were out-of-work dockers, there was no sewing work available for them to take in, and they had nothing left to pawn. But, stressed Hollingshead, these people weren't criminals: they were honest and hard-working.

In mid-January, bakers' shops and eating houses were attacked all along Whitechapel and Commercial Roads, and the food looted. Mounted police were called out, but could not control the huge crowds. Unemployed dockers took to hanging around the Thames Police Court in Arbour Square, where the magistrates distributed small sums out of the limited resources they had available. The situation was given publicity in the newspapers, and readers sent in donations. The vast majority of those helped were:

Irishmen, who always suffer naturally by the suspension of business in the docks, on the wharves, and on the river, and whose precarious earnings at all times are very small, though engaged in the most laborious and roughest work of the Port of London.

Out of work dockers

Fr Kelly issued his usual appeals for alms through the Catholic papers, but most help came from the generosity of the wider public. The magistrates expected applicants to bring a letter of recommendation from a local clergymen to confirm their bona fides, and lump sums were given to the clergy for direct distribution: the biggest such amount, £20, went to St Mary and St Michael's. Handouts at the Police Court continued until nearly the end of January, when the weather improved, and employment went back to normal.

Between crises which hit the headlines, the needs didn't go away. The clergy gave what they could, but they had very little to give. The poor boxes at St Mary and St Michael's yielded on average just over £1 a month, to be divided between Fr Kelly and his three curates, and this was supplemented by Fr William O'Connor, at the wealthier parish of Lincoln's Inn Fields, who passed on the sum of £4 each year to each of the Commercial Road priests. So each of them had at most 3s week to dispense to the worst cases they came across during their pastoral visits. The Sisters of Mercy, in their parish visiting work, also distributed small sums of money entrusted to them to help the poor.

A fresh blitz on the church debt

Meeting government standards to qualify for grants meant, paradoxically, that the parish needed to raise even *more* money for its schools than before. However Fr Kelly argued that as a result they now had far better schools, giving their children educational opportunities just as good as their Protestant neighbours. Although each school still operated in a single large schoolroom, the children were now divided into classes, organised on the basis of attainment, not age. The poorer children often remained stuck in the lower classes, struggling to master the basics: it was difficult for them to learn, because their attendance was so irregular, and they were less self-confident and motivated. The higher classes got more attention from the qualified teacher, were usually smaller (because most students never reached them), and comprised overwhelmingly the children from better-off families.

It therefore made excellent sense to introduce a sliding scale for school fees, charging more for the higher classes, and Fr Kelly launched such a scale in January 1861. The customary flat rate of one penny a week per child would continue, but Fr Kelly opened a separate book for "voluntary contributions". In Red Lion Street and Johnson Street, children in the first class were urged to pay 4d a week; in the second and third classes 3d; and in all other classes 2d. In Pell Street, at the rougher end of the district, first and second classes cost 2d, and all other classes were free (except for the standard penny). Fr Kelly regarded Pell Street as essentially a "free school", but parents of children attending the other two schools did, on the whole, pay up. This ensured that, for the next few years at least, "the schools pence nearly supported the teachers".

Over a five-month period from May to early October, Fr Kelly carried out another parish census, and drew up fresh lists for the collectors. Like the first time it was a fascinating experience, and he felt it enabled him to get to know his parishioners spiritually:

> *The average weekly earnings of the people are less than at my first visit, yet their rooms are now tidier, cleaner, and have more things of value in them. Objectionable prints have given way to Scripture pieces; and there is now hardly a dwelling that has not the*

Crucifixion, Virgin and Child, &c., &c. It was no unusual thing for the people to say to me on my second visit, 'Father, what an extraordinary change has taken place, the past few years in our congregation, it must be they are more enlightened, they are not the same people at all.' Yet with all this improvement they are not able to give so much to the new church as at my first visit. Since that visit most of them have joined burial clubs, and hence have had to reduce the amount they used to pay towards the church. There is yet a vast amount of work to be done here, and amongst other things, there are as many children in this parish alone to be looked after as would fill all the Catholic orphanages in and about London, but whilst the debt lies heavily upon us, the space of our activity is paralysed.

Fr Kelly had enough hands-on knowledge of working-class household economy to warn other Church leaders that if they kept hammering away at the poorer Catholics, for money they genuinely couldn't afford, it would drive them out of the Church. He also warned against the unrealistic expectations of well-meaning organisers of good causes who blithely assumed

that the working man after paying rent, supporting his family, paying for his children at school, paying his family doctor, his Sunday contribution towards his church, his club money, the expense arising from occasional deaths in his family, and contributing to alleviate the distress of his fellow workmen who meet with accidents &c., has a considerable balance remaining out of his fifteen or eighteen shillings a week to give in charity.

In October 1861 Fr Kelly called a big meeting of parishioners at Johnson Street School. Fundraising for the church debt had gone on well for about a year after the opening,

but death became then and since active amongst some of our collectors – some left the congregation, and the employment of others became incompatible with the duty of collectors.

He acknowledged frankly that his decision to get involved in the workhouse campaign had made it impossible for him to give sufficient attention to getting the fundraising back on track, and the situation was now at crisis point. There'd been two years during which fundraising dipped so badly that virtually everything that came in was swallowed up by the interest payments, so that the parish was only marking time on clearing off its debt. If the congregation didn't recommit itself to regular, systematic collections, he threatened, it might be necessary to re-impose the old expensive seat prices – in which case St Mary and St Michael's would become "the church of the few instead of the multitude". John Michael Calnan compared the state of church and school when he was young, to how it was now. Calnan would have been about six or seven in 1813, when the original charity school moved to Chapman Street. He remembered it as being in Walburgh Street (which crosses Chapman Street, so perhaps it was on the corner) and having only about 20 children:

What a difference now-a-days when we have one of the finest, if not the best, church in England, situated not in a hole and corner like Virginia-street Chapel, but in the best street in this part of London. Shame on the congregation, then, if they did not put their shoulders to the wheel, one and all, and by paying of the debt show their gratitude to God for blessing them with such excellent schools, and such a noble church. (Applause.).

Fr Kelly concluded with a word of thanks to the collectors, who: "without a fee or earthly reward, spend their only day of rest in collecting pence and half-pence from their brethren to pay off the debt on the Church." There were 68, headed by Mr Crogan Batt and Mr Rooney. Before long, hoped Fr Kelly, the collections would be going so well that the Cardinal might feel able to consecrate the church. But on Lady Day 1862, when he made up his accounts, the debt still stood at £9,842 10s 0d.

Even very poor schools usually got a summer outing, and the local Protestant chapels were always taking children off for excursions, paid for by West End philanthropists. With his church and schools so deeply in debt, Fr Kelly couldn't afford it, but it was terribly hard on the children. A modest outing was therefore organised in summer 1863. In order to avoid the main roads the children were marched to one of the smaller local train stations. This caused serious problems, as the platform wasn't big enough: the station master was instructed by the directors of the railway company *never* to allow it to happen again, for safety reasons. For 1864 something more ambitious was planned. A committee was set up under William Flinn to organise and fundraise, and one fine day in August 700-800 children were marched off towards Shoreditch Station. (Shoreditch was then one of the main London stations; it was only replaced by Liverpool Street in 1874.) The march started from Red Lion Street, picking up the contingents from the other schools on the way. "When all were in line the sight was striking and pretty", wrote Fr Kelly. "The parish flag was flying in front, followed by our amateur brass band and the schools' fife and drum band. Each school had its peculiar flag carried in its front ranks, and each school wore distinctive rosettes peculiar to its school and flag..." The flags and rosettes had been made by the Sisters of Mercy, and would hopefully ensure children didn't get lost. The Sisters had also made special efforts to see that the children's general appearance was reasonably neat. The bandboys were wearing green sashes, so passers-by could see that this was an Irish Catholic turnout:

We soon found ourselves in the crowded thoroughfares where various sights were to be seen and odd things heard; many instinctively drew up their horses and vehicles to the side of the road out of our way, whilst here and there some few others seemed intent on riding us down, when in an instant some one, frequently strangers, would spring from the footpath, seize the horses' reins, and force them back to the kerbstone, telling the coachmen they were greater brutes than the horses they were driving...

Arrived at Shoreditch Station, we were soon on our way, and in less than one hour arrived at Buckhurst Hill, up which our young ones scampered as lambs frisk about in May. As soon as the flag-bearers arrived at the enclosure attached to the Bald-faced Stag, a crow-bar was procured, and the flag staves planted in the ground. For lunch in the morning, and tea, &c, in the evening, each school assembled around its own flag. The weather was magnificent, and the day passed away, enjoyed as town children alone know how to enjoy such a time.

The striking of the flags in the evening, and military precision with which each school took its proper position in the march, was a pleasing sight. The air down Buckhurst Hill to the railway station was made melodious by some of our best English hymns, and the carriages to Shoreditch as a great choir doing its best. After the usual number of scrimmages here and there with waggoners, we landed safely and soundly in the church with all our children, and, blessed be God! not one accident coming or going befell any of them. After several hymns were sung, Benediction of the Most Holy Sacrament was given, and never did I hear these young voices join in the singing more lovingly, more gratefully, or more cordially. Every one present felt it was a glorious day fittingly ended.

Nevertheless, concluded Fr Kelly, "no consideration could again induce me to bring so many children to or from Shoreditch Station." Some other route would have to be worked out for future years.

Curates

Gradually Fr Kelly was building up a team of assistant priests who were a real help, men he could depend on. Fr James Foley moved on in 1860 to take charge of a mission of his own, and the promising young Fr Thomas Cahill, after only a couple of years at Commercial Road, moved on at the same time. But in their place came Joseph Padbury, who was to remain for 22 years. Fr Padbury was notoriously eccentric: according to Fr Langton George Vere "His brusque manner of speech, his almost American nasal twang, his intense sincerity and honesty, his almost 'brutal' truthfulness, were so peculiarly impressive that they can only be expressed in one word – they were entirely 'Padberian!' I never knew another man like him." He was unthinkingly plain and blunt, but very well-liked by his fellow clergy, who used to call him "Dear old Pad!" and much-loved by the boys in the parish, with whom he was always kind and patient. Fr Vere admitted however that "Those who did not understand him, especially ladies, thought him rather trying." He was particularly devoted to the sick, giving scrupulous attention to the many sick calls which could come at the most inconvenient moments. Even in the middle of the night, the priests were liable to be summoned urgently to the bedside of someone who was supposed to be dying, and the St Mary and St Michael's district could easily have up to ten deaths in one day. But Padbury saw his availability for sick calls as being like "standing on the ramparts", ready to repel the assault of the enemy and snatch a soul for heaven. He would happily "stand on the ramparts" all day long, and he hardly ever bothered to take time off. The parishioners said that his life amongst them "was one continuous sermon, teaching self-denial and fidelity to God."

With Fr James Connolly, though he was only briefly at St Mary and St Michael's, Fr Kelly formed a lifelong friendship. Fr Thomas Francis Gorman had trained with the Pallotine Fathers, but decided to leave the congregation and be ordained for Westminster Diocese: St Mary and St Michael's must have been his first mission, and he stayed for 32 years, becoming one of the most valued priests on the team.

Fr Thomas Seddon, who arrived in 1863 just after Gorman, and would stay for four years, was very committed and hard-working. Fr John Bernard Sheppard, who joined the team in 1866, was described by Fr Kelly as "one of the most gentle, humble and pure-hearted of men. He professed a high and splendid intellect, of the full powers of which he was not conscious." He loved the parishioners, and they loved him. Another talented and energetic curate was Fr Leopold Pycke, who arrived in 1868. He was a Belgian, born at Hoorbeke, Ghent, on 22nd August 1839, educated in the minor seminary in Ghent, and had completed his training for the priesthood at the English College in Bruges 1861-64. He never quite managed to lose a slight Flemish accent, but he didn't like being treated as a "foreigner", arguing that his experiences as a priest in London, and "all the good Irish beef and butter" he'd eaten, entitled him to be regarded as an honorary Irishman.

Death of Cardinal Wiseman

Ample accommodation was now available in the parish schools, but their capacity was woefully underutilised due to low, and erratic, attendance levels. Attendance at Pell Street was particularly poor, partly due to competition from the schools in Spicer Street run by the French Marist Fathers at St Anne's, who received financial support from France, and could offer "inducements" to draw in more children. (All schools tried to offer inducements for good attendance it, ranging from occasional distributions of sweets, buns or pieces of fruit, to parties and outings. Fr Kelly's problem was that he couldn't afford any.) At one point the teachers in the boys' schools all threatened to resign unless action was taken to address the problem of "about 400 four hundred children little weeds thrown on the bosom of the Thames floating between Spicer St Schools and Commercial Road Schools". Children who kept switching backwards and forwards from one school to another wouldn't clock up enough attendances at either school to qualify for the capitation grant; they also wouldn't learn anything, and so would fail the examination, and get the teachers into trouble.

In 1862 St Boniface's German Church gave up its premises in the City and moved to Whitechapel where, as well as providing pastoral care for German Catholics from all over London, it was made responsible for the local, mainly Irish, Catholics within a small district carved out of the one belonging to St Mary and St Michael's. Fr Kelly protested angrily, citing Cardinal Wiseman's promise not to subdivide the district for ten years, but his protest was ignored. Church receipts at St Mary and St Michael's inevitably went down, and the Pell Street schools faced added competition from a new English-medium poor school opened by St Boniface's. Early in 1865, as the Cardinal lay dying, preparations went ahead for starting two more new missions in Tower Hamlets. A school-chapel for Bow, served from Stratford but destined to become independent as soon as possible, was planned and pushed through by Fr McQuoin. The other project entailed an invitation to the Oblates of Mary Immaculate to establish a new mission at Tower Hill.

Cardinal Wiseman died on 15th February. Huge and respectful crowds, largely made up of non-Catholics, lined the streets as the funeral procession passed along the seven miles from St Mary Moorfields to Kensal Green Cemetery. Such a turnout was entirely unexpected, and the practical arrangements weren't good enough. The procession became mixed up with the traffic and disarranged, at the cemetery the ground was a sea of mud, the carriages were stopped at the gate instead of being allowed to proceed to the grave, and no police were on duty inside to control the spectators. It was the parishioners of St Mary and St Michael's who saved the day: at a moment's notice their clergy were able to mobilise a team of willing and dependable volunteers to keep order. The cemetery chaplain, Fr Bennett, wrote afterwards to Fr Kelly to thank "the generous band of Irishmen" who had made it possible for the burial to be carried out with decency:

It must have been a dreary time for you all standing for so many hours on the cold mud. I fear many of you must have had but a scanty supply of refreshments to support you. Still we cannot but rejoice that the police were not there – your influence on the many hundreds who knew you and Father Toomey must have done more to preserve order than any body of police could have effected, and no guard could have been more appropriate to the Cardinal's grave than the affectionate zeal of his own children.

Fr Robert Cooke OMI moved into lodgings in Tower Hill, improvised a chapel and celebrated Mass. There had as yet been no public announcement about the new mission, and the congregation comprised only a dozen people, but very quickly word got around and hundreds more assembled in the street. Someone suggested a nearby railway arch, and Fr Cooke duly sallied forth to the railway arch to address his new parishioners for the first time. When Fr Kelly heard what was going on, he went through the roof. Fr Cooke initially tried to counter his protests by publishing Wiseman's authorisation for Tower Hill. However Fr Kelly pointed out that it had not been signed by Wiseman, but by Canon Hearn on his behalf, and insinuated that the dying Cardinal had been harassed into agreeing to the decision when he was too weak to argue back. Fr Cooke forebore to reply to this, and the correspondence lapsed.

What a regiment of soldiers could not effect

The cholera epidemic of 1866 was almost entirely confined to East London, and 93% of the deaths occurred in districts served by the East London Water Company. "The cholera is here in our midst and no mistake," began a letter from Fr Kelly published at the beginning of August, by which time the death toll was 924:

The clergy are out all hours of the day and night. God's will be done. The Archbishop of Westminster called here last Sunday and considerately gave £5 to be spent in cab-hire and messengers… May I express the hope that these good examples may be followed by many others. From long experience I have found that all physic or doses prescribed for those seriously attacked by cholera have, as a rule, failed. Amongst the poor during the cholera of 1853-54 Lord Edward Howard sent us several gallons of first-rate French brandy – brandy distilled, not from Irish whiskey, or other spirit, but from the produce of the grape. For the poor who cannot fulfil the numerous conditions required for the success of other remedies, brandy, as above described, is, in my opinion, by far the most successful remedy, as was proved here in numerous cases in the above-mentioned year.

I have, therefore, to ask ladies and gentlemen to look into their cellars and see what they can do for us in this line, and not only for us, but for all the Priests and people in the east-end of London. Best dry pale sherry and dry port wine are anti-cholera mixtures for the clergy.

The need to provide medicines, alcoholic or otherwise, was only part of the problem: the stricken people and their families might need help to buy food or blankets. A lay committee was formed in the parish, and donations came in to St Mary and St Michael's from the Mansion House Fund organised by the Lord Mayor, as well as from charitable individuals. Rev M'Gill gave £20.

Because cabs were proving impossible to get hold of in a hurry, and his curates were near to breakdown, Fr Kelly used some of the funds sent to him to hire a carriage to be permanently on hand while the emergency lasted. The Sisters of Mercy helped nurse the victims. The fact that they were teachers, not nurses, didn't matter since few nurses as yet received any specialised training: any common sense care, by devoted women willing to brave the risk of infection, would have been greatly appreciated.

Cholera

One night when Fr Kelly was the only priest still in the house, the public health officer called to ask him to come down to Harris Court to help organise the removal of the body of a cholera victim. Harris Court was in Ratcliffe, off the Highway. The dead woman's daughter lay upstairs, close to death herself, and several small children in another bed in the same room, but the rest of the family wouldn't allow the corpse to be taken away. "I went with him at once, and as I travelled along, I thought for an instant of the wonderful change that is going on in society."

He was reflecting on how the British authorities were at last beginning to realise how much trouble could be avoided by a little sensitivity to people's religious and cultural beliefs:

The greased cartridge was the immediate cause of the Indian mutiny, and here is the Sogarth Aroon called upon to do what a regiment of soldiers could not effect without slaughter – to break up the Irish 'Wake', so sacred in the eyes of the Irish peasant.

At the house the health officer and the police "stood by and most judiciously abstained from all interference," leaving Fr Kelly to handle the situation. Several of the mourners were already drunk, but he jollied them into giving way:

One girl fought to the last and seized the coffin. I said to myself, this is a glorious girl. She is fighting for an ancient custom, so I took her gently in my arms, and put her sitting in a chair, on which she sank down as gently as a baby." The coffin was taken away. 'The next day the girl that offered such resistance came to beg pardon; and I said to her, yes, I forgive you, but I shall inflict upon you a dreadful penance, which is to take this half sovereign to your poor father.

The cholera seriously depleted the resources poor families had to fall back on, and on the heels of the epidemic came another harsh winter, with thousands thrown out of work. To make matters worse, a poor 1866 harvest had pushed up the price of bread, the staple food of the poor.

Finally, the ship-building industry in the riverside districts collapsed: this meant the unemployment would be far worse, and far longer-term, than usual. The resources of the Poor Law were stretched to the limit and failing to cope, and once again bread riots broke out. Voluntary relief funds and soup kitchens were set up all over the East End. Thames Police Court sent £10 to Fr Kelly, and the London Dock Company £5, but it "disappeared in no time": however an anonymous individual donor sent £20, and another £5. Around the middle of January the Lord Mayor received a number of letters and deputations. Immediately a Mansion House Committee began making grants to the district deputations: the one from St George's in the East, headed by Rev M'Gill, got £300. Fr Gorman helped set up a committee to co-ordinate relief measures in the locality, and represented the Catholic community on it. The St Mary and St Michael's parish committee, which had organised relief during the cholera epidemic, was revived to face the new crisis.

The Ratcliffe Soup Kitchen

To have the law fairly and impartially administered

Relations with the Stepney Guardians, already difficult, had grown worse. The Guardians had never allowed regular Catholic instruction sessions in their workhouses in Ratcliffe and Wapping, and Fr Kelly hadn't made an issue of it, because all too often none of the priests had time to do it. But visits had always been arranged around Easter, to allow inmates to make their Easter duties by going to confession. However in 1861 Stepney suddenly decided not even to allow that. The Poor Law Inspector, Mr Farnall, spent two hours pleading and arguing with them, but got nowhere. He advised Kelly that the only way forward was to press for a change in the law. Accordingly a Parliamentary Select Committee on Poor Relief was set up to investigate the Catholic complaints. It eventually presented its report in 1864. Fr Kelly, who had been among those called to give evidence, ploughed through all eleven volumes and was delighted: his complaints of unfair treatment were entirely vindicated. Farnall had also given evidence, and had made an overwhelmingly strong case against Stepney Union.

Through the Catholic papers, Fr Kelly publicised yet another telling case study of one of the parish families. 12-year-old Ellen Cadey had been left an orphan when her father died, and because she had a dislocated hip she had no chance of getting a job as a servant. He'd done the best he possibly could to provide for her:

Cadey had his life insured in the St. Patrick's Burial Society for £13 and had £3 in the savings' bank. Of these amounts, £6 was paid for his burial and his relatives had spent £4 in feeding and clothing Ellen Cadey. I hold the remaining six pounds.

Fr Seddon had tried everything he could think of to get Ellen into a Catholic institution, in which case her father's savings would be handed over to go towards her keep, but he'd got nowhere: most homes could only afford to take children if promised regular sponsorship of £12 a year. The outlook for Ellen was looking grim:

In consequence of Ellen Cadey's relatives (working people) having several children of their own, they have informed me that after the six pounds are spent they must put her into the Workhouse. Now when Ellen Cadey, who has partly been educated by the Nuns and made her first Communion and received a medal as a reward for proficiency in Catechism… finds herself in one of the Stepney Workhouses, she will, beyond all manner of doubt, be compelled to learn the Protestant Catechism and practise the Protestant religion.

Fr Kelly had advised Catholic leaders to build orphanages around London, and then campaign for a change in the law so that Boards of Guardians could transfer Catholic children to them, and pay a weekly sum for their maintenance out of the Poor Law funds. The necessary legislation had gone through in 1862, but it was permissive only: none of the London Boards could be induced to transfer children, so the orphanages were standing empty. All the priests in London were therefore asked to call public meetings in their districts, and try to set up parish committees to support a lobby of Parliament. The meeting at Commercial Road took place quite promptly in January 1865, with Fr Kelly in the chair, flanked by all his curates. He urged the parishioners to stand up for themselves, and have confidence in the democratic process:

There is no doubt in this country a party of malignant bigots ready and willing to light again the fires of Smithfield; but the overwhelming mass of the Catholic and Protestant people have become tired of and disgusted with such atrocities, and are determined never again to allow such scenes to be enacted. At all events, the best way to prevent their recurrence, and bury in oblivion such sad recollections, is to have the law fairly and impartially administered as between man and man.

The main speeches were delivered by two lay parishioners: Francis Scannell, and Dr Lawrence Mahony, an Irish surgeon who had settled in Stepney some ten or so years before with his English wife Anne, living at 20 Colet Place. Fr Seddon's involvement with Fr Kelly's campaign for destitute orphans must have been a key influence in his career: when he moved on from St Mary and St Michael's he became the diocesan expert on the issue, and devoted the rest of his life to fighting for the Catholic children of London.

An 1867 enquiry showed that 1,708 Catholic children were being held in London workhouses (more than previously estimated), and so far only four had been handed over. Copies of a further petition to Parliament were therefore circulated for signing at all the churches and chapels in the Westminster Archdiocese, and on 31st July 1868 Parliament duly passed "an Act to make further Amendments in the Laws for the Relief of the Poor in England and Wales".

On the Sunday after the news reached him, Fr Kelly arranged for a Te Deum to be sung at St Mary and St Michael's. For thirty years he had "watched with keenest interest the condition of our poor in the workhouses, and, though in sorrow at the time, he could not refrain from announcing a solemn thanksgiving for their release from Protestantism and dissenting thraldom." But immediately after the Te Deum the altar was draped in black. A telegram had arrived on Friday, notifying Fr Kelly of the death of his mother, Catherine Kelly of Ballynacarrig, at the age of 96. He was unable to go over to Ireland for the funeral, but held a Requiem Mass for her at 9.00 on Monday morning.

With unflagging spirit

The guilds of Fr Moore's time had passed away, and their place was taken by sodalities of continental inspiration. The first "canonically erected" confraternity at St Mary and St Michael's was that of the Most Holy Rosary, established by Fr Horrabin, and granted a faculty from Bp Wiseman shortly before the Restoration of the Hierarchy. At the time of the opening of the church, it was the only one Barbara Fitzgerald knew about. Others had been initiated since, but membership was often little more than a formality.

In October 1868, however, Fr Pycke established at Commercial Road a branch of the Archconfraternity of the Holy Family – a Belgian sodality designed specifically to meet the spiritual needs of working-class men – and this made a very significant impact.

Twice every year from then on a solemn service of consecration was held, in which new members were formally enrolled into the confraternity, and everyone received Communion. The first such ceremony took place six months after the initial launching, and enrolled 330-40 men. The members were organised into smaller and more manageable guilds, mostly neighbourhood-based, though with separate guilds for the younger age-groups. Each guild was under its own lay prefect who reported to the prefect general, Michael Barry, who in turn reported to the secretary John Marks, who gave Fr Pycke a complete run-down every three months on the situation of each member. Additionally, each prefect had a sub-prefect, and Marks had an assistant secretary, a Mr Feyer, to help him in his work. Participation, and loss of interest or drop-out, could be monitored quite accurately because the prefects kept careful registers. The active members covered a wide social range, some were "influential", but others were "very poor, some blind and some lame..." Within the first year they had raised £25 to buy themselves a banner, and thereafter came a series of successful fundraising projects for the needs of the church: for altar vessels, or vestments, or a sanctuary carpet. Before long St Mary and St Michael's had the largest Holy Family branch in London, if not in Great Britain. The London City Missioners, who went from door to door labouring to convert people to their own strongly Evangelical brand of Protestantism, loathed the Archconfraternity: it was much more difficult to get a toehold in Catholic households once people were properly organised, and well-informed about their faith.

Fr Sheppard started a branch of the Holy Family for women, with Anne Flinn as prefect general. She and her husband William, who was a Customs Examining Officer, lived on Commercial Road at 21 Arbour Terrace, a few doors along from the Convent of Mercy: they were in their late fifties, with no children still on their hands, and sufficiently well-off to keep a servant. Both were very active in parish affairs, and Anne had launched a Maternity Society, as a revival of the old Society of Charitable Sisters, to provide help for poor women while they had their babies. The men's Holy Family Confraternity met in the church each Tuesday night at 8.00 for "prayer, exhortation and Benediction", and the women's on Wednesdays at the same time.

Young unmarried women were encouraged to aspire to join the Children of Mary, whose president was Maria Grace; enrolment was dependent on exemplary behaviour, and the Guild of St Agnes acted as feeder and testing ground for underage candidates. The zealous 21-year-old Kate Scannell decided to make Fr Kelly "a magnificent cope and veil, richly embroidered", collected money from her fellow-parishioners for materials, and was helped and advised in the work by the Sisters of Mercy. Kelly promised that when he wore the cope to give Benediction at Pentecost, he would ask for "a special grace and blessing" for everyone who'd contributed.

Besides running by far the most successful of Commercial Road's confraternities, Fr Pycke did a course in Curwen's tonic solfa system, then used this method to revitalise and greatly expand an existing choral society in the parish. Whereas strictly devotional associations were *never* mixed, boys and girls, young men and women were all welcome in Fr Pycke's Tonic Sol Fa Choral Society. The group was seen as a great asset, both for its temperance implications (providing people with an alternative to going round the pub) and for its fundraising potential. It had about 120 voices, put on frequent concerts at St Mary and St Michael's, and provided artistes for charity events in other East London Catholic missions. It also served as the church choir. Even working-class missions liked to stage elaborate sung Masses by Haydn or Mozart: St Mary and St Michael's couldn't afford to engage professional singers like the central London chapels, so they were overjoyed to have their own star vocalist, Lizzie Emblem, to do the higher-pitched solos. Mary Shea of Arbour Square, one of the children taught to sing by Fr Pycke, was confirmed early at the age of eight because she was about to emigrate with her family to America. She never forgot how happy she'd been at Commercial Road: 50 years later, when she revisited England with her husband and children, she came back to see the old church, and kept exclaiming in a strong American accent over everything that brought back happy memories.

William Flinn organised a ball every year, to raise money for the schools. For the one in 1867, held at Johnson Street, the premises were beautifully decorated with holly and flowers, and "an Irish harp, ingeniously formed of leaves – doubtless the work of some fair hands – attracted some admiration." Fr Kelly arrived just before midnight and was welcomed with an outburst of applause. Refreshments were served, after which "The dancing was resumed, and kept up with unflagging spirit until four o'clock, when the long line of carriages which filled the street received their freights." John Roper Parkington, who acted as Master of Ceremonies, was still in his early 20s but had already started his own business, a wine shipping company based in the City.

In early June 1869 a very grand three-day bazaar was held, also at Johnson Street School, in aid of the Convent of Mercy. Fr Gorman and Roper Parkington deployed a huge team of women and girl parishioners as stallholders and willing workers, and several City companies chipped in with support: Milner and Wright supplied wines at cost price, and Roper Frères & Cie, which shared office premises with Roper Parkington's, provided the sherry. This was emphatically *not* a temperance event, nor was it aimed at a working-class clientele: the whole idea of parish bazaars was to draw in fashionable outsiders, with serious money to spend on amusements and purchases of no practical use. As a crowning touch, M Eugene Rimmel of the Strand supplied a fountain which played eau de cologne.

The School Board Election

Under the 1870 Education Act, support for voluntary schools was to continue, but from now on local authorities would also be permitted to set up their own schools, to be managed by a specially elected local school board – and the school boards would have a say in policy-making for all schools. Manning did not want any Catholic children going to board schools, which (in common with most non-Catholic church leaders) he regarded as "godless", but he urged all parishes to continue to co-operate with government requirements and qualify for grant funding, to keep their schools going, and he was keen for Catholics to secure a voice on the school boards. A few weeks before the first London School Board elections were to be held in late November 1870, several of the local Catholic priests were invited to take part in a meeting at the London Hospital. Tower Hamlets was supposed to elect five representatives, and the idea of the meeting was to get everyone to agree on just five candidates, so as to avoid a contest. It was proposed to have two Anglicans, two Nonconformists, and one Catholic. This was felt to be fair, since virtually all schools were run by the churches. Fr Kelly nominated someone he thought suitable: the English-born son of an Irish immigrant. But unfortunately the meeting failed to reach unanimous agreement on five candidates, so an election had to be held after all.

The priests of all seven Catholic missions in Tower Hamlets (Commercial Road, Poplar, St Anne's, Tower Hill, St Boniface's, Mile End and Bow) came to Fr Kelly's presbytery to talk to his nominee, and agreed to invite him to stand. Next each mission elected delegates to a committee of laymen which would meet at St Mary and St Michael's several evenings a week in the lead-up to the election. But at the very first meeting, the clergy's candidate was summarily rejected "by an overwhelming majority of lay Irishmen", on the grounds that he was non-practising. Once this point was settled, despite being temporarily without a candidate, the committee quickly went out and bought street lists, and sent out canvassers "in every direction". Eventually, Arthur Langdale, son of the late Charles Langdale, agreed to stand, and everyone agreed he would fit the bill. In view of the antagonism that has sometimes been postulated between the Irish immigrants and the English Old Catholics, it's interesting that an East End lay committee should so decisively prefer a devout scion of the English recusant aristocracy to a lapsed Irishman. All the Tower Hamlets priests accepted the new situation, and endorsed the replacement candidate, and the lay organisations – above all, the well-organised Holy Family confraternity – swung into action to turn out the Catholic vote. Langdale polled fifth, but it was enough: there was a Catholic representative on the School Board.

Antibilious pills

Fr Kelly had had to promise that the intensive parish collections would come to an end as of Christmas 1867, because the parishioners were exhausted. Thanks to their heroic efforts, the debt had been reduced to the point that the annual interest payments were well under £200. That was still a lot of money, and it was an awful pity for the parish to have to keep paying it out, year after year, but the burden could just about be sustained. However Abp Manning's declared policy was establish more missions in slum districts, to plant the Church among the poor. Yet another slice was cut off Commercial Road's district when the formerly Congregationalist Salem Chapel in Mile End Road was purchased in 1868 and re-opened as the Catholic Church of the Guardian Angels. Most of the new Mile End district was carved out of St Anne's, but part of it came from St Mary and St Michael's. Poor Fr Kelly! The German Church, Tower Hill, and now Mile End: "These three operations" had deprived his church "of nearly four hundred a year, just as if a person put his hand into my cash-box and abstracted that amount annually. Ever since those separations took place, this mission, as far as local resources are concerned, has been simply insolvent in all its branches."

Fr David Hickey

High in Manning's list of priorities was the establishing of a mission actually within densely Irish-populated Wapping. Fr David Hickey was assigned to this task, and he celebrated the new mission's first Mass in the schoolrooms in Red Lion Street in October 1871. Within a few months the congregation was bursting at the seams. "I would advise any body" wrote Fr Kelly in his 1872 fundraising appeal for the debt still weighing on his beautiful church and presbytery, "who proposes erecting such buildings to purchase at least one hundredweight of antibilious pills. He will find them indispensable. Since I commenced to erect those buildings, three new missions and a portion of a fourth have been cut off, in other words, six hundred pounds have been annually taken away from this mission, and that before the debt has been paid off." Nevertheless some progress had been made during the past two years, as the mortgage was now down to £2,500.

34-year-old Fr Sheppard wasn't well, and although he was being properly looked after and cared for at the presbytery, Dr Mahony advised a rest cure in the country. But in June a telegram arrived, a parishioner named Miss Conway rushed off to nurse him, and a week later Fr Gorman had to go with one of the Scannells' small boys to administer the last rites. Fr Kelly went the next day, and was with Fr Sheppard when he died that evening, of cerebro-spinal meningitis. His body was brought back to Commercial Road, where Abp Manning and fifty priests attended the funeral. Later in the year Fr Kelly accompanied 300 members of the Holy Family women's section to St Patrick's Cemetery, Leytonstone, to erect a memorial stone on his grave.

In 1873 Abp Manning issued a directive banning women from church choirs. The change, which was to bring London into line with liturgical reforms being promoted throughout the worldwide Church, was widely considered a positive one: some of the professional singers had been rather over-the-top. But a lot of poor missions had had women volunteers, and there was concern about having to start from scratch to train boys to replace them, and that the boys would want to be paid. A local music-lover wrote to the *East London Observer,* expressing confidence that the St Mary and St Michael's parishioners would accept the archbishop's decision, but lamenting the loss of Lizzie Emblem's "rich magnificent voice, which so often rang through the aisles of their spacious church, *Ad majorem Dei gloriam*."

By now the parish's annual ball had become so big and successful that it no longer had to be held on the cheap at Johnson Street: instead the Beaumont Institute, in Beaumont Square, was hired for the night. Doors opened at 8.30, dancing began at 9.00 and continued until 4.00 in the morning. Tickets cost 5s for gentlemen, 4s for ladies, or 8s 6d for a couple. John Roper Parkington was still helping to run the ball, but he was no longer living in the parish: he'd moved to Coborn Terrace, Bow Road. He married in 1873, and then or soon afterwards left East London. Headed for the big time, he was to acquire numerous honours during a distinguished career, including a knighthood.

A series of meetings was held around the parishes of the Westminster Diocese to discuss the setting up of a Catholic Association. As the meetings progressed, the need to revive the temperance movement emerged as a priority: Fr Kelly, in particular, stressed its importance. The third meeting was held at Commercial Road, chaired by Abp Manning. In his address he encouraged Catholics to join existing temperance associations, but also announced his plans to start a new one for the whole of London modelled on the Association of the Cross which had been founded 25 years previously in Canada: prospective members could choose between two pledges: one of total abstinence and one of temperance proper – that is, moderate drinking. Another speaker at this meeting was Dr Herbert Vaughan, founder and director of the Mill Hill Missionary Society, and applause broke out as he recalled how he acquired his own missionary experience at St Mary and St Michael's.

As the new temperance movement came together, the double pledge option was lost sight of, and Manning himself took the total abstinence pledge. By no means all working-class people supported the temperance movement, and many were strongly opposed to it, but those who were for it often felt very strongly about the issue, and had a clear preference for total abstinence rather than "half measures": in creating his Catholic Total Abstinence League of the Cross as a strictly teetotal movement, therefore, Manning was simply responding to popular demand. St Anne's, Underwood Street, and St Peter's Italian Church in Clerkenwell, promptly got involved, followed by Tower Hill. (In all three cases an existing temperance association was transmuted into a League branch.) But St Mary and St Michael's held aloof, because Fr Kelly wasn't happy with the League's teetotal line.

St George's in the East

Ecumenical ups and downs

With agreement from the Rector of St George's in the East, an experimental Anglican mission had been established in Wapping by Charles Lowder, an enthusiastic product of the Oxford Movement in the Church of England. At first the Irish threw things at the missioners, but they bravely stuck it out, and after a fortnight or so they were agreed to be harmless, and left in peace. Within a couple of years, they established a permanent centre in Wapping, and one in Wellclose Square. In 1859-60 the team was targeted by Protestant extremists who whipped up a ferocious campaign of anti-ritualist rioting. Yet Rev Lowder refused to give up, and donations from sympathetic supporters enable him to purchase a site in Wapping on which to build a permanent church. St Peter's, London Docks, opened in the summer of 1866, just as the cholera epidemic was breaking out. The dedication of his mission teams to the sick and dying impressed everyone who witnessed it, and broke down the widespread prejudice against High Anglicanism. The Wellclose Square mission centre was being looked after by three promising young clergymen: George Akers, who'd been working with Lowder since December 1864, Edward Shapcote and Francis Windham. The plan was for the mission to become an independent district, whereupon Akers would be the first vicar. Coming from an upper class and wealthy family, although he wasn't the only son he'd inherited a personal fortune amounting to thousands of pounds: out of the £5,000 pledged for the building of the new church, £4,000 was to be from him.

An attack on the clergy house in Wellclose Square during the 'Ritual Riots'

During February 1868 the Oblate Fathers gave a mission at English Martyrs Church, and Akers, Windham and Shapcote decided to attend. The experience put Akers into a personal crisis. On the Sunday, most unusually for him, he preached a strongly Protestant sermon at St Saviour's. On the

Monday morning Windham went off to visit a sick relative in Kensington, but didn't come back until lunchtime the following day. After lunch he spent several hours talking to Akers, and they left the house together. Rev Lowder only found out on the Wednesday that both of them had been received into the Catholic Church. Shapcote was on holiday, so he sent a message for him to return immediately, but Akers and Windham intercepted him at the railway station where he had to change trains, and persuaded him, too, to convert. Akers had been very popular with his Anglican flock, so a lot of them contacted him, wanting to discuss his decision, and about 60 ended up following his example.

St Peter's, London Docks

Though periodically ruffled by such incidents, the tenor of interfaith relations in East London was normally as smooth as a millpond. Any really major dissensions were more likely to occur within confessional bodies rather than between them – as indeed was the case with the St George's Ritual Riots, which never touched the local Roman Catholics at all. Other parts of Britain, and other parts of London, experienced major civil disturbances during the 1860s, due to Irish mobs responding violently to provocation by travelling evangelists (sometimes ex-priests) who specialised in abusive anti-Popery, or admirers of Garibaldi making rude remarks about the Irish Brigade. But the parishioners of St Mary and St Michael's simply ignored everything of that sort. Fr Kelly wrote to the papers to recommend their laid-back approach to his fellow-countrymen:

> *There is hardly one foreign Apostate, or native Souper, who obtained a momentary fame in London, that has not placarded and lectured in various buildings in my Mission; yet not one of my congregation interfered or went near them. Indeed I never found it necessary to give any caution to my people on the subject.*

Board schools usually charged 2d or 3d a week, and most Anglican and Dissenting schools charged more, but virtually all Catholic schools charged only 1d, and let children off if they said they couldn't afford even that. Since many parents genuinely couldn't afford the requisite pennies, and the government was moving towards making attendance compulsory, the Poor

Law Guardians were authorised to pay the poorest children's fees: however interested parties were going to have to lobby their Guardians to obtain action. So it was that in February 1873, Fr Kelly and some of the local Anglican clergy got together a joint deputation. The Vicars of St Matthew's Commercial Road, and Christchurch Watney Street, accompanied Fr Kelly to see the Guardians of the St George's in the East, sending in a written request signed by themselves, and also by the St George's Rector J L Ross, and by Rev Lowder and his colleague Robert Linklater at St Peter's. Fr Kelly acted as spokesman, urging that the Guardians take steps to pay fees for parents on out-door relief, and suggesting they pay them direct to the school managers, who would keep a careful account. Rev Fidler of St Mathew's confirmed that all the Anglican clergy supported the proposal, and he was sure the Nonconformists would also agree. The Guardians took this démarche sufficiently seriously to call a special meeting to discuss it. Nevertheless their decision was negative. Ecumenical good feeling was strained in September 1873, by a sermon delivered by Rev Linklater in which, going by the newspaper reports, he'd taken a thoughtless dig at the Catholic clergy:

Two-thirds of the population in the neighbourhood of the London Docks were Irish Roman Catholics, who were loyal to the back-bone to their faith and Church. Even if it were desired it would be useless to attempt to interfere with that faith. It was with them a matter of race and nation. But it was sad to see how they were neglected by the priests of their own communion. Possibly they might be ministering to richer congregations in other parts of London. These poor Irish were left uncared for, their children were bred in ignorance and vice, and the Anglican clergy were powerless to influence them. Any attempt to do so was met by language the most bitter, violent and obscene.

Kind friends lost no time in drawing this to the attention of Fr Kelly, who penned an angry reply turning the accusation on its head. During his periodic parish visitations for census purposes, he riposted, *he'd* never come across any non-Catholic clergy doing their rounds, or even any lay auxiliary workers like Scripture readers. In 1854, during the cholera epidemic, "I had the place all to myself, and people of every religion and no religion were delighted to see me amongst them. Over and over again, when I made enquiries of Protestants, they would ask me to enter their rooms and have a chat with them; but I had no time for that, as I was then building the church in the Commercial-road East."

Since 1st July he'd been busy conducting yet another parish census, starting from Leman Street (which was currently the boundary with the Tower Hill district), and had got as far as Sutton Street. Once again he'd not met a single clergyman other than his own four curates, who were constantly at work, around the streets or in the schools.

An edifying spectacle

Fr Gorman was spiritual director of the schools in Johnson Street, and in charge of organising the First Communions. Thanks to his efforts, allied to those of the Sisters of Mercy and the lay teachers, the alarming rent-a-mob atmosphere of the 1850s had been completely transformed. At a ceremony involving 130 children in the spring of 1874, a newspaper reported that the demeanour of 56 boys from Johnson Street "evinced the most profound recollection, and after receiving they returned slowly, and with hands clasped devoutly, to their seats. It would be hard to conceive a more pious sight. All present were deeply impressed, and many shed tears of religious joy." The boys were dressed neatly, all wearing "nice collars and neckties" given them by Fr Gorman, and with their Confirmation medals round their necks.

The London Hospital in the eighteenth century

Another area in which Fr Gorman was deeply involved was hospital work. The London Hospital had no public funding. Originally, it was supported by wealthy subscribers, and to be accepted as a patient you had to obtain a recommendation from a subscriber. By the 1870s this archaic system was breaking down, and being replaced by mass fundraising, but there was still a confused feeling that donating money earned the right to treatment. Abp Manning therefore ordered all Catholic churches to participate in the Sunday Fund, started in 1873, for which collections were held in all London churches on "Hospital Sunday" in June, and also backed the Saturday Fund, which targeted the non-churchgoing working-class. Being poor, the Catholics might only be able to contribute relatively small amounts for the hospitals, but the important thing was to show that they were part of the general effort, and therefore just as "entitled" to receive treatment as everyone else. In the same spirit, Fr Gorman represented the Catholic community on the governing body of the London Hospital, and every morning after his Mass, the sacristy was filled with people – not necessarily Catholics – seeking recommendations. He was also on the board of the East London Children's Hospital, which was started by a young married couple – a doctor and a nurse

– in 1867, and worked to sign up wealthy Catholic subscribers – people like the Duke of Norfolk, who had no particular interest in East London at the time, but was brought on board by Fr Gorman's explanations of how helpful the new initiative was to the East End Catholics. When a "Lying-in Home" (Maternity Hospital) was started in Shadwell in 1884, Fr Gorman was brought onto the board of that, too. The Maternity Hospital was later to move to Commercial Road, just a few doors along from the church.

East London Children's Hospital: an illustration from Charles Dickens' *The Uncommercial Traveller*.

It was Fr Gorman who started a branch of the League of the Cross at St Mary and St Michael's, in May 1874. Abp Manning attended the inaugural meeting at Johnson Street, and announced that the new branch "would make the seventeenth in existence in London and Southwark. He looked on these branches as seventeen regiments, and he hoped that the new regiment at the Mission of SS. Mary and Michael's would be foremost in the ranks of teetotalism." 84 men then took the total abstinence pledge at his hands.

By this time the League had 28,000 members in London, and August that year saw its first mass rallies: 20,000 turned up to a demonstration on Tower Hill, and 12,000 a week later at the Crystal Palace, where Fr Pycke was among the organisers and helped stage a concert using child singers as one of the day's features. Each branch had both a priest president and a lay president, and a committee, and met weekly. League members in good standing could be promoted to the rank of "Guard" and be entitled to wear a uniform comprising a cap and a broad, ornate, sash in green picked out with gold. There was a regular monthly parade round the parish, and for larger events they'd march right across London. Catholics were chary of staging specifically religious activities in fully public spaces like main roads or squares, for fear of attack, but temperance demonstrations could count on a fair measure of approval from all faith groups. It was a matter of pride to have beautiful banners, for which they'd save up their pennies, and to establish their own brass, or drum-and-fife, band (or both). The bigger marches featured open air temperance talks by Abp Manning and other speakers, often delivered from a wagon if a temporary platform could not be conveniently erected at the spot. Special events were organised four times a year to mark the festivals of the League: St Patrick's Day, Whit Monday, a summer event at the Crystal Palace in August, and 10th October which was the birthday of Fr Mathew.

Fr Cahill

Fr William Kelly did not live to a ripe old age, and Abp Manning always said that he gave up his life as a martyr to the building of St Mary and St Michael's church. Although he struggled to keep up his usual round of energetic activity, his constitution was packing up. His friend Fr James Connolly came give him the last rites, after which he made a partial recovery, but it wasn't long before he suffered a relapse. He died in the presbytery at Commercial Road on Christmas Eve 1874 "after a severe and protracted agony, in the 59th year of his age and the 37th of his priesthood."

After careful consideration, Fr Thomas Cahill was chosen to succeed Fr Kelly. Now in his mid-forties, Cahill had spent most of his career at St Mary

The Calvary which was severely damaged in

the 17th March 1945 V2 bombing.

It was never displayed again but the crucifix was restored

and is now positioned at the entrance to the church.

Sisters of Mercy at prayer in the old Convent Chapel

OUR LADY'S HALL,

JOHNSON STREET, COMMERCIAL ROAD, E.

A GRAND

ASSAULT-AT-ARMS

Will take place

ON THURSDAY, JUNE 4th,

In aid of the Funds of the Young Men's Catholic Association.

TOMMY BURNS

Champion of the World, who is a Catholic, will spar with

PAT O'KEEFE

TICKETS, 10/- ; 5/- ; 2/6. Doors open 7.30.
No Admission without Ticket. No Money taken at doors.
Apply at once to Father MAGRATH, SS. Mary and Michael's, Commercial Road, E.

Father BERNARD VAUGHAN, S.J.

WILL SPEAK.

A poster for one of Fr Bernard Vaughan's talks at Our Lady's Hall.

World Heavyweight Boxing Champion, Tommy Burns, in attendance!

Date: June 4th 1908

The East End comes to a standstill for Canon Ring's funeral in August 1941. Cardinal Hinsley and several other bishops were present, along with an array of local politicians and dignitaries including future prime minister, Clem Attlee, who was shortly to become Churchill's deputy prime minister.

Mayor and local MP, Walter Edwards, with Canon Fitzgerald and pupils in St Mary and St Michael's Primary School in the early 1940s.

Bishop Challoner girls busy under the watchful eye of a Sister of Mercy

St Michael is hoisted up into place in the early 1950s

Corpus Christi procession leaves the
Convent of Mercy in Hardinge Street

Parish pilgrimage to Lourdes 1956

Rosary Procession in the 1950s

Moorfields, keeping church and district running smoothly so the Administrator, Mgr Daniel Gilbert, could attend to his duties as a canon and Vicar General of Westminster Archdiocese, and founder-director of the famous Providence Row night shelter for homeless people. Mgr Gilbert had a very high regard for him. Any balance still outstanding on the church debt will have been settled by Fr Kelly's life insurance, so Fr Cahill could start with a clean slate. The title and rights (whatever they amounted to in practice) of Missionary Rector were conferred on him, and he was looked to with confidence to provide the key quality of overall leadership needed by such a large and important parish.

His first step was to call for the church to be given a thoroughgoing wash and brush-up. All the stonework was rubbed down and the walls distempered; the stations of the cross and altar were carefully repainted by two parishioner volunteers, Michael Calnan (John Michael's son) and Miss Minoch; and the Holy Family Confraternity raised £37 for new choir stalls. An eminently sensible move taken around this time was to drop one of the Sunday Masses – the earliest one at 6.00. Now the numbers had been reduced by the dividing of the district, six Masses weren't necessary. But after only a few months in post, Fr Cahill's health broke down. He became so ill that he had to go to the Isle of Wight to be looked after by his younger brother, Fr John Baptist Cahill, who was parish priest of St Mary's Ryde. By the end of the 1875 it was clear that he would never be able to return to Commercial Road, and he sent in his resignation. He died early the next year on 31st January. The funeral took place in Ryde, where his brother was to survive him for many years (eventually becoming Bishop of Portsmouth), and Cardinal Manning presided over a Requiem Mass at St Mary and St Michael's.

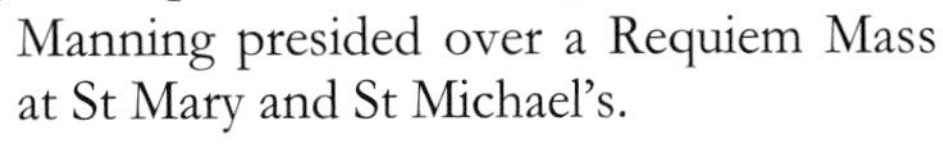

Father Patrick O'Callaghan

All-powerful with his cheerful, winning, and peaceful smile

37-year-old Fr Patrick O'Callaghan, who replaced poor Fr Cahill, had started off his priestly career as a curate together with him at St Mary Moorfields, and since then had been in charge of SS Anselm and Cecilia, Lincoln's Inn Fields, for about fourteen years. Due to slum clearances, the central London chapels were losing most of their population, so moving to St Mary and St Michael's meant taking on more responsibility, for a larger and more important mission. According to an emotional eulogy delivered at the farewell meeting in Lincoln's Inn Fields:

All priests... were good, but none could be better than the beloved clergyman they had lost and they could never cease to think of his cheerful smile as he walked about amongst them doing good... Day and night Father O'Callaghan was always ready to attend the call of the poorest of his flock; and as he walked through Wild-street, Lincoln's-court, and other places, fighting and quarrelling were put an end to at his approach. Their good priest was all-powerful with his cheerful, winning, and peaceful smile. Why, he did more in one instant to quell the most terrible rows than all the police of Bow Street assembled together in the majesty of law (loud applause).

Many of the poorer, older and more marginalised parishioners were Gaelic-speaking, and they were devastated to lose Fr O'Callaghan because he was one of the rare priests in London who understood their language; he promised to come back from time to time to hear their confessions. Thanks to the language skills of the curates, confessions at Commercial Road could be heard in French, Flemish, Dutch and Italian, as well as Irish. The cook-housekeeper at the presbytery during O'Callaghan's time was Elizabeth Kelly.

The boys' and girls' schools at Johnson Street, and the boys', girls' and infant school at Pell Street were all doing well, and getting positive reports in the government inspections. But because Johnson Street didn't have an infant school, a number of quite small children were being admitted to the boys' and girls' schools and taught with them in the same big rooms – which can't have been good either for them or for the older children. After 1st January 1877, when school attendance was to be made compulsory, not only should the existing schools be full, but more accommodation would have to be made available – or else a great many of the parish's children would be compelled to attend non-Catholic schools. In appointing Fr O'Callaghan to Commercial Road, therefore, Cardinal Manning told him his first priority must be to expand the schools, to take at least another 400 children.

The original school at Johnson Street was surrounded by quite a large playground, with plenty of space for an additional building, and plans were quickly agreed from Young and Sons for a two storey structure. The ground floor would become an infant school, while the top floor would be used to start a "middle school" for boys, named St Joseph's, as a counterpart to the girls' convent school. Schools could charge fees of up to 9d a week and still be eligible for government grants, and St Joseph's would therefore charge 9d a week. The parents who could afford such a princely sum would expect social exclusivity (some of the kids in the main boys' school were probably quite rough), so Fr O'Callaghan assured them that the middle school would be "completely separated from the other schools".

The infant school opened in September 1876, under the Sisters of Mercy, and immediately enrolled 200 children. St Joseph's middle school opened at the end of the year, under a headmaster named James Cassidy, with two very talented assistant teachers, and Frs O'Callaghan and Pycke helping out with Latin and French lessons. Within just a few years it was achieving excellent exam results, and winning prizes at the annual diocesan inspection for Religions Knowledge: two boys went on train for the priesthood, and others were known to have landed very good jobs. The new building cost £2,000, and to raise this amount quickly Fr O'Callaghan had to tie up the school endowments for the next 20 years. The capital was safe, and about half the income – £150 a year – would become payable to St Mary's and St Michael's once again from 1893, but not until 1896 would the usual income of £300 a year be available.

The organisation of the "ecclesiastical conferences" (essentially, deaneries) in the eastern part of Westminster Archdiocese was changed: whereas previously the Tower Hamlets missions had been grouped with some of the central London ones in a conference headed by St Mary Moorfields, the new grouping excluded anything west of Aldgate, though it included the scattered missions in Essex out to Southend. Within this new grouping St Mary and St Michael's was pre-eminent. Fr O'Callaghan became president of the conference, and was appointed Dean. He also took charge of the New Common Fund, for the support of aged and infirm priests of the dioceses of Westminster, Southwark, and Portsmouth.

Until recently there'd not been all that many priests, and their chances of living long enough to retire were slim, but from around 1877 demand began to outstrip the available resources, so Fr O'Callaghan had to work hard to build them up. Taking responsibility for a relatively unglamorous, but very necessary, project may have suited his temperament: whereas some of the London priests enjoyed media attention, he didn't like to talk about himself much, and preferred to stay slightly in the background.

The large plain-glass window behind the sanctuary in St Mary and St Michael's had to be covered by a large red curtain, as otherwise the light was so strong that the congregation couldn't see the altar. So in August 1878 a fundraising drive was launched to install stained glass, commissioned from Mayer and Co of Grosvenor Street. It was agreed that the new window should be a memorial to Frs Horrabin and Foley who had bought the church site, and Fr Kelly who built the church. The work was expected to be completed in four months, but it took a lot longer than that, because the fundraising ground to a halt when London was hit once again by harsh winter weather conditions, and a severe trade depression.

Not until March 1879 was the stained glass window unveiled: it featured the crucifixion in the centre, flanked by various saints including Michael and Bridget, and the final cost was £520, of which £55 was donated by non-parishioners. Something also needed to be done about the heating – Cardinal Manning said St Mary and St Michael's was "the coldest church in London" – but Fr O'Callaghan had to defer this for a few years. When he eventually installed a new system, he got the Cardinal to come down specially to tell the parishioners about it, and urge them to dig deep to pay the bill.

Membership of the parish's Holy Family Confraternity, Men's Section, peaked at 846 in 1880, and at the half-yearly consecration in November 620 received Communion. It was unquestionably the most successful parish association in the whole of London. But at the end of that year the popular Fr Pycke moved on, to become parish priest of St John the Evangelist, Islington. The successive curates who looked after the group from then on tried really hard, and Sr Stanislaus Purcell encouraged the schoolboys to join as soon as they'd made their First Communion, but gradually the numbers began to fall. At the time of Fr Pycke's departure Michael Barry was still prefect-general, and the secretary was a Mr J Maunsell. By 1888 a new set of lay officers had taken over: the prefect-general was John O'Loghlen, and the secretary was J Browne. John O'Loghlen, a longstanding parishioner, came from Broadford, Co Clare, in Ireland, while his wife Mary was a Londoner: they lived at No 59, Bromley Street, and John's professional work as a chemical analyst (at the government laboratories in Somerset House) allowed them to keep a servant. Membership was down to about 400, and the Sunday Mass which concluded a confraternity retreat – during which the distinguished Fr John Spencer Vaughan, Dr Herbert Vaughan's brother, "occupied the pulpit and delivered an impressive discourse on the enormity of sin" – saw just 300 Communions.

Charles Fay was a key leader in the League of the Cross, and he got a juvenile branch started: Fr O'Callaghan declared that "the success of their branch of the league, which was equal to any throughout London, was mainly due to Mr. Fay's labours." The vice-president was a Mr M Burns, and a Mr Raher was Captain of the Guards. Linked to the League was a women's group called the Guild of Our Lady of the Immaculate Conception.

Cardinal Manning quite often arrived late for events where he was supposed to be the main speaker, so organisers needed to be quick on their feet, and arrange substitutes to keep up the momento until he made his grand entrance. One might wonder if his lateness was sometimes contrived and planned for, to increase the dramatic effect – but Manning clearly had a very crowded diary, and sometimes he was running so late that he didn't turn up at all. Once he arranged to address a League of the Cross meeting in Harris Court, and the neighbourhood went wild with excitement:

The houses were decorated, banners and flags were suspended across the street, and the windows were filled, and every vantage spot, even to the roofs of the houses, crowded to obtain a view of the beloved Cardinal-Archbishop. But the good people were doomed to be disappointed, for his Eminence, delayed at the confirmation at S. James's, Spanish-place, was unable to attend.

On that occasion, though substitute speakers had to be put up for the open-air event, the Cardinal did make it to Commercial Road for the evening service. In August 1881, when he arrived late for a much bigger League rally, on Tower Hill, he explained that he'd had to attend a meeting in St Mary and St Michael's to appeal for funds for a new residence for the Sisters of Mercy, because their house was far too small. He took the opportunity to deliver a little plug for the Sisters to all the people assembled at Tower Hill, and hoped it would generate some donations for them.

No 535, Commercial Road, had been too small when the founding Sisters first arrived, but the community now numbered 14, and during the day the house also had to accommodate 100 girls attending the convent school. The Sisters continued to teach in the three girls' schools and three infants' schools in Johnson Street, Pell Street and Red Lion Street, a total of 1,340 children. Exhaustion and cramped living conditions were telling on their health, and several quite young Sisters had died. A working committee was set up and a subscription list started, and Cardinal Manning kicked off the appeal by handing over a cheque for £50. Nevertheless there was no chance of raising enough to purchase land and put up a really suitable building, so the only solution was to spread the community and its activities over two terraced houses in Commercial Road, instead of just one. The Sisters therefore arranged to take over the adjoining house, No 533: this would require £150 for moving in expenses, and £80 a year from then on to pay the extra rent.

Due to slum clearances Tower Hill district lost a lot of its congregation, and in spring 1882 it was agreed that the parish boundaries should be changed, and part of the Commercial Road district – including Pell Street – be transferred to Tower Hill. No longer having to staff the Pell Street schools relieved the Sisters of Mercy of a significant part of their crushing workload. Later they also gave up the Wapping schools, so as to be able to concentrate all their efforts on Commercial Road.

Ordinary channels

The work of the Guardians of the Poor was unpaid, and meetings were usually held during the day, so candidates needed to be self-employed, or have a private income. The local notables who sat on the Boards usually succeeded in getting themselves re-elected every time or, if any had chosen to retire, bringing in friends to fill the vacancies. It wasn't at all easy to break in to the charmed circle. Where children were clearly identified as Catholics, the Boards could now be compelled to transfer them to Catholic orphanages. But partly for lack of room in the Catholic homes, and partly for other reasons, many remained in the Poor Law institutions. The Boards were supposed to do everything they reasonably could to have them brought up as Catholics, but a lot of pushing was required, and Fr Seddon, as secretary to both Cardinal Manning and the Westminster Diocesan Education Fund, took on the main responsibility for keeping up the pressure. Boards would argue and haggle over the religious identity of each individual child, and trying to make arrangements with them for religious instruction, and Mass attendance, could be a nightmare.

Heated arguments arose on the Board of St George's in the East: they didn't want to allow Mass to be celebrated at the Plashet school, yet the alternative was to march the children all the way to the Stratford Chapel every Sunday. Anti-Catholic remarks began flying around at Guardians' meetings, and were reported in the local newspapers. This sparked off a furious reaction at St Mary and St Michael's, and at the elections in 1875 it was decided to put up two Catholic candidates: John Michael Calnan, and Mr Malone. A Guardian named Shaboe, though he was a Protestant and insisted he was "as determined an opponent of Roman Catholicism as any man" was so annoyed with the Board that he resolved to withdraw in favour of a Catholic: this meant that however badly the Catholic candidates performed in the election, one of them ought to get in. In fact, the parishioners worked so hard that not only did both get in, they headed the poll. At first their inexperience created some embarrassment: they didn't understand the proper procedures, and sometimes even got the issues confused. But they did their best, and at a later election were replaced by two other parishioners, Dr Mahony and J M Sullivan. Being in a minority, the Catholic Guardians couldn't change everything overnight, but a foothold on the Board at least made it possible to ask awkward questions, and challenge unfair decisions and bureaucratic inertia. As they learned the ropes, gradually established a good working relationship with the veterans, and showed they were pulling their weight, they came to be accepted and respected.

Applying to the Guardians was always an absolute last resort: people did everything they could to get help from charitable sources instead. In January 1881, when yet again a snow storm and frost had thrown everyone out of work, the priests wrote notes for a number of parishioners, vouching for them, and sent them over to the Police Court in Arbour Square where the magistrates were once again distributing relief. As usual, there wasn't enough to go round, and many were disappointed: they couldn't understand why other people had been helped, and they hadn't. The priests tried in vain to explain. Eventually, Fr Padbury resolved the misunderstanding in his own inimitable way. He went over to Arbour Square and stated the problem in open court, saying he "wished to have his worship's answer publicly so as to satisfy these poor people" because there were over a thousand parishioners needing help. The magistrate, Mr Lushington, complied, explaining that the funds held by the court came from voluntary donations and were very limited: they tried to relieve "special cases of distress and suffering", but couldn't help everyone. He was quite sure there were many others genuinely in need, but he could only refer them to the "ordinary channels" (which meant the Poor Law). Leaving the court, Fr Padbury was followed by "at least a hundred poor people, who had come over with him anxiously awaiting the magistrate's reply."

Home Rule

Charles Stewart Parnell

There was in England both considerable sympathy for the Irish national movement (which could mean different things to different people), and a natural chariness of its terrorist fringe. Cardinal Manning condemned the violence of the Fenians, but insisted on the need to address the grievances of Ireland which had provoked that violence. From around 1870, O'Connell's constitutional approach was reborn in the Home Rule movement, which was generally understood to mean devolution rather than independence. Within a year or so Home Rule Associations were springing up among the Irish diaspora in London: by 1872 that there were branches in Poplar, Whitechapel and Wapping, and they were eventually federated into a Tower Hamlets Association. From 1879 the Home Rule movement was consolidated under the leadership of Charles Stewart Parnell, and formed a close alliance with the Catholic Church: the clergy strove to encourage constructive and peaceful attitudes and discourage violence, and in return for their blessing, the nationalists supported the Church over the education issue. The Tower Hamlets Home Rule Association, for example, made a point of backing the Catholic candidate in School Board elections.

Like other local parishes, St Mary and St Michael's formed a branch of the Catholic Young Men's Society (CYMS), which had been founded in Ireland in 1849, and become very strong in the north of England. It aimed both to keep lads in the Church after they'd left school, and to channel their idealism and energies away from Fenianism and into constructive channels – which, it was accepted, could include non-violent campaigning for Irish Home Rule, and social change. Donald Horne H McFarlane, MP for Carlow, came to give them a lecture on the Irish Land Question. It was one of the big topics of the day. Successive bad harvests in Ireland had reduced the peasantry to destitution. While appeals were launched for famine relief, families who couldn't pay their rent were being evicted from their farms. In response the National Land League organised rent strikes and boycotts, and called for transfer of land ownership to the tillers of the soil.

Meanwhile in England, whenever anything awful happened – such as the massive blaze at the Royal Victoria Dock in February 1881, which caused half a million pounds worth of damage – there was a knee-jerk assumption that the Fenians were to blame. Though understandable, it was very tough on law-abiding and peaceful Irish residents. In March 1882 Queen Victoria experienced an assassination attempt, but the attacker turned out to be a deranged Scot. J M Sullivan made a point of getting to his feet at a meeting of the St George's in the East Board of Guardians to move "That this Board expresses its horror and indignation at the dastardly attempt on the life of Her Most Gracious Majesty, and desires to congratulate her Majesty on her providential escape." His gesture was appreciated. But from 1883 the American Fenians, over whom Parnell had no control, launched a series of terrorist attacks in London using the new invention dynamite. Some of the targets were symbolic sites like the House of Commons and the Tower of London, but several bombs were planted in the tunnels of the London Underground. Fortunately nobody was killed, though quite a number were injured. The bombs did succeed in spreading terror, and fuelling hostility towards the Irish. A lot of Irish people lost their jobs, because employers were frightened of employing someone who might turn out to be a secret terrorist.

Capable and willing to hold office

Half hour weekly instruction sessions, and Sunday services, for children in the huge and dreadfully regimented Poor Law residential schools where they were all terrified of being singled out as "different", could be no more than a temporary stopgap. Gradually but surely, more Catholic orphanages were opened, and the Guardians were induced to transfer the children to them. While continuing to follow up transfer applications, Fr Seddon then turned his attention to lobbying for more realistic maintenance payments. The Local Government Board recommended 6s per head per week as reasonable, so Fr Seddon wrote round to all the Boards of Guardians, asking them to pay 6s. Several East End Boards refused, but St George's agreed without debate, and he wrote a nice letter thanking them for their decision. Shortly afterwards two non-Catholic Guardians, Sly and Crowder, reported back positively on a school committee inspection visit to the Catholic orphanages, and Sullivan made a point of thanking them. The old hostility had largely been overcome: when in 1883 a third Catholic candidate came forward – Michael Calnan, son of John Michael – he was actually "recommended" by the sitting Guardians for one of the vacancies (an endorsement which carried considerable weight with voters) and duly elected. Sullivan was to serve on the Guardians for 29 years, and his tact and courtesy were a major factor in achieving fair treatment for the Catholic community.

Catholics were supposed to be allowed out on Sundays to attend Mass, and it was generally believed that a lot of inmates put themselves down as Catholics in order to get a day out, and go on the razzle. Certainly a tendency had long been noted for Massgoers to return to the workhouse very late, and very drunk. The obvious solution was to arrange for Mass to be celebrated in the workhouses, and this would also benefit the large numbers of paupers who were too old and infirm to go out. But even if the Guardians were willing, the clergy were reluctant to take on the extra duty unless they were paid for their time. They were already putting in a tremendous amount of work at the Poor Law institutions, all of which had Anglican chaplains on a comfortable salary, while they didn't get a penny.

From the start of their campaign about the Poor Law, St Mary and St Michael's had been demanding chaplaincy stipends. Unfortunately a legal opinion had been handed down in 1873, saying that Guardians weren't allowed to pay for non-Anglican religious services, but in 1883 the issue was being raised once again. Carefully observing all the proper forms, Dr

Mahony introduced a motion asking the St George's Guardians to petition Parliament for a change in the law, as some other Boards had decided to do. After some discussion, and despite strong opposition from a few of the Guardians, they voted 18 to 11 in favour. The law was indeed changed soon afterwards. There was no direct benefit to St Mary and St Michael's, because all the Poor Law institutions had been relocated outside the parish. But St George's paid £80 a year to the priests in Wapping, for the pastoral care of its workhouse and infirmary in Prusom Street (which later became St George's Hospital), and even Stepney eventually started paying its Catholic chaplains.

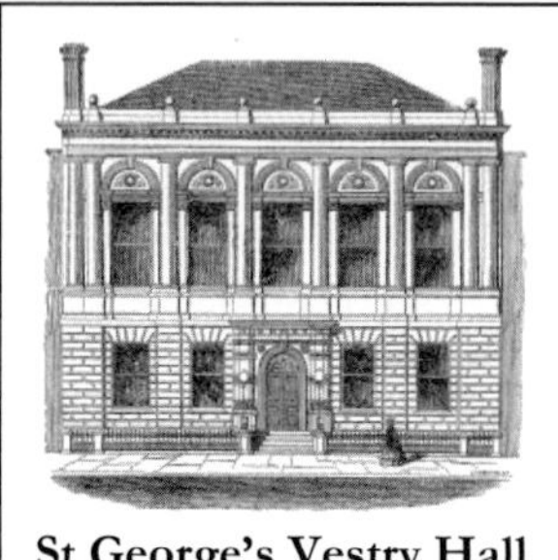
St George's Vestry Hall

A number of the Guardians also sat on the St George's Vestry, among them Michael Calnan, and Abraham Benabo, a Jewish house agent with offices a few doors along from St Mary and St Michael's. However the Vestry had recently been infiltrated by a "reforming group" who were very hostile both to the sitting members (the "old party") and to the minority communities. The "Reformers", had a whole lot of bees in their bonnets, and flared up at any attempt to subject their ideas to a reality check. A meeting in March 1884 grew very heated, with sharp words exchanged between a Mr Watts and the Clerk, who fumed that "If Mr. Watts wants to get rid of an Act of Parliament, there is a legal way of doing it." The next item on the agenda was nomination of overseers, and Frederick Dellow "nominated Messrs Petherbridge, Calnan, Benabo and Hammond". Suddenly, as reported in the *East London Observer*, "a scene" erupted. The Reformers started making facetious counter-nominations, then became openly abusive:

Mr. E. DAVIS protested against going outside the Vestry to find candidates for office and used some strong language as to the name of one of the candidates stinking in the nostrils of every respectable person. There were men on the Vestry capable and willing to hold office. Why did they not elect them instead of a Jew.

Mr. MOYLE: I would not sit on the Board with a blasted Jew. ('Oh! Oh!' and 'Order')

The CHAIRMAN remonstrated with the last speaker…

Mr. BALLARD at some length opposed the nomination of a Jew and a Roman Catholic, and amid calls to order, spoke of one of the candidates as a renegade Jew, and also used other expressions, which brought

Mr. CALNAN to his legs to resent the allusion to him as a Roman Catholic. He held that as he was elected by the ratepayers of the parish, he had a right to fill any office in the parish. He defied Mr. Ballard, or anyone else, to put him out.

Another scene erupted at the last meeting before the Vestry elections, and things got so bad that the chairman walked out. The longer-standing members had had enough: they quickly formed an alliance with the Catholics and the Jews, who were equally fed up with the "Reformers" and wanted them out. Election handbills were printed up and circulated to local households, drawing their attention to the newspapers reports of "scandalous scenes", "violent conduct", "most improper language" and "scurrilous remarks made of a most intolerant nature with regard to Roman Catholics and Jews". A German version, signed by Benabo, and quoting the relevant passage from the *Observer* in German translation underneath, went to the Jewish households. After the election the *Observer* congratulated the "old party" on "having secured the return of all but one of their thirteen nominees, and relieved Messrs. Watts, E. Davis and Hall, jun. of the responsibility, worry and excitement of parochial office."

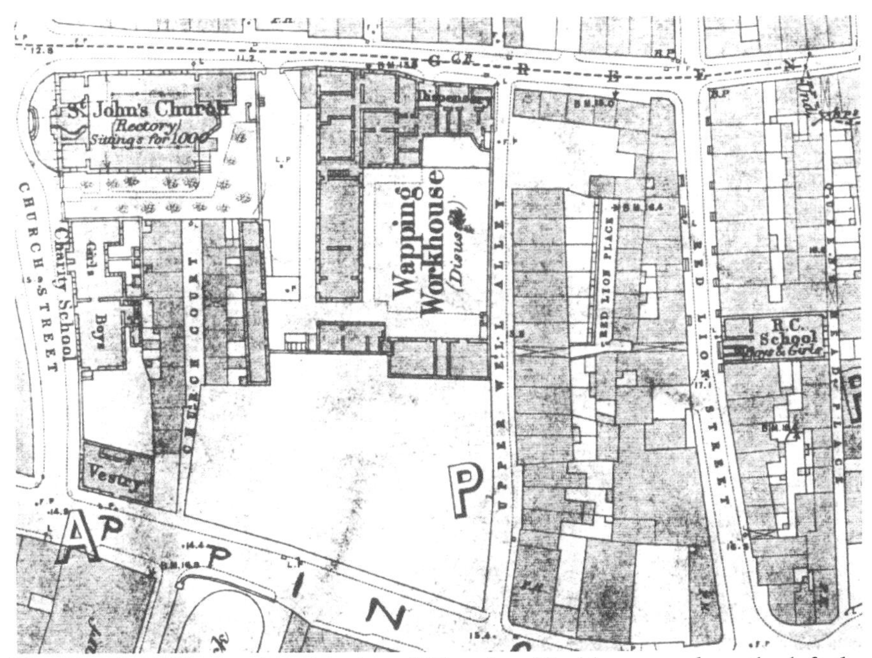

Wapping in 1873 showing the site of Wapping Workhouse and on the left the Red Lion St school. Wapping Workhouse has been immortalised in Charles Dickens' collection of articles, *The Uncommercial Traveller*.

Every three years when the School Board election came round, the Catholic community in Tower Hamlets worked to get a Catholic representative elected. After Arthur Langdale had served two terms, Fr Angelo Lucas agreed to stand for election in 1876. The only son of Frederick Lucas, the convert from Quakerism who founded the *Tablet*, he was then parish priest of Guardian Angels, but soon after beginning his term on the School Board he was moved to Wapping. His predecessor Fr Hickey had secured a site for a church: the former Wapping Workhouse, disused since 1863.

Stepney Union must have been pretty desperate to get it off their hands to sell to the Catholics, but sell they did. On Sunday 15th July 1877, the Wapping parishioners marched in procession to the workhouse grounds, where Cardinal Manning met them and made a speech from an improvised platform. The site had cost £7,250, which was quite expensive – and Fr Lucas ironically thanked the Cardinal for his generosity in dumping such a heavy debt on him. However the Cardinal wanted the church built in an Italianate classical style, because it would enable the basic building to be got up quite quickly and cheaply. Sure enough, Fr Lucas secured a contractor willing to do it for £4,000.

St Patrick's Church Wapping

The new St Patrick's church was opened on the Feast of the Assumption, 15th August 1879: it wasn't finished, and would not be finished until 1892, but it was usable, and would do for the time being. However when the next School Board election came up in November, Lucas refused to stand again: he reckoned it was impossible to attend all the meetings, including sub-committees, and do all the additional work that was expected, such as the inspection and visiting of schools, while also running a busy parish. Since the

School Board was practically a full-time job in itself, though unpaid, it wasn't easy to find another candidate, but Cardinal Manning came up with a willing West Ender. Colonel Lenox Prendergast, who'd fought in the Crimean War, had been working for some years as diocesan inspector for Catholic orphanages, so he already had a lot of relevant experience.

The work of getting him elected was organised by Fr Gorman, with the help of the Holy Family Confraternity. Their first job was to find the Catholics who were eligible to vote, and make sure they knew they were eligible, and were registered. A lot of women, as well as men, could vote in School Board elections (though not in parliamentary ones) and they often didn't realise that, so needed to be told. Then it was necessary to go over all the details very carefully with each voter, to make sure they knew how where to find the right polling booth, when it would be open, and how to cast their vote when they got there. Because there were five seats for Tower Hamlets, each elector had five votes, but you could cast them all for the same candidate if you wanted. So the Catholics were all told firmly to write "5" against the name of the Catholic candidate.

On the day of the election, the canvassers went into the courts and alleys to round people up. Polling booths in strongly Catholic areas experienced a heavy rush of voters in the lead-up to closing time at 8.00 pm. The majority were still hopelessly confused about what they were being asked to do, but nobody tried to challenge their right to vote, and the returning officer did his very best to help them, and decipher the illiterate scrawls on the ballot papers. Colonel Prendergast proved a dedicated and hard working member of the School Board. He wasn't a political animal, and never bothered to charm the voters, or even turn up in Tower Hamlets on polling day, yet his election was always considered guaranteed. The consensus agreement which had been established from the start, in 1870, persisted: if the Catholics of Tower Hamlets wanted a representative on the Board, they should have one.

The Bitter Cry

In Wiseman's time, all parts of London were socially quite mixed, and some of the worst slums were in the West End, check-by-jowl with the mansions of the rich. But slum clearances and redevelopment had changed all that, and West Enders now knew less about the more deprived areas of London than about the interior of Africa – and seemed to care less, too. But "The Bitter Cry of Outcast London", a sensationalised penny pamphlet issued in October 1883, succeeded in creating intense public concern about living conditions in the East End. A Royal Commission on Housing, on which Cardinal Manning sat, struggled in vain with the dilemma of how the poor could be properly housed if local government was not allowed to provide, or subsidise, housing they could afford. Slum clearances only made things worse: the evicted families moved into cheap lodgings in the surrounding streets, which became even more overcrowded. They couldn't afford to move outside London, far away from the places where they might find work, and rents for the "model dwellings" put up by philanthropic companies to replace the slums were just slightly too high. Rev Samuel Barnett, Vicar of St Jude's, Whitechapel, and his wife Henrietta, launched the East End Dwellings Company to target the worst-paid manual workers, but found the difficulties overwhelming. During the 1890s, therefore, they modified their approach slightly in order to attract a better social mix: Cressy and Dunstan Houses in Stepney Green are examples from this later phase.

Benjamin Costelloe

Samuel Barnett referred to the "Bitter Cry" in a talk he gave to a group of university students in Oxford, out of which developed the settlement movement, which offered people from privileged backgrounds the opportunity to spend a few weeks or months really getting to know how the other half lived. The first settlement, Toynbee Hall, was established in a romantically designed complex of buildings in Whitechapel. Unlike later settlements which usually had a specific religious or philosophical ethos, Toynbee brought together people of all religions or none. Among the Barnetts' Catholic friends was graduate lawyer Benjamin F C Costelloe, who spent some time living in the East End, and was very involved in all the discussions around setting up Toynbee Hall. Later he helped establish the first ever Catholic settlement, Newman House in Southwark Diocese.

Toynbee Hall

Another initiative which arose out of the "Bitter Cry" furore was the development of the East End Methodist Mission by Rev Peter Thompson, who was posted to Cable Street in 1885. Women volunteers arrived to help by carrying out systematic visiting work, a doctor and a chemist started a medical mission, and substantial and regular financial support came from Methodists throughout the country. Peter Thompson managed to turn some of the local "dens of iniquity" into mission halls. His first such triumph was the takeover in 1887 of the White Swan public house on Ratcliffe Highway, much patronised by the local Irish, and better known by its nickname "Paddy's Goose". The following year he acquired Wilton's Music Hall, popularly known as the "Old Mahogany Bar", and eventually he acquired the building on Commercial Road which would become his main headquarters.

The Old Mahogany Bar taken over by the East End Mission of the Methodist Church in 1885 kept the name The Old Mahogany Bar until 1956. In the first dock strike of 1898 it served 2,000 meals a day to the strikers and was the HQ for the people of the East End who gathered to stop Mosley's fascists in the famous 1936 Battle of Cable Street, and in World War II gave shelter to a badly blitzed community. In 1956 it was sold and used as a rag warehouse

Continuing migration into East London swelled still further the overstocked labour market for poorly-paid, casual, unskilled or semi-skilled work, so that the district grew steadily poorer. Local industries relied on having available a very large pool of labour, unorganised and desperate, which could be quickly taken on in busy periods, and got rid of as soon as the rush was over. The position of women garment workers was particularly vulnerable – and many women were forced to work, either to supplement the inadequate income of their family's male breadwinner, or because there wasn't a male breadwinner present. Desperate single mothers with small children wailing for food would compete to undercut each other, offering to work at ever lower rates of pay,to get *something* to put in their mouths. In 1883 a woman making trousers might earn 1s for working a 17-hour day, with no meal breaks. For making men's shirts she was paid 10d a dozen. In St George's in the East not only women, but children as young as seven, toiled at home making sacks for just one farthing per sack: sack-making and tarpaulin-making were local industries which employed a large number of Irish women, though the employing firms were mainly English. The situation on the docks was worse now than at the time of Mayhew's survey, because far more men were competing with each other for whatever work was available.

On top of its "normal" miseries, East London suffered another economic depression 1884-1887. A Committee on Permanent Distress in London, set up in 1885 by the Lord Mayor, and on which the Catholics were represented by Cardinal Manning, Mgr Gilbert and Colonel Prendergast, spent almost a year searching for solutions, but all it could come up with were thrift, sobriety, friendly societies and emigration. As the recession in London dragged on over the next two years, Cardinal Manning addressed committees, led deputations to the Prime Minister and wrote letters to the Times, urging relief measures. He was already on record as holding that everyone has a natural right to the necessities of life, which takes precedence over property rights; he supported trade unions and collective bargaining; and he warned the Church to take the aspirations of the working class seriously.

Thanks to a reduction in the property qualification for voting in parliamentary elections, and a redistribution of the constituencies, far more Catholic men in East London got the right to vote, and their votes counted for more: Tower Hamlets had previously been one constituency with two MPs, but it was now divided into nine constituencies, each with its own MP. Across the country, a great many Irish immigrants and their descendants were enfranchised, and Charles Stewart Parnell responded to the opportunity by putting more effort into mobilizing the Home Rule movement in England. Claiming to be able to influence a significant bloc of voters, he was in a position briefly to flirt with both the major political parties, playing them off one against the other.

In the lead-up to the 1885 General Election, Cardinal Manning instructed Catholics to ask candidates whether they would support the faith schools, and vote accordingly. The Conservatives were generally more sympathetic to faith schools than the Liberals, so if the Catholics did as he urged, they would in most cases end up voting Conservative. Coincidentally Parnell instructed

William Gladstone

Irish voters *not* to support Liberal candidates, in order to put pressure on Gladstone for his failure to commit himself more definitely on the Home Rule question. As the ballot was secret, we don't know for sure how people voted: only that the Conservative Charles Thomson Ritchie – sitting member for Tower Hamlets – won St George's in the East, whereas most of the other new constituencies in Tower Hamlets returned Liberals. But there is compelling evidence that Fr O'Callaghan voted Liberal, despite all the urging not to. He was cited in a court case by the unsuccessful Conservative candidate for Stepney, who decided to contest the result because Fr O'Callaghan and some other Liberals had voted twice. The fact that the Missionary Rector of St Mary and St Michael's had voted twice must have been widely known, and also the fact that he'd definitely voted Liberal. Because the church and presbytery buildings straddled the boundary between Stepney and St George's, he was legally entitled to vote in either constituency, and he genuinely believed himself entitled to vote in both. The law on the matter appears to have been unclear, and his entire good faith in the matter was openly acknowledged: this may have been another reason why the court agreed to take his vote as a test case. The judgment actually made no difference to the election result in Stepney, because Fr O'Callaghan had cast his first vote there, and the judges agreed that *that* one was therefore valid – but the second vote, cast in St George's, wasn't.

The overall result of the 1885 General Election was Liberals 335, Tories 249, which meant a hung Parliament with the Irish Nationalists holding the balance. At first the Conservatives formed a government, and set up the Cross Commission, with Manning among those appointed to sit on it, to make enquiries into the working of the Education Act. In December Gladstone committed himself decisively to Home Rule, and on 1st February his party resumed power, but the Home Rule Bill which he introduced only brought his government down, and another General Election in July 1886 resulted in a clearcut Tory victory. Ritchie then joined the cabinet as Chairman of the Local Government Board and, as one of the new breed of Tory Radical, set about establishing the London County Council (LCC) to replace the antediluvian mish-mash of administrative structures which was blocking progress in the nation's capital. Meanwhile, through all the political ups and downs, the Cross Commission continued its work and eventually presented a report in 1888, recommending that rate aid be extended to the faith schools. This was politically very contentious, so no immediate action was taken.

Demographic changes

We have no reliable figures for Mass attendance at St Mary and St Michael's in the 1880s, but it was probably falling. Confraternity memberships undoubtedly were, and so was income, and there's plenty of evidence that better-off and more established Catholics were moving away from St Mary and St Michael's parish, going to Mile End or Bow, or out of the East End altogether: improved transport facilities were making it easier for better-paid breadwinners to move their families out to leafy suburbs, and commute in to work. Tower Hamlets was nevertheless becoming ever more over-crowded, but those coming in were much, much poorer than those who were leaving. A high proportion were Jews. Unlike earlier Jewish immigrants, who were skilled and German-speaking, those who'd been flooding in since 1881 were mostly desperate refugees from the stetls of Russian Poland. English and Irish people displaced by slum clearances in central London also pressed into Tower Hamlets, as did farm labourers fleeing depressed rural districts in Essex, while immigration directly from Ireland also continued, though at a fairly low rate.

Fr O'Callaghan was finding it impossible to make ends meet. Each year when he added up his accounts at Lady Day, they were deeper and deeper in the red, and the school expenses, particularly the teachers' salaries, were his biggest headache. A desperate appeal for help had been launched in 1887, when the debt stood at £772: £342 for the church and £430 for the schools. By 1st May 1888 the school deficit had grown to £508. Despite handing Pell Street over to Tower Hill, and although Limehouse had been separated off as an independent mission, with its own school, St Mary and St Michael's still had very high numbers of school age children. Whenever any additional accommodation was made available, there always seemed to be Catholic children waiting to move in. When space wasn't available, they either had to attend board schools, or keep well out of the way of the attendance officers. The 1888 St Mary's and St Michael's school enrolment, at 813, was still the highest of any Catholic mission in London.

Fr Gorman's Silver Jubilee – the 25th anniversary of his ordination – was an ideal opportunity for everyone to show their appreciation. Contributions poured in not only from parishioners, but from all sorts of other local people who thought highly of him – including several of the Anglican clergy – and the final total was £172. The presentation at the Johnson Street school was attended by many distinguished non-Catholics, particularly Dr F C Carr Gomm, the current Chairman of the London Hospital; Rev Dr P R Carter, Anglican Rector of St John's Wapping and Chairman of the Lying-in Home; Dr C Cheston and Mr Warner, Chairman and Secretary of the East London Children's Hospital; and various other dignitaries and doctors from the voluntary hospitals.

Each year on St Patrick's Day, Fr O'Callaghan preached a panegyric in Irish. It was greatly appreciated, although even in Ireland most people now spoke English, and relatively few London Irish could have understood him. Their keenness to identify as Irish nevertheless remained strong. In early August 1888 Dr Mahony presided over a public meeting at Johnson Street School to set up an Irish club. Fr James Maher was on the platform, and a parishioner named M T Lalor, as prime mover behind the initiative, was called on to explain the plan:

> *Entertainments would be given at which purely Irish songs would be sung. It was enough to make any Irishman's blood boil, said the speaker, to hear the so-called Irish songs give at the various music halls, and they should be condemned by Irishmen on every possible occasion. (Hear, hear.)*

An employment society would be attached, to help Irish people find jobs, and the Irish National League could meet on the premises. 15 Irish MPs had agreed to become honorary members. One of them was present, and gave a speech in which he pointed out that another advantage of the club would be to help get people registered to vote – and then turn out Charles Ritchie at the next election. Everyone hissed at the mention of Ritchie's name. Since Gladstone had nailed his colours to the Home Rule mast, the Irish Nationalists had come to identify totally with the Liberal Party, and see the Tory and Liberal records on the Irish Question in unrealistically black-and-white terms.

The proposed St Columba's National Club and Institute would need premises in which to operate. Whether the project succeeded, and if so for how long it flourished, is unclear, but a branch of the Irish National Foresters (a longstanding Nationalist association which was also a friendly society) was established at No 158, Commercial Road, under Lalor together with a Mr M Lyons. In the spring of 1890 the group was doing well, and the priests were joining it. However all the Irish clubs and associations will have been badly affected by the split in the Irish Party which followed the fall of Parnell later that year.

The dockers' tanner

Ben Tillett

Several local strikes had ended successfully for the workers, and when in August 1889 a dispute broke out at the West India Dock, and the casuals there resolved to strike, they were quickly joined by those at the East India Dock, and some of the stevedores and other permanent dock workers began to come out in sympathy. The casuals were demanding an increase in pay from 5d an hour up to 6d (a "tanner"). Their union leader Ben Tillett wrote to the directors saying he would call for an answer with 10,000 men, and on Friday 16th August an impressively large procession set off along Commercial Road, led by two bands and with banners flying. As they approached Aldgate they were joined by John Burns, a charismatic figure and excellent public speaker who was to prove a great asset to the strike and – despite his reputation as a dangerous agitator – do a great deal to maintain friendly relations between the strikers and the police.

Dock Strike Meeting
Cardinal Manning is seated at back in the centre with, in the front, Ben Tillet on the left and John Burns on the right.

It was Burns who announced the directors' reply: they would make no commitment about a pay rise, but only hinted they might consider it favourably if work was resumed immediately. There was no question of the men accepting such a dusty answer. Over the weekend the Victoria and Albert men joined the strike, and so did the powerful stevedores' unions. On Monday the workers at the London and St Katharine Docks, and some of those at Millwall, joined the daily procession to the City. By the end of the first week the numbers involved were up to 50,000 or more, the strike had extended eastwards to Tilbury and southwards to the Surrey Commercial Docks, the lightermen were out, and the Port of London had been brought to a standstill. Groups of other workers began to strike in sympathy, including the girl ropemakers at Messrs Frost next to St Mary and St Michael's. The press and public opinion had grown sympathetic to the dockers, and were largely on their side.

At the end of August the left-wing novelist Margaret Harkness went to call on Cardinal Manning. Old Newman, the Cardinal's butler, let her in. "Religion?" he asked, pointing to the chapel. "No, politics." "The Cardinal isn't as young as he was," mused the butler. But when Harkness saw Cardinal Manning half-an-hour later, he sent her to fetch a list of the docks directors, and then set off towards the City. Picking up Alderman Sir Andrew Lusk, who was acting Lord Mayor, on the way, he went to see the Joint Docks Committee presided over by C M Norwood at Dock House. He pointed out that he did know something about their line of business, as his father and brother had been chairmen of one of the dock companies, and he strongly urged the committee to make concessions. Norwood was polite but wouldn't move an inch. The crowd of strikers outside in the street nevertheless appreciated the attempt to mediate, and loudly cheered the pair when they emerged from the company offices. Cardinal Manning issued a diplomatic statement to the press, but confided to the strikers that he had never 'preached to so impenitent a congregation!'" Food tickets were distributed to the strikers, and local tradesmen in the East End agreed to accept them in lieu of cash. As long as sufficient funds were available, 25,000 tickets were issued each evening at 6.00, and double tickets for Saturday. They were distributed in collaboration with the gangers, who could identify their men and help expose fraudulent claims. No money was available for rent, but local landlords were told to wait patiently: two banners were hung across Commercial Road, one at Hungerford Street and one at Star Street, warning them not to bother calling. The Star Street one said:

Our husbands are on strike; for the wives it is not honey,
And we all think it is right not to pay the landlord's money.

Everyone is on strike, so landlords do not be offended;
The rent that's due we'll pay you when the strike is ended.

Another banner hung across the Highway near Paddy's Goose. Most of the landlords did wait patiently – or at least held back from evicting strikers' families. Local shopkeepers made regular donations to the strike fund, either in money or kind: many of them put up a notice outside stating how much they intended to donate. From the first week some of the East End churches and missions began offering help, and before the end of August Paddy's Goose was being used by its local dockers' committee for distributing shilling tickets, while the mission workers sang hymns to the men waiting their turn. Free breakfasts were provided to the strikers at the Goose, and a midday soup kitchen for their wives at the Old Mahogany Bar.

General Booth

In early September, when the Jewish tailors also came out on strike, General Booth ordered the Salvation Army Hall at 272, Whitechapel Road, opened as a relief depot. A large piece of bread and a bowl of soup could be had for ½d, and meals were also available in return for tickets: 10,000 were estimated to have been fed on the first day.

The Salvation Army was reimbursed at least partly from the strike fund, which made sense since encouraging people to use big centres, where food could be purchased and cooked in bulk, was the most cost-effective way of keeping them fed. But the strike fund figures do not include other money contributed by sympathisers among the general public directly to churches, or other independent relief organisers, usually for feeding the women and children. The situation was getting desperate. If the men could only hold out for another week or so, the ship owners would surely force the directors of the dock companies to reach a settlement. But it looked as though they'd have to give in, because the strike fund was almost exhausted. Then suddenly a telegram arrived to say that money was on its way from Australia. The generosity of the Australians could be explained by simple big-heartedness, or working-class solidarity, but the fact that so many of both the Australian population were of Irish ancestry, as were the strikers, may have had a lot to do with it. There'd been a lot of suffering, and the suffering would continue even after the strike was won, but at least it wouldn't have been wasted. Fr O'Callaghan issued an appeal through the Catholic papers:

It is now three weeks since the large multitude of labourers employed at the docks of the port of London have been thrown out of work, and as a consequence thousands of families have been brought to extreme poverty. A large number of dock labourers are Catholics, and unfortunately at the best of times a majority of them belong to the class of casual labourers. They live in a state of chronic poverty, and are unable to lay by any reserve for special emergencies. Many of them are also blessed with a numerous offspring of young children, and for these reasons the enforced idleness of the last three weeks is particularly distressing. The strike will probably be over when these words are read, but it will take these poor people many weeks, and perhaps months, to regain their former position. In the meantime I consider it a duty, as the pastor of some thousands of those poor families, to appeal in their behalf to the charitable readers of THE UNIVERSE, *who are always willing to give generously for every work of charity. In the present emergency I ask for help to provide for the most necessitous food and fuel, and if our means permit it to redeem from pawn-offices the clothing which has been pledged to procure the necessaries of life. Help is urgently needed. 'He gives twice who gives promptly.'*

Bishop of London Frederick Temple

The Lord Mayor, James Whitehead, arrived back in London and called a meeting at the Mansion House, to form a Conciliation Committee to negotiate an end to the strike. The Anglican Bishop of London, Frederick Temple, and Cardinal Manning were among those present, and a telegram was sent to ask John Burns and Ben Tillett to attend.

The Committee agreed to recommend the 6d per hour rate, but wanted to negotiate a delay before it came into effect. The date of 1st April 1890 was rejected with disgust by the strike leaders – the men would inevitably have made comments about "April Fool's Day". Mid-March was then suggested, but Burns protested at this: "I appeal to your Eminence, and to you, my Lord Bishop; and to Mr. Buxton, whether the men in this strike had not behaved with a 'sweet reasonableness'?" Manning replied: "My son, they have." "Then I do not think they ought to be asked to wait until March for this small advance." Eventually the strike leaders *provisionally* agreed to 1st January, though pointing out that they could not agree definitively without consulting the men. Actually, the January offer wasn't as good as it looked at first sight, and the men turned it down. By 1st January the docks would be in their slackest season of the year, during which most of them weren't able to get any work at all, and business wouldn't pick up again till April – so the men *would* be "April Fools" to accept the deal. They were all skint after so many weeks on strike, and they needed the wage increase *this* year, while there was still some work available. Among the crowds gathered outside the Wade's Arms many of the wives were heard agreeing that the men should not go back to work until the tanner was paid. The wage increase must begin 1st October.

THE DOCKERS' CARDINAL
From *PUNCH* 1889

The announcement that the directors' offer had been refused provoked, initially at least, a fierce backlash of opinion against the strikers. Bp Temple was furious and wanted to have no more to do with the negotiations, while the Lord Mayor was also hurt and angry. The strike leaders, for their part, were sore at being accused of bad faith. But on Monday afternoon the Conciliation Committee was in session once again at the Mansion House. Cardinal Manning and Sidney Buxton, MP for Poplar, met and talked to the strike leaders before they entered the meeting room, in order to calm them down.

The Cardinal's Peace

On Tuesday Cardinal Manning went down to Poplar, accompanied by Buxton, to hold a private meeting with the Strike Council at the Catholic schools in Wade Street. The meeting lasted three hours, and the 81-year-old

Cardinal made a point of going carefully through all the issues so as to understand why they were so important to the men.

John Burns was fascinated by Manning, and several of the other strike leaders were also deeply impressed with him. According to Tom Mann:

Cardinal Manning

The Cardinal was a very slender man; his face was most arresting, so thin, so refined, so kindly. In the whole of my life I have never seen another like unto it. He spoke of the dockers in such a quiet, firm and advising fatherly manner, that minute by minute as he was speaking one could feel the mental atmosphere changing.

At the end of the meeting, as described by Smith and Nash, Manning summed up:

In an address which deeply moved his hearers, he reviewed the arguments on both sides. He himself was accountable to no human authority for standing there; he was responsible only to One above. Unaccustomed tears glistened in the eyes of his rough and work-stained hearers as he raised his hand, and solemnly urged them not to prolong one moment more than they could help the perilous uncertainty, and the suffering of their wives and children Just above his uplifted hand was a carved figure of the Madonna and Child, and some among the men tell how a sudden light seemed to swim around it as the speaker pleaded for the women and children. When he sat down all in the room knew in their own minds that he had won the day, and that as far as the Councils were concerned that was the end of the strike – the Cardinal's peace.

The strike leaders signed a document indicating acceptance of a wage increase to begin in early November – provided the Cardinal could get the dock directors to agree. He deliberately left both sides to stew for another day before meeting with the directors on Thursday. On Friday the negotiations continued with the Lord Mayor also present. Manning found the directors much harder going than the strikers, but on Saturday 14th September, agreement was reached: all the strike demands were met, and the casuals would get their "tanner" in November. The Cardinal was the hero of the hour, and as a token of appreciation the dockers collected £160 for a presentation, which he used to endow a bed at the London Hospital. In a brief statement on his reasons for intervention, he concluded:

What we may hope will come from this strike is a registration of labourers and an organisation of dock labour. This will clear the dock gates and the East of London of thousands who year by year flow in from the country without knowledge of skill. They become a floating population of disappointed men; indolent because unemployed, living from hand to mouth, and dangerous because they have nothing to lose; starving in the midst of wealth and prosperity from which they are excluded.

Sure enough, the Dockers' Union was recognised, and work was henceforward reorganised so as to ensure that the main body of dockers were allocated sufficiently regular work, at the new pay rates, to enable them and their families to lead a more normal life.

It was a great victory for unionisation and collective bargaining, and banners carried in London's first ever May Day processions the following year bore portraits of Karl Marx and Cardinal Manning.

Unfortunately, however, only a limited number of dockers were covered by this arrangement. Notwithstanding Cardinal Manning's hopes that it would discourage fresh in-migration, a lot of men who were already permanently settled in the East End found themselves worse off after the strike, because their chances of finding any work at all was drastically reduced. Concerns expressed by priests in the riverside parishes show that many of their parishioners were among those who lost out. When Fr O'Callaghan wrote again to the Universe to thank donors for their contributions, he showed he was already aware of the dire prospects facing some of the families at St Mary's and St Michael's:

Pope Leo XIII

The strike is now over, and no doubt the condition of the regular hands is greatly improved. The position of the casual labourers, however, is worse than ever, as very few of that class will be required in future. Until they obtain some other employment, their suffering will be terrible. Through the school we have excellent opportunities for discovering and relieving the most necessitous cases. Hitherto we have been 'feeding the hungry.' Who will now help us to 'clothe the naked?' Winter is fast approaching, and scores of our little school children are barefooted and in rags. God will bless those who befriend them for His sake.

The strike had lasting ramifications of course, both politically and in the fields of ethics and, it's not too far-fetched to say, theology, - to the extent that Pope Leo XIII was influenced by it in his issuing of *Rerum Novarum.*

A big surprise and a shock

The St Mary and St Michael's League of the Cross branch had lost Burns and Raher: both of them moved to Stratford, and became officers in the branch there. Fortunately the captaincy of the Guards was taken over by Michael Whelton, under whom they won awards for well-drilled marching, and who according to Fr Maher "seemed like a magnet in drawing other good men around him." Whelton was one of the men who stood at the back of the church every Sunday collecting door money, and had been one of the regular outdoor collectors for the last 20 years: everyone liked him because he always very courteous, and absolutely trustworthy. He was a Gaelic-speaker, and famous for his repertoire of Irish-language songs, a great asset at League meetings which, unless an outside speaker or entertainer had been invited, were dependent on the members' amateur talent. The branch's 15th anniversary in May 1889 was celebrated by inviting contingents of Guards, with their bands, from all the other East End parishes, and guest speakers like Inspector Askew of E Division, one of several police officers prominent in the League. Highlights of the gathering were presentations to Captain Whelton, and to Mrs Bannon, president of the Guild of the Immaculate Conception. At the Crystal Palace rally in 1890, St Mary and St Michael's was well represented by dockworkers – "strong, stalwart men, many of them losing a day's pay to attend the great demonstration." Shortly after that rally, when Cardinal Manning made a Sunday afternoon visit to Commercial Road, to inspect the juvenile League, 100 adult men members were present, all in uniform, together with 50 members of the Boys' Guild and 70 from the Women's Guild.

Over the past few years Fr O'Callaghan had definitely noted a falling off in Mass attendance, which saddened and worried him though he charitably ascribed it to his parishioners' "fearful poverty". The deficit on parish and schools mounted higher and, as the regular collections were not bringing in enough, "annual sermons in aid of the mission and schools", became a regular event, supplemented by additional blitz collections whenever a suitable opportunity arose. Competition from the rate-aided board schools, and constantly rising standards mandated by the School Board, were pushing up the amount of voluntary funding which the faith schools had to raise to impossible levels. All the poor Catholic missions were struggling desperately. Their teachers' salaries were on pitifully low rates compared with board schools – and because of the low pay, Catholic boys rarely chose teaching as a career, so that women vastly outnumbered men on the staff of parish schools.

Teachers in all schools in poor areas were aware that many children came too hungry to learn anything. Some hadn't eaten at all; even the luckier ones had usually had only plain bread and butter for breakfast, and been given a little packet of plain bread and butter for their lunch at midday. The government made no official provision, so charitable groups had sprung up to provide low-cost meals for children in local schools. Most worked on a shoestring, serving a limited number of children (selected by the teachers as the most needy) in a specified school, and operating for two or three days a week during the winter months only. Catholic schools usually had to make their own arrangements. St Mary and St Michael's used to issue an appeal for help in feeding the hungriest of the schoolchildren during the worst of the winter months, when their fathers were likely to be out of work. The appeals stressed that the meals (hot soup or stew, with a large slice of bread), could only be provided insofar as donations came in to cover the costs.

In a crucial vote on 30th January 1890 the London School Board passed a resolution that schools in receipt of state grants should be free. So far it was only a resolution, but it flagged up the way public opinion was changing on the issue, and it was obvious that as soon as the Liberals got back in, they'd abolish school fees in the board schools, without doing anything to help the voluntary schools – and that would be the finish of them. So the Conservative government pre-empted them with the 1891 Education Act, which abolished fees for the board schools, and gave voluntary schools which followed suit an additional government grant – of 10 shillings per child per year – to make up.

In the lead up to the 1891 School Board elections, ostensibly enthusiastic meetings were held in various parts of Tower Hamlets to promote Colonel Prendergast's candidature, including several presided over by Fr O'Callaghan of the "East End Cathedral", and Fr Gorman buzzed round with his usual "zeal and energy". So it came as a big surprise and a shock when Prendergast was defeated. The *Catholic Herald* conducted an investigation, and concluded that the state of Irish politics was to blame. Parnellites and anti-Parnellites wouldn't work with each other, so there had been "no proper canvas, and no interest whatever shown by the large body of the people in the result".

The minority of the politically aware were rigidly polarised: "it was enough to tell some of our people that Colonel Prendergast was a Conservative in order to prevent them voting for him; as if Conservatism or Liberalism or any other ism had anything whatever to do with the matter." (And the West End English Catholics were no better, having refused to vote for Catholics who were Liberals or Home Rulers.) The rot had set in long before the election, nothing having been done to ensure that Catholic voters were even on the electoral register. As for those who were on the register, fumed the editorial:

> *Some of our voters would not go to the poll, because the priest did not call upon them; others would not go because a conveyance was not sent for them. Men who received canvassing books simply went home, and neglected to bring up a single voter.*

The St Mary and St Michael's school roll was still growing, and by 1892 it would be up to 1,100. Yet there was now no Catholic on the School Board to protect their interests. Worse still, Colonel Prendergast – who understandably felt very let down – said he wouldn't stand again, and for the next six years no other lay Catholic candidate could be found.

Fr Gorman was asked to stand in 1894, but refused, whereupon Fr James Lawless, the grand old parish priest of Poplar, came forward. Lawless was so well-liked, everyone was sure he'd get in, but he lost – by just a few votes.

Whatever happened to Fr Moore?

After his sudden departure from St Mary and St Michael's in 1852, Fr John Moore spent a few rather difficult years in charge of Stratford (during which he appears to have been arrested, and briefly imprisoned, for debts connected with the Johnson Street school), then moved around rather frequently for a bit until, in 1862, the War Office agreed to make an allowance for a chaplain to look after Catholics among the troops stationed at Shoeburyness. Fr Moore, now aged 56, agreed to take on the job. He rented a house at No 3, Capel Terrace, Southend, and made the upstairs front room into a chapel. The congregation at his first Mass on 15th May 1862 consisted of his faithful housekeeper, and a little nephew or great-nephew who was staying with him. Only four other practising Catholics lived in Southend. Each Sunday morning he got up early to hear confessions in the chapel, then walked four miles to say Mass at 9.00 for the soldiers and their families at Shoeburyness, and walked back to celebrate the main Southend Mass at 11.30 for his congregation of six. Gradually things improved. The military authorities agreed to send a cab to fetch him and take him home, and the Southend congregation slowly grew larger. Moore fitted folding doors between the chapel and the back room so it could accommodate up to fifty people.

One Sunday he asked the people "to join him in the Litany of the Blessed Virgin on behalf of an intention he did not disclose, but which sought a place worthy of God's worship. Within a fortnight a carriage drew up to his door and he received a visit from a lady he had not previously known." It turned out to be Miss Helen Tasker. The Taskers had been an important family in Essex for several generations, and lived at Middleton Hall in Brentwood. Helen's only brother Joseph was drowned at sea, and when her father – also Joseph – died suddenly she inherited all his money. It came to half a million pounds, and over the next 27 years she carefully spent it on helping to build churches, schools, convents and hospitals. Like the Duke of Norfolk, she was involved to a minor extent with a very wide range of Catholic charities, and – for example – was listed among the patrons for the very grand 1869 bazaar in aid of the Commercial Road Sisters of Mercy, but inevitably she had to be selective about the projects to which she made a major and very substantial commitment. Having introduced herself to Fr Moore, she arranged to stay in Southend for a couple of days and look around. She was looking for a site for a church, and when she found it she bought the land and presented Fr Moore with a cheque for £1,000 to start building. The church, dedicated to St Helen, was opened by Archbishop Manning on 26th October 1869 – though it was still unfinished and only just usable: very bare inside, with a temporary wooden altar.

A reminiscence of Fr Moore in his final years was published in the Brentwood Diocesan Magazine in 1923: "he was a wonderful figure. In spite of his years (and rumour ran riot on the matter of his age) his personality was striking and his walk majestic, and his voice suggestive of a strong, determined will. Children loved him and were not afraid to call him to order when, as frequently happened, he gave out fifteen aves for one decade of the Rosary and five for the next. Father Moore's hearing left much to be desired." He died in December 1890, aged 84. A number of East End parish priests, including Fr O'Callaghan, travelled down to Southend for the funeral, at which Fr Lawless preached. Referring briefly to the early part of Fr Moore's career, he said he would not "touch upon the troubles of those first days, but he bore everything – for he recognised it was the Hand of his Master – with no complaint." In St Helen's Church, Southend, there is a stained glass window in memory of Fr John Moore: it shows St John the Baptist baptising a soldier.

Like a wise man, from the East

Cardinal Herbert Vaughan

Cardinal Manning died in January 1892. Such huge numbers wished to pay their respects – over 100,000 on one day – that the lying-in-state had to be extended. After a solemn Requiem Mass at the Brompton Oratory, delegations from the League of the Cross and various trades unions formed up with their flags and banners to march in procession behind the hearse, and the entire four-mile route to Kensal Green cemetery was thickly lined with people. The new Archbishop after Cardinal Manning was Herbert Vaughan, who already had some acquaintance with Tower Hamlets – especially St Mary and St Michael's – and whose friend Lady Herbert of Lea was very involved with Poplar. However he would need to carry out a very careful visitation of the whole diocese to update himself on each local situation. He was particularly worried about East London, because it had such a high concentration of Catholics, and because their economic problems were so serious. On 27th April he wrote to Lady Herbert: "I imagine there will be great wants of everything as soon as I am able to master the East End and to formulate, after conference and discussion, a plan of action." The visitation had to be postponed because he caught a cold, but on 15th May he wrote again, "I am going into the East today as my first visit. Commercial Road and Poplar (your Poplar) are the points of beginning, and then work West, like a wise man, from the East." There was in fact a whole series of visits: Vaughan wanted to get a feel of each parish, to see how best to take things forward. On one occasion he was taken by Fr Maher round the district which had been his "beat" during his very brief period of pastoral experience at St Mary and St Michael's as a young priest. Meanwhile Fr O'Callaghan was honoured by being made a canon. A committee in the parish organised the customary presentation of an illuminated address, together with a cheque for £112, and he was deeply touched, promising to hang the address in his room, and saying he'd been given to understand that even the poorest parishioners had insisted on contributing 6d or 1s towards the impressive total. Abp Vaughan's formal, canonical visitation of St Mary and St Michael's was concluded on a Sunday in early December, when he preached at High Mass to a congregation of 3-400, giving not so much a homily as a harangue to the troops. The total Catholic population was thought to be 6,000 (almost certainly an underestimate, because no proper census had been carried out for quite a while.) but only about 2,000 were attending Mass, and he urged those who *were* attending to bring those who were not – as if it were that easy!

While he was at it, the archbishop had a go about the poor level of financial giving. Regular income now came in in three ways: entrance money, an offertory collection, and the outdoor collection. Vaughan was keen to abolish the collection at the door, which tended to give the impression that you weren't allowed in if you couldn't pay. The offertory collection, by contrast, was seen as voluntary – and people naturally felt free to put nothing in the offertory if they'd already paid the entrance tariff, and couldn't afford more. Paying on the door could not, however, be done away with unless the offertory collections went up – and unfortunately, the usual experience of parishes which abolished door money was that offertory giving did not rise to compensate.

Canon O'Callaghan had been looking forward desperately to 1893, when the schools' endowment funds were out of hock, and once again bringing him in an income of £150 a year. In June 1893 the government grant arrived: £609 7s, plus £324 as the special new grant in lieu of fees. (The fees grant was based on an average attendance of 650 children, and since we know that the total roll was well over 1,000, it gives a good idea how appalling the attendance rate was, even after nearly two decades of "compulsory" schooling!) Soon, surely, the deficit could be cleared? But just then a demand arrived from the School Board to make "all sort of improvement in the school premises. Most of the alterations," noted Canon O'Callaghan, "are simply impossible, but those which can be effected will involve a heavy outlay." Next it became clear that the school drains were blocked, and "the workmen soon discovered that the stoppage occurred at a spot where a railway company had recently erected a large buttress. The obstacle, on probing it, was found to be hard substance – apparently solid masonry – and as there seemed no hope of removing it" there was no option but to build a new drain. This involved closing down the schools for five weeks. Canon O'Callaghan was worried that all the pupils would enrol in board schools and never come back, and relieved when the school re-opened, and the "little angels" all returned to the fold. But the work on the drains cost £160. He was convinced the railway company was responsible, but they refused to admit liability. To get redress he would have had to bring an expensive lawsuit, which he certainly could not afford.

The Catholic Social Union

Cardinal Vaughan lacked his predecessor's radical streak. He was very concerned about the wretched poverty in which the vast majority of his flock lived, but in searching for answers instinctively turned to the Catholic upper class from which he sprang. Well-off Catholics must be mobilised to establish settlements in poor parishes, get to know how the other half lived, and be personally involved in running socio-pastoral projects – especially youth clubs, to reduce the heavy rate of lapsation among school leavers. For this he needed a large pool of volunteers who would not only work unpaid, but cover all their own expenses, and contribute a generous share towards the running costs of the projects. The most likely source would be women from "good families", who were not allowed to take paid work, and were often only too delighted to have something useful to do with their time. With Lady Herbert's help, therefore, the Cardinal began making initial approaches to potential women recruits, while also doing his best to enlist men. In November 1893, after doing as much preparatory spadework as he could, he launched the Catholic Social Union (CSU). By then several projects were ready to roll. The first clubs were started at English Martyrs, Tower Hill, with the Dowager Duchess of Newcastle in charge, and were closely followed by a Boys' Club at Mile End. Meanwhile preparations went ahead for the first CSU settlement, which was started in Mile End in February 1894 by Lady Margaret Howard, sister of the Duke of Norfolk. Named St Philip's House, it started a Girls' Club and a Mothers' Meeting. The Duchess of Newcastle started a second CSU settlement in Tower Hill, named St Anthony's House. Another CSU stalwart was Lady Edmund Talbot, who was married to Lady Margaret's younger brother Edmund. Edmund's surname had been changed from Howard to Talbot because he was a major beneficiary under the will of Bertram Talbot, the last Catholic Earl of Shrewsbury. Lady Edmund was born Mary Caroline Bertie, daughter of Lord Norreys who was a convert to Catholicism. Soon after the couple married, in 1879, she ran away to France with another man, but her husband persuaded her to come home, they put their marriage back together, and twenty-odd years later she was as zealous and active a Catholic as he was. To start with, Lady Edmund concentrated on organising clubs in Sheffield, where the Howard family were important landlords. But she also helped the Duchess of Newcastle at Tower Hill, and in 1895 she started a Girls' Club in Commercial Road, aimed specifically at "the rougher class of factory girls" – *not* the "better class girls" who were the natural recruiting pool for the parish sodalities. Her experience had taught her that when starting off, it was best only to admit the most marginalised girls, and make sure they felt welcome and at home. Once the club was properly up and running, daughters of the more socially respectable and active parishioners could be invited to get involved as well, and would make a useful contribution.

A Boys' Club was started shortly afterwards, by men volunteers. Johnson Street School was the venue for both clubs, and they were open on as many nights of the week as the volunteers could manage. As they were aimed at working teenagers, members were expected to pay 1d each evening they came, but each club still needed to be subsidised to the tune of £50-60 a year. Evening classes, usually with paid instructors, were a staple activity. Like Toynbee Hall, the CSU clubs aspired to bring some higher culture into East End lives, but the most popular subjects were usually practical – especially sport and physical training – and the girls enjoyed sewing and cooking, singing and dancing. The Girls' Club had a lending library stocked with books and magazines, though it was small, and the books had to be read and re-read again and again. There was a strong religious ethos: on the third Sunday of each month the members were all asked to attend a specified Mass in the parish church, and receive Communion together, and a service was held once a month at the club, with rosary, a sermon and Benediction.

Arundel Castle

Before the end of the summer the Girls' Club had its first excursion – a treat for the most regular attenders – to the Howard family seat, Arundel Castle. Lady Edmund arranged periodic entertainments, usually concerts or operettas, using her contacts to bring in artistes – both professionals willing to give a free performance in a good cause, and good quality amateurs. It wasn't long before club members began developing their own talents, and taking part in the concerts. Full advantage was taken of the CSU magic lantern, which toured the clubs accompanied by two men volunteers, one to operate the apparatus and one to deliver the commentary. Various topics were offered. Most of the entertainments were for the girls' club only, but the magic lantern shows were enjoyed by girls and boys together: one on the Bible drew a "phenomenal" attendance.

It is not my choice…

George Akers, erstwhile curate at St Peter's, London Docks, had been ordained a Catholic priest in 1870, and assigned as curate to St John the Baptist, Hackney. He'd soon begun to branch out on his own, demonstrating the leadership skills which had previously attracted him to Charles Lowder's mission, and made him such an asset to it: he had an impressive capacity for mobilising teams of lay activists, and was only too happy to put up with the gruelling workloads, and harsh living conditions, which were so often the price of pioneering a new mission. He successfully pioneered two. The first was Homerton, where he sank a lot of his personal money into the Church of the Immaculate Heart of Mary and St Dominic. During his time there he also played a key role in helping a French congregation, the Servants of the Sacred Heart, to establish themselves in London; an English branch of this congregation later became the Chigwell Nuns.

Canon Akers

Fr Akers then spent a period at St Edmund's College helping to train priests (he had an MA from Oxford University), before going to semi-rural Hampton Wick, forming the scattered Catholics there into a community, and getting a church built. Since 1889 he'd been a canon of Westminster Archdiocese. Despite having given a lot of money away, he still enjoyed a comfortable private income – though it's doubtful that he spent much of it on himself. In October 1895 a large crowd of Hampton Wick parishioners crowded into their school, to celebrate his Silver Jubilee. But not long afterwards they received some very unwelcome news: Canon Akers was being transferred.

Canon Patrick O'Callaghan was 66. Fr Gorman had recently retired to Isleworth, and he may have felt it was time for him, too, to move to a small, quiet mission with a light workload. But then again the decision may have been Cardinal Vaughan's. The Cardinal wanted to install Canon Akers at St Mary and St Michael's, and charge him with starting what was described as an Apostolic College, to which all Westminster's newly ordained priests could be sent to gain pastoral experience, in the same way as he'd done himself years ago. To support Canon Akers in this work, the Cardinal thought he should have a second community of active nuns, so he requested Mother Mary Angela Potter, foundress of the Little Company of Mary, to make a foundation in St Mary and St Michael's parish. The Little Company was a nursing congregation. Most sick people – even serious medical and surgical cases – were cared for at home, and many religious and philanthropic bodies deployed nurses who would come round for free. Catholics were encouraged to use nurses of their own faith if at all possible, to guard against any risk of proselytisation, and because committed Catholic nurses were an important source of spiritual help for patients and families. Since 1880 St Mary and St Michael's had been able to call on the Little Sisters of the Assumption in Bow, but they were a small community serving the whole of the East End, and must have been very overstretched. From now on the parish would have its own nursing Sisters.

Mother Mary Angela Potter

The Nottingham superior came down to London accompanied by Sr De Sales, who was to be part of the new community, and leased two small houses in Commercial Road from the Mercers: Nos 326 and 328 (next to Abraham Benabo's house, and a few doors along from St Mary and St Michael's church). Shortly afterwards two more nuns arrived from Rome, and they all got stuck in, sorting the house out, and making one of the rooms into a chapel. In the middle of everything, inevitably the bell rang, and it was Cardinal Vaughan come to call: he was given a cup of tea in the kitchen, sitting on an empty packing case. The superior was Mother Etheldreda (Emily Stonor), and their first Mass was celebrated on 21st January 1896. The colour of their habits made it easy to distinguish them from the black-clad Mercy Sisters, and the parishioners usually referred to them as the Blue Nuns. Fr Lawless called on Canon Akers when he first arrived at Commercial Road, partly to welcome him to East London, but also curious to know why, given his very poor state of health (he had Bright's Disease) he wanted to undertake a completely new piece of work. "With tears in his eyes, Canon Akers said, 'It is not my choice, but I feel I should be wanting in obedience as a priest if I uttered a word of opposition.'" The presbytery at Commercial Road would continue to house the usual team of Missionary Rector and four curates, and with them would live two or more additional priests, straight from seminary: Akers paid £206, which must have come out of his own pocket, to have the house thoroughly cleaned and redecorated. The whole clergy team was reorganised, and the only one of Canon O'Callaghan's assistants to remain was Fr John Nicholson, a former Jesuit who'd left the Society in 1894, transferred to Westminster Archdiocese, and been at Commercial Road ever since. Cardinal Vaughan persuaded one of his most zealous younger priests, Peter Emmanuel Amigo, to become Canon Akers' second-in-command. Fr Amigo was originally from Gibraltar, though he'd been educated in England since the age of 14, and like Canon Akers he'd spent some time teaching at the seminary in between parish assignments: he was now 32.

Fr Peter Emmanuel Amigo

Fr Amigo quickly came to feel that he was having to do the lion's share of the work. Certainly he, or the other curates, must have had to take care of anything requiring physical exertion, but Canon Akers did as much as he could. On top of his responsibilities as parish priest and with the Apostolic College, and as Dean, he was much in demand as a guest speaker, and as a retreat-giver for religious communities of women, and he still found time once a week to travel to Hampton Wick to visit his former parishioners, and hear confessions. The number of Sunday Masses at St Mary and St Michael's was put up once again to six: on the hour, every hour from 7.00 to 12.00. This was probably more to accommodate the extra priests than for the convenience of the parishioners.

Inside and out

St Mary and St Michael's church struck Canon Akers as so horribly unappealing, he thought it was probably putting people off coming to Mass. So he decided his first priority should be to beautify the building. Launching a fundraising drive, he told the parishioners it was their duty "to preserve and adorn the noble church which their fathers, hard-working people like themselves, had built", but also did his best to interest outside donors. It took a year or so to rake in enough money, whereupon he commissioned designs from the architect Frederick A Walters, and immediately got the parish started on an organ fund. Lady Edmund Talbot and the other CSU workers helped by organising a bazaar. The heating installed by Canon O'Callaghan was no longer effective, so Canon Akers accepted a quote by John Grundy to install his patent "warm air" system for £125. Unfortunately, instead of warm air all it produced was "choking smoke", and the church remained bitterly cold in winter. The Girls' Club was doing well. The Boys' Club was still functioning but – like all the other CSU boys' clubs – was struggling: the improving activities on offer held little interest for most boys, and the men volunteers became very discouraged. The League of the Cross was still a large London-wide movement, but Cardinal Vaughan wasn't a teetotaller himself, and couldn't possibly bring to it the same enthusiasm as Cardinal Manning. Commercial Road still theoretically maintained men's, women's and juvenile sections, but at the fortnightly meetings the 300 who usually turned up were almost all women.

The Guild of Ransom – founded in 1887 by two converts, Fr Philip Fletcher and Mr Lister Drummond – had established branches in several of the neighbouring parishes. A cheerful group, the Ransomers worked with buoyant optimism for the wholesale return of England to the Catholic faith, and boldly carried out symbolic reclamations of territory through outdoor processions and pilgrimages. All Catholic churches used to hold devotional processions, especially for Corpus Christi, but almost always inside churches, or in the grounds of Catholic institutions: an explicitly *religious* procession through the streets was a startling innovation.

The first one was undertaken at Tower Hill in September 1892, on the evening before a contingent of pilgrims was due to depart for Lourdes. Led by Fr Fletcher and Drummond, together with some of the Oblate Fathers, they ventured out with some trepidation to march around a mostly Jewish neighbourhood. The priests wore cassocks and cottars, some banners were carried, and hymns were sung. Fr Fletcher could never remember clearly whether a statue of Our Lady was carried, though other participants were sure there had been. In any case, everyone got back in one piece, and the Jews had been very nice about it. Other London parishes began to take up the idea. Attempts in some places, by militant Protestant groups, to attack the processions were countered by obtaining police protection, but trouble in the East End was almost unheard of. In 1896 Tower Hill, St Anne's and Wapping staged quite elaborate ones. Contingents from other parishes took part in all of them, but nobody from St Mary and St Michael's. However both Canon Akers and Fr Amigo were friends of Fr Fletcher, so it could only be a matter of time. The 1897 Lenten mission was conducted by the parish clergy, but while the other priests held services in the church, and were available there for confessions, Fr Amigo went out to preach in the courts and alleys, returning each night in time for the main evening service leading a crowd of people reciting the rosary. A lot of them must have been the supporters who'd accompanied him out, but these evangelistic forays were also successful in bringing in quite a number of people who'd not been to Mass for 20 years or more. Other lapsed Catholics were brought along by the Blue Nuns through their visiting work. During Canon Akers' first year or so in charge, thanks to the Blue Nuns and the settlement workers, several thousand additional Catholic families living in the parish were identified. St Mary and St Michael's held its first outdoor procession in May that year. It formed up inside the church on a Sunday afternoon, with Fr Amigo and some local Ransomers doing the organising, and at 5.00 sharp moved out into Commercial Road. The statue of Our Lady, adorned with flowers, was carried by the Children of Mary in blue cloaks and veils, and in front marched all the parish groups: the League of the Cross Guards, the Holy Family and other confraternities, the Guild of St Agnes, and the little children's Guild of the Angels, all carrying banners and interspersed with bands. Representatives came from all the other East End parishes, with especially large contingents from Limehouse, St Anne's and Poplar, and the altar boys from the German Church in white cottas and scarlet tippets. Following the statue came the all-male and surpliced St Mary and St Michael's choir, Canon Akers in the cope which was now standard wear for the principle clergyman in the procession, all the curates, and the clergy of the neighbouring missions. The procession was over half-a-mile long, 2,000 took part, and the march lasted two hours. The police, according to the *Tablet*,

> *maintained excellent order along the route, which was densely crowded with people thoroughly respectful and reverent. In many streets the houses were bright with lights and flowers, flags and drapery, and with pictures of the Madonna displayed in witness of the faith.*

A parish branch of the Society of St Vincent de Paul (SVP) was developed.

Traditionally the SVP recruited from among relatively well-off Catholic men, with time and money available, and membership was rarely very large. Only six or seven joined the Commercial Road conference, but soon they were collecting and distributing between £50 and £75 a year. The clergy stopped handling relief themselves: if they came across someone who seemed genuinely in need, they took the name and address and referred them to the SVP.

The Charles Booth Survey

Around the end of November 1897 Canon Akers hurt his knee quite badly, and for the next two months – all over Christmas and into the new year – he was stuck in his room. So he may have been quite pleased when towards the end of January, a young lady arrived to interview him. The hard facts and figures about poverty in London were being set before the Victorian public, in volume after volume, thanks to a massive survey organised by Charles Booth. He'd begun his systematic investigation into socio-economic conditions in the 1880s, and was currently building up an overview of the efforts of clergy and charitable workers to address the problems. The interviewer was impressed by Canon Akers' "handsome face and fine clear cut profile" and thought that if he wasn't a priest he'd have made a good soldier. He had "a most sympathetic voice and manner, and his speech is of a highly cultivated gentleman." In response to questions, he stated that there were 8-9,000 Catholics in the parish of St Mary and St Michael's, mostly Irish and of the labouring class. There'd been some shifting of Catholics out of the district, partly due to the Jewish influx at the western end, and also to the shipping moving further down the river. The Convent of Mercy had 12 Sisters, and the new convent seven, and Lady Edmund Talbot was thinking of starting "a small settlement for ladies" like those in Mile End and Tower Hill. The church could seat 700-800 – so the permanent seating must have been hugely reduced since the opening of the building, with a lot of space now left empty. Of the six Sunday Masses the 10.00 attracted the largest and poorest congregation, with sung High Mass at 11.00 not so popular. Total Mass attendance was 1,800-2,000, and there were about 2,000 regular communicants. (Most of them will have received Communion only once a year, around Easter.) The Sunday evening service, Canon Akers thought, drew 6-700 hundred – but other evidence suggests that this estimate was vastly over-optimistic. Attendance of children at Sunday afternoon catechism was 300-350, but that wasn't good enough so he'd started catechism classes on Thursdays after school, and 700-800 were coming then. The schools were full to bursting, and needed more space: there were about a thousand children on the roll of the free schools, plus 60-70 boys in the "middle class 9d" school, and a similar number of girls in the convent school.

Leaving aside the schools, the income for the parish, which had no endowment, came to about £500 a year, partly paid over in church, and partly to the collectors on their rounds. "The East Ender is generous, the more so in proportion to the slenderness of his resources," explained Canon Akers, and showed the researcher a bag full of coppers which had been handed in yesterday in the church. This income met all the regular expenditure. If there was any special project on, like the current one for an organ, they had to appeal to outsiders, but the parish was essentially self-supporting. The researcher made a special note of this: Protestant churches in poor districts were *never* self-supporting, and it was quite amazing how the Catholics managed to do it. However although what Canon Akers said was essentially true, he didn't mention that whenever there was any special extra expense, he paid it out of his own pocket: without his private income, the parish would have constantly been going into the red. Rev H Henman, Vicar of St Mary's Cable Street, struck the researcher as shy and nervous, and "quite lacking in enthusiasm", so it didn't surprise her that his average morning congregation was about 15 adults, and 60-70 in the evenings, mostly women and girls. On the other hand he had 1,200 children attending his Sunday School. (This attendance pattern was quite common for Protestant churches in the East End.) Out of 600 families in the parish that he had some contact with, 331 were nominally Church of England, 94 Nonconformists, and 81 Roman Catholic.

The men were almost entirely unskilled labourers, with a small sprinkling of skilled artisans, but since the Dock Strike their chances of work had become more regular, and their financial position had improved. Ten years ago, when he arrived, there were no Jews living locally, but now they were scattered throughout his parish, and they'd taken over the whole west side of Lucas Street (Lukin Street). He'd noticed that young people, when they got married, tended to move away from the district. His Catholic counterparts looked after "their own people" well, and he was very friendly with them. As well as interviewing all the local clergy, the researcher picked several Sundays to make a tour around the churches, dropping in on services and trying to get a feel of each one. She arrived at St Mary and St Michael's during the first reading, after which the notices were given out. People were still coming in (late), and she reckoned the church would be about a third full by the time they were all settled. At the door, just inside as you came in, were two men with brass plates in front of them. Everyone paid a penny, and if they needed change they asked for it and got it. The researcher visited again for the evening service, but found a smaller congregation. In the evening the men with the brass plates were at the door once again, but it seemed you didn't have to put anything in if you didn't want to. She wholeheartedly agreed with Canon Akers about the interior décor: "This is not an attractive place of worship but it has the usual business like aspect of Roman Catholic places of worship."

St Cecilia's House

Lady Edmund Talbot started the East End's third CSU settlement – St Cecilia's – in a rented house in Albert Square. Those of the volunteers who could, took turns to live there for short periods, and it served as a base from which to organise the work. Parish visiting, Lady Edmund reckoned, could easily occupy three women for four hours each a week, if only she could find that many faithful volunteers. There were religious instruction sessions for children not attending Catholic schools, the Girls' Club, a Mothers' Meeting and a Boys' Guild. Boys' Guilds had been trialed at the Tower Hill settlement, and seemed to work well: they ran organised games, and targeted a younger age group than the CSU Boys' Clubs, which needed to be run by men. The school premises were used for all the larger group activities, but instruction sessions, and classes for small groups, took place at the house. Lady Edmund's own children must have been at boarding school by 1898, so there was nothing to stop her coming to live at St Cecilia's from time to time, and she was able to speak from personal experience about how actually living in an East End settlement enabled you to get to know the local people much better than if you only came down during the day. Florence Ashton, as co-leader of the settlement, provided an ongoing presence when Lady Edmund could not be there. The CSU workers tried to take an interest in everything that was going on in the parish, and Miss Ashton made a point of attending one of the League of the Cross meetings. Another CSU worker, Miss Raynes, set up a Provident Club for the parish's mothers: they gathered each Thursday night to pay in whatever they'd been able to put by during the week, and she entered the amount in the Club books and in the member's own book (as a receipt). Payout came just before Christmas, when they received ½d interest on every shilling if they drew their savings in cash, or 1d if they drew the equivalent value in coal or groceries. The preferential interest rate was meant to encourage the mothers to use the money in ways the workers considered "sensible", and particularly to discourage spending it on drink.

Lady Edmund appealed through the *Tablet* for more volunteers: women who could either live at the settlement for several weeks at a time, at periodic intervals, or else commit to coming along on a regular weekly basis to take responsibility for certain tasks. Fr Nicholson was very supportive of the CSU and the settlement, and penned a letter to the *Tablet* to explode the myth that the East End was full of dangerous savages, among whom it wasn't safe for respectable women to venture. "I have asked the ladies at the settlement in this parish," he wrote, "and sisters and nurses in the London Hospital, if they have at any time of the day been insulted in the streets of this neighbourhood, and they have unanimously resented such an aspersion on the manners of the people."

The Tower Hamlets Catholic League

Benjamin Costelloe agreed to stand in the 1897 school board elections, and his first meeting to drum up support was held at Johnson Street in mid-October: Canon Akers chaired, and parish lay leaders John O'Loghlen and Mr Maunsell were on the platform. Costelloe stood as an independent, but as the former LCC member for Stepney he was already well-known as a Liberal, and several local Liberal associations pledged support, as did Sir Samuel Montagu, Liberal MP for Whitechapel and very influential with the Jewish community. He won his seat, and Tower Hamlets once again had a Catholic representative on the School Board.

In 1898 an effort was made to get all the parishes to form a joint association – the Tower Hamlets Catholic League – to promote Catholic education. Commercial Road parishioner Patrick Considine was among the prime movers, and executive meetings were initially held at Johnson Street School, because St Mary and St Michael's was the most central parish, and because Canon Akers was Dean. He was also made a vice-president (an honorary position) but it was not really his baby, and neither he nor Fr Amigo took much interest. Complaints were raised about Johnson Street being too noisy, and how the proceedings were constantly interrupted by trains going past. But though not ideal, the school was used for all sorts of functions, so the complaints probably reflected the fact that the executive body was unmanageably large: in an effort to secure broad-based support, 12-15 lay delegates had been invited from each parish, plus all the clergy, making a total of 156. Attendance quickly fell off, and most of the priests found they had more important things to do with their time. Holding executive meetings in each of the parishes in turn only made things worse. One or two of the 15 St Mary and St Michael's delegates, though they were labouring men working long hours, usually did make the effort to turn up, but from some parishes nobody ever came, and the meeting was quite often cancelled for lack of a quorum. When people mobilise, they usually mobilise round an issue, and just at this point there didn't seem to be any clear, burning (and potentially winnable) issue to mobilise round. Ironically, the campaigns of the East End Catholics in past years to win equal rights had been so effective that there were no really obvious injustices for people to get worked up about, and it wasn't so easy to interest people in longer-term, bread-and-butter organising.

Cardinal Vaughan kept calling for a diocese-wide census of the Catholic population to be carried out, and the League leaders was firmly agreed that a proper "canvas" of the Catholics in Tower Hamlets would be an invaluable exercise. The two tasks could easily have been combined, if only there was the will to do the work – but there wasn't. Canon Akers was, in fact, facing an immediate, hands-on crisis over the parish schools in Johnson Street. Shortly after he arrived, they were condemned by the Board of Education on the grounds that they were too small for the number of children, the sanitary arrangements were inadequate, and the main boys' school had no playground. Unfortunately, the League wasn't designed to help with that sort of problem. The neighbourhood was by now very built up, and there was no vacant space, but Canon Akers planned to purchase some houses in Lucas Street, round the corner from the church, demolish them and build new schools on the site, and then use the old Catholic cemetery behind the church as a playground. The plan actually depended on being kept very quiet, but unfortunately it was leaked, and when the landlord discovered that the site was wanted for Catholic purposes, he pulled out of the deal.

A lofty and richly covered reredos

The alterations to the interior of St Mary and St Michael's were carried out at the end of the summer of 1858, and a grand reopening service was held at the beginning of October. Some of the steps into the chancel were eliminated, and the altar rails which had stood in the middle of the sanctuary area were moved forward to the lowest step: this was to enlarge the sanctuary, and create more room for ceremonials. The new look also featured "a lofty and richly covered reredos", elaborate wrought iron screens in the arches between the sanctuary and the side chapels, and "a rich pavement of encaustic tiles" covering the floor of the chancel. Walters' design included a rood, with figures of the crucified Christ flanked by Our Lady and St John, but this had to be left out because there wasn't enough money. The new organ was not built in the original organ chamber designed by Wardell, but in, or in front of, the Lady Chapel, in such a way as to block or restrict access to the corner chapel. This suggests that the corner chapel had never really been used much, perhaps because there'd never been any money to furnish it properly.

Newly-minted priests continued to come to Commercial Road for their pastoral experience. Theoretically they came two at a time, for six months, but adjustments must have been made depending on the individual, and on how many new priests were coming through the system, and there could be as many as four in the Apostolic College. Some were actually ordained at St Mary and St Michael's, as was Bartholomew O'Doherty in 1897. 1898 was a bumper year for ordinations, and on the last Sunday in October the revamped sanctuary offered a fine setting for the priesting of William Bendon and Thomas Bullivant, by Auxiliary Bishop James Paterson. As soon as Mass was finished everyone queued up to kiss the new priests' anointed hands, and everyone attending later Masses that day, or other services, was offered the same opportunity afterwards.

In August 1899 Canon Akers, now aged 62, was in the middle of giving a week-long retreat to the Dominican nuns at St Catherine's Convent, Bow when, on the Thursday, he suddenly became too ill to continue, and had to be brought home to Commercial Road. The immediate cause of his collapse was diagnosed as gastritis. As the doctors held out no hope, Fr Amigo administered the last rites on the Friday, and Canon Akers' family were summoned. On Sunday a message was sent round to the church to say he'd died, but this was followed by a correction, as he'd unexpectedly shown signs of life. He did die at 5.15 the following afternoon, Monday 14th August. His sister, brother-in-law and nieces were present, and all the St Mary and St Michael's priests. A notice placed at the entrance to the passage leading to the presbytery was "scanned with mournful interest by hundreds of passers-by." His family wanted Canon Akers buried in the family vault at Malling Abbey, but were persuaded to agree to St Patrick's, Leytonstone. From Wednesday Canon Akers lay in state in the church, and the Sisters of Mercy, the Sacred Heart Sisters from Homerton, and the Bow Dominicans sent relays of nuns to keep up a constant prayer vigil.

Dr Lee of Lambeth

The funeral was on Friday: Bp Brindle officiated, and Fr Lawless delivered a panegyric. Over 150 priests were present and 130 nuns. Canon Akers was still persona non grata with the clergy and people of St Peter's, London Docks, but a few other Anglicans who'd known him attended the funeral. Dr Frederick George Lee, Vicar of All Saints, Lambeth, where Canon Akers had been a curate for a short while, took his place among the priests, and spent ten minutes praying devoutly before the Blessed Sacrament. One of the High Anglicanism's most extreme "romanisers", Lee had gone to the length of obtaining episcopal consecration from a schismatic Catholic bishop, so as to be able to reintroduce a valid Apostolic Succession into the Church of England. He retired shortly after Canon Akers' funeral, and All Saints was demolished to make room for an extension to Waterloo Station. Lee was to be received into the Roman Catholic Church in 1902, six weeks before he died. Fr Frederick Higley, parish priest of Limehouse, always said the move to Commercial Road had shortened Canon Aker's life. He left £8,261, bequeathing half to the Archbishop of Westminster and half to his family. Homerton Parish launched a fundraising drive for a suitable monument to its founder, and in due course erected a beautiful marble altar with a commemorative inscription.

Dawn of the 20th Century

Fr Amigo succeeded Canon Akers, and was duly appointed Missionary Rector, though not Dean, since it was only fair that that title should pass to Fr Lawless. He inherited the problem about the schools, and began drawing up plans to build on the old cemetery: the work would cost £6,000, and the parish began fundraising. Meanwhile the new organ was installed, and Fr Amigo declared it would be a memorial to Canon Akers, who had worked so hard to save up for it. For the next year or so, most of Amigo's attention was necessarily devoted to the school. He didn't only concern himself with the plant, but also took great interest in the children, who thought the world of him. He liked personally to prepare the boys' class that was coming up to First Communion, and after the ceremony provide the customary breakfast, and distribute medals and scapulars. Unfortunately, when he was ready to present the rebuilding plans, he was told that an 1884 Act of Parliament had made it illegal to build on a burial ground. Meanwhile he and Lady Edmund Talbot attended a meeting at Archbishop's House, chaired by the Cardinal, at which Fr Segesser, who'd pioneered the Catholic Boys' Brigade in Southwark, gave an impressive presentation on his work. Boys loved the military-style uniforms and drill: it provided an effective carrot to keep them involved with the Church, and was seen as character forming because it required smartness, punctuality and reliability. It *did* cost money, because the uniforms and kit had to be subsidised by the parish, but Fr Segesser argued it was worth it. Diocesan authorities, parish priests and CSU were all convinced, and all gave their wholehearted backing. Guardian Angels was first to act, and St Mary and St Michael's quickly followed suit.

St Cecilia's moved to a larger house on the main road, next to the Convent of Mercy: No 531 Commercial Road. Besides the "lady" volunteers, who came and went, three paid domestic servants were permanently based at the settlement: volunteers when in residence were expected to contribute 25s a week for their living expenses, including their share of the servants' wages, and the house rent. There were currently 17 volunteers, though the number in residence at any one time was usually three or four, as the house couldn't hold more. As the school leaving age was being raised to 14, and as the CSU clubs were specifically intended for leavers, their minimum age was made 14. But this flagged up a need to do something for the younger girls, still at school, so St Cecilia's started a junior club. Girls and women were taken to make short retreats at the Cenacle in Stamford Hill: the retreatants paid part of the cost, and although the settlement had to subsidise them, it didn't involve major expense. On Christmas Day, dinners were provided at the settlement for the poorest parishioners, and Lady Edmund and her husband used to give up their own Christmas to come and help serve, with Lord Edmund in charge of the carving.

One day some nice Protestant women came to discuss a situation that had arisen with a Bible Class they were holding in the evenings for local children. Quite a lot of Catholic children were attending, but they would be quite happy to send those ones over to St Cecilia's, if something similar could be arranged there. It transpired that 75 Catholic children were attending the Bible Class, with the permission of their parents – who thoroughly approved, because they "learnt something useful" and it kept them off the streets. Such practical ecumenism was entirely normal for Tower Hamlets, but the settlement workers, clergy and nuns, none of whom were East Enders, were aghast. It was agreed to begin after-school classes at the settlement, starting with 10- and 11-year-old girls coming up to First Communion. The classes were held twice a week, and made interesting with stories, pictures and magic lantern slides, and an altar which the children decorated themselves. The settlement workers were naturally drawn into helping out on the First Communion Day itself, together with the Sisters of Mercy: getting the girls dressed, and organising the breakfast. Afterwards they ran "perseverance classes" for them, while beginning preparation classes with the next year's cohort. Involvement with First Communions became a regular part of the settlement work, and in some years Lady Edmund personally provided all the requisite white dresses. Initially, the CSU had tried to make it a rule not to give out money, but this rule was soon broken, and the volunteers were allowed to use their discretion: you couldn't talk to people about religion if they had nothing to eat. The St Cecilia's House volunteers soon learned how to make limited amounts of money provide maximum effective help, and about the range of non-Catholic charities and agencies to which they could refer people. Lady Edmund encouraged them to be ready to learn from the poor, especially from the good example they gave by "their wonderful patience, long-suffering, and charity one to another, their resignation and trust in God". "Relief dinners" were provided every weekday during the school term for the neediest children: they had to obtain tickets from the clergy, who would only give them to those with a record of regular attendance at both school and Sunday Mass.

Commercial Road houses similar to those occupied by Convent of Mercy and St Cecilia's

Cardinal Vaughan's dream of recruiting massive numbers of better-off Catholics into the CSU had never been realised: the membership remained quite small, and almost exclusively female. To give it a fresh lease of life, therefore, Lady Edmund persuaded Vaughan to start an English branch of the Ladies of Charity of St Vincent de Paul, to complement the SVP which was an all-male organisation. All the CSU volunteers were encouraged to join the Ladies of Charity, and the CSU settlements and clubs carried on as before, but now as Ladies of Charity projects. This change brought the advantages of being affiliated to an internationally well-known network with an established charism and history, and a very strong presence on the ground in France. It also offered opportunities to link up with other parts of the Vincentian "family", like the Sisters of Charity. The Dowager Duchess of Newcastle became President of the Ladies of Charity, and Lady Edmund was Secretary.The Tower Hamlets Catholic League, still struggling for survival and achieving very little, had gone back to meeting at Johnson Street School. Very suddenly Benjamin Costelloe was taken ill, and died on 22nd December

Fr Francis Beckley

1899: he was still a young man, but he'd always burned the candle at both ends. The League approached the School Board to ask that Fr Francis Beckley, rector of Wapping, be co-opted to replace Costelloe, and this was courteously agreed. At the next School Board elections in November 1900, since it still hadn't been possible to find a lay Catholic candidate, Fr Beckley stood and was duly elected, coming in second of the five successful candidates. Fr Amigo had worked very hard on his behalf, but the turnout of Catholic voters should have been a lot better, and everyone knew Fr Beckley's return was due as much to the apathy of the electorate, and goodwill of the local political establishment, as to the efforts of the Catholic community. It still hadn't been possible to carry out the much-needed census and canvassing work.

Elementary schools were not really geared to stretch older children, so the School Board was beginning to set up higher grade central schools for them, with an enriched curriculum. Something which very much needed discussing, therefore, and for which the Tower Hamlets Catholic League meetings offered an ideal forum, was whether to set up a Catholic central school. Unfortunately, as Fr Higley (who was keen on the idea) pointed out, it couldn't even be discussed unless all the parish priests were present, and they never were. Most of them were in fact chary of it, because it would cream off the most promising students from their own parish schools. The only joint project Higley could move forward was building an extra infant school, the Good Shepherd, at the point where the boundaries of his own parish, St Mary and St Michael's, and Guardian Angels met. Each parish was asked to contribute just a few hundred pounds, and Fr Higley's Protestant father, a carpenter, did a lot of the work for free.

A situation fraught with the gravest danger

Francis Bourne, Bishop of Southwark, had tried to headhunt Fr Amigo soon after he came to Commercial Road. Fr Amigo was deeply interested in the whole question of providing an improved training and spiritual formation for the diocesan clergy, which was why he'd been put in to help Canon Akers with the Apostolic College. He'd quickly decided the College wasn't working, and got fed up, so when Bp Bourne invited him to join him in Southwark and help start something different, he was very willing to listen. Cardinal Vaughan had flatly refused to release him, so nothing more was said, but early in 1901 Bp Bourne renewed the invitation, and this time the Cardinal agreed.

Francis Bourne Bishop of Southwark
later to become Cardinal Bourne Archbishop of Westminster

Within a few hours of getting the news, the parishioners were holding a packed meeting in the school. They hadn't been told *why* Fr Amigo was leaving. Dr W Grandy took the chair, and speaker after speaker rose to point out how indispensable Fr Amigo was. They "were face to face that night with a situation fraught with the gravest danger to the best interests of this important mission," averred Mr J P Donovan, headmaster of St Joseph's (popularly known during his time as "Donovan's"). He "referred in detail to the many-sidedness of the rector's labours, dwelling especially on the extremely valuable work which Father Amigo had done for the schools. In conclusion, he appealed to all present to leave no stone unturned to avert the calamity with which they were threatened." Mr Jordan, headmaster of the main boys' school, spoke of how well Fr Amigo knew the parishioners: he "might truly say like his Divine Master, 'I know My sheep, and My sheep know Me.'" Deputations were formed "representing every branch of spiritual, educational, and social activity in the parish" to plead with Fr Amigo to change his mind, and appeal to the Cardinal, but could not get the decision reversed.

Just two Sundays later, the parishioners gathered again at Johnson Street to say goodbye. A lot of people couldn't squeeze into the room, and had to stay in the corridors. There was no leaving present, because Fr Amigo had said very firmly that he didn't want them collecting money for him; he'd rather they devoted their efforts to giving every possible support to his successor. But speeches were free, and there were plenty of them. Patrick Considine kicked off by declaring that Fr Amigo was "one of the best rectors the mission had ever possessed", and his only drawback was his modesty. He was glad Fr Amigo wasn't an Irishman,

> *because people would then say that Commercial Road had thought much of Father Amigo for his nationality alone. It was a splendid object-lesson of the broad spirit of the Church which asserted that a good Catholic and a good priest should receive the fullest measure of congratulation and support, no matter what his nationality might be.*

The departing rector was eventually given the floor, whereupon he asked the parishioners not to blame either him or the Cardinal, assuring them that

> *they were the best people that any priest was placed in charge of, and he parted from them with great sorrow. The sacrifice was, therefore, all the harder for him. It was the duty of the priest to do the will of God, and in discharging that duty he… left dear old St Mary and St Michael's parish.*

He thanked everyone, particularly the other priests, the schoolteachers, the Sisters of Mercy (who, he reminded everyone, had been there much longer than he had), and the Little Company of Mary "who had done so much good in the parish". Finally he distributed to everyone present "a little devotional gift".

Give my love to your mother

Timothy Ring was born in Co Kerry, Ireland, in 1858, and trained at the Killarney Seminar and the Irish College in Paris. Ordained in 1884, he was expecting to work in Ireland, but Cardinal Manning was appealing desperately for priests, Fr Ring was enthusiastic to respond, and his bishop agreed to send him over to London. He did his first curacy in Clerkenwell, then in March 1887 was moved to Wapping, where he spent a memorable few months under Fr Beckley. In June the Vicar General, Mgr Gilbert, asked him to pioneer a new mission in Silvertown. Fr Ring had never heard of the place, and objected that he was too inexperienced, didn't really belong to Westminster, and had no money. But a day or so later he was summoned by Cardinal Manning, and masterfully sweet-talked into it. An empty barber's shop had been hired by a Mr Harrington to hold catechism classes for a few children. On the following Sunday, Feast of the Sacred Heart, Fr Ring celebrated Mass there for a dozen people. He had to sleep in the attic, and really rough it, only eating properly when someone invited him for a meal. Cardinal Manning once asked him where he was going for his holiday, and he replied that since he had no money, he was going home to Ireland to stay with his family. At this the Cardinal "took out of his old musty purse a sovereign and gave it to me, saying, 'This will help you with the fare, and give my love to your mother.'"

He'd been told there were about 90 Catholics in the district, mostly Poles, but that if he investigated the local factories he'd probably find quite a lot of Irish people working in them. Sure enough, within just a few years he'd tracked down thousands, and built a school and a church. A demand from his own bishop for his return "called forth a correspondence between Ireland and London", as Cardinal Manning was very eager to retain him, and the upshot was that Fr Ring was permitted to transfer permanently to Westminster. While remaining parish priest of Silvertown, he pioneered a second mission at Custom House, building a church there too.

The young Fr Timothy Ring

At the same time he confidently entered the political arena, standing for the West Ham School Board: in successive elections he came top of the poll, and was made Chairman of the Board. When the school boards were scrapped, Ring was co-opted onto the Education Committees of both West Ham and Essex County Council. He was one of the most active members of the CPSC, and of the Catholic Education Council which later replaced it. His solid achievements, combined with (let's be honest) an outstanding talent for self-publicity, made him a very well-known figure in London's Catholic community, and his friend Fr John Crowley was sent to ask him if he'd take over St Mary and St Michael's. But he was in the middle of his building projects and couldn't really walk away just at that stage, so he begged off.

Commercial Road's financial situation was critical, with the deficit mounting at a rate of £10 a month, and the Catholic population moving away and being replaced by Jews. The school problem appeared insoluble, and a rumour was going round among the diocesan clergy that Cardinal Vaughan had suggested dividing up the church, since most of the space wasn't going to be needed any more, and making part of it into a school. People were saying the parish was doomed, and would soon be closed down. Nevertheless someone was found to take it on. A product of Maynooth, Fr Thomas Dunphy had been brought over from Ireland in 1898, and assigned as troubleshooter to sort out St Edmund's, Millwall, which was going through a really bad patch. Now 40, he was ready for St Mary and St Michael's.

Lifted out of the mud

Fr Dunphy knew he had to ensure that the fundraising efforts for the new schools were kept up (even in the total absence of viable plans for rebuilding), yet at the same time bring the parish debt under control. Sensibly, he didn't institute a total freeze on non-essential expenditure, but went ahead with a number of low-cost improvements around the church: all the statues were repainted, a hymn board was installed in front of the pulpit and a Calvary inside the main entrance, large lamps were placed just outside the doors, and the tattered old notice board was replaced with a nice new one. He also encouraged a small fundraising campaign for new Stations of the Cross. Getting the parishioners to work towards small, concrete and quickly achievable goals would help raise morale, and thereby boost both regular giving, and longer-term fundraising drives.

Key figures in the liturgical life of the parish were the chief Master of Ceremonies James Thomas Doyle, loyally assisted by his brother John; the organist Joseph Cunningham, and a new choirmaster, Mr Dunn, who quickly had the choir well in hand. The League of the Cross was at a low ebb all over London, but a big push was on to revive it, and Fr Dunphy threw his weight behind the revival of the parish branch. He reintroduced the custom of the League Guards attending Mass once a month as a body, and receiving Communion, wearing their regalia. Well-known guest speakers were booked to give talks at the fortnightly meetings in the school hall, during the winter months when there were few rival attractions: the first was given by George Elliot Anstruther, a journalist destined to spend many years running the Catholic Truth Society and editing the *Universe*, and to have a long and fruitful relationship with Commercial Road.

All sorts of concerts and shows were staged in aid of the new schools, ranging from small and semi-private affairs put on by the Sisters of Mercy and their convent school children, and by the settlement workers at St Cecilia's, to a grand concert organised by Joseph Cunningham at Limehouse Town Hall. Fr Dunphy went into the schools to check attendance, and found the total present in all the schools put together was 1,369: this was 300 more than any other mission in Westminster Archdiocese. The Infant School was particularly crowded. But despite the huge difficulties, all the schools were doing an excellent job, getting very good reports from both government and diocesan inspectors, and earning the maximum possible grant. Everyone was praying to Our Lady, Help of Christians, for a solution to the impasse on finding a new site.

Fr Matthew Towmey

Fr James Carey, though he'd only been ordained and joined the Apostolic College in 1898, was now senior curate. He took over the moribund Confraternity of the Sacred Heart, and put tremendous effort into building it up: soon it was the biggest in the diocese, and a real powerhouse. Both men and women could belong, and the leader of the men's section was a police constable named Charles Berg. Members received medals and, like the Holy Family in its heyday, were divided into sections and put on a register, with a prefect in charge of each section. They were urged to attend the devotional service which was held in the church every Friday evening, and thanks to Fr Carey's talks, the Friday night congregation was built up to impressive numbers. Fr John Augustine Davidson, a former Franciscan, older than Fr Carey but less experienced in parish work, was chaplain to the new Boys' Brigade company, which was shaping up well and becoming one of the best in London. It had already got its own band, and could be relied on to bring credit to the parish if taken anywhere on an excursion. On parade Sundays the Brigade all sat at the front of the church, gave a "general salute" at the Elevation, and afterwards marched round the parish. Fr Davidson was busy trying to set up a bicycle corps. The latest recruit to the clergy team, Fr Matthew Twomey from Co Cork, collaborated with Sr De Sales in looking after the Children of Mary and Guild of St Agnes. In poor health himself due to rheumatic fever contracted as a child, Fr Twomey took the girls out for frequent excursions into Epping Forest to benefit from the fresh air.

1st station of the Way of the Cross installed St Patrick's Day 1902

The new Stations of the Cross were ready in time for St Patrick's Day 1902, and were erected as a memorial to the pastorate of Fr Amigo. Over 1,500 attended the 10.00 feastday Mass, and in the evening there was an Irish entertainment at Limehouse Town Hall. After a new Lady Altar had been installed, the next of the smaller fundraising projects was for a new pulpit. All these items were commissioned to gothic designs, to match the church. For the 1902 outdoor procession the parish band, led by drum major Peter Hubbert, wore their black and green uniforms for the first time. The Boys' Brigade band also took part, while the rest of the Brigade strode along looking smart, and flying the papal flag. Lady Edmund Talbot marched with her Girls' Club, and the Boys' Guild wore red and gold sashes. The Blue Nuns walked together behind the Children of Mary carrying the statue, while the Mercies were dispersed through the procession, supervising different groups of children: they'd kitted some out as "Rosary Children", with sashes in red, blue and mauve to represent the Glorious, Joyful and Sorrowful mysteries, and carrying appropriate white satin bannerettes and pictures. Fr Fletcher, as usual, took part in the march and preached in the church afterwards.

In 1901 Cardinal Vaughan's brother Bernard (15 years younger than him, and a Jesuit) was transferred to the fashionable Farm Street Church in West London, where he achieved fame as a high society preacher. There was standing room only at his 12.00 sermons, and not because he flattered the rich: on the contrary he never tired of telling them how sinful and selfish they were – but they lapped it up. Those who *didn't* like Fr Vaughan accused him of only being interested in "confessing countesses". But he quite soon informed his brother that there wasn't enough work for him at Farm Street, and he wanted also to work in the East End. The Cardinal agreed for him to move into the presbytery and help out at Commercial Road, only he didn't think to consult the parish clergy, or even inform them of the arrangement – they first heard about it from reading the newspapers.

Fr Vaughan began staying in the parish for a couple of nights each week. He took a children's service on Tuesday afternoon, and after tea he went out preaching in the streets. Previous instances of street preaching from St Mary and St Michael's had always been connected with mission services in the church, and laid a heavy emphasis on sin, and the need for repentance, because traditional missions made it their overriding objective to get people into the confessional. But Vaughan focused more on simply preaching the Good News to the poor, gently scattering the seeds, and leaving them to grow in their own time. Journalists were soon taking a keen interest, and his forays were covered quite extensively in both the Catholic and the national press. One account described how, on a bitterly cold day in December 1902, Blue Nuns, settlement workers, League Guards and other supporters could be seen going round, ringing hand bells and directing people to School House Lane, "within ear-shot of Dr. Barnardo's Homes". At 4.00 sharp the service started with "Hail Queen of Heaven", after which Vaughan began to preach:

> *The learned preacher set before his poverty-stricken audience, the whole scheme of man's redemption, in words so simple, that the young children could understand and follow him, yet so telling, that the grown men and women were listening with rapt attention to every word.*

Leading up to the Nativity story, he stressed that since the infant Christ was poor like them, poverty was clearly no hindrance to religion.

> *And then, when that day came that the Master's bell would be rung in the courts of Heaven to summon their souls before their Judge, some, maybe, from School House Lane would hear their Lord's 'Well done' spoken to them, and would enter into His joy. At the conclusion of the address, all present knelt and recited the Rosary with great fervour. This was followed by the singing of the Act of Contrition, after which the crowd gradually dispersed.*

The hymns had to be sung without accompaniment until the Duke of Norfolk, Lady Edmund Talbot's brother-in-law, donated a harmonium on wheels. Fr Vaughan soon turned his talents to organising entertainments to raise funds for East End causes. His family background gave him entrée into the upper reaches of society, and at Farm Street he was well-placed for networking with the Catholic elite. He showed tremendous flair for talking big name artistes into performing for free, and retired ones into making exceptional come-backs. The *Daily Chronicle* described Fr Dunphy as "one of the most active religious workers that the 'docker' district of East London has ever known." In a year and a half he raised £1,200 from the local congregation alone, mostly towards the rebuilding of the schools. This was nothing like enough, so to make sure the work could go ahead as soon as a site had been secured, £2,500 was taken from the Richard Neale Fund as a loan, repayable by the parish over 30 years. As Fr Carey put it – Fr Dunphy had "given us fresh hope, fresh life, and practically lifted us out of the mud." So it was a big shock to the parish when he was taken ill, and had to go to Ireland for treatment. Fr Carey took charge in his absence. At a League of the Cross meeting in July he read out a letter from Fr Dunphy, who was at the Mater Misericordiae Hospital in Dublin. He had a serious hernia, and the doctors had thought he needed an operation, but had now decided that he didn't, and he was getting better: he expected to come back to London in August.

Sure enough he did, and was able to attend the League of the Cross rally at Crystal Palace in August, taking with him Frs Jerome Deady and John Cauldfield, the two current inmates of the Apostolic College. The first anniversary of the revival of the parish branch was coming up in October, and the number of Guards was up to 25: Dunphy said he wanted that figure doubled by next year's rally. Fr Dunphy took Michael Welton off the outdoor collecting so he could devote all his energy to the temperance cause. A register was made of all those who took the pledge, but most of them had fallen off the wagon: Whelton was to go round visiting everyone, and try to reclaim them. He must also divide the membership into sections, each with a Guard in charge to keep an eye on everyone. His efforts were supported by those of his second-in-command, Lieutenant Spelling, and of Patrick Considine who was hon secretary of the parish's League branch, attended meetings regularly, and performed in the amateur concerts they put on.

Dean Lawless died in October 1902. Dunphy attended the funeral together with all his curates, but within just a few weeks he himself was rushed back into hospital again. A letter arrived from the Vicar General, saying he would need complete rest for quite a while, but quite soon afterwards came another letter, saying he'd undergone an operation which had left him in such a critical condition that it was doubtful he could ever work again. In those weeks of crisis, Fr Vaughan lifted everyone's spirits by holding a Christmas concert at Johnson Street. The teachers and parish collectors worked hard selling tickets, while Fr Carey undertook to pack the hall like a sardine tin –

and succeeded. On the night, Vaughan boasted, he sold the programmes "at 'popular prices' but gave no change till the light was turned down (if then)."

Dean Dooley's Dockers

Andrew Dooley was born in Ireland in 1864, and ordained for the Diocese of Waterford, but "lent" to Cardinal Manning for London. He'd spent six years as curate to Fr Beckley in Wapping, then in 1892 was offered his own parish, whereupon he was permanently transferred to Westminster. After doing a marvellous job for ten years at Canning Town, he was transferred to St Mary and St Michael's, and as the position of Dean was now vacant, it was given to him along with the appointment as Missionary Rector. The Sunday he arrived was the eve of the Feast of the Immaculate Conception, the anniversary of the opening of the church, and Dooley referred to this in his introductory sermon.

He had been a neighbour of Father O'Callaghan's both at home in Ireland, and in London, and when stationed in Wapping, he had always spent his 'off' evenings in Fr. Maher's room. He had made short meditations by the side of the grave of Father Kelly, the good priest, who had built the Church. He had been a friend of the late Canon Akers, and also of Father Amigo, therefore he felt that he did not come among them as a stranger. With their late Rector, Fr. Dunphy, he had been very closely connected. They had been at Maynooth College together... They had been ordained in the same year, and had maintained their friendship ever since.

The new pulpit was unveiled just before Christmas. It was made of marble and alabaster, beautifully carved, and cost £150. Dean Dooley urged the parishioners to work hard to pay off the balance of £70 still outstanding, and think of it as a memorial to Fr Dunphy who had started them collecting for it, and approved the designs before he fell ill. (Contrary to the doctors' expectations, Dunphy made a full recovery, and in due course returned to the active ministry.)

At the first League of the Cross meeting after his arrival, Dean Dooley presided, sang "The Wearing of the Green" and "The West's Asleep" to great applause, and pledged his full support to the cause of temperance. Fr Deady was now looking after the League, and at one of the fortnightly meetings he and Patrick Considine, between them, gave an excellent talk on the history of the parish. More Guards were invested with the green and gold sash, including sizeable contingents of women: they used to hold a monthly march around the parish, and attended any larger rallies that were on, especially at Tower Hill. The men Guards became such a pillar of parish life that they were nicknamed "Dean Dooley's Dockers": the church was thoroughly cleaned and painted by a group of them working in the evenings: P O'Shea, Peter Hubbert, F Cullander, J Donovan, R Jackson, R Regan, W Henshaw, T Crawley, T O'Shea. Irish language evening classes taught by Fr Twomey, which had been announced by Fr Dunphy before he left, went ahead as planned: parishioners were strongly encouraged to attend them, and also the classes in Irish dancing and music. This was all part of the Gaelic cultural movement which became very strong over the turn of the century, as an apolitical and uncontentious way of affirming an Irish identity. Twomey also started, and nurtured, a parish branch of the Irish National League, which *was* political.

The 1902 Education Act was about to place the country's faith schools in a relatively secure financial position. In future their staff salaries and running costs would be paid for by public funds, though the religious bodies to which they belonged would still be responsible for all major building work. Directly elected school boards were to be abolished, and their responsibilities taken over by the educational committees of the county councils. Influencing the LCC would require a different approach from the old tactic of putting Catholic candidates in for local School Board elections, and it was perhaps this change that put the final nail in the coffin of the Tower Hamlets Catholic League. In the spring of 1903 it was wound up, and the small balance of funds in hand given to Fr Higley, to help pay off the debt on the Good Shepherd School.

Dean Dooley had had a brainwave about expanding Commercial Road's school accommodation: to pull down the condemned portion of the existing schools, and construct a larger and better-quality building in its place. Unfortunately the lease on the Johnson Street site didn't have much longer to run. The Mercers were willing to extend it, but only for another 40 years, and to rebuild on that basis would not be cost-effective. However Dean Dooley went to see them, showed them his plans and explained the situation in detail, and got their agreement to an 80-year extension, on condition that the cost of the new building be at least £6,000. This was very generous of them, especially since the ground rent was now only £5 a year.

Robert L Curtis was the architect, and Calnan and Sons were contracted for the building work, which went ahead in the autumn of 1903. Before demolishing the old school, they erected a prefabricated iron building in the presbytery grounds, and this inevitably pushed up the cost: the total contract was for £8,100. The parish had so far raised about £2,000 towards this total, and Cardinal Vaughan (shortly before he died) agreed that part of the schools' endowment – Commercial Road's share of the Wilkinson Fund – could be sold off, realising another £3,880. (In the rush everyone forgot that a third of this belonged by rights to St Patrick's, Wapping, and this led to a fuss when it eventually came to light.) For the next eight months, classes were organised for 500 children in the iron building and in the presbytery.

Fr Vaughan, in order to have more freedom and avoid the risk of being a nuisance, had moved out of the presbytery at the beginning of 1903. He rented a room at No 33, Lucas Street, for 2s 6d a week and, having furnished it with a camp bed, two chairs, a gas fire and a frying pan, set about learning how to shop and cook for himself. Early one morning he went out to buy some milk, but didn't realise he was supposed to bring a jug to put it in. The shopkeeper agreed to lend him a lemonade bottle so long as he left 2d deposit, but he insisted on leaving a sovereign, which got her worried because she thought he was a madman on the loose. As he became known in the neighbourhood, attitudes changed: an old man who sold hot potatoes at the street corner used "to consider it a privilege to give him a couple to carry home with him." Like the settlement workers, if Vaughan wanted to help a parish family in need, he often gave tickets instead of money, but then he discovered that the bread shop where the tickets were redeemed was giving short weight. Loaves were sold by weight, and if necessary an extra slice was supposed to be added, but the baker was arguing that he didn't have to do that for recipients of "charity". Fr Vaughan was furious, went round with a crowd of mothers, told the baker to give him the scales so he could do the weighing himself, and declared, "Ladies, this is not charity, but my gift of bread to my very good friends."

The street preaching was now well established. A small boy would come to fetch Fr Vaughan, and walk in front carrying "a tall and vividly painted crucifix". They usually called first at the Convent of the Little Company of Mary to pick up the harmonium, and borrow a bell, a box or stool to stand on, and some Sisters. The party then proceeded deep into the back streets, ringing the bell and collecting a crowd of excited children on the way. Once arrived at a suitably dingy court or alley, Fr Vaughan would put on the stole given him by Pope Pius X, jump up on the box and begin a service, with the Sisters and Children of Mary joining in the hymns. Occasionally the Duke of Norfolk came along to take part – no one ever recognised the hereditary Earl Marshal of England, and he was given the job of ringing the bell. The people always listened spellbound throughout and had a quick way with hecklers. At the end Fr Vaughan might produce a bag of sweets for the children, but this wasn't a regular feature, and children, like adults, enjoyed the services for their own sake. His Christmas 1903 concert was held at the People's Palace

The People's Palace in Mile End Road

in Mile End Road to raise funds "for the poor, sick, and suffering of St. Mary and St. Michael's", and Madame de Navarro (Miss Mary Anderson), who'd been a top actress in her time, sang two songs and gave a reading of the famous balcony scene from *Romeo and Juliet*. According to the *East London Observer* there was a "capital attendance" of well-heeled West Enders. The following night, again at the People's Palace, over 4,000 children from all the East End Catholic schools were treated to a party, with refreshments, conjuring tricks and a magic lantern. Madame de Navarro appeared and sang some songs, and at the end called for three cheers for Fr Vaughan.

In May a very, very important Sunday evening service was held at St Mary and St Michael's, and for this the huge church really was filled. The event wasn't due to start until 7.00, but by 6.30 all the seats were taken, and the League Guards were putting out forms and chairs in all available spaces. Even then, latecomers had to stand in the porch where they couldn't see or hear what was going on: altogether there were about 3,000 present, which was far larger than for the closing service of even a successful parish mission. Peter Amigo was due back for a visit, and he was now Bishop of Southwark, Francis Bourne having been made Archbishop of Westminster. During the service he confirmed 384 people: 50 adults, 130 boys and 184 girls. Mr Jordan sponsored the boys, and the girls were shared between Lady Edmund Talbot and Madame de Navarro.

During the first week in June, the parish clergy blessed and opened the new school buildings in Johnson Street. There was accommodation now for 1,209 children, divided into five departments: senior boys, junior boys, senior girls, junior girls, and infants. Of the £8,100 cost, £6,000 had already been paid. No great ceremony or fuss was made about the opening, but Dean Dooley quoted the text "Unless the Lord build the city, in vain do they labour who work thereon", and thanked everyone who'd given support – above all Our Lady, Help of Christians. The iron building now became the parish hall. Sadly, the school opening was the last service Dean Dooley was ever to perform for the parish. According to the *Tablet* "the seal of early death was upon him", which probably meant he had TB. Taken seriously ill, he moved to Ramsgate for the sake of the sea air, and both Bp Amigo and Bp Fenton, one of the Westminster Auxiliaries, visited him there. He died in August. Fenton conducted the funeral at St Mary and St Michael's, with Bp Amigo also present and a hundred priests, including some who'd come over specially from Ireland. The League Guards bore the coffin from the church, and to the graveside at St Patrick's Cemetery.

In my short time here…

Fr Vincent McNabb

Fr Timothy Ring was no longer so resourceless that he had to go home to his parents for his holidays, and he'd developed a taste for foreign travel. That summer he embarked at Hull for a cruise to Norway with some friends, but before the ship left he was handed a letter telling him he was being transferred to St Mary and St Michael's. It rather spoiled his trip. The new Dean and Missionary Rector addressed his parishioners for the first time on Rosary Sunday, October 1904, paying tribute to the Sisters of Mercy, who were still teaching in Wapping when he was a curate there: "I well remember that when all my efforts failed to get certain hardened sinners to Holy Mass, I had only to send for Sr Patrick and the work was done." He took care to mention the Blue Nuns as well, the "other kind and devoted Sisters who watch by the bedsides of the sick and dying, and visit the homes of the poor."

The curates were already a strong team, and once again Fr Carey had coped marvellously. Membership of the Sacred Heart Confraternity was up to well over a thousand, well-known speakers like Fr Vincent McNabb OP often came to give talks, and their monthly joint Communions had to be split between two Sundays: Dean Ring thought them "the salt of the parish". Though girls and young women were well provided for, he noted that there wasn't much for boys: they could be altar servers or join the choir, but the Boys' Brigade was going through a bad patch due to opposition from the Irish nationalists, who feared it would encourage them to enlist in the British Army. Fr Deady's League of the Cross was in reasonably good nick, but the old Holy Family Confraternity was at a low ebb, and as all the adult associations were now mixed there was nothing specifically for men. Early in

1905, therefore, Dean Ring invited the new Archbishop, Francis Bourne, to come and relaunch the Catholic Young Men's Society (CYMS). Bourne was sceptical: the CYMS had never caught on at all in London, so he said "he would watch them very closely." Supervised by the junior curate Fr Timothy Murphy, the group soon had hundreds of members, and they quickly raised £50 to buy equipment for their club activities in the parish hall. But then disaster struck: Fr Murphy was moved, and the LCC insisted on the demolition of the iron building, as it had only been permitted as a temporary structure. The CYMS continued to meet at Johnson Street, but both membership and enthusiasm fell off sharply.

Dean Ring was sensible enough to reserve judgment on many aspects of parish life, until he'd had the chance to study all the ins and outs, but there was one thing that had him bothered:

In my short time here I notice an extraordinary disposition to beg from the clergy, and to associate religion with material benefit. I think it is a decided loss to the moral fibre of our people not to have induced them in the past to do more for religion. I fear multitudes of them look on the priests as Protestants regard parsons viz. as clerical relieving officers.

He was shocked to discover that the schools were dependent for their outings on the Protestant Ragged School Union, and the children had to wear RSU tags for the day. It never bothered *them* where their treats came from, but Dean Ring wasn't having it: he told the schools to hold concerts for the children's parents to raise funds for excursions, or else do without. When they did raise enough money, and got their outing, the boys and girls who'd gone on the free outing from the East End Methodist Mission were excluded – all the children agreed that was fair. Dean Ring was also shocked to discover that the parish's total regular income was only about £10 a week, which was nothing like enough. For the time being, door money would have to continue. The work of the 12 outdoor collectors was vital, and he assiduously cultivated them, formed them into a committee, and gradually built up their number to 16. Their names were posted up inside the door of the church.

While constantly nagging on about the duty of parishioners to support the parish's regular running costs, Dean Ring launched a whole series of special extra fundraising projects, which he urged them to be generous to as well – though for most of those he was also willing to appeal outside the parish. Having endured one freezing cold winter, he arranged to install new central heating in the church. A hot water system recommended by Robert L Curtis cost £700, but unlike Grundy's patent system it actually worked, so the parishioners could appreciate the benefit while they fundraised to pay off the money. Nevertheless, Dean Ring toyed with the idea of ripping out the electric light fittings and reinstalling gas, to save money, because gas was cheaper. He was very relieved when a whole lot of essential maintenance work on the church – repointing the stonework, and clearing blocked drains which were undermining the foundations – was carried out by volunteers, with scaffolding loaned by Calnan's and Gibbs', so that only the cost of materials had to be paid for. Much to his surprise the volunteers insisted that their names not be publicised, not out of modesty but for fear that other parishioners would have a go at them about it.

Fr Carey had started a parish magazine, and its success inspired Dean Ring to launch *Rector's Realm*, a customised insert in the monthly *Messenger of the Sacred Heart.* Costing 1d, it was available from the church and the convents, or from several dozen parishioner distributors, and became a wildfire best seller. People who missed an issue would pay way over the odds for one that somebody else had finished with. Local firms bought advertising space, politicians trembled under the lash of Dean Ring's editorials, and local newspapers gleefully reprinted some of his choicer diatribes. He unashamedly played to the gallery by publishing his correspondence with local government officials, with comments on the correspondents – such as "This man whose ignorance does not excuse his stupidity…" Reporting on the success of his first parish mission, in 1905, he wrote that some of the men who turned up admitted that the last time they'd spoken to a priest was when Fr Mathew came over in 1843. During 1906, in the lead-up to the church's Golden Jubilee celebrations in December, the magazine featured a serialised parish history. Rehearsing the money worries of his predecessors, Dean Ring quipped that the present rector was glad that "the time of sending priests to prison for debt is past. He is fast qualifying for it." Parishioners who were generous in their giving were openly named and praised; those who were not were left mercifully anonymous, but their feeble excuses were analysed with biting sarcasm. In the interests of transparency and trust, the accounts for the outdoor collections, fundraising drives, and parish groups were always published in the magazine.

For parishioners living along the route of the outdoor procession to set up shrines in the windows of their houses was now a well-established tradition. They were often very elaborate, and Dean Ring warmly defended them against critics who muttered about their being a waste of money. The procession used to halt at each one to pray a Hail Mary. In 1906 two working men, Michael Harrington and Mr Shea, spent weeks preparing a 12 ft high altar on a street corner along Brook Street (the eastern stretch of Cable

Street): Harrington invested nearly £30 in it, and during the procession Fr Fletcher knelt there for a whole decade of the rosary. The procession always went along Commercial Road, then south to Cable Street and along that, and then back to Commercial Road to return to the church. Slight variations of route were possible from year to year, but it never went north of Commercial Road: this was because actually crossing the road, and then crossing back, would have completely blocked the traffic for most of the afternoon. A fruitful source of strife in the parish (one of many) was the procession's *not* going down streets where some of the parishioners lived, and Dean Ring had to keep explaining that it couldn't go everywhere.

The majority of participants were children, and the children were the star of the show. Little girls loved dressing up in white dresses and veils, and plenty of women were involved in organising the children, whereas the men were naturally inclined to feel self-conscious about it. So unless they were actually in the band, or serving as stewards, or needed to form small "guards of honour", most men preferred to stand on the pavement and watch: that way, they were not making a spectacle of themselves, and inviting "remarks" from their non-Catholic workmates. But it also meant that if any spectators did start poking fun at the procession, a fight would start. The organisers had identified this problem early on, and urged that no Catholics should ever watch from the pavement: they must all take part, as a way of bearing witness to their faith, and they must remain in the procession regardless of any provocation, relying on the police to deal with trouble-makers. Dean Ring was determined to have the men parishioners walking in the procession. Even Charles Berg was reluctant, but Dean Ring insisted and got his way. At first he could only get about 50 or so men to join him, but gradually the numbers built up.

He described himself as a constitutional Irish nationalist, and had friends in all parts of the national movement, including those by no means committed to constitutional means. He prided himself on his ability to speak Gaelic. On St Patrick's Day shamrock was given out from the altar, and the children sang hymns in Irish. For Christmas Midnight Mass, the best-attended service of the year, entrance was by ticket only, obtainable from Michael Welton: the tickets were free, and their purpose was to exclude potential troublemakers. Two ethnic churches were currently operating within the parish: one for Lithuanians on the corner of Christian and Cable Streets, and a Polish Chapel in Mercer Street, Shadwell. The Lithuanian Chapel eventually moved back to Bethnal Green in 1912, but the Polish Chapel remained in Shadwell until 1930, when it relocated to Islington. Polish and Lithuanian contingents regularly took part in the outdoor processions. The Queen of Saxony attended Mass at St Mary and St Michael's in 1905, and in 1906 Queen Natalie of Serbia sat in on one of Fr Vaughan's children's services.

Bernard Vaughan loved his work in the East End, but was naturally aware that his position there was somewhat anomalous, so he'd initially been quite nervous about such a forceful new character as Timothy Ring taking over. What if they failed to hit it off? Some people were definitely anticipating a bust-up, but as Dean Ring put it, "We fairly disappointed the prophets. I early saw in him a surprising humility and charity, and I think he credited me with some feeling for the poor. This was for him sufficient." A new curate, Vincent Magrath, was trying to build up the Boys' Brigade, and Vaughan picked up on the financial difficulty about uniforms, which led him to start a clothing club. He appealed for second-hand clothing and boots, obtained donations of new items from certain factories in Lancashire, and mobilised his Children of Mary to sew for the cause. The sales side was run from the Blue Nuns' convent. Parishioners could go round any Thursday or Saturday night, and purchase items very cheaply – often below cost – but there was no giving things away for nothing, and Dean Ring warned that Mother De Sales had "a bucket of water up her sleeve for cadgers and humbugs". All proceeds went back to the Farm Street Children of Mary to purchase more materials for their sewing.

Around the end of August each year, special trains took thousands of working-class families from Tower Hamlets and Southwark out into the countryside, to fill the seasonal need for large influxes of unskilled labour during the fruit and hop harvest. It was hard work, in extremely basic living conditions, but as well as a welcome opportunity to earn some extra money, it was the nearest they ever got to a holiday. About one in five hop pickers were of Irish Catholic descent. Dean Ring noted that about half the parish schoolchildren went hopping, far more than in previous generations when a higher proportion of parishioners were relatively well-off. He praised poor women hop pickers who made a point of leaving their weekly outdoor collection pennies with Protestant neighbours, to be given to "the Chapel man" with an explanation for their absence.

No proper arrangements had as yet ever been made for pastoral care of Catholics out in the hop fields, though Anglican missions and other charities were quite active. This changed after Bp Amigo made a visit to Maidstone in 1904, to see for himself how the hop pickers lived. Shortly afterwards he received a letter from one of the local Anglican curates, urging him to do something for the Catholics, and in August 1905 the first mission team was set up: a couple of priests, a couple of Sisters of Mercy, and some lay volunteers drawn from the Franciscan tertiary movement. Young laymen served as "scouts", riding bicycles round the hop fields to look for Catholics, and invite them to Mass and evening entertainments at the mission bases, which were large tents borrowed from the Catholic Boys' Brigade. One of the early scouts recorded that he would always claim to be personally acquainted with each hop picker's parish priest: this immediately got them talking, because even though many of them were non-practising, they had the greatest respect for their parish priest. The Hop Pickers' Mission became a regular annual apostolate. Kent was still part of Southwark Diocese, and each year Bp Amigo used to pick a Sunday to go to the hop fields, where he would celebrate Mass at one centre, and preach at others. His visits were very popular with the pickers, and they flocked to see him.

Many a loving deed of mercy

Sisters of Mercy Commercial Road 1904

The Sisters of Mercy had at last managed to lease a plot of land, in Hardinge Street, to build themselves a proper residence to replace their cramped and damp premises on Commercial Road. Rev Mother Alphonsus Gilson, who was superior over the turn of the century, supported by Mother Aloysius Sheridan, took out a loan of £3,000 to allow the building work to begin, while a "Homeless Nuns" appeal was launched to pay off the debt. Early in 1906

Dean Ring chaired a meeting at the Sisters' existing house, and spoke powerfully on their behalf. The Hardinge Street Convent would be:

a centre from which the light of the Faith and many a loving deed of mercy would radiate to the furthest bounds of Stepney, a central refuge for all in sorrow or need.

A Ladies' Committee was formed to help with the fundraising, with Patrick Considine's wife as president, and Miss Maggie Browne and Miss Powell as secretaries. Two local Liberal MPs, William Wedgwood Benn (St George's in the East) and William Pearce (Limehouse), lent their names as patrons (neither of them were Catholics). Present parishioners, former curates, former pupils who were now in positions of wealth or influence, Bp Amigo and Fr Vaughan, all rallied round. A Grand Concert at the People's Palace in February, with a troupe of artistes mobilised by Frank Graham of the Actors' Association, and his wife Madame Emily Tate, served both to raise money and to publicise the appeal far and wide.

The Sisters took possession of their Hardinge Street home, and began moving in, in March 1906, but the official opening was not until November, when the chapel, with its beautiful marble altar, was ready for use. One of the settlement workers had paid for the floral arrangements, and it was "exquisitely decorated with white lilies and chrysanthemums". Dean Ring celebrated Mass, and Abp Bourne preached, speaking of how:

in the midst of the darkness of East London, these patient, noble spouses of Christ had toiled for fifty years... Year after year they had worked in silence and retirement. The back street, the dark alley, the crowded schoolroom had been the scenes of their devoted labours... But now it was time that the splendid work of the Sisters should be more widely known, and he appealed to all present to speak of it to their friends far and near and do their utmost to clear away the debt that still remained on the convent.

Mme Adeline Patti

Fr Vaughan preached at Benediction that evening, when the service closed with the singing of "Mother of Mercy".

Arrangements were made for the parish to lease from Mr Calnan a piece of ground in Johnson Street, just opposite the schools, and behind the new Convent of Mercy. A parish garden fete was held to raise the £270 to secure it, and Abp Bourne came to bless the foundation stone, which was then ceremonially laid by the Duchess of Norfolk. The entire cost of the new parish hall – £3,000 – was raised by Fr Vaughan, who begged for it widely and tirelessly. At his biggest concert ever, this time at the Albert Hall, yet another retired artiste – Mme Adeline Patti (Baroness Cederström) – made a sensational reappearance which completely filled the venue.

Constructed by Calnan and Sons, the two-storey building was opened in April 1907. The actual hall, complete with stage, was on the first floor, downstairs there were clubrooms and children's play areas, and Vaughan had been promised a grand piano and a billiards table. The building's primary purpose was to accommodate the CYMS club activities, but there was plenty of space for other groups, even in the evenings (let alone during weekdays, when it was used by the school): Dean Ring assured the parish that there would be a room for young ladies – and that by young lady, he meant anyone under 90. Fr Vaughan wanted it named in honour of Our Lady, while Dean Ring wanted to call it the Vaughan Memorial Hall, in honour of both the late Cardinal and Fr Bernard himself. Both names stuck: the upper floor was always known as Our Lady's Hall, but the bottom half came to be referred to as the Vaughan Club.

The battle for the schools

England's faith schools were eyed with deep hostility by large and vociferous interest groups. Secularists disagreed with religious education altogether. Nonconformists wanted to extend the existing system, whereby public funds paid for "simple Bible teaching" in the council schools, but objected to "their" rates going to pay for Catholic or High Anglican doctrinal teaching.

Both groups threw their support to the Liberal Party, on the understanding that it would overturn the 1902 Education Act. The LCC, which had a Liberal majority, actually passed a resolution protesting against being required to levy rates for faith schools. However some Liberal candidates in East London sought to distance themselves from their party's stance, because they recognised the very high level of support for faith schools in Tower Hamlets among Catholics and High Anglicans, and also among the Jews: Catholics and Jews were mostly Liberal supporters, and should not be alienated.

LCC inspectors came round to all the "non-provided" schools (ie schools where voluntary bodies, as opposed to school boards, had provided the buildings) and in a large number of cases condemned the buildings. This had nothing to do with sectarian bias: most of them were in an appalling state. A lot of Anglican schools had to close. The inspector who came to Johnson

Street had a go about the inadequacy of the playground, which was a parish responsibility, but studiously ignored the fact that the infants were sitting on makeshift benches made out of old scaffolding planks: Dean Ring pulled him up sharply. St Mary and St Michael's, having so recently rebuilt its Boys' and Infant Schools, wasn't as overwhelmingly threatened as many other Catholic parishes, which faced impossibly high demands. Nevertheless £1,180 had to be spent upgrading the new schools. In the Girls' School, which still occupied the original, unaltered, 1840s building, so that several classes had to operate in different corners of the large schoolrooms, £2,500 had to be spent putting in partitions, and iron staircases for access to the upper floors.

Meanwhile Dean Ring joined Fr Beckley, the Duke of Norfolk and the architect Robert L Curtis on a special committee to study needs across the Archdiocese. The cost of bringing all the schools up to LCC requirements, they reckoned, would be £100,000, so they launched a campaign to raise this sum. It was a massive struggle, but the target was eventually reached, and of the 85 Catholic elementary schools in London, not one had to close. Ring was always said to have been the main driving force behind the fundraising. Fr Beckley's work on the London School Board had been highly regarded, and Wedgwood Benn had agreed to get him co-opted onto the Education Committee of the LCC, but didn't. Dean Ring never forgave what he saw as a broken promise.

At LCC insistence the two boys' schools were united under Donovan, and the second headteacher post suppressed. The managers offered to keep Mr Jordan on at the same salary as before (presumably making up the balance from parish funds), and Donovan promised to be as accommodating as possible, but Jordan refused to accept demotion: in the end he had to be physically compelled to leave the premises, and then he tried to sue the school – albeit without success, as the judge immediately ruled that there was no case to answer. The LCC was cutting down staffing levels in the Catholic schools, and also keeping teachers' salaries on the old, terribly low, scales. When proposals for bringing them into line with LCC scales were eventually unveiled, there was an uproar because (to keep rates increases down) it had been decided not to recognize previous service in fixing initial salaries. This meant that a lot of senior teachers' salaries would go *down*. Grade I headteachers in Catholic schools previously received a minimum commencing salary of £175 for men and £140 for women, but under the new LCC proposals they would receive a maximum of £130 for men and £116 for women. (It never occurred to anyone to pay equal rates to women for equal work!) Mr Donovan chaired a big protest meeting of London Catholic teachers, in July 1905, at the schools of St Peter's Italian Church.

A key aim of the 1902 Education Act was to make secondary education more widely available, while firmly rejecting any suggestion that it should be available for everyone. The very brightest children in the elementary schools would be creamed off, by means of scholarships and free places enabling them to attend private grammar schools. A wide range of scholarships, from the LCC or from charitable foundations, were open to anyone, and Catholic schools encouraged children to compete for them. Since the St Mary and St Michael's school endowments were no longer needed to help with running costs, it was agreed with the diocese that the Richard Neale Fund be used in future to provide a tiny number of scholarships for children from all the parishes in Tower Hamlets. These scholarships were only open to Catholics, and *had* to be taken up at Catholic grammar schools: Howrah House in Poplar for girls, or St Ignatius, Stamford Hill, for boys.

Meanwhile, £500 of the Fund was set aside for building a Catholic central school. It was understood that this would be a very long-term project, and no one had any idea when, or how, it could be made a reality. Lady Edmund Talbot started scholarship classes at the settlement, to coach potential winners. Every child in the parish schools who won a scholarship had to write a letter to Ring, and the letters were published in the parish magazine. Looking to the future, the Sisters of Mercy sent four young nuns to teacher training college for two years: it had never been necessary before, but soon it would become essential. Both they and Mr Donovan were becoming increasingly concerned about the fate of school leavers in the job market. It was the easiest thing in the world for a 14-year-old boy to step into a job, because employers liked to take on young lads for running messages and making deliveries, but once they reached 17 or 18 and could expect a man's wage they were sacked, and often found it impossible to get steady work again for the rest of their lives. Donovan urged parents to put their sons into apprenticeships. To provide opportunities for the girls, evening and Saturday classes were started at the Convent of Mercy in typing, shorthand and book-keeping, each at a few shillings a term.

Meanwhile the prospects for Catholic education took a turn for the worse, after the Liberals won a landslide victory in the General Election of January 1906, and introduced a swingeing new Education Bill which would have turned all the non-provided schools into council schools. Parents' meetings were called in parishes through London, and on Sunday 23rd April, Catholics from all over Tower Hamlets flocked to a big open-air protest meeting in Harris Court, where they were addressed by Dean Ring. Their schools "were raised, he said, by the pennies of the poor, without any help or endowment, and they intended, come what may, to keep them as Catholic schools.

(Cheers.)" Patrick Considine and Fr Higley also spoke. With banners flying and bands playing, everyone then marched to Dellow Street. Dean Ring spoke again, and Considine read out a letter from Wedgwood Benn MP: "Please apologise for my absence… As regards the Education Bill, would you please make it clear that I am fully determined to carry out in every way the pledges I gave at the election for the safeguarding and protection of the Catholic schools." More speeches were then made, and resolutions passed condemning the Bill.

In May Abp Bourne presided over an impressively huge turnout of London Catholics at the Albert Hall, demonstrating that the Church's rank and file were solidly behind their hierarchy on this one. The Nonconformists' were campaigning under the slogan "Rome on the Rates", asking how the Catholics dared to demand public funding for "sectarian" doctrinal teaching; Bourne riposted with the counter-slogan "The Rates on Rome", pointing out that the Catholics had been subsidising the rest of the British population for years, by contributing heavily to maintain their own schools, while also paying rates to maintain the board schools which their children didn't use.

The Irish Party fought the Bill in the Commons, and the Catholic peers fought it in the Lords. Although the Irish MPs were willing to negotiate a compromise, the peers were intransigent, and the government decided to drop it. Before the end of the year, however, trouble broke out in St George's over the Stepney Borough Council elections. A leaflet attacking the Catholic schools was circulated by the Liberals. About 300 Catholic voters attended a meeting at the Town Hall where all the Liberal candidates were on the platform. Each one in turn stated that he did not agree with the leaflet – yet their names were on it, and a note saying it had Benn's approval. Ring took the floor and spoke for over half an hour, to loud cheers, then declared "that next March, at the County Council election when he is to stand as a candidate, he would teach them what Liberalism meant."

A Catholic Federation, on a model pioneered in Salford Diocese, was started in Westminster in 1907. Immediately a Stepney branch was launched at Commercial Road, and it soon had 180 members drawn from several local parishes. Edward Brennan, a longstanding Commercial Road parishioner and League of the Cross member who was now on Stepney Borough Council, was president, and the honorary secretary was John Doyle. Dean Ring pushed it hard, and he was also on the diocesan committee set up to co-ordinate the various branches. Efforts were made to ensure that the Westminster Federation was not seen as a Conservative stalking horse (as the Salford version was), and the Hon Charles Russell (a Liberal politician) was made overall Chairman. Ring's decision to stand for election that year to the LCC seemed only natural, given his considerable past experience in local politics. Like most of the London Irish, he described his politics as "Progressive" (ie Liberal), but as a priest he saw himself as above party politics as such. In an enthusiastic meeting at St Patrick's, Wapping, interspersed by musical interludes from the St Mary and St Michael's band, the local Federation pledged its backing to both Dean Ring, and Dr J W Lynch of 372 Commercial Road, to stand for St George's in the East in 1907 as "Catholic Independents".

The Conservative candidates – Percy Simmons and Dr W R Smith – fell over themselves to be nice to Ring, because their best chance of getting in was for the Catholic candidates to split the Liberal vote. The East End Methodist Mission's newsletter jumped into the fray in support of the Liberals. Dismissing some of its statements as seriously inaccurate or misleading, the pro-Liberal *East London Observer* urged Peter Thompson to "correct the zeal of his youthful editor", while the *Catholic Herald* (also pro-Liberal) accused the Wesleyan deaconesses of "going round in a most insidious and unfair way, misrepresenting the Catholic position". As Dean Ring's attitude hardened, he grew increasingly hostile to the Liberals, and began making abusive comments about their candidates, the sitting members Harry Gosling and J Smith, and sounding more and more Conservative in his speeches. The *Catholic Herald* accused him of hatching a plot with the Conservatives whereby Dr Smith would stand down, and *he* would become the second Conservative candidate along with Simmons. The Liberals promptly bought up large quantities of the *Herald* and distributed a free copy, carefully marked, to every voter in the division. A protest letter to the *Herald* signed by Patrick Considine (the paper's local stringer), and a long list of other Commercial Road parishioners, failed to elicit a retraction. Despite repeated scathing criticisms of the Ring-Lynch candidature, the *Herald* nevertheless urged the Catholics to vote for them. Poor Dr Lynch began worrying that they might really win, and made a point of being out of town on election day.

The pro-Conservative *East London Advertiser* rated Ring's chances as excellent, but when the votes were counted, the highly popular Gosling headed the poll, and Simmons won the other seat, while Ring trailed in fourth place. The *Catholic Herald* complained bitterly that the debacle had achieved nothing except to enable the Conservatives to capture a safe Liberal seat. The *Jewish Chronicle*, which had taken a keen interest in the elections because seventeen of the candidates, including Simmons, were Jewish, remarked primly that "two candidates are stated to have stood as Catholics pure and simple. We are glad that nothing of the kind occurred as far as our community was concerned." However Dean Ring expressed satisfaction, insisting that he'd achieved his aim of teaching the Liberals a sharp lesson. Simmons made sure to keep in his good books by making donations to all the parish good causes, and arranging for the LCC to provide plenty of equipment to the schools, including two pianos: he even attended a parish bazaar, and bought an expensive hand-embroidered stole for one of the curates, Fr William O'Farrell. For a politician to be *allowed* to make donations like this was actually an honour: politicians whom Dean Ring disapproved of had their donations angrily returned.

The Liberal government kept on introducing Education Bills, and though none of them got through, tensions remained high. In March 1908 the Catholics of Stepney held a protest meeting at St George's Town Hall. According to the *Universe*: "the platform included all classes, Irish and English, working men and professional men, clergy and laity, school managers and Catholic officials – all alike were there to testify with united voice their opposition to Mr. McKenna's Education Bill." Also present were Percy Simmons LCC, and Wedgwood Benn MP. The audience was close-packed and noisy, with a large crowd outside of people unable to get in, but eagerly joining in the cheers and shouts. Dr Joseph Jerome Reidy chaired.
Born in Limerick, Reidy had arrived in England in the early 1890s, and there met and married his wife Frances, a nurse from Co Derry. They came to Commercial Road in 1905, and Dr Reidy built up one of the largest medical practices in East London: he became a Life Governor of the London Hospital, while Frances joined the Committee of the Children's Hospital, and was very involved in fundraising for all sorts of local charities. Dean Ring spoke first, followed by Councillor Edward Brennan, and Fr Bernard Vaughan. Other speakers were John W Gilbert, nephew of Mgr Daniel Gilbert and Secretary to the Providence Row Night Refuge, who was emerging as an expert on Catholic education, and Anstruther. Benn got up and tried to speak, unfortunately bypassing the Chairman (which didn't go down well), and got a very hostile reception from the audience. At Dean Ring's request they agreed to allow the MP five minutes, but quickly changed their minds and shouted him down. The meeting was then tactfully brought to a close with a verse of "God Bless Our Pope."

I declare this altar now unveiled

A parish census identified approximately 9,000 Catholics living in the parish: 3,000 men, 3,850 women and 2,150 children. Average adult Mass attendance had fallen slightly to around 1,700 (1,000 women and 700 men), though it was still nearly double that of any other East End parish. The attendance of the

1,300 schoolchildren was policed by 40 prefects (20 boys and 20 girls), who took a register each Sunday, and would check up later on anyone who was missing. Dean Ring noted that some of the children had no shoes, even in winter, but they still came to Mass. He knew that adult parishioners usually wouldn't attend if they had nothing to wear except their soiled workclothes, and he was sympathetic to their embarrassment, though he tried to point out that God would understand. Missing Mass because you had to work on Sunday he regarded as a valid excuse. 300 of the children still attended the afternoon Catechism, for which attempts to secure higher attendance levels had been abandoned as a lost cause. (It kept going into the thirties, but by then Dean Ring was slamming it as a total failure because it attracted "only" about 100 children!) Home visits were carried out systematically, with the parish divided into five districts, and one of the five priests responsible for each. As in most parishes, visitation was linked to the outdoor collection: the lay collectors called weekly for a small sum (about 1d) from each parishioner household, but once a month the priest would come instead, and then it was a matter of pride to give at least 6d.

Sacred Heart numbers had begun dropping since Fr Carey moved on to become parish priest of Bow Common, but Holy Family membership had been built up again to 400, Children of Mary was 300, and the League of the Cross 100. Captain Brooks, instructor for the Boys' Brigade, was working hard to knock it into shape, and present well-executed drill displays and band music to showcase its work, and persuade parents to let their sons join. The CYMS was doing well, and had started a junior section for teenage boys, supervised by Brooks and Dan Whelton: men and boy members together came to about 400. Football and swimming were popular: the 1907 swimming contest was held in the Thames and won by Mr Heggarty, while the runner-up Mr Spollon had earlier that day saved the life of someone who fell in the lake at Victoria Park. A concert or a lecture was organised every other week, and talks on Irish issues were featured whenever a suitable speaker was available: Charles Russell gave one on Wolfe Tone. In 1908 Dean Ring presided at the first CYMS annual dinner, for 50 members, at the London Tavern in Fenchurch Street.

With no diversions such as television people made their own entertainments. All parish groups enjoyed putting on concerts and shows, which generally doubled as fundraisers. The CYMS and the Children of Mary held dances in the parish hall. The regular annual bazaar, for which all parish groups had their own stalls, usually made £300-£400. The proceeds from bazaars and fetes were usually boosted by money donations from local politicians and businesses: the Spiegelhalters, a German Catholic family of clockmakers and jewellers, who had had a shop at No 82 Mile End Road since 1828, were among the benefactors. The parish was always fundraising for something, and once the school improvements were paid for, Dean Ring launched a big appeal to build the church spire, and install bells – so that the Angelus could be rung, and parishioners summoned to Mass on Sundays. Abp Bourne sanctioned the appeal on condition that no work be started until all the money was in hand. A special bank account was opened up, and donations began to come in, but it had to be put on the back burner when other priorities came to the fore.

The parish was becoming quite famous, and a growing number of well-to-do outsiders were taking an interest in it. Some were brought along by Fr Vaughan or by the settlement (whose supporters moved in similar circles), while others were Dean Ring's own contacts. They made frequent donations, small or large, for the church or schools, or to help poor parish families, and thanks to them, it became easier to put on regular parties and excursions for all groups in the parish. Dean Ring didn't necessarily have a problem about free treats, provided they were both offered, and accepted, in what he felt was the right spirit, and provided that any strings attached were aimed at building up the parish, not undermining it. All treats were therefore strictly reserved for specific groups, and for those with a regular track record of faithful attendance and participation. Starting to come to something just before a treat was due, and disappearing afterwards, was an established little cottage industry in the East End, but Dean Ring was on to it, and all such "cadgers" were ruthlessly weeded out. Particularly generous benefactors were the Metcalfe family of Thorpe Bay, Essex, who'd got to know and admire Dean Ring while he was at Silvertown, and Madame Deschamps, who held a dance in Our Lady's Hall to which she invited both society friends (including two Russian émigré princesses) and local parishioners.

The 1908 Eucharistic Congress was held in London, and Ring urged all parishioners to participate in the closing event, an open air procession on Sunday afternoon. The schoolchildren were taken along on Saturday by the teachers, wearing badges in yellow and white (the Papal colours), and as they approached Westminster Cathedral they all cheered Cardinal Vincenzo Vannutelli, the first Papal Legate to come to England for 350 years, standing with the bishops on the balcony. In an essay published in *Rector's Realm*, Mary Ann Driscoll wrote: "It was so quiet and orderly that the Protestants there said there must be something in the Catholic religion to make the children behave so nicely." The Sunday procession went ahead, but there was a lot of anger because the Prime Minister, Asquith, had caved in to a minority of ultra-Protestant agitators, and banned the carrying of the Blessed Sacrament.

Pope Pius X

Fr Bernard Vaughan, asked what he thought of Asquith, quipped "Why, we think so much of him that we intend to make him legate (leg it)!" Almost immediately afterwards came a pilgrimage to Rome, to mark the Golden Jubilee of Pope Pius X. Dean Ring signed up to go, and so did at least two parishioners, though they didn't travel together. When the Dean returned, Fr Deady joked that he'd been hoping to get the spire built while he was away. He gave talks to the League of the Cross and Holy Family Confraternity about his experiences, distributed (to Holy Family members only) a lot of holy medals that he'd got the Pope to bless during a private audience, and on the next Sunday evening solemnly passed on a blessing to all the parishioners from the Holy Father.

During 1909 the parish published its own Catholic Hymnal. The celebrations for the Silver Jubilee of Dean Ring's ordination to the priesthood, in June that year, were held in Our Lady's Hall. Fr Vaughan presided, and handed over a cheque for the 210 guineas collected by the parishioners, and a solid gold celtic cross. He also did most of the talking – though he wasn't the only speaker, and Dean Ring enjoyed "a humorous speech" by his friend Jeremiah McVeagh, an Irish MP, "on my capacity for extracting silver coins from recesses which the hands of specialists only could reach".

Most transport was still horse-drawn. Motor traffic was gradually increasing, but people still weren't used to it, and there wasn't enough of it to dissuade children from playing in the streets. In a tragic accident two little girls, Jane Neville and Katie Kilduff, were killed by a newspaper van outside their homes in Brook Street. Following the Requiem Mass in St Mary and St Michael's, Dean Ring assured their parents that their pure souls were in heaven, and advocated the public lynching of drivers who sped recklessly through the streets at 10 miles an hour. However not all change was for the worse. A high proportion of East Enders had never been able to save for their old age, and when they were too old to earn a living, they went to the workhouse. Barbara Fitzgerald, when interviewed for the parish history in 1906, was living in St George's Workhouse. Nobody got up in arms about this, because it was normal: the workhouse was better than being thrown on the street, and conditions for elderly inmates had improved quite a lot since the bad old days. Now however Lloyd George, Chancellor of the Exchequer,

Lloyd George
Architect of Old Age Pensions

was going to bring in Old Age Pensions. The parish clergy were inundated with requests from people all over the country for documentation on their baptisms, so they could prove they were over 70: most of them didn't offer to pay expenses, but Dean Ring did all he could to help. He also devoted a large amount of space in the parish magazine to explaining how the pensions worked, and how to apply.

The League of the Cross, over five years, had collected £120 for a new high altar, and a separate collection had raised £90 for a memorial to Dean Dooley. When Madame Deschamps agreed to contribute £300, the money was all put together, and a new altar commissioned, to a gothic design by Robert L Curtis, from R S Boulton and Sons. It would weigh ten tons, so before it could be installed a new foundation had to be constructed: the old altar had stood on a concrete base only 6 in thick, on top of a 12 ft high platform filled with loose mould. Meanwhile the old altar was offered to East Ham, but as the church there hadn't even been designed yet, it was carted off by the contractors to be stored while awaiting a purchaser.

Cartoon of
Sir John Knill

Sir John Knill, a prominent south London Catholic, had been elected Lord Mayor of London, and on the Sunday before Christmas he came to St Mary and St Michael's together with his Lady Mayoress and the Sheriff. A cheer went up outside the church as the state carriage arrived, and the mayoral party in their official robes were led along a red carpet, flanked by lines of smartly uniformed Boys' Brigaders, to a place of honour at the front. Abp Edward Bagshawe (retired Bishop of Nottingham) stood in the centre of the sanctuary facing the congregation, and said: "I declare this altar now unveiled", whereupon the cover was whipped off, candles lit, and High Mass begun. The frontal had a single panel depicting the Last Supper, based on Leonardo da Vinci's famous painting, and the reredos held statues of St Patrick, St Joseph, Our Lady, St Michael, St Augustine and St Andrew – this last statue chosen specifically because the altar was intended as a memorial to Dean Dooley. The ceremony went off without a hitch, and the well-trained men and boys choir handled the unaccompanied Gregorian chant with "admirable efficiency".

The chapel to the right of the altar, originally designated St Patrick's, had become the Sacred Heart Chapel, and the Sacred Heart Confraternity was raising funds to beautify it. That to the left had always been the Lady Chapel, as originally intended. Dean Ring was inclined to defer its beautification until he could also move the organ. He always said the position of the organ was "like a toothache" to him, because it meant the chapel in the far left corner could hardly be used, and (in his view) it also spoiled the appearance of the Lady Chapel. Shifting it, however, would be a really major operation.

A year of elections

Lloyd George drew up what he called a People's Budget to tax the super-rich (not all that heavily) in order to finance the Old Age Pensions. When the House of Lords threw out the budget, the Liberals vowed to take the issue to the people, and called a General Election for January 1910. The Catholic bishops issued a joint Pastoral, stressing the importance of establishing where candidates stood on the schools issue, and voting accordingly. Dean Ring and his clergy went all out to urge their flock to vote for the Conservative Percy Simmons, rather than the Liberal sitting member Wedgwood Benn. Even from the pulpit, though names were scrupulously never mentioned, they were told in meaningful tones that they ought to vote, as their priests directed them, for "the man who would support the religious education of their children."

However most of the parishioners, besides being Liberal supporters by long tradition, and convinced that the Liberals were the only hope for delivering Home Rule to Ireland, wanted the People's Budget. They naturally got very upset about the line their clergy were taking, and the parish split into two factions. A small group rallied to the priests' support, but the vast majority – something like nine out of every ten – found themselves in the doghouse. It was alleged that local Catholics were being told they would go to hell if they didn't vote as the priests directed. This probably wasn't strictly true, but it did indicate the pressure people felt was being put on them.

Many parishioners belonged to the United Irish League, which operated virtually as a Liberal constituency association. On the evening of Friday 7th January, the League planned a big meeting at St George's Town Hall, Cable Street, to promote Benn's candidature. Speakers would include Benn himself, Harry Gosling, and Charles Mathew, a prominent barrister who was a great-nephew of the Apostle of Temperance Fr Mathew. A huge crowd began to assemble outside two hours beforehand, and grew to about 2,000 by the time the speakers were due. They were being escorted from Wapping Station in a procession, led by a drum and fife band, and when the band was heard approaching the town hall doors were opened. Everyone surged forward, and on one side of the door the iron railings collapsed and a number of men fell through into the area. At the sound of shrieks the crowd eased back, while inside the building, the caretaker rushed down to the basement. Looking up, he spotted Dr Reidy on the pavement, shouted to him to jump down, and caught him in his arms. Nothing could be done for one man, who must have been killed instantly when a huge block of fallen masonry crushed his head. Ten others had been injured, four seriously. Inside the Town Hall, Mathew went up to the platform and announced that the meeting was cancelled. Benn moved a vote of condolence and sincere sympathy with the relatives of the deceased man, who was later identified as Andrew Ramsay, a 51-year-old sailor from Dundee.

Throughout his campaign, Benn reiterated his promise to protect Catholic interests if elected, but this cut no ice with Dean Ring. On the evening before the election, the St Mary and St Michael's clergy issued a circular alleging that Benn would turn the nuns out of the schools and destroy them: "Catholics of St George's-in-the-East, follow your priests, who never lead you astray, and do not vote away the religion of your children." The Dean's followers cunningly distributed the circular outside the Town Hall, as people were leaving *after* a Liberal meeting: this was so the Liberal speakers wouldn't have the chance to confute it – though when they found out what was happening they called the people back in and continued the meeting, in order to answer the allegations in the circular. Pro-Liberal parishioners were extremely angry about the election eve circular, and a young Benn supporter named Daniel Hunt spoke his mind rather strongly. Lucy Fleming, the presbytery housekeeper, and a Mrs Mary Donovan complained that he had called Fr Ring "a dirty rotter", and that if he wasn't "turned off the altar" they would get up a petition. A few days later Fr Magrath walked into the Vaughan Club, where Hunt was playing billiards, and ordered him out. Patrick Considine took details, and a headline appeared in the *Catholic Herald*: "YOUTH EXPELLED FROM CATHOLIC CLUB". Hunt, a senior altar server and a teetotaler, was generally considered an exemplary Catholic, yet according to the *Herald* he had been expelled for refusing to support Simmons. Fr Magrath filed a libel suit again the *Herald.*

Benn beat Simmons by a comfortable 434: the vast majority of the Catholics *and* the Jews had voted for him. The Liberals won across the country, though their majority was much reduced, making them dependent on the Irish and Labour votes in Parliament. Despite the close result, the Lords accepted that the government had been given a clear mandate, and passed the People's Budget. But the underlying constitutional question – whether the Lords had the right to block legislation indefinitely – remained. It was a burning problem for the Liberal administration, because the Lords were overwhelmingly Conservative, and inveterately hostile to virtually all the key policies which the Liberals wanted to implement. In particular, the Lords were determined to block any attempt to give Home Rule to Ireland.

After what happened in 1907, both Liberals and Conservatives had decided that one of their two candidates in the 1910 LCC elections for St George's in the East had better be a Catholic. The Conservatives picked John Gilbert, whom they'd already co-opted onto the LCC Education Committee, and the Liberals chose Charles Mathew Mathew wrote to the Borough of Stepney Catholic Federation, asking to be allowed to address a meeting, but they refused, and shortly afterwards announced that they were officially endorsing Gilbert. They then invited both Gilbert and Mathew to hold a debate, but Mathew felt, reasonably enough, that they were trying to set him up, and angrily refused the invitation. On the Federation's instructions, John Doyle then published the correspondence in the local newspapers, in a blatant attempt to discredit Mathew (which may well have backfired). As the election date approached, Gilbert published a very pointed letter of support from Bp Amigo:

I most earnestly hope that the L.C.C. will continue to have you on its Education Committee. Your zeal and devotion have made you appreciated on that committee, and your presence there as a Catholic educationalist has ensured their knowing the needs of the Catholic body. With the best intention in the world, justice cannot be fully done to us in this important matter of education, unless we have a Catholic like yourself to explain our position. We in London know your work on our own Education Committee and as manager of a large school. You are standing for a part of London very near to my heart, and I am sure that my old parishioners will do all they can to ensure your election. Wishing you every Grace and Blessing.

Mathew simply declared: "On all general questions I am a whole-hearted and enthusiastic Progressive. On the school question I am an Irish Catholic." Charles Russell sent Ring a letter inviting him to come "to discuss an election tangle in St. George's-in-the-East." Ring had to explain that "unfortunately I was the tangle." However he insisted he'd been away when the local Federation adopted Gilbert, and a thoroughgoing enquiry held at Our Lady's Hall, with a solicitor in attendance, confirmed that it had been a democratic decision by the membership. In any case, notwithstanding all the efforts of Bp Amigo, Dean Ring and the Catholic Federation, Mathew and Gosling won St George's by a comfortable margin against Gilbert and Simmons: Gilbert received only 887 votes to Mathew's 1,492. Gilbert was mildly disappointed at his defeat, but not too upset. The Conservatives got him onto the LCC as an alderman, which actually suited him a lot better than having to kept standing for election every three years. He was to devote his life to London's local government and to Catholic education. His work was always greatly appreciated by the bishops, and he remained a lifelong friend of Dean Ring.

The dissensions at St Mary and St Michael's were only an extreme symptom of trouble in parishes across the country. People in Southwark Diocese were scandalised when a priest threatened to "call down from the Altar the curse of God" on the United Irish League activists if they didn't desist from distributing leaflets outside the church after Mass. The Liberals were determined to push through constitutional reforms to limit the power of the House of Lords, so another General Election was called for December 1910, and Lloyd George exercised his talent for demagoguery all round the East End, addressing vast audiences of working men (no women were allowed in, for fear of suffragette hecklers!) and poking fun at a parasitic landowning class who neither delved nor span, but yet enjoyed lives of luxury. If the hierarchy's political advice was going to be totally ignored by large sections of the laity, the hierarchy needed to backtrack, fast, and reign in the Catholic Federation before it caused any more damage. At a Federation Council meeting in the Cathedral Hall, therefore, Lister Drummond solemnly moved "That this Council... does not consider it advisable to submit questions to candidates at the forthcoming election the issues not directly affecting Catholic interests." He affirmed that this policy had "the strong approval of his Grace the Archbishop", and the resolution was passed.

It was during the December 1910 Election that Fr Magrath's case against the *Catholic Herald* was finally heard. The priest admitted in court that he always took the *Herald*, as it was very interesting, though he didn't agree with its political line. He was himself a Liberal and a Home Ruler, but thought the education issue took priority. Asked if it was normal in the Catholic Church to expel someone from a club on the basis of women's tittle-tattle, without making any proper enquiries, he insisted that a whole lot of "reasonable people" in the parish had complained about the language used by Daniel Hunt about Dean Ring; however he himself had never actually heard him use the words "dirty rotter". Hunt stated on oath that he was very fond of Dean Ring, and had never used insulting language about *him*, only about his circular. But John Doyle, who had been helping distribute the circulars, testified that Hunt took one, tore it up, threw it on the ground, stamped on it and said, "He's a dirty rotter." Counsel solemnly asked whether the word "rotter" was an offensive term. "It is considered by some to be offensive," was the equally solemn answer. The judge raised a laugh by enquiring whether "in some cases it would be considered merely a term of affection?"

Patrick Considine testified that as a result of Dean Ring's political campaign the atmosphere in the parish was "something awful": the two sides weren't talking to each other, and priests with whom he had previously been on the friendliest terms would cross over the road to avoid meeting him. Dr Reidy confirmed that they were "all at sixes and sevens", and that several other court cases were in progress; someone had just threatened *him* with a writ. Counsel for the Plaintiff asked how a 90% majority could be made to feel boycotted by a minority of 10%; the answer of course, though nobody quite felt able to explain it to an outsider, was the immense emotional influence exercised within an Irish Catholic parish by the priests. The jury found for Fr Magrath, but thought the *Herald*'s reporting was "partly true", so only awarded £10 damages with leave to appeal. St Mary and St Michael's proud tradition of active participation in local government was as strong as ever, but it had come of age, and the laypeople were doing things *their* way. Dr Reidy had recently joined Brennan on the Borough Council, while Mrs Reidy, Ed Gibson, George Lewis and other parishioners were active on the local Boards of Guardians.

No tradesman's entrance

The 1911 parish mission was given by the Jesuits, with Fr Bernard Vaughan heading the team. On the first Sunday evening, before the mission was due to start, he led all the priests and altar boys in procession round the parish, with the Boys' Brigade band playing and League Guards acting as stewards, and stopping at intervals to give short talks and invite people to come to the service. At the church, his opening sermon contrasted the people of the East End with those of the West very much to the detriment of the latter: intellectuals, and men of the world, were "too clever to acknowledge God", but there was no child at St Mary and St Michael's "with his little capless brow and his little shoeless feet who would not put his arms round his (Fr. Vaughan's) neck and tell him that he came from God, and at the end of his life would go back to God." On day two of the mission a platform was set up opposite the pulpit, and a skit staged in which Vaughan, speaking with a Cockney accent, played the part of Michael, a typical Bad Catholic who had to be persuaded (by his colleague Fr Patrick Hassan) of the error of his ways and brought to the mission, notwithstanding a string of excuses.

> *He'd "eard tell of this 'ere mission' and wanted to know what is was. Fr. Hassan patiently explained in a manner which obviously impressed 'Michael.' 'Well, I'll come and 'ave a look, Father, and if it's all right I'll come every night,' said 'Michael' in a tearful voice. 'Do you ever go to Mass?' suddenly shouted Fr. Hassan. 'Michael' was obviously ill at ease. 'Well – well – er,' then brightening as he caught at a straw, 'me missis does.' 'Your missis won't help you on the day of judgement,' said Fr. Hassan seriously.*

Eventually the wretched Michael promised to comply, and then, "the Dean'll 'ave no more cause to get at me.' At the end of the skit, Fr Vaughan

> *suddenly changing to his own personality, applied the moral, and concluded by hoping that he would meet them all one day 'at that great central door of the Heavenly mansion, where there is no servant's bell and no tradesman's entrance, but only a visitors' bell for all.'*

Another parish census was being carried out, and though it was only part-completed, Ring believed the number of Catholics was down to around 7,000. Abp Bourne was pushing hard for all parishes to establish a Blessed Sacrament Guild. Dean Ring's initial reaction, like a lot of the priests, was that this top-down directive would only mean unnecessary duplication, and extra work for nothing. Guilds and confraternities might have different names, but a lot of what they actually did was the same, and there was a tendency for them to get into a rut. Nevertheless, as part of the mission that year, Fr Vaughan launched a Blessed Sacrament Guild for the men and boys in the parish, and Dean Ring agreed to look after it. It took over the Wednesday evening slot previously allocated to the Holy Family, and men members of the Holy Family and Sacred Heart were treated as belonging automatically to the new group (while women Holy Family members were shifted to Fridays). Attendance was made compulsory for the CYMS, and strongly urged on the Boys' Brigade and older schoolboys. Charles Berg was appointed Master of the Guild, Tom Whelton was Secretary, and among the first prefects were Edward Brennan and Tom Bryan.

The format for confraternity devotions was fairly standard: rosary, an address from a priest, and Benediction. But Dean Ring made sure the Wednesday meetings got really interesting and educational talks, either by himself or by a well-chosen guest speaker: Fr Bede Jarrett was booked to give a series in August. By then there were over 500 members – 167 lived to the east of Hardinge Street, 173 to the west, and 120 north of Commercial Road, while a few came from outside the parish. A stained glass window was installed in the Sacred Heart Chapel in memory of Fr Twomey (who'd left Commercial Road for health reasons but died in 1910), showing Our Lady with St Mathew and St Agnes, in recognition of the late priest's name saint, and the sodalities he'd been in charge of. Its unveiling was scheduled for a Wednesday night, and his brother Fr Patrick Twomey, who came to give Benediction, was duly impressed by the large turnout of men. Beginning in January 1912, Ring began a tradition of holding a New Year's reception for the men of the parish, with coffee, tea, minerals and "smokes", and musical entertainment. The prefects reciprocated by hosting an annual "smoking concert", with Ring as honoured guest. John Gordon designed a Christmas card each year, which went to all members, and Miss Minnie Gordon (who played the organ for the children's Sunday Mass at 10.00) came each Wednesday to play for the Guild service. The Guild held a Blessed Sacrament procession in the church once a month, and in the annual outdoor procession they marched as a bloc, wearing their scarlet sashes.

Charles Berg had completed 25 years of service with the City Police, and was about to retire on a pension. On Sunday 3rd March 1912 he participated as usual in the Men's Guild Communion, and carried the procession banner at the evening service. On Monday afternoon he was on plain clothes duty as usual at the entrance to New Court, the Rothschilds' banking house in St Swithun's Lane. Shortly after 5.00 Leopold Rothschild's car came through. The vehicle was slowly trying to turn in the narrow lane when suddenly a man leaped forward with a revolver, and fired several shots through the back window. The chauffeur knocked the man off the running board and Berg grabbed him, but he then shot Berg in the throat before being overpowered by a passer-by. He was identified as a Jew named William Tebbitt, probably suffering from mental problems, and probably mistaking Leopold for his elder brother, Lord Rothschild, who'd left shortly before him on foot. (They'd met at the office to observe yahrzeit prayers for the anniversary of their mother's death.) Berg was taken to St Bart's in a critical condition, with the bullet embedded in his throat, though still conscious. He was in hospital for over a month, and Cardinal Bourne sent a message of sympathy, and his blessing. When the time came for the outdoor procession that summer, he was well enough to march as usual and carry a banner. He ascribed his narrow escape from death to his devotion to the Blessed Sacrament, and the prayers of the Guild. In the New Year Honours he was awarded a medal from the King.

The Blessed Sacrament Guild, now the main association for men parishioners, was often referred to simply as the Men's Guild, while the

Sacred Heart Confraternity became effectively the Women's Guild. As time went on, Dean Ring began to discourage participation by large contingents from other parishes in the outdoor procession, at the same time as encouraging *all* parishioners to take part, without exception. He assured them it didn't matter if they were shabbily dressed, what mattered was to be there: "The dockers, the coalies, the casual labourers, the men of the rank and file, who build our churches and whose children fill our schools." By 1914 the procession was 90% parochial, and men and boys slightly outnumbered women and girls.

Ladies and Sisters

While focusing particularly on St Mary and St Michael's, Fr Vaughan fundraised for, or provided other forms of support to, a wide range of East End causes. All the CSU settlements were close to his heart. He collected donations in money and kind for their boot and clothing clubs, and each year he used to take 20 horse-drawn vans full of children to Epping Forest, always breaking the journey both out and back at the Dowager Duchess of Newcastle's house in Woodford. She was too old and infirm now for settlement work, and not long for this world, but she loved to see the children, and do her bit for their day out.

When the Sisters of Mercy moved to Hardinge Street, St Cecilia's took over their former convent, so it now stretched over three houses: Nos 531-535. The work of the settlement had expanded and changed. Laywomen from the leisured and monied classes still set the tone, but as there were never enough of them, Lady Edmund Talbot arranged for four Sisters of Charity to join the team. They moved into No 533, and reopened it as a Convent of Charity on 9th December 1911. They received free accommodation, with Lady Edmund covering rates and other expenses, and additionally paying £140 a year maintenance (£35 per Sister). As soon as they moved in, Dean Ring gave them names of 135 Catholic men in just two streets who were refusing to join the Guild, for them to "make saints" of. Pope Pius X had lowered the age of First Communion, and the Sisters of Charity made it their responsibility to look after the smaller boys and ensure that their First Communion wasn't also their last. Sr Mary Ware got very cross with the boys' parents, and said she wanted to "give a right good talk" to them, because without their co-operation all her efforts were wasted.

Sisters and lay settlement workers served on the Care Committee which handled a range of issues for the parish schools in Johnson Street, including health and hygiene, and also feeding: school meals were still not provided on a systematic basis, only as an emergency measure for children in special need, and they were still heavily dependent on voluntary groups. A close collaboration developed between St Cecilia's and the LCC, which provided qualified teachers for a Domestic Economy Centre at the settlement. Girls from the school came during the day for classes in cooking, laundry and housewifery, and in the evenings older girls who'd left school could come for evening classes – taught by the same teachers. The settlement ran a school clinic, approved by the Board of Education and partly financed by the LCC, with Dr Reidy as Medical Officer. There was also a cleansing centre, where children found to be verminous could be sent for bathing and treatment. (This was considered a terrible disgrace, but the Sisters may have found ways of making it easier for the children than if they went to a council-run facility.) District visiting and follow-up of children being treated at the clinic was carried out by the Sisters, under LCC supervision. Miss Pearson worked in the clinic, while Miss Hill liaised with the Children's Country Holiday Fund, and other agencies, to organise breaks outside London for women and children: these were heavily subsidised or free, depending on what people could afford.

From the St Cecilia's House Annual Report

Work carried out September 1910 – September 1911

Visits paid to the poor in their homes	2094
Christmas dinners given to destitute children	250
Women, girls and children sent to country and convalescent homes	215
Excursions during the summer for the day	93
Numbers attending Retreats in Stamford Hill	184
Girls attending Senior Club	35
" " Junior Club	75
" " Drill Class	30
" " Millinery Class	15
" " Sewing Class	50
" " Mothers' Meeting	66
Baptisms	20
Conversions	12
Lapsed Catholics brought back to the Church	14

The King of Portugal had been assassinated in 1908 together with his eldest son, and two years later his younger son, who succeeded him as Manoel II, was overthrown by a republican revolution. The Royal Family took refuge in England, living very simply at Twickenham where they became parishioners at the local Catholic church. Queen Mother Amalia became very interested in

St Mary and St Michael's: she came down incognito, and was taken along by the settlement workers and Sister of Charity when they visited poor families around the parish. She also asked to sit in on a meeting of the Men's Guild. Elizabeth Hyde, a young music student, worked hard to put on a concert every year in aid of the school debt: later the parish repaid her by helping her raise money to go and study music in Italy. Mabel Quinlan, an Australian who'd spent some time at the settlement around the turn of the century, came back after a gap of eight years and told Dean Ring she was amazed at what had been achieved with the Men's Guild.

It is our right to have a living wage

The standard form sent out to all the parish priests in 1911, to be completed as part of that year's round of visitations, included the question: "Have secret societies, spiritualism, or socialism obtained any footing among your people?" Ring replied: "Not to my knowledge". In many parts of the world, "Socialism" was closely allied with revolutionary terrorism and militant atheism, and in the higher reaches of the Catholic Church its every manifestation was viewed with very deep suspicion. Priests and people in the East End of London, though for the most part genuinely wary of extremism, had learned to see the issues in somewhat more nuanced terms. One non-practising Catholic hunted up by the Jesuit missioners said he didn't go to Mass because he thought the Dean was too sympathetic to the suffragettes and the socialists – though the excuse fell apart when it emerged that he'd stopped going well before Dean Ring's time.

Winston Churchill at the Seige of Sidney Street

Political attitudes were becoming increasingly polarised. January 1911 had seen the Siege of Sidney Street, with the police and the army, directed by Home Secretary Winston Churchill, trying to batter their way into a house to arrest a group of foreign anarchists: when the house caught fire, Churchill refused to let the fire brigade through. During a dock strike in the summer of 1911 a young Belgian priest named Joseph Cardijn had a meeting with Ben Tillet, at the Dockworkers' Union in Mile End Road, which helped inspire him to set up the Young Christian Workers (YCW) movement. The 1911 strike succeeded, but as further strikes broke out across the country, Churchill kept wanting to call out the army, while at the other end of the political spectrum a great many English, as well as Irish, people were infuriated over the Ulster Unionists being allowed to get away with defying Parliament over Home Rule, while disproportionate violence was used against other groups which seemed to have a legitimate grievance. A second London dock strike began in the spring of 1912, and the sweated tailors in the East End struck at the same time. The (Jewish) tailors and the (English and Irish) dockers held joint meetings on Mile End Waste, and when the tailors' strike ended in victory, the Jewish families provided meals for the hungry dockers' children.

Dean Ring spoke up for the strikers: "Trusts, Combines and Companies are treating men as cab-horses, and no wonder the poor 'cab-horse' kicks. This system cannot last and the 'agitators' of today, like the Irish agitators of a generation ago, will rank as patriots if the grinding, pig-headed policy of shareholders is not radically modified." By June, parish families were suffering terribly, and he wrote to the *Tablet*, saying he'd spent £3 that day providing bread for people who were literally destitute – no question of meat or milk, they were happy just to get some dry bread. The response to his appeal was overwhelming. A committee was set up comprising himself and two curates, all the leading men in the parish, and Mother De Sales, and they began issuing food tickets to the most needy families. Five shilling tickets were given to each of 545 homes that week, all paid for by *Tablet* readers except for an overspend of £16 which was soon made up. Meanwhile Dean Ring appealed to the *Catholic Times* and the *Universe* as well, and several national dailies took up the story: Tom Whelton went round to the newspaper offices pleading with them to publicise the cause. Donations came in from Italy and St Petersburg, as well as from various parts of Ireland. The Blue Nuns, with their nursing experience, confirmed that some of those helped were weak with hunger. The children were getting free meals at school during the week, but the committee was able to organise meals on Saturdays as well, getting the food cheaply from the Alexandra Trust. Inevitably some nasty letters came in, condemning the strikers and accusing Dean Ring of prolonging the strike. He reacted with high sarcasm, asking the critics if it wouldn't be a good idea to put all the shiftless poor into a big ship like the Titanic, take it out to sea and sink it – or else string up 130,000 strikers at Tower Hill? The employers, led by Lord Davenport, were really digging in their heels; Ben Tillet, haranguing the strikers at Tower Hill, was urging them to chant "O God, strike Lord Davenport dead!" and riots broke out as the dockers battled with police and blacklegs, but eventually they could hold out no longer and returned to work. Thomas Burke, as treasurer, published the committee's final accounts. £1,350 7s 8d had been received, and used mostly for food tickets for families and for the children's dinners, with a small amount on special needs like children's boots.

Fr Vaughan was away on an extended overseas trip. He'd been overtired and badly needed a proper holiday, but couldn't be persuaded simply to stop, so undertook a lengthy preaching tour of North America. After having a marvellous time (though it was hardly a rest cure) he returned via the Far East, arriving back in London in April 1913. Early in May he came along to St Mary and St Michael's for the second anniversary of the Blessed Sacrament Guild, and nearly a thousand members turned out to welcome him home: "The church was crowded from end to end by men, with the exception of one aisle reserved for and fully occupied by their women folk." The Guild had proved an outstanding success, and Dean Ring was delighted with it. He reckoned it had rejuvenated the Catholic life of the East End generally, not just St Mary and St Michael's, and he'd noticed that if a young man asked a girl to go out with him, the first thing she wanted to know was: "Are you a member of the Guild?" He, too, had come to see membership as a litmus test of Catholicity: those who made the excuse that they "weren't good enough" were told it was for ordinary Catholics, not special people, and those who still failed to join he pilloried as "blacklegs".

On round-the-world trip, Fr Vaughan had travelled 30,000 miles and addressed half a million people. But on returning to England he'd found more and more people saying they had no use for religion, and churches closing down all over the place and being turned into cinemas. In the depths of his despondency, he'd said to himself

'Let me get away down to Commercial Road that my heart may expand and my soul may be lifted up to see the working men living on less than a pound a week rallying to the Master and more fervent in their Catholicity than in the days when they counted for more.' Jesus Christ is proud of you… you who are the wage-earners, you, who have to put out your lives for a sweated wage, you have His sympathy, and when this work-a-day world is done, and the pay-day of the eternal Sabbath shall dawn, He will make it up to you and to your children… You know Him and love Him, and you express your love in terms of service and translate that service into deeds of sacrifice. You are simply splendid men. You are the men for whom the Life and Death of Jesus Christ was worth while.

Cardinal Bourne and Fr Vaughan both attended Dean Ring's New Year reception in January 1914, and spoke about the dock strike in which many of the 500 men present had taken part. The Port of London Authority had handed over a week's pay, which had been kept back in lieu of notice in May 1912, in time for Christmas 1913. But many of the men were still out of work. Fr Vaughan said he hoped the PLA would be generous and give them their jobs back, but insisted:

> *it is our right to have a living wage… It was a terrible thing to know that down there in the East End there were people working for 4d., 3d., 2d., and even ½d. an hour. They must recognise these things as wrongs. They must lift up their voices demanding that they cease. He was grateful to the Socialists for having revealed these sores of humanity and having forced the country to look into the by-ways and hovels and slums and garrets holding the living and the dead. He thought the country was awakening… and with such a tremendous force they would bring about justice and liberty for the poor.*

Take cover

Jeremiah McVeagh wangled a seat for Dean Ring at the House of Commons so he could witness the passing of the Irish Home Rule Bill, but its implementation was suspended due to the outbreak of war with Germany. John Redmond, leader of the constitutional wing of the Irish nationalists, urged the Irish people to give every possible support to the war effort. Within a month or so, 147 parishioners had joined up. The first to be killed was John Dremond, of Newton's Rents. Over 300 wounded Belgian soldiers were brought for treatment at the London Hospital, and Dean Ring went there to say Mass: the Blue Nuns set up a temporary altar, the patients shuffled in swathed in bandages or hobbling on crutches, and people said it was "like a morning at Lourdes". Parish enlistment continued apace: the CYMS had to close down, because virtually all the members were "with the colours", and half the membership of the Blessed Sacrament Guild also volunteered. Hundreds of women parishioners swore off alcoholic drinks for the duration as an "offering of penance… for the honour of God and the safety of our people". At Christmas the usual Guild card was sent to as many of the members overseas as could be contacted, together with gifts of tobacco and cigarettes.

Fr Bernard Vaughan

War conditions led initially to shortages and price rises, and soldiers' dependents were treated shamefully, but before long many parishioners were benefiting from full employment, and high wages in munitions work. Dean Ring encouraged wives to save some of it, not spend it all in riotous living. Following the sinking of the Lusitania by a German submarine in May 1915, German homes and shops in the East End were attacked and looted, but he expressed satisfaction that Commercial Road parish hadn't suffered as much from the riots as some of the others, and that some of his parishioners had formed a guard to defend the premises of "generous and charitable" local Germans like the Spiegelhalters. The outdoor procession was held as usual, though no statues were carried, only a crucifix, and parishioners were told that the shrines need not be as elaborate as usual; soldiers in khaki were among those who marched. At the Guild meeting on Wednesday 8th September 1915, Dean Ring spoke of the wisdom of making a good Act of Contrition before going to bed, a lesson reinforced by a zeppelin raid later that night in which 106 Londoners were killed. A bus was hit and the conductor William Hammond, a Commercial Road parishioner, lost an eye. The parish had quickly to raise £32 to pay for air raid insurance, and the schoolchildren contributed 11s 6d in farthings towards the total. Miss Pearson left St Cecilia's to volunteer as an army nurse.

Fr Bernard Vaughan was much in demand as a speaker at patriotic rallies across the country, and at fundraisers for the Red Cross and the Irish units in the armed forces. He'd never pulled his punches about anything, and in a speech at the Mansion House in January 1916 he declared bluntly: "Our business is to keep on killing Germans." When a letter of protest from the German Province of the Society of Jesus was published in all the British newspapers, he commented that their feelings were perfectly reasonable, but so were his. There were a number of specifically Irish divisions and regiments, which London Irish volunteers could opt to join if they wished, and on St Patrick's Day that year, the Mayor of Stepney approved a flag day in aid of extra comforts for the Irish troops.

Roger Casement

Notwithstanding the prevailing mood of common Anglo-Irish patriotism, some of the more extreme of the Irish nationalists resolved on an armed uprising. On Good Friday, 21st April 1916, a German U-boat landed Sir Roger Casement at Banna Strand, Co Kerry, but locals tipped off the police, and he was quickly arrested and taken to London. An accompanying ship bringing a consignment of arms, intended for the conspirators, was intercepted and forced to scuttle. Despite this debacle the Easter Rising went ahead: it wrecked the centre of Dublin and resulted in 318 civilian deaths, widespread looting and economic disruption. Casement was at once transferred from Brixton Prison to the Tower of London. Meanwhile 3,500 people were arrested in Ireland, many of whom had nothing whatsoever to do with the Rising, and the courtmartialling and shooting of the ringleaders began to give them a halo of martyrdom, and turn public opinion sharply against the British government. Summary proceedings against Casement were out of the question, because he was an internationally famous humanitarian figure.

Nevertheless he was sent back to Brixton, where he gave his religion as Catholic. He stood trial for treason at the end of June, was found guilty, condemned to be hanged, transferred to Pentonville, and stripped of his knighthood. While he waited for his appeal hearing, extracts from the diary he maintained of his sex life were deliberately leaked in order to blacken his reputation. He lost the appeal. Though he was now asking to be formally received into the Catholic Church (he'd been brought up a Protestant), Cardinal Bourne hesitated. He had no sympathy for Casement or his cause, and doubted the sincerity of his conversion – but in any case, everyone was still expecting a reprieve. However once it became clear Casement would indeed go to the gallows, the Cardinal sent two of his priests to Pentonville,

to reconcile him to the Church, with a message that I would pray for him, that I wished for him every grace and blessing of Almighty God and that I would offer my Mass for him on the day of his death.

The choice of Dean Ring for this mission was a kindly touch, and it was he who heard Casement's first, and last, confession.

Completion of the new communion rails of marble and alabaster, paid for by Mrs Metcalfe in memory of her father Charles Crawley, was delayed by the war, but they were installed in 1916. They spanned the whole width of the church and cost over £500. By May 1917, about a thousand St Mary and St Michael's parishioners were in the forces, and a framed roll of honour with all their names was put up in the porch of the church. It was noted with pride that the remaining Guild members faithfully attended the meetings and monthly Communions, despite terribly long working hours, and occasional air raids. Letters arrived from absent members in Gallipoli, Palestine and Egypt, France and "somewhere in the Balkans". Tom Whelton wrote from India: he'd been promoted to Sergeant Major, and enclosed 10 rupees for anyone in need.

The first really serious air raid by planes, as opposed to zeppelins, came just before noon on 13th June 1917. Most people were more curious than frightened: they stood out in the open watching, or even climbed up on roofs or stood at windows to try to see what was going on. However 104 people were killed, 154 seriously injured, and 269 slightly injured in the East End alone, and the King and Queen visited next day to express sympathy. Though the air raids continued, no mechanism was set up for giving warnings until mid-August, when the police were made responsible for notifying the public. From then on, when a raid began, constables were sent out in all directions carrying notices saying "Take Cover". But usually the news spread quicker by word of mouth, and the streets emptied before they arrived.

The Mayor of Stepney was supposed to serve for one year, and then hand over to someone else, but the Borough had got into the habit of rotating the office round a select few, and an argument broke out about this in November 1917. Some Councillors wanted Hugh Chidgey, the outgoing Mayor, to serve a fourth term. Others objected to this, and Alderman James Kiley, who was also MP for Whitechapel, nominated Dr Reidy. The nomination was seconded by Harry Kosky. A straw poll showed the Council almost evenly split, so a ballot was taken: Chidgey got 26 votes, and Reidy 28. Reidy was declared duly elected, invested with the official robe and chain, and sworn in. It was the first time Stepney had ever had a Catholic Mayor. The civic service for new mayors was traditionally held at St Dunstan's, but Reidy insisted that his be at St Mary and St Michael's, and the following Sunday he came to Mass "in State", accompanied by the other Catholic Council members.

Mrs Reidy was a striking figure: "Tall and fair and smartly dressed, her head is usually adorned by a wonderful creation in millinery." She was said to have worked harder than any other Stepney mayoress. A lot of people couldn't understand how the pair managed to achieve so much, since he was still holding down a busy practice, and she had eight children under 11 (though they *did* have a nanny). The Chairman of the London Hospital issued an appeal for "a million half-crowns" (£125,000), and Dean Ring wrote to Mrs Reidy suggesting she try to raise a thousand from Stepney. "You may count on me for forty" he added. Mrs Reidy took up the idea with enthusiasm. To help meet the target she organised a concert in July at the People's Palace, with a talk by Fr Vaughan for good measure. Princess Beatrice attended, and Fr Vaughan gave one of his rip-roaring patriotic speeches – hitting out at both the "Prussians" and the pacifists, and lauding the Royal Family – which went down a treat.

Altogether during their mayoral year, the Reidys raised half a million pounds, either for the war effort or for philanthropic causes. Meanwhile Ed Gibson's tireless work as Secretary of the Stepney War Savings Committee was to win him an OBE.

At a meeting of the Stepney Board of Guardians, of which Fr Higley was now Chairman, everyone stood for a moment in silence to pay tribute to John Redmond, who had recently died, and to his brother Willie who had been killed on the Western Front. Another item on the agenda was to hear the report of a committee, interdenominational but including Edward Brennan and Fr Higley, on the establishing of a Catholic chapel at the Stepney workhouse, as a comfort to elderly residents. One of the non-Catholic Guardians, A E Garner, immediately handed in a donation of £10 towards adapting a room for the purpose. Stepney Guardians had come a long way since the 1860s.

In March 1918 Redemptorist Fathers Francis Prime and Richard Marsh came to give a Lenten mission at St Mary and St Michael's. Arriving at the presbytery on Saturday night, the first thing they heard was a cry of "Take Cover" which, as the *Tablet* coyly related, "was followed by an unmusical programme, which they did not appreciate." Anti-aircraft guns started up once more after the evening service on the Sunday, and on Monday, Fr Marsh was interrupted yet again in the middle of a discourse on "Death". He asked the congregation to stand up and sing "Faith of our Fathers" before moving to the shelters, and "they obeyed with the order and precision of calm and disciplined soldiers of Christ."

In September Dean Ring was made a canon. His parishioners collected more than enough to pay for his robes (which cost about £70), so they also gave him a cheque for £120 as a "war bonus". At the presentation, which was attended by the Mayor and other local Catholic politicians, Fr Bartholomew O'Doherty, parish priest of Guardian Angels, remarked that "Canons had a habit of going West, he hoped, however, that Canon Ring would live among them for many years to come." Dr Reidy stepped down as Mayor in November, shortly before the Armistice which ended the First World War.

Oil paintings

The parishioners of St Mary and St Michael's commissioned an oil painting of Fr Bernard Vaughan, and presented it to him as an expression of gratitude for all he'd done for them. He planned to give it to his old school, Stonyhurst. In his speech of thanks, he spoke about growing old (he was 73) but said that

> *he had found comfort in saying to himself: 'You have only been a poor servant, but after all if I had a servant who had served me for 50 years as I have served my Master,*

I don't think I would give him notice. I think I would give him the Old Age Pension. (Applause).'

The parish was quite into oil paintings. Any pilgrims coming to Commercial Road towards the end of 1919, according to the *Universe*, would have noted:

> *the ancient Romanesque font, now serving as a holy-water stoup; the Calvary in its bold architectural setting; the pulpit of coloured marble with white statuettes in niches of beautiful design; the unconventional placing of the organ, so that the gay pipes form a background to the Lady Altar; the homely and beautifully clean red and blue tiles, like the floor of a farm-house kitchen; and the mysterious, inaccessible chapel seen through some fine arches in the north-east corner. But perhaps he will be most struck by the great show of mellowed oil paintings in subdued frames. These works are not all good; but it must be remembered that if we unhooked at random an equal number of canvases from the walls of a Royal Academy Exhibition there would be a great many bad ones among them. While most of St. Mary's and St. Michael's pictures are soundly executed copies of works by Murillo, Vandyck, and other old masters, I was assured on the day of my visit, and I hope it is true, that some of them are originals of considerable value. Whether copies or originals, they certainly help to give a Catholic feeling to what would otherwise be rather a bare church.*

Most of the paintings had been donated by Amand Bamberger, a Parisian artist who lived in the parish during the war years. The *Universe* correspondent also mentioned an almost life-sized portrait of the late Pope Pius X, greatly revered though not yet canonised, which hung near the Calvary – and he was pleased that the choir largely abided by Pius' ruling about plainchant. Sung Mass was conducted "briskly", and over in 50 minutes: "We heard no sermon, and no Epistle and Gospel in the vernacular, and as for the notices, the genial rector settled them in the fewest words." However Canon Ring *did* mention the results of the recent Borough Council elections, which closely affected the parish.

The Stepney Labour Party comes to power

All men over 21 now had the right to vote in parliamentary elections, and also women over 30. Following a reorganisation of constituencies, most parishioners lived either in Whitechapel and St George's, or in Limehouse, while north of Commercial Road was in the Mile End constituency. Lloyd George, the Prime Minister who'd led Britain to victory, had held a General Election as quickly as possible after the war ended, and won hands down in Great Britain – though Ireland, where Home Rule was still on hold because of the determined opposition of the Ulster Unionists, voted overwhelmingly for Sinn Fein, which repudiated Redmond's constitutional approach and demanded total independence under a republican government. Meanwhile, however, the Labour Party was establishing a very solid power base in many parts of the country. Most Catholics, as soon as the Home Rule Bill went through, had dropped the Liberal Party and gone over to Labour. Oscar Tobin, a Jewish chemist in Harford Street, joined his Mile End Labour group up with the Limehouse Labour Party, led by the Catholic trade unionist Matt Aylward, to form the Stepney Trades Council and Labour Party. The way to power in East London, Tobin realised, was to build up an alliance between the Jews and the Catholics – albeit without excluding people like Clement Attlee, an atheist from a public school and university background who'd been drawn into the East End through settlement work, and was now living in a flat in Commercial Road.

Clement Attlee

In November 1919, Labour won a majority of seats on Stepney Borough Council, and made Attlee Mayor. Fifteen Catholics had been elected, and two more co-opted as Aldermen. Commercial Road parishioners Edward Sexton and George Groves were among the successful Labour candidates, while others had won seats as Liberals – Dr and Mrs Reidy, for example, and Dr Reidy's cousin Fr Callaghan Joseph Irwin, an assistant priest at St Mary and St Michael's since 1907. The *East London Advertiser* described Irwin as "Slim in build, a pale face contrasting with dark hair, his somewhat solemn expression is completely changed by a smile of great charm." Though not an eloquent preacher, "he is a clear speaker who marshals his facts and arguments in such a way that they are presented in orderly and convincing sequence." He was keen on sport and very popular with young people.

The CYMS invited all the successful Catholic candidates, regardless of party affiliation, to a celebratory concert and dance at Our Lady's Hall. Canon Ring's glee outweighed any old misgivings about Liberal intentions towards Catholic schools, or fresh ones about Socialist intentions towards private property. He made a speech saying how proud the Catholics of Stepney were of having seventeen representatives on the Council:

> *none of them were elected on religious grounds but because their neighbours thought that they were competent and capable administrators of the borough... there was no*

Catholic favour and no Catholic privilege desired or expected of them, and he hoped they would never advocate or support any policy that did not apply to every section of the community.

It was an irresistible opportunity for him to give the Borough Council a piece of his mind about the political priorities:

He hoped at once to see that the slur of insanitary dwellings would be removed from the name of Stepney. There was another matter that the Council may not have powers to tackle, but organized labour, if true to itself and to its programme, should tackle it – that was unscrupulous rent-raising. The rates were going up through nobody's fault, and property should bear its share of the increased cost of living. What did we find here? We found profiteering landlordism throwing the whole increased rate on poor helpless tenants by increases in rent from 2½d. weekly for a room up to 1s. 6d. or 2s. for a flat of three rooms.

The new Council *did* pay serious attention to housing conditions: 40,000 repair orders were served on landlords, tenants' advice bureaux were set up, and an army of sanitary inspectors and health visitors deployed. Meanwhile the news from Ireland remained disturbing. Large numbers of English ex-servicemen, recruited to help fight a guerrilla war against the Irish Republic Army (IRA), and nicknamed "Black and Tans", were earning a horrific reputation for brutality. Ring felt so let down by the British government's treatment of Ireland that he made no objection to the Sinn Fein flag being displayed alongside the Union Jack at parish events. Even Fr Vaughan, gung ho imperialist as he was, when addressing an East End audience denounced "the Black-and-Tan mob". Lord Edmund Talbot was promoted to the peerage as Viscount FitzAlan of Derwent, and appointed Ireland's very first Catholic viceroy. Lady Edmund, now Viscountess, insisted on accompanying her husband to Ireland, despite the risk. Viscount FitzAlan also denounced the Black and Tans, and managed to win the respect of many nationalists, but he couldn't stop the violence.

Look unto the Rock whence you are hewn

St George's in the East was badly in need of repair, and the Rector applied for a faculty to sell some of the church plate, arguing that his income had been badly hit by the continuing immigration of Jews and Irish Catholics into an area that had once been, at least nominally, Anglican. Canon Ring jokingly offered to buy the premises and take it off his hands. While church attendance for most denominations was already depressingly low, and continuing to fall, average adult Mass attendance at St Mary and St Michael's bottomed out and stabilised at around 2,000.

The outdoor processions were restored to their full glory. In 1920 the parish put on an even greater effort than usual, because the event was being filmed.

There were tableaux depicting Joan of Arc (canonised in 1919) and the Irish martyr Oliver Plunkett (beatified that year); someone lent a horse for Joan of Arc, but unfortunately the film didn't turn out well. The custom of selecting a girl as May Queen was introduced, greatly adding to the processions' popular appeal. In Protestant festivities the climax was the crowning of the May Queen, but in the Catholic version she crowned the image of Our Lady. It was a great honour to be chosen, and the honours were spread around by also selecting courtiers, pages and maids-in-waiting. The nuns in the school had the main job of organising all this, and drilling the selected youngsters. Everyone knew that a factor in the selection process was their families' reputation and level of parish involvement, but also their economic status, because the family had to provide the expensive special dresses and shoes.

Outdoor procession in Commercial Road

In June 1920 Canon Edwin Burton, an expert on Church history, delivered three historical sermons at St Mary and St Michael's. Quoting the text "Look unto the Rock whence you are hewn" (Is 51: 1) the first sermon began with the unknown Saxons who built the original Stepney Church which became St Dunstan's, and told the story of the Catholic faith in East London up to the

Henrician Reformation, and Tristam Swadell who was appointed to St Dunstan's by Mary, and "deprived" in 1562 – presumably for refusing to accept the Elizabethan Settlement. The next week, Canon Burton spoke about the Stepney Martyrs. The third and final sermon took the text "I the Lord have built up what was destroyed" (Ez 36: 36), and carried the story through the Penal Times to the Virginia Street Chapel, and the opening of the present church in Commercial Road. The talks hadn't been written down beforehand, but speeches at parish events were beginning to be recorded by enterprising youngsters needing shorthand practice, and they were published as a pamphlet shortly afterwards. Canon Burton was invited back later to give a series of talks on the English Martyrs. He went into particular detail on the Thames boatman, John Roche, who'd helped Margaret Ward to rescue a priest from prison, and been hanged for it: here was a London riverside worker of Irish descent, with whom the parishioners should surely be able to identify.

When Tom Whelton was demobbed and got back home, he immediately went through the Men's Guild registers to check on attendance, and go after any of the prefects who'd let things slide. The Boys' Brigade was never revived after the war. The CYMS was, but within a few years Canon Ring noticed that the members were no longer attending Wednesday devotions, or even Sunday Mass. Even the committee was no longer seen in church. The club was often closed over the summer months anyway, when attendance was very low, and in 1921 it wasn't permitted to reopen. Miss Pearson, the settlement nurse, was back at St Cecilia's, and it was agreed that she would re-launch the CYMS after a suitable interval, with the latest contingent of boy school leavers, and with the rules about church attendance strictly enforced. Soon the club was thriving once again, with a select membership of 60-70, but thoroughly part of the life of the parish. St Mary and St Michael's usually had no problem fielding a good male-voice choir, either from the Men's Guild or the Boys' School, but the old ban on female choirs in church had been quietly forgotten since shortly before the war. Both St Cecilia's Club and the Children of Mary took singing skills very seriously (St Cecilia's used to win prizes at competitions), and provided choirs for some of the Masses. Both groups also had a dramatic society.

The collection of door money from people coming in to Mass continued. Among the longest-serving collectors were Con Crane, a devout League Guard who earned a meagre living selling newspapers on the street, and Tim Murphy, an old docker now in his 80s, who still faithfully tended the plate at the early 7.00 Mass. However since Michael Whelton died a lot of people were refusing to pay, and the takings had gone down. Ring pointed out tartly that non-payers were often flash young men earning nearly £5 a week, while ill-clad girls from the poorest streets in the parish scrupulously handed over their pennies. "Of course," he wrote, "the theory is that the extra penny is given in the offertory. Observation is kept on that also, and the stingy at the door remain stingy till they go out."

Over 150 parishioners had been killed fighting overseas. A stained glass window was commissioned for the Sacred Heart Chapel – which was also now the Blessed Sacrament Chapel – as a memorial to the 134 Men's Guild members who'd given their lives. In acknowledgement of the dual purpose of the Guild Chapel, the window showed St Margaret Mary and the vision of the Sacred Heart, flanked by four saints specially connected with the Eucharist: Tarcisius, Clare of Assisi, Pascal Baylon and Juliana of Liege. A framed list of all the parish's war dead was placed in the Calvary shrine.

Women's Sodality of the Sacred Heart processing along Commercial Road

An Irish jaunting car

Quietly and unobtrusively, Attlee managed to keep peace between the Jewish and Catholic factions on Stepney Borough Council. When, in November 1920, it was time to elect a new Mayor, he appealed to them to keep "the religious question" out of it. The Labour Group negotiated between the respective nominees, Oscar Tobin and Joseph Cahill, and it was agreed Tobin should be Mayor. Cahill shook on it, but then went back on the deal. Word of the split in the Labour Party did the rounds, and at the Council meeting the galleries and public benches were packed with spectators. Sure enough a huge row broke out. It was mainly between the Catholics – at least, they were the ones getting most excited, becoming white with rage and shaking their fists at one another. Edward Sexton said that an Irishman's word should be his bond, and Cahill should have honoured the Party's agreement, whereupon Councillor O'Brien caused an uproar by calling Sexton a Black and Tan. Cahill won the final vote, which did not entirely follow religio-ethnic lines: a number of Catholics voted for Tobin, whereas Jacob Woolf Rosenthal voted for Cahill. As proprietor of the Pavilion Theatre in Whitechapel Road, the celebrated home of Yiddish drama, and as a Liberal, Rosenthal may have preferred Cahill because he saw him as less left-wing than Tobin. Attlee handed over the chain to Cahill, though without offering the usual congratulations, while pandemonium broke out among the spectators. People were shouting "Traitor!" and threatening the new Mayor, and one man had to be forcibly removed by the police. Next Sunday Mayor Cahill, wearing his chain, processed with a good number of (mostly Catholic) Aldermen and Councillors from the Town Hall in Cable Street to attend Mass at St Mary and St Michael's. The party was met at the main door by Canon Ring. Councillor Fr Irwin assisted the celebrant, and Ring preached on peace and goodwill, and the unity of the Catholic Church. Noting that "There was not the same unity in secular government, and even in the small area of the Municipal Council Chamber differences occurred", he urged them to cling more closely "to the divine teachings".

The first couple of years after the Great War had been a time of prosperity, but recession was now setting in, and large numbers were unemployed. A great many St Mary and St Michael's parishioners were thrown out of work. During his mayoral year Joseph Cahill did his duty by all the usual charitable events, so redolent of British patriotism and loyalty to the monarchy: Alexandra Day (mainly organised by Mrs Reidy) raised a record total of over £800. But Cahill also organised Sunday afternoon rallies at Tower Hill on Ireland and Unemployment. The first one, in March, had four bands, including one from St Mary and St Michael's. Cahill reckoned 5,000 came to hear the speeches and sing the songs. To resounding cheers, he put in a plug for the *Catholic Herald* as an appropriately pro-Ireland and pro-Labour paper, sold 250 copies with no trouble, and ordered 500 for the following Sunday. £10 was collected for the Irish Distress Fund.

Canon Ring needed to expand his schools. This was partly to provide more accommodation, but Ring also had in mind Fisher's Education Act of 1918, which provided for an ambitious extension of schooling with nursery schools; more secondary and central schools; and compulsory daytime "continuation classes" for teenage school leavers. Ring planned to have one of everything: a secondary and a central school, a continuation school and a nursery. Initially, the continuation school seemed to be the highest priority. Building costs had risen massively since the war, but when a large piece of land in Lucas Street became available in 1921, Canon Ring chanced his arm and laid out £1,775 (which he didn't have) to acquire it. He'd been trying to acquire that land for years, and had earlier been willing to offer far more, so he felt he'd got a bargain.

Fr Fletcher blesses a street shrine near Commercial Road in 1920

To pay off the debt, he asked that each of his parishioners contribute £1. Con Crane immediately promised £2, one for himself and one for Mrs Crane – and as he couldn't afford it all at once, began paying 2s a week. The Cardinal gave £300, and the Sisters of Mercy £100. A grand three-day bazaar was opened by King Manoel and Queen Augusta of Portugal, with the Mayor of Stepney arriving in an Irish jaunting car. Fr James McCarthy had the brilliant idea of asking families which had street shrines during the outdoor procession to put out a collecting box for donations, in aid of the school building fund, and this worked so well that it became regular practice.

The Labour Party had been very embarrassed by Cahill's coup, and determined to let nothing of the sort happen again: it partly disowned him, and refused to regard him as a Labour mayor. Shortly before the time came to elect his successor, he and his key supporter O'Brien were attacked in the street and beaten up. At the Council meeting O'Brien, very worked up, started shouting and offering to fight any man who cared to step outside. He continued heckling while Jack Sullivan proceeded to nominate Oscar Tobin. Whether or not the main issue the previous year had been religion or ethnicity, this time it was more clearly politics: a lot of people suspected Tobin was a Communist, and most of the Catholics were profoundly anti-Communist. Tobin won by 32 votes to 26, whereupon a shout went up: "Don't put the chain on his shoulders, Joe!" Cahill nevertheless handed over the chain, and Tobin responded with an eirenic speech, deploring the attacks and hoping the perpetrators would be caught.

The Anglo-Irish War was ended by the signing of a treaty in December 1921, creating the Irish Free State, but IRA irregulars immediately started a civil war against the leaders who had signed the treaty. In 1922 the Labour gains on Stepney Council were rolled back by an equally multi-ethnic Conservative-Liberal coalition, calling itself the Ratepayers' Party. But in the General Election that same year the Labour Party gained four parliamentary seats in Tower Hamlets, including Limehouse (won by Attlee) and Whitechapel.

A memorial to Fr Vaughan

Fr Bernard Vaughan died in October 1922. At Canon Ring's request his fellow-Jesuit Fr C C Martindale, who shared his interest in the East End, wrote a biography which he dedicated to St Mary and St Michael's. But Canon Ring also had in mind another idea. The government had got cold feet and never implemented Fisher's Act, choosing instead to slash the entire education budget by a third, while continuation schools were dropped as unworkable. This left him free to modify his plans for the Lucas Street site, and he decided to use it to build a central school, as a lasting memorial to Vaughan. It would provide a quality education to a wide category of children whose abilities were going to waste in the elementary schools, yet who were either not quite bright enough to get into secondary schools, or couldn't see the point of trying.

Fr C C Martindale

For most local children, aiming for a place at a central school was more realistic than trying to get into a secondary school, and made better sense for other reasons. The secondary school curriculum was very academic, which was OK if you were planning to go on to university, but hardly any East Enders ever dreamed of that. Central schools, alongside the academic subjects, offered courses in typing, shorthand and book-keeping, which were virtually banned in secondary schools, but much more likely to land you in a decent job. Yet at present there was only one Catholic central school in the whole of London, established by the Oratory.

All the Tower Hamlets parishes agreed to collaborate in the fundraising, and Canon Ring launched a nationwide appeal to everyone who had known and admired Fr Vaughan. He placed adverts in the Catholic papers, and wrote huge numbers of letters to royalty, politicians, businessmen and media celebrities. King Manoel of Portugal agreed to be named as patron, though the Queen of Spain returned the standard polite excuse that she had too many other calls upon her. Former parishioner John Roper-Parkington sent a nice little note and a cheque for £50. By the beginning of March Canon Ring had sent out 981 letters, and raised the first £1,000, from 103 donors. Now for the *second* £1,000. Over the next couple of weeks he wrote another 167 letters, which must have left him very tired and needing something to lift his spirits. The St Patrick's Eve concert in Our Lady's Hall was a disappointment, as he noted in his diary: "It was a poor performance for an Irish night and a poor attendance." But on the feastday evening he popped round to Limehouse Town Hall, which he found "glowing and full." An advert in the *Tablet* called for a thousand people to send an Easter donation, pointing out that if Fr Vaughan himself could have preached at Farm Street that Easter, £1,000 would have been subscribed in no time. In just one week in April Ring wrote 291 letters. News of the appeal reached America, and generated some publicity there.

By July over £2,000 was already in the bag, and it was hoped that the £3,000 mark could be reached fairly soon. The St Mary and St Michael's children put on a concert at Limehouse Town Hall, and marched through the streets with a box saying "£12,000 needed for Catholic Central School": so many pennies and halfpennies were thrown in that it became too heavy for them to carry, and altogether they raised £30. The band of the Metropolitan Police played for a garden party on the school site in Lucas Street, which raised £52, and a concert by the Children of Mary raised £70 15s 10d. The parish organised a "Shillings Fund" and the first shilling was handed in by Con Crane's three-year-old son. By the end of the year the Shillings Fund raised £115, while a few parishioners, and Ring himself, quietly slipped in donations of hundred pounds or more each. Contributions arrived from a number of non-Catholics, and the local Jewish community was very supportive: J W Rosenthal made the Pavilion available for staging "The Shaughran" by the "Veteran Irish Players" (all proceeds to the central school fund), and the current Mayor of Stepney, Harry Kosky, sent 5 guineas.

Nevertheless the momentum slowed, and by December the total stood at only £2,587. Donors may well have been discouraged by the apparent impossibility of getting the necessary official permission. The government was trying desperately to roll back expenditure on education, and determined to block the opening of any new faith schools, if only for reasons of cost. Ring was told that in any case it would be useless to have a central school "in that neighbourhood, because of the low level of attainment in the East End," but he was undeterred.

Meanwhile a General Election resulted in a hung Parliament, but with Labour holding more seats than any other single party, and in January 1924 James Ramsay Macdonald became Britain's first Labour Prime Minister. His MPs were sufficiently dependent on Catholic support at constituency level to respect sensitivities about education – and were in any case very keen to expand educational opportunities for working class children. Thus it came about that Canon Ring extended his "blessing" to the Labour Party. Writing in his parish magazine, he pointed out that previous governments had "refused Catholics in all parts of the country permission to open Catholic schools," yet "In five months the Labour government has sanctioned the building of these hitherto forbidden schools… Catholics are receiving from the Labour Government better treatment than either of the other parties extended to them."

More hurdles lay ahead, but the prospects were looking brighter, and fundraising for the central school picked up. During 1924 the Shillings Fund brought in £375, and a parish bazaar in July a whopping £730: together with contributions from other parishes and outsiders, the fund by the end of the year had passed the £5,000 mark. By St Patrick's Day 1925 there was £5,599 19s 2d.

Due to increasingly stringent LCC space requirements, it was impossible to squeeze all the parish's Catholic children into the existing school buildings. Part of the problem seems to have been that there was no lower age limit, so a lot of space was taken up by under-fives. The Sisters of Charity and the Blue Nuns were hunting down Catholic children in non-Catholic schools and sending them along to Johnson Street, and the Sisters of Mercy were turning them away for lack of room. Ring therefore decided in 1923 to start an overflow school in the Vaughan Club, and asked Sr Bernard O'Shea, who'd just finished teacher training college, to run it. The "Academy" started on 15th October, with 74 children aged from 2½ up to 5. There were no seats (and no heating), just two large billiard tables. The children sat on floor, and kept rolling under the tables, emerging "more like Blackamoors than

Londoners", so the Johnson Street headmistress, Sr Evangelist Seaborne (a native of Poplar, and one of the very few Londoners ever to have joined the community, which had always been almost entirely Irish) agreed to provide 40 desks. By Christmas the number of children was up to 100. Many had previously been attending council schools, but the parents were persuaded to withdraw them and send them to the Academy.

In 1926 Sr Evangelist resigned as headmistress, and Sr Philomena Conway was appointed to replace her. Mr Donovan retired later the same year, and was succeeded by Frank Greenan. He was to remain at Johnson Street for many years, and his nickname there was "Bumpy Greenan" – this was apparently a reference to his manner of wielding a cane. The fact that he used the cane, as virtually all teachers did in those days, didn't mean he was callous: he cared tremendously about the kids, and was very aware of their difficulties – such as that you'd sometimes find two boys in a family coming to school on alternate days, because there was only one pair of shoes between them. The senior classes in the Girls' School were very large, usually 60-strong, which made it very difficult to give individual attention to any child, so Sr Philomena proposed to Ring that a special "coaching class" of 30 be established in Our Lady's Hall. The LCC agreed to fund this. The little children's school downstairs was neither recognised nor funded by the LCC, but the Sisters of Mercy generously taught it for free.

Premierland

G K Chesterton

For the 1924 Men's Guild New Year reception G K Chesterton agreed to come and give a talk, and so as to fit everyone in, it was held at Limehouse Town Hall. On the day itself there was a rail strike, but Tom Whelton got hold of a car and drove to Beaconsfield to fetch Chesterton and his wife. The success of the event gave Ring the idea of organising a big new year's rally for men from all the East End parishes. The other parish priests all agreed, and he booked Premierland for 13th January 1925.

A large hall in Aldgate, Premierland was actually meant for boxing matches, and not really suitable for a large meeting with speeches from the platform, as there were no microphones. But microphones were quite a recent invention, and most public figures still knew how to make their voices carry without. It was supposed to be able to hold at least 4,000, seated or standing. Tickets were sold in all the parishes, and all of them co-operated to push the event and make sure the hall was filled. Mayor of Stepney Jack Somper (one of Canon Ring's many devoted non-Catholic friends and admirers) welcomed Cardinal Bourne, and paid tribute to the contribution of Catholics in local politics – both among his own Ratepayer allies and on the Labour Party. The Cardinal gave the main talk, and in it he stated very loudly and clearly that Catholics were free to belong to any of the three mainstream political parties: Conservative, Liberal or Labour – though he added a warning to Labour supporters to avoid class warfare. This groundbreaking speech both strengthened Labour in East London, and stiffened the resolve of the Labour Catholics to combat Communist infiltration. At the November 1925 elections, Labour won back its majority on Stepney Council.

Premierland became an annual event. Most of the audience arrived early to be sure of a seat; sometimes up to 5,000 squeezed in, and hundreds of latecomers had to be turned away. The gathering presented an unique opportunity, and Ring was always able to bring in at least one top-quality keynote speaker, usually to deliver a morale-boosting talk on Catholic history, and also to discuss current affairs, while his regular allies among Catholic writers, politicians and aristocrats could be relied on for subsidiary speeches. Cardinal Bourne usually attended, whether or not he chose to speak, and so did the current Mayor. Community leaders, of whatever party or religious allegiance, could arrange to have seats reserved for them on the platform, and local politicians knew it was worth their while to be present. The event was essentially men-only, though a few women dignitaries might be on the platform, and sometimes a box was reserved at the side for any other women wishing to join the audience. Labour mayors made a point of not wearing the traditional red robes, but they did wear the mayoral chain, and were preceded by the mace-bearer. In 1926 Fr C C Martindale, moving a vote of thanks to Mayor Joseph Hurley, said he'd recently been chatting to Pope Pius IX, and

> *the Holy Father told him to tell the working people of England that he knew the working men well, that a great part of his youth had been spent among them, that he knew their nature and character, and that it was a good nature and character, and that he trusted them and thought of them always with special affection.*

Hurley was succeeded as Mayor by Jack Sullivan, and in January 1928 George Groves became the third Catholic mayor in succession to welcome the Cardinal to Premierland. The main speaker that year was Dr William James O'Donovan, English-born son of an Irish immigrant customs officer, a skin specialist who combined a Harley Street practice with consultant posts at the London Hospital, and was Coroner's Pathologist for East London. O'Donovan was subsequently to enter politics, but he always said he'd never dreamed of public speaking until Canon Ring roped him in for this Premierland talk. Among the newer faces on the scene was John R A Oldfield. Educated at Eton and then at Cambridge, where he converted to Catholicism, Oldfield had developed an interest in social issues, come to live at Toynbee Hall, got involved with the Labour Party, and was now on Stepney Council. He normally attended Mass at St Mary and St Michael's, where he, along with O'Donovan and Dr Reidy, gave a lot of help to the CYMS. O'Donovan and Oldfield became respectively chairman and vice-chairman of the Westminster Catholic Federation, but it was already past its best before date, and there was nothing they could do to breathe life into it.

Deus Vult

By January 1927 £8,500 had been raised for the central school, mostly from local working-class people, and at a meeting of all the parish priests, at Commercial Road, it was decided to submit plans to the Board of Education and the LCC. Despite some local opposition, and an appeal to the Board of Education, Canon Ring received the go-ahead. Another £4-5,000 still needed to be raised before construction could begin at the Lucas Street site. But then an alternative opportunity came up. Due to demographic changes, the overall number of children of school age in Tower Hamlets was going down, so it was decided to dispose of some of the LCC schools. Canon Ring bought one in Baker Street (Damien Street), near the Commercial Road end of Sidney Street, paying £10,000 for the freehold, and another £5,500 for alterations. He put in art rooms, science laboratories, medical inspection and dining rooms, central heating and electric light. The dining rooms were needed because he was determined that meals should be provided for all children who had to come from a distance; the meals would be delivered by the LCC, at a cost of ½d each.

The new central school was to be named St Bernard's, after Fr Vaughan's name saint, Bernard of Clairvaux – whose crusading war cry "Deus Vult" ("God wills it") featured on the school badge. It would take both boys and girls, not as a mixed school but in separate departments, each with accommodation for 200 students. The Boys' Headmaster was Edmund McGann, a graduate of Manchester University, and the Girls' Headmistress Sr Emmanuel FCJ, who had a BA from London University. At Canon Ring's entreaty, Sr Emmanuel had agreed to give up the headship of Howrah House to come and help launch the new central school. The LCC took a helpful and generous line, providing £1,450 to cover furnishing costs, and appointing John Gilbert as its representative on the managing body. Gilbert had had a very successful career, serving as Chairman of the LCC Education

Committee, and of the LCC itself, and gaining a knighthood; since 1927 he'd also been Chairman of the Catholic Education Council. The appointments of the two headteachers were dated from the end of November, so they could spend the first few weeks of December visiting the feeder schools and interviewing pupils. For the initial intake contingents of 11- and 12-year-olds, and a few 13-year-olds, were selected from each of the Tower Hamlets Catholic schools, and some children from Hackney and south of the river were also offered places. On 1st December Cardinal Bourne came to bless and formally open the building. A procession made its way from St Mary and St Michael's to Baker Street, collecting a huge audience on the way. The Cardinal was welcomed to Stepney by the Mayor, Dan Frankel, and in thanking him declared that Jews were in the same position as Catholics in holding that "definite religious teaching was essential in properly ordered education". Viscount FitzAlan made a speech stressing that more money was still needed (partly to pay off a small amount of remaining debt, but also if possible to provide maintenance grants for poor students), and his vote of thanks to the Cardinal was seconded by Dr O'Donovan. St Bernard's School commenced classes on 8th January 1929, with a speech from Canon Ring after the first assembly.

A celebratory year

For the first round of celebrations for the 1929 Centenary of Catholic Emancipation, in April, Canon Ring organised a big rally for over 2,000 East End children at the People's Palace, where Sir John Gilbert delivered an inspirational talk about the heroic conduct of Catholics during the Penal Times. At the end Canon Ring joked that

> *his audience would see why the L.C.C. had chosen Sir John Gilbert for the Chairmanship of the Educational Committee, when they saw how he had got a shy and nervous man like himself to speak.*

At the Emancipation Congress in September, 500 men from St Mary and St Michael's joined the march, led by Amigo, from Southwark Cathedral to Westminster.

In that year's outdoor procession the St Bernard's pupils marched en masse, in their smart uniforms, behind a beautiful banner crafted for them by the nuns at Howrah House. A start was made at last on curing Ring's "toothache" by moving the organ. Though it wasn't being moved far, adjusting its position required a complete rebuilding operation, but as soon as that was finished, work would begin on redecorating the Lady Chapel, and installing a new stained glass window and altar. All this required a great deal of fundraising, but at the same time the parishioners went ahead with a presentation to mark the 25th anniversary of Canon Ring's arrival at St Mary and St Michael's. With Dr Reidy as chairman and treasurer, and Charles Berg "general hustler for success", £450 was collected; this included a substantial contribution from Police Superintendent Sygrove and his men at King David Lane, who weren't Catholics but saw Canon Ring as their ally in keeping down the crime rate. (Men gambling illegally on the street would take no notice of the police, but if Canon Ring came along they'd scarper immediately.) Alderman Kiley, another non-Catholic, declared his respect for all that he had achieved:

It was impossible for anyone to benefit one section of the community without helping all sections. He had once asked Canon Ring to what his success had been due. Canon Ring had answered, 'I do not dictate to my people. I tell them what I am going to do and why I am doing it, and it is for them to decide whether they would follow.

Afterwards the Infant School gave an entertainment, dressed as fairies and wishing the parish priest "happiness, friends, and health and wealth". One of them declared solemnly:

My wishes are more wise, friends. Through the parish they extend
Of St Mary and St Michael's, in this wonderful East End:
Although it cannot boast the scenes that County Kerry shows,
It is just as dear to Canon Ring, as everybody knows.

Sir John Gilbert, Cardinal Bourne, Canon Ring and Auxiliary of Westminster, Bishop Bidwell.

More celebrations in December marked the beatification of 136 of the English Martyrs, including Stepney Martyrs William Dean and John Hewett, and John Roche. On Wednesday 4th December the auxiliary bishop, Joseph Butt, came to consecrate the church. Ring was very cross that the work on the organ was delayed, and couldn't be finished in time, so they'd have to manage without music, but some choristers from the Cathedral came to help. Bp Butt started work at 10.00 am. It had been raining earlier on, but the rain had cleared up, and as he put the oil of consecration on the altar "the sun shone gloriously through the pictured windows and made the figures in them appear to join us in the sacred chant..." The schoolchildren were all brought in for High Mass at 12.00. On Sunday the Cardinal came for a celebratory High Mass, and the Mayors of both Stepney and Poplar were present, together with many of the Councillors and Aldermen. The church now had permanent seating for 1,400, and Canon Ring had purchased about 100 extra temporary chairs for the event, but large numbers had to stand.

The outward and visible sign

John Scurr

The deal whereby religious bodies provided and maintained their school buildings by voluntary fundraising was becoming an insupportable burden. Sir John Gilbert calculated that since the 1902 Education Act, the East End Catholics had had to raise a total of £150,000 in voluntary income to keep up their school buildings. Commercial Road alone had raised £39,000. Proposals to raise the school leaving age to 15 caused consternation, not because Catholics were opposed to educational progress, but because it would require a major expansion in their school accommodation costing nearly £1 million. Catholics all over the country, including the Commercial Road parishioners, bombarded their MPs with letters and postcards. Finally John Scurr, Catholic Labour MP for Poplar, moved an amendment to block implementation of the School Attendance Bill unless the faith schools got more help. The Scurr Amendment passed by 282 votes to 249. A tidy number of Labour members disregarded their Party whip to support it, including many Catholics but also including Jimmy Hall, MP for Whitechapel, who was not a Catholic but had a healthy respect for the concerns of his minority constituents. Attlee did not, however, and all the parish groups wrote angry letters to Attlee.

Feted as a hero by the Catholics for putting religious principle before party loyalties, Scurr was execrated as a traitor by many ill-informed Labour supporters. But the real betrayal of Labour came shortly afterwards when, faced with ever-rising unemployment and a financial crisis, Ramsay Macdonald lost his nerve, and replaced his old cabinet with a new Conservative-dominated "National Government". A General Election was then held, in October 1931, against a background of general hysteria, with Macdonald demanding what he called a "doctor's mandate", to do whatever might be needed to rescue the economy. In Mile End, Scurr was defeated by co-religionist Dr O'Donovan, standing as a National Conservative (he'd become very anti-socialist following an experience during the General Strike, when the electricity supply to the London Hospital was cut off), while Whitechapel went to a National Liberal, Barnet Janner. Both these non-Labour candidates benefited from the nationwide swing in favour of the National Government, plus an added edge from the support of their own ethno-religious communities. Both knew the results were largely a fluke, so O'Donovan made huge efforts to build up grassroots support for Conservatism in his constituency, and court the Jewish community, while Janner, a well-known champion of Jewish causes and an ardent Zionist, worked hard to demonstrate that he was also as profoundly supportive of Catholic interests as was Hall. Most parliamentary constituencies in Tower Hamlets remained solid for Labour: George Lansbury (Bow) and Clem Attlee kept their seats, becoming respectively the new Leader and Deputy Leader of the Labour Party, and of the official Opposition. However control of Stepney Council swung back to the Ratepayers' Party. Now that the Lucas Street site was no longer needed for a central school, the 75-year-old Canon Ring decided to use the land for a new junior school. Providing alternative accommodation for the 7-11 age-group would free up space in Johnson Street, and allow more children to be admitted to all departments. Including the St Bernard's students, St Mary and St Michael's Parish would then have 1,800 school places altogether. Barnet Janner MP got Ring a personal interview with the Minister of Education, Sir Donald Maclean, who was persuaded to give permission. Ring had no money in hand, so he borrowed it, entering into a bond for £12,000. Tenders were invited (the lowest, and successful, one was received on St Patrick's Day), the remaining tenants in the old houses were got out in April, and demolition and building work began. On a Sunday afternoon in May the whole parish processed over from the church, where the Canon blessed the foundation stone before it was ceremonially laid by Sir John Gilbert. The parish's school system, declared Ring, was

the outward and visible sign of great sacrifice and generosity on the part of the working classes of the district, and it represented in the last 30 years an outlay of about

£40,000 derived in a large measure from the pennies of the poor. It was also evidence of the importance that the workers of the district attached to religion, and when people wrote on the decay of faith in the East End of London, they might in justice and in truth make an exception for the Catholic body."

Viscountess and Viscount FitzAlan

The end of October saw Lucas Street gay with flags, banners and bunting, and lined with cheering children and parents, to welcome Cardinal Bourne when he came for the formal opening of St Mary and St Michael's Junior Mixed School: the school hall was solemnly blessed, and a crucifix hung on the wall. Whereas at the time of the LCC takeover there had been 85 Catholic schools in London, there were now 99, and this would be the hundredth. The architect was John Sterrett. Total cost of the building was £10,059 10s, and the Cardinal donated £250. Lady FitzAlan, who'd done her bit to help with the fundraising, came for a guided tour and was taken up to the roof playground, and Barnet Janner (who couldn't attend the opening because he was in America) had a special visit all to himself in November, when the children performed songs and dances in his honour. The new Junior School wasn't paid for, and fundraising was to continue for the next few years. Charles Fay, who'd moved away but still kept in touch, sent £5 with a letter saying that out of all the really old parish families that went back to Virginia Street, only the Wheltons and the Dohertys seemed to be left. The new Junior School actually opened for business on 2nd November. The roll was 479, and actual attendance during the first week was 456 – which was gratifying, but slightly worrying as the official accommodation capacity was only 440, and a spot inspection would have got the school into trouble. However attendance rates of 90-95%, which were considered "very good", were too good to last: they continued up to Christmas, and then attendance began to drop. During hop picking, nearly half the school was absent, but that was expected and normal – the teachers only got worried when the rates dropped for no obvious reason. If large numbers of unexplained and suspicious absences persisted for as long as two weeks, they drew up lists of names and sent them to the Attendance Officers so that investigations could be made. There were 12 classes, each with about 40 children. Occasional educational trips were organised to the Tower of London, the Houses of

Parliament (by boat down the river), Hampton Court, the London Docks and Greenwich, and the teachers took it in turns to visit other local schools, to make sure they were keeping abreast of all the latest methods.

Even with the expanded accommodation, the Vaughan Club continued to serve as an overflow school. Certain classes, such as sewing and knitting, were held there, and it was used to serve the dinners for specially needy children. The LCC gave permission for an open air class to be held from April to October each year on the recreation ground (the old cemetery), with desks under a large awning for children who were considered delicate and in need of fresh air. All parish children started off in the Infants in Johnson Street, then went on automatically to St Mary and St Michael's at seven. Joan Donovan, who made her First Communion at the new Junior School and was also confirmed there, remembered it as a lovely school. The children wore navy blue and yellow berets marked "St Mary and St Michael's", but no uniform apart from that as far as she could remember. Sr Philomena Conway was headmistress. Later on, children who didn't get in to St Bernard's went back to Johnson Street, to the Senior Boys or Senior Girls. Sr Joseph Cleary was headmistress of Senior Girls, and Frank Greenan headmaster of Senior Boys. Sr Scholastica Fallon, a Sister of Mercy borrowed from Chelsea, remained headmistress of the Infant School until 1936, when Sr Bernard took over.

When the first St Bernard's boy won a scholarship in March 1930, the event was recorded in the logbook. Canon Ring arranged for a change to be agreed in the operation of Commercial Road's and Wapping's share of the Richard Neale Fund, so that instead of providing ten scholarships for Stamford Hill and Howrah House, it would provide forty for St Bernard's. Before long all the East End parishes followed suit. Their 11-year-olds sat the scholarship exam together each spring, in the St Bernard's school hall. Successful scholars won £5 a year initially, upped to £10 from the age of 14. Even a few shillings a week relieved the pressure on them to find paying odd-jobs to do before or after school, instead of homework, and also to leave at 14 to get a job; it might also mean their parents could allow them a little pocket money, so they wouldn't feel completely left out when their working mates were flashing around their shillings. Other pupils from low-income families benefited from LCC scholarships.

Canon Ring, like other East End clergy, always strongly supported the right of families to take their children hopping in September, regardless of missing school, and when the LCC tried to take a parish family to court over it, he engaged a top solicitor to defend them. The benefit from the fresh air and sunshine greatly outweighed any (doubtful) benefit from whatever they could learn in the elementary schools. But St Bernard's pupils were *not* allowed to go hopping. Hardly had the Central School opened before Canon Ring was planning an extension. He was to add yet another new wing in 1935, pushing capacity up to 291 girls and 262 boys, from an even wider catchment area covering 34 Catholic elementary schools.

St Bernard's had a proven success rate for getting leavers into the sort of jobs local families considered the acme of ambition: girls were being offered starting salaries between 17s 6d and 27s 6d a week, and boys were landing white collar jobs with commercial and shipping offices, solicitors and chartered accountants. St Bernard's had much of the ethos of a grammar school – the teachers often wore their academic gowns in class. Parents were therefore increasingly eager to get their children in, and allow them to stay on until at least 15, if not 16.

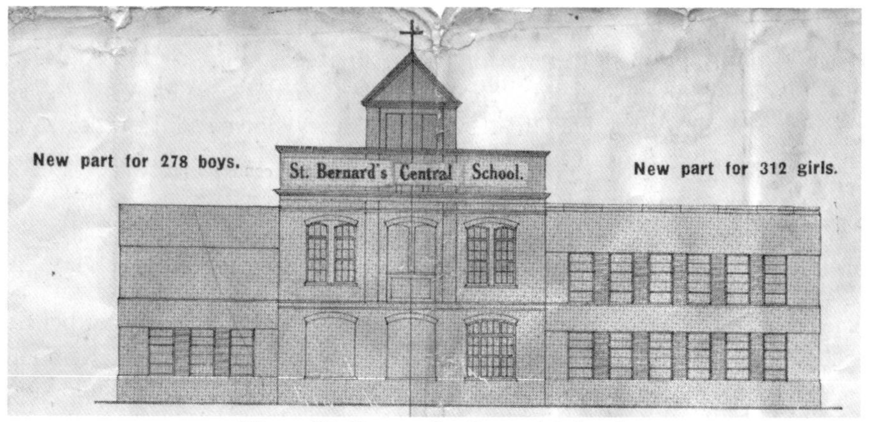

Plan of St Bernard's Central School

A menace to peace and prosperity

Boards of Guardians had been scrapped, and replaced by Public Assistance Committees (PACs) under the LCC, but the old Poor Law mentality carried over. Those thrown out of work by the Depression were entitled to unemployment benefit – the "dole" – but the PACs ruthlessly applied the hated Means Test introduced by the National Government. If a family had any savings or assets, or a close relative who was working, their benefit was reduced accordingly. The long-term unemployed were liable to be sent by the PAC to a labour colony at Belmont for "residential training", and if they refused, their dole was stopped. Critics pointed out that the training was useless, and referred to Belmont as a "slave camp".

In the House of Commons and at local meetings around the country, Dr O'Donovan became known as a staunch opponent of divorce and contraception. He could talk the hind leg off a donkey, and determinedly talked out several bills for easier divorce – on one occasion by quoting lengthily from the marriage service in the Anglican Book of Common Prayer. The Catholic bloc on Stepney Borough Council continued to vote down any publicly-funded promotion of artificial birth control. Their determination was stiffened by the open concern of so many of their leading opponents to reduce the number of potential benefits claimants. The tendency to become unemployed was widely believed to be a hereditary disease – though this didn't save the jobless from being held morally responsible for their plight! John Oldfield alleged that a local PAC sub-committee chairman had told him the children of a relief applicant "ought to be put into a lethal chamber". Meanwhile, despite contraception steadily gaining ground among the upper classes, the birth rate in St Mary and St Michael's Parish remained in a very healthy state. Large families were the norm, and Juniper Street, which was mostly Catholic, was locally referred to as "Incubator Street". It was calculated that over fifty Catholic families left the parish each year, moving out to the big new housing estates in the suburbs, yet the number of baptisms continued to rise. Canon Ring turned to haranguing the Ratepayers' majority on the Borough Council on the need for action on slum clearance, and building decent houses for local people: he alleged that since they took over, "not a brick" had been laid in St George's or Whitechapel. However when Jack Somper, now an Alderman, protested that this was simply not true, he was allowed space in *Rector's Realm* to reply on the Ratepayers' behalf. Among other new residential developments, they were planning to build some housing on the site next to the church, which had previously been Frost's rope factory, but had been acquired by the Council some time before, and was still standing empty. Somper bore no grudge. Everyone knew that in the last resort, Canon Ring was supremely impartial in his politics: he would work with politicians of any party or none, handing out accolades whenever they delivered what he wanted, and grief when they didn't. Most East Enders had learned to accept him the way he was.

After the Labour Party gained control of the LCC, in 1934, directives were issued that unemployed men who were married no longer be sent to labour colonies. Canon Ring hailed the move with a blisteringly outspoken Easter sermon, appealing for more humane treatment all round:

> *The poor had a right to the amenities of the land and it was hoped that the*

browbeating and abuse of applicants for public assistance would be stopped. Officials had a tendency to regard applicants for relief, to which the law fully entitled them, as trespassers and cheats. If they only realised the humiliation experienced by the majority of men who had to apply for the help to which they were entitled, the Relief Committees would insist that they should be given sympathy and not censure. Harsh administration made the law hated, and the offensive treatment of mothers implied that the duties of married life and parenthood were unworthy of approval.

This outburst was slammed by the conservative-minded as a pro-Labour manifesto, but the Labour Party knew better than to view the Canon as a safe asset. When Somper rose in a Council meeting to propose that one the new block of flats going up in Shadwell be named after Ring in his lifetime (rather than after his death), the Labour members opposed the motion. Dan Frankel said he had

the greatest admiration for Canon Ring's religious work though that did not follow that he had the same for his political activities, and personally he felt that members of the cloth should be above politics.

The vote was split, 27 for and 27 against, whereupon the Mayor "exercised his casting vote in favour of the resolution." Somper was very pleased: he was in poor health, and longing to retire, but he'd hung on just to be sure of pushing through this honour for his old friend. In the borough elections later that year his Ratepayers Party was to go down to final and absolute defeat, with all 60 seats on Stepney Council going to Labour.

The first St Mary and St Michael's school concert, held at Limehouse Town Hall, was a great success even though the new Junior School had only been functioning for six months. The most popular item was a "Canon Ring on Trial" skit in which the parish priest (played by Elsie Harrison) was charged:

That during the years 1904 and 1934 in the County of London, chiefly in the parish if Stepney, he did by public speaking as well as by propaganda in the form of a parish magazine cause strife in certain families in Stepney, in which parish he is now regarded as a menace to peace and prosperity.

Witnesses for the prosecution included a girl who'd been made to donate her lipstick money to the school building fund; a woman whose husband turned the house upside down with his "Get this ready, get that ready, Canon Ring wants all the men at the Guild", and a man who didn't want his children going to good schools and learning more than him. Witnesses for the defence were a mother of ten whose grown-up children all had good jobs thanks to the parish schools, and a man who "proved that the Canon had brought happiness to a formerly miserable home." He was declared Not Guilty. The proceeds of the concert went towards his forthcoming Golden Jubilee.

Dr Reidy and Canon Ring

Hailed by the local press as the Grand Old Man of East End Catholicism, Canon Ring received congratulatory messages from the Pope, Cardinal Bourne (a fellow-jubilarian), four archbishops, seven bishops, and Rabbi Joseph Stern. All 1,800 schoolchildren were given a concert and tea party in the church grounds in the afternoon, and in the evening the whole parish gathered in the school hall in Lucas Street. Dr Reidy presented the Canon with a cheque for a thousand guineas, together with a leather-bound book, embossed with jewels, containing the names of all the subscribers. The Sisters of Mercy and Junior School presented him with an oil painting of himself, which thenceforth hung in Our Lady's Hall. Canon Ring remarked that this was his fourth jubilee: his parishioners in Silvertown had celebrated a Copper Jubilee for him on the tenth anniversary of his ordination, and since then he'd had two Silvers and a Golden at Commercial Road (not to mention numerous subsidiary tributes in between). He hoped he'd live to celebrate a fifth jubilee.

The next jubilee was actually organised in 1935 – not for Ring, but for King George V. The King and Queen drove, very slowly, in an open-top car along Commercial Road to Limehouse Town Hall, where all the East End Mayors and MPs were waiting to meet them. All the local schools, and some other organisations, were allocated stretches of pavement, but the Lucas Street and Johnson Street schools, and St Bernard's, refused this offer and proudly announced that they would make their "own arrangements". Canon Ring arranged for stands to be erected inside the parish grounds, facing the road, so all the parish schoolchildren were accommodated in comfort, with a marvellous view of the whole parade over the heads of the people on the pavement. Later that summer a Jubilee Fair in the church grounds helped pay off some of the school debt.

Thomas More

1935 was the 400th anniversary of the executions of Thomas More and John Fisher, and their canonisation went through that year – in the middle of the Royal Jubilee. They were the first of the English Martyrs to be canonised, and the first new English saints since the Reformation. The secular press, by and large, hailed the canonisations as an honour conferred on two distinguished and patriotic Englishmen. At that time the execution site on Tower Hill was part of Trinity Square Gardens, a private park belonging to Trinity House: it was not open to the public, though nearby householders could obtain a key if they were willing to pay a guinea a year. The *East London Advertiser* announced Stepney Council's intention of acquiring the gardens for public use "as a priceless asset to this congested neighbourhood and, while so doing, to reveal the scaffold site to the public, with a memorial appropriate to its poignant memories."

John Fisher

Invitation to breakfast

Whenever anyone wrote to the papers bemoaning the irreligion of the East End, and alleging that hardly anyone still went to church, Canon Ring would issue a challenge, inviting the writer to come to St Mary and St Michael's on any Sunday morning to count for himself the 2,000 – 3,000 worshippers, and then join him for breakfast in the presbytery afterwards. He also pointed out that St Mary and St Michael's was entirely self-supporting: he regularly collected £20-30 a week from the congregation. (This was despite his constant whingeing about people refusing to pay door money!) Very few of local Protestant churches were self-supporting. The East End Methodist Mission received massive amounts of help from outsiders, most of the money being used to provide a wide range of social services for local people regardless of creed: a cinema screen and projection equipment had been installed in the church, and lots of Catholic children were among those queueing up for the Penny Pictures each afternoon, and saving up their tickets to qualify for the Christmas party and summer outing.

Canon Ring's outlook was a long way from what would later be regarded as properly ecumenical. He enjoyed warm and friendly relations with people of all different religions, and he loved to listen to them explain and defend what they believed – but mainly in order to gain a clearer perspective on why he totally disagreed. Anyone who'd been hoping he would meet them halfway was doomed to disappointment – and if they took it personally, he would be completely mystified as to why.

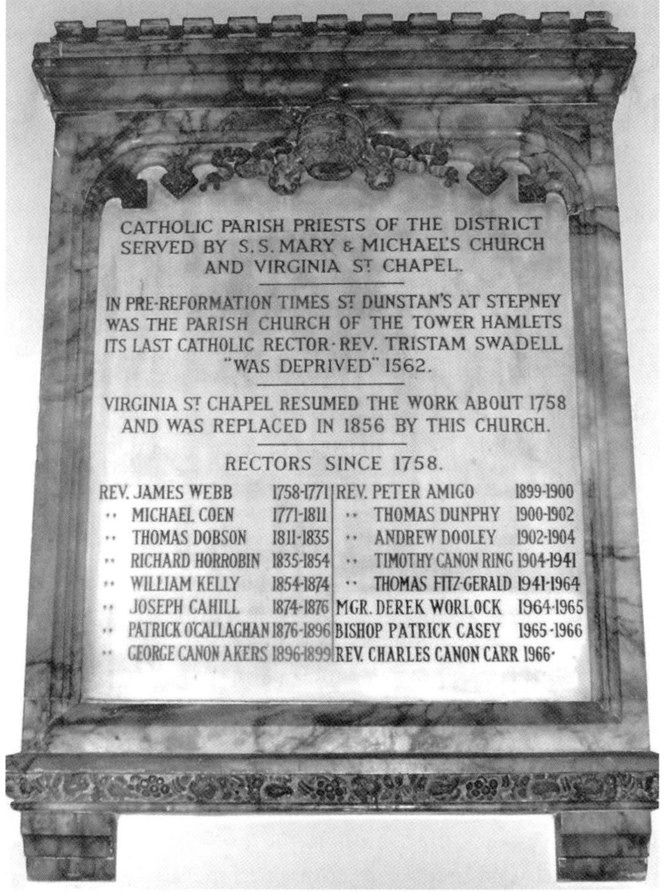

Marble tablet, framed in alabaster, in the church porch listing the names and dates of Parish Priests of St Mary and St Michael's

Since the pioneer days of St Peter's, London Docks, many more of the local Anglican churches had gone "High" – St Mary's Cable Street, and Christchurch Watney Street - being outstanding examples. They taught their adherents to believe in Catholic teaching and call themselves Catholics, and regard the Church of England as the legitimate continuation of the pre-Reformation Church. All Canon Ring's predecessors had treated such claims as nonsense, and so did he: like them, he dismissed the Anglo-Catholics as campaigning under false colours. Ironically this was one issue where he found common ground with a great many local Protestants. The fact that Rev John Groser at Christchurch, and some of the other Anglo-Catholics, were so radically left-wing as to be happy to collaborate with the Communists, did nothing to sweeten his feelings. He proudly flew the Papal colours on the 75 ft flagpole erected outside the church in 1930, another gift from Mrs Metcalf. Around the same time a marble tablet, framed in alabaster, was placed in the church porch, listing the names and dates of the Catholic priests of St Mary and St Michael's: the main list was preceded by a reference to pre-Reformation Stepney, and the deprivation of its "last Catholic Rector" Tristam Swadell in 1562, after which – as far as Canon Ring was concerned – there had simply been a gap until "Virginia Street Chapel resumed the work about 1758…"

Practically ever year, St Mary and St Michael's had a full-scale mission around Easter, spread over three weeks and with a specialist mission team. The first week was usually reserved for the children, and by the 1930s this was so firmly established that they all attended regularly and punctually, and behaved themselves perfectly, with no need for the clergy or nuns to ride herd on them. Canon Ring regarded the children as the best evangelisers in the parish, and once the adult mission started, a lot of non-practising parents were brought along by their children's insistence. Often there were men-only sessions, and he urged the women to pick up their brooms and chase their husbands out of the home to make them come: in return, the men would be allowed to baby-sit later during the women-only sessions. A big feature of the adult mission was the Men's Guild procession on the second Wednesday night, with nearly a thousand participants.

Of course there were always Catholics living in the parish who refused even to attend Mass, let alone join a sodality, but they were well-advised to stay out of Canon Ring's way. Whenever he came round personally on visitation, the man of the house would often hide in the outside loo until the coast was clear. As far as the Massgoers were concerned, he'd ensured that virtually all of them belonged to one of the parish associations, and largely as a result of this, the number of Communions had more than doubled since before his time. (Most people received Communion along with the other members of their association once a month, on a specified Sunday, and it was almost unheard of for anyone to approach the altar rails on the weeks in between.) Big families remained the norm. The annual garden fete in the presbytery garden usually featured a baby show: Matt Henderson, who won it one year, was Mrs Henderson's eighth child, and she went on to have two more – Marie and Monica. Parishioners' children joined the associations prescribed for their age group as they became old enough, and then graduated from one to another as they grew older: it was automatic, it was what you did. Your life was not your own, but cradle-to-grave care was assured, as in the case of Hanna Hearn, a 34-year-old dinner lady at St Bernard's School who belonged to both the Children of Mary and the Women's Guild: when she was knocked down in Commercial Road by a "motor-coach" (as they were still called in 1931, before the horse-drawn type was forgotten), one of the curates was with her in minutes to give her the last rites, accompany her to the London Hospital, and remain with her until she died during the night. After Dr Reidy died, in 1936, both his practice and his role in the parish were taken over by Dr O'Toole.

While everyone virtually *had* to belong to one of the main associations, some were more optional: the Knights of St Columba, for example, which Ring was initially chary of because he thought the subscription too high, or the Legion of Mary which was introduced by Fr John Halvey. Fr John Leigh's parish branch of the Catholic Social Guild held a study circle every Tuesday evening in the Junior School, to hear a paper on some topic like Private Property, Communism, or Trade Unions, which they would then discuss: the local secretary was James Coveney of 60, Bekesbourne Buildings. An East London Catholic School of Social Study was developed. Jesuit speakers Paul Crane and Cyril Clump gave a course of lectures on "The Christian State" at St George's Library, and the final lecture was graced with the presence of Fr Leo O'Hea SJ, the distinguished head of the Guild, and Principal of the Catholic Workers' College in Oxford. A large and important sub-group within the parish were the hospital nurses, who often got together for fundraising initiatives.

All the associations took part in the outdoor processions, which were the biggest and best publicised in the East End. Ring himself was a flash of colour in his red canon's robes, and sometimes all the other canons of Westminster Cathedral came to join him. It became standard practice for the Mayor of Stepney, if a Catholic, and all the Catholic Councillors, to take part, and be allocated their own special place in the march. Depending who was around, sometimes there were other special contingents, such as Catholic doctors and barristers, the National Irish Foresters, or the Knights of St Columba. John Oldfield, who after serving briefly as an MP was LCC member for Whitechapel for many years, walked with the CYMS, carrying a statue of Christ. Talks used to be given from the first floor windows of some of the houses with street shrines, either by priests or by prominent lay activists like Oldfield or Anstruther. The League of the Cross was in steady decline, but the parish Guards, now captained by Dan Whelton, still marshalled the processions. Ring insisted on strict discipline – everyone was to joining in saying the rosary, or singing the hymns (they must keep time with the music!) and avoid any unnecessary talking. When Fr Philip Fletcher, Master of the Guild of Ransom, died in January 1928, he was buried from St Mary and St Michael's, and the famous Ransom Cross was carried in the cortège. Anstruther came every year up to 1938 when – very old and ill – he wrote to say his doctor wouldn't let him come. Ring expostulated: "Oh! these doctors! Mussolini is not in it with them!" That year Oldfield compared the procession to the League of Nations, because there were Poles and Germans, Indians and Africans, all marching together. Whole families took part in the procession. When James Boland died, his son carried his banner in the next year's. On the day of the procession, the men in Joan Donovan's family used to go off at 3.00 am to Covent Garden to buy lilies, gypsophilia and irises (blue in honour of Our Lady), and when they got back her mother and the older girls all got busy decorating their house's street shrine, and getting the younger children ready to walk in the procession. Joan's brother Terry was in the parish band, which played at all the outdoor processions, fetes and functions. The kerbs were painted white, and bunting hung across the street. The collecting boxes at the house shrines were a useful earner (a lot of the money was donated by non-Catholics who enjoyed the show) and any other opportunity for fundraising was eagerly seized: Joan recalled that if you held a ribbon from the banner you had to pay 6d. The money went to whichever cause had been announced on the programme – usually the current school project. Excited Protestant and Jewish children used to follow the processions round for hours, wishing they could take part.

Parish excursions usually involved spending a day somewhere in the Essex countryside. It was financially and practically impossible for whole groups from working class parishes to make overseas pilgrimages, but organised parish pilgrimages even to shrines in England seem not to have been a regular practice in the interwar years. In 1930 35 girls from Johnson Street made a pilgrimage to Westminster Cathedral, to the newly installed shrine of the English Martyr John Southworth. In 1931, to mark the recent successes and achievements (mainly those of 1929), the parish began saving up to send a delegation on the 1931 national pilgrimage to Lourdes, but the collection didn't go well. The parishioners had fundraised very hard for the beautification of the church, so may be they were exhausted – or maybe they didn't see the pilgrimage as being so relevant. However an outside benefactor suddenly agreed to cover the balance for two tickets. Henry Martin and Ada Goldsmith were alarmed to be summoned to their respective headteachers' offices at St Bernard's School (Ada was wondering what she'd done wrong), but it was good news: they'd been chosen to represent the parish at Lourdes. Later in 1931, Mother Emmanuel was able to arrange a school journey in France for some of the St Bernard's girls: they went to Bayeux, and stayed in a Benedictine convent. The boys's school journey was to Yorkshire, to study fossils.

Richard Totman was CYMS Secretary. For some years the annual dinner was held at Wickham's Restaurant. Wickham's was a huge department store, the Harrods of the East End: its beautiful new building spread over where Nos 69-79 and 83-89 Mile End Road had previously stood – only the effect was rather spoiled by No 81 remaining stuck in the middle, because Spiegelhalters refused to sell! From 1935 on the dinner was held in Our Lady's Hall, though still catered by Wickham's. The new Archbishop of Westminster, Arthur Hinsley, was guest of honour in 1937, when the group's chaplain happened to be Fr Edward Hinsley, a fellow-Yorkshireman, and distantly related. Totman told the archbishop that the club was facing a serious problem: the building wasn't big enough for everyone who wanted to come. The dinners were always mixed, and the club itself had been opened to members' wives – though it was said that some of the men left when women were allowed in! At first only men could be members, but they could bring in women as visitors. Thus the CYMS began a process of transformation into a club for all the family: grandparents, parents and children. By 1939 women were allowed to be members in their own right. Canon Ring encouraged everyone in the parish to join what was now called the Vaughan Club, as it was good wholesome fun.

Over the years there had been repeated attempts to set up a parish Boys' Club. The CSU settlement had tried, and the CYMS had tried, but boys were always difficult to work with, and the arrangements kept breaking down. However in October 1937 Fr John Leigh and Frank Greenan agreed to try again. For boys aged 14-20, the new club offered boxing (with Tom Brooks as instructor) or PT at the Vaughan Club on Tuesday nights; various other games on Thursday night, including use of the men's billiard tables; and more games on Friday night at Johnson Street School. A lot of equipment was purchased specially, and within a couple of years it had 100 members. The SVP group continued to meet in Our Lady's Hall at midday every Sunday,

run by Frank Greenan, who also served as choirmaster. But many local needs were met by neighbourliness rather than in any formally organised way. For example, hardly anyone had a car but when Tommy Henderson had to go into hospital with leukaemia, the undertaker Alf Ta[illegible], who lived at the end of Hardinge Street, used to go and bring him home for visits. The caretaker, who lived in the lodge at the front of the church, was Mr Dunne, and "you couldn't get past him, he was a wonderful old man." A small but steady stream of boys from Johnson Street and St Bernard's went on to train for the priesthood. Two sons of George Groves, George and Alex, became priests, and in 1937 Joe Doyle was ordained at Westminster Cathedral in the morning, and came to Commercial Road to march in the outdoor procession in the afternoon. John Coughlan, of Whitehorse Street, had noticed that lack of pocket money was a serious factor dissuading boys from staying on at school, and was concerned that the parish might be losing vocations because of it. So he and his wife agreed to devote their hard-earned life savings towards providing £10 a year pocket money for one seminarian. Canon Ring wanted the scheme to be called the John Coughlan Fund, but "he would not hear of it", so Mrs Metcalfe, who chipped in another £100 and set the thing up, named it the Canon Ring Fund. The first beneficiary was 15-year-old Victor Guazzelli, the seventh St Bernard's student to be accepted for seminary training. Victor had been outdoor collector for Twine Court and Solander Street for over five years. Though he was the only son, his father Cesare gave his blessing, and Victor departed in September 1935 for the English College in Lisbon. Cesare died a few years later, and Victor never saw him again. The family café, at No 406 Commercial Road, took his brother-in-law's name and was known as Tolaini's, but Canon Ring always referred to it as "Mrs Guazzelli's restaurant".

The Canon fires a salvo

By the mid-1930s people everywhere were losing confidence in the capacity of a democratic system to resolve the world's devastating economic crisis, and turning instead to extremist political movements. In Tower Hamlets the governing Labour group was perceived as corrupt and ineffectual; unwilling to allow genuine debate, especially from the left wing of the Party; and too heavily dominated by Catholics. Significant numbers of East Enders – especially Jews – were joining the Communist Party. That option was not open to practising Catholics, who tended instead to be attracted to Oswald Mosley's British Union of Fascists (BUF).

Constant clashes between the Reds and the Blackshirts drove a spiral of violence in the lead-up to 1936, when the outbreak of the Spanish Civil War sharply polarised the situation. Reports that thousands of priests, nuns and devout laypeople had been murdered in Spain by Republican forces were airily dismissed by most of the British population. The Labour Party tried to distance itself from a rally organised at St George's Town Hall by the Stepney Council for Peace and Democracy, which they considered a Communist front. Nevertheless Isidore Vogler, a prominent Jewish Labour Councillor and former Mayor, agreed to chair, and Monica Whateley, a Catholic and budding Labour politician, gave an eye-witness account which was firmly pro-Republican: she'd been in Barcelona shortly before the outbreak of hostilities, and had seen "the nuns and priests were walking about in the streets happy and secure". She was probably genuinely unaware of the slaughter that took place *after* the fighting began – for the horrifying tales were in fact true. Half-a-dozen Catholics, including Councillor Jerry Long, and John Oldfield LCC, began shouting protests, the meeting dissolved into uproar and Vogler had eventually to ask all the protesters to leave. Excoriated for embarrassing Vogler, the Catholics felt themselves unfairly blamed and deprived of a fair hearing, and took refuge in "non-political" rallies where their religious leaders praised them for sticking up for their principles. Oldfield's understanding of the rights and wrongs of the Spanish conflict was actually quite well-nuanced, but most local people had no way of evaluating the issues, and saw it in highly glamourised terms as Good versus Evil, on a completely different plane from politics as ordinarily understood. Jews, and many other non-Catholics, saw it as a people's struggle against Fascist terror, whereas Catholics saw it as a crusade, with heroic Christians battling for survival against the forces of international Bolshevism.

Local Communists boasted of how they'd successfully taken up collections for Spain outside St Mary and St Michael's, after Mass, but it's impossible to know whether some of the parishioners were really pro-Republic, or (more likely) misunderstood which side the collection was for. For most East End Catholics, anti-Communism was a tribal badge. It was claimed at the time that "hundreds" of them joined the BUF out of solidarity over Spain. But we don't have firm figures and, more importantly, we know very little about how long most recruits to Fascism stayed in the movement. The BUF always publicised numbers of new members, but carefully never mentioned how many left: its membership was actually a very fast-revolving door! Abp Hinsley, and the local Catholic clergy, took a strong line against anti-semitism. On 4th October, a planned Fascist parade along Whitechapel High Street was prevented by a mass turnout of a hundred thousand protesters: in what came to be called the Battle of Cable Street, Catholic dockers from the riverside districts joined the Jewish, Communist and Anarchist groups which were blocking the roads at Aldgate and defying the police.

Canon Ring in procession with the Mayor and Mayoress preceded by the macebearer

Despite this show of East End solidarity, tensions persisted and grew. The dominant figures in Stepney politics were Jerry Long and Morry Davis. Davis was President of the Federation of Synagogues, and had achieved a great deal for Jewish causes, but his operating style was profoundly undemocratic, and he was too fond of controlling everything personally to want to nurture younger leaders. Some of the other prominent Jewish Labour politicians, including Vogler, were subjected to disciplinary procedures for failing to distance themselves sufficiently from the Communists. Dan Frankel became MP for Mile End, but for a long time there were no more Jewish Mayors. A lot of people were under the impression that the Mayor was always a Catholic (which wasn't true), and saw the Catholics as having everything sewn up. To

Harry Fitzer as the King of Siam in the Rodgers and Hammerstein musical *THE KING AND I* presented at Our Lady's Hall in March 1972.

Maureen Hayward as Widow Corney and Harry Fitzer as Mr Bumble in the production of Lionel Bart's *OLIVER* shown at Our Lady's Hall in January 1973.

Irish dancing at the St Patrick's Night Ceilidh 2007
in Our Lady's Parish Community Hall

Rosie Armstrong and Sister Lawrence enjoy
the St Patrick's Night Ceilidh

Three ladies happy at their task: Sheila Crawley, Patricia Cartwright and Tara Aves arrange the flowers in church.

The church cleaning team relaxes during a tea break. Some on the team have carried out this wonderful service to the church for over 50 years.

October 2007: parish catechists preparing material for the First Communions course.

October 2007: staff of St Mary and St Michael's Primary School off on their annual retreat.

Vitoldas Preibys finishing the restoration of the statue of the Madonna and Child which had stood for many years on the wall of Our Lady's Hall in Johnson St.

August 2007: the blessing of the restored statue of the Madonna and Child outside the new Our Lady's Parish Community Hall.

The restored crucifix from the Calvary destroyed in the V2 bombing of 17th March 1945

Ayline Chowrimootoo works on the restoration
of the statue of St Michael the Archangel

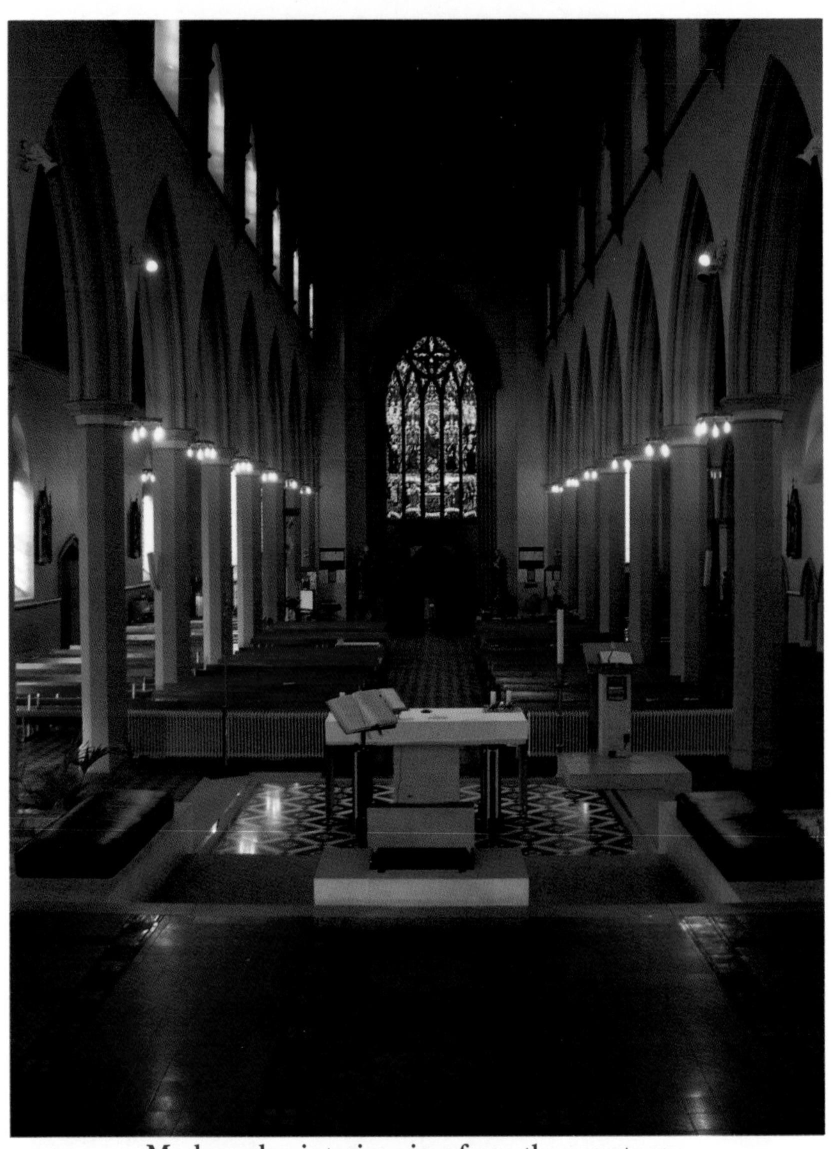

Modern-day interior view from the sanctuary
of the 'Cathedral of the East End'

the many Jews who looked to the Communist Party as their only reliable bulwark against Hitler, the vehement anti-Communism of the Catholics, their resistance to any co-operation with Communists, and above all their sympathy with Nationalist Spain, made all of them – including the vast majority who wouldn't have touched Mosley with a bargepole – appear as crypto-Fascists.

The 1937 Commercial Road outdoor procession was the largest and most elaborate to date, with 2,500 parishioners taking part, including close on a thousand men. Shortly beforehand, the Propaganda Administrator of the BUF wrote to Canon Ring to inform him that a planned Blackshirt march had been postponed so as not to clash with the religious event. His reaction to this attempt to curry favour was prompt and furious: he wrote back to say he had already heard of the proposed march, and intended to denounce from his pulpit "any men calling themselves Catholics" who dared to take part. He also published his letter in the *Universe*:

> *It is an abominable disservice for Catholic men to associate the Catholic Church with Communism or Fascism... It is an offence against truth for Communists to say they are speaking as Catholics. But it seems to me that it is a greater offence for Fascists, as pretended friends, to do so... This effort to drag the unity and solidarity of our people into the service of freak movements, is unworthy of members of the Church. I bear grateful witness to the kindness and helpfulness of my Jewish neighbours for over 30 years, and I am annoyed at the attacks on them by political tramps, and strangers to the locality. It is an outrage on the Catholic Church to associate it with the repulsive 'isms of fanatic champions, or to imply that it has any sympathy for race hatred.'*

The Fascists raged impotently against the "ill-mannered" Canon. Just one month later (no doubt by pure coincidence) came the news that the Pope had appointed him a Domestic Prelate. Henceforth he would bear the title "Right Reverend Monsignore."

For the 1937 LCC Elections, the BUF put up two candidates for Limehouse. Charles Wegg-Prosser was from a prominent Catholic family, and he tried hard to obtain some sort of endorsement from Abp Hinsley, asking him to make a Premierland-style statement that it was OK for Catholics to vote Fascist: Hinsley refused. The Labour candidates, Richard Coppock and Monica Whateley, won a resounding victory, each gaining over 8,000 votes, but the two Fascists each got slightly over 2,000, which was a lot better than anyone (except themselves) had expected. Coppock angrily complained that most of those who voted for them were Catholics. It's certainly very likely that a lot of Catholics wanted to register a protest vote against Whately, and

Wegg-Prosser had gone all out for Catholic support. However Mgr Ring was furious about how he'd presented himself as "a pious promoter of the St Vincent de Paul Society." In his parish magazine he fulminated against outsiders who suddenly descended on Limehouse making a big play of being Catholic, although "there is no Catholic issue and no Catholic interest to be served", and expecting "to range us all on their side... We are supposed to be odd if we do not swallow his clap-trap. He is beaten, and we see no more of him. He disappears and leaves us to swab up." Quite soon afterwards, Wegg-Prosser left the BUF, having become disgusted with its anti-semitism, and before long was repentantly making anti-Fascist speeches at Jewish gatherings.

Valiant Women

Mother De Sales, the first of the Blue Nuns to arrive in Commercial Road, and superior since 1907, remained and worked in the parish for thirty years and was dearly beloved. When she left, having been promoted to Provincial Superior, the Children of Mary saved up to pay for a stained glass window to be placed in the Guild Chapel in her honour. It was executed by Arthur Orr, and unveiled in May 1927. The centre light showed St Francis De Sales; on either side were depicted the raising of Jairus' daughter (symbolising the Sisters' nursing vocation), and the death of St Joseph (symbolising their role in bringing spiritual comfort to the dying); and at the top was an idealised image of religious nurse.

There was consternation in the summer of 1933 when it was announced that the Little Company of Mary had decided to withdraw its Sisters from Commercial Road. A petition to the Superior General was signed by thousands, and when she came over to Hillingdon Court, on a visit from Rome, a deputation from the parish went there, but in vain. To make matters worse, in 1934 the Sisters of Charity also decided to withdraw. Their congregation had houses in most of the East End parishes, and was overstretched, and Lady FitzAlan's maintenance grant wasn't going as far as it had in 1911. The visitation part of their work in St Mary and St Michael's parish was taken over by St Philip's House, the former CSU settlement in Mile End, which had also become a Convent of Charity. As the Girls' Club activities were mostly evening classes, Lady FitzAlan held discussions with Edith Ramsay, Head of the LCC-funded Stepney Women's Institute, and with Miss Pearson, and it was arranged that they could continue under LCC auspices at Senrab Street School. She asked Sr Bernard, who was going to take over the Children of Mary from the Blue Nuns, to "look in now and then" on the evening classes as well, but somehow the Sisters of Mercy got drawn in deeper than they'd intended, and became quite heavily involved with the Girls' Club. Meanwhile Lady FitzAlan made arrangements to bestow the St Cecilia's settlement property – the three houses on Commercial Road, of which she now held the freehold – on the trustees of the Archdiocese of Westminster for the use of the people of St Mary and St Michael's: it would be known as the FitzAlan Trust. Sr Bridget Leahy, who had entered the Convent of Mercy in 1884 when already a qualified teacher, and been superior for 11 years 1919-1930, died in January 1937, aged 96. According to the *East London Advertiser*:

She was a lady of great culture and refinement. The great crowd of children and parents at her Requiem showed how much the poor respected her. She had always an excuse and an explanation for their shortcomings. Canon Ring referred to her... as the 'Valiant Woman' of religious life, to whose self-denial the poor of the parish owed much... It was a tragedy, he declared, that those who spouted stupidities about convents did not come in contact with those brilliant women who gave up home and country and fortune to labour for the enlightenment and happiness of the poor in community life.

A "large and representative" congregation attended a High Mass of Thanksgiving at St Mary and St Michael's on Easter Monday 1937, with the Children of Mary choir, to celebrate the marvellous news that the Blue Nuns were back. The FitzAlan Trust had made it possible, and they were to move into St Cecilia's. Shortly afterwards the Mercy Superior, Mother Evangelist Seaborne, proposed to Mgr Ring that her Sisters withdraw from supervision of the Girls' Club, but he asked her to carry on until the end of the summer term on 1st July, to give the Blue Nuns a chance to settle in and get themselves organised. However in August he suddenly demanded that the Sisters of Mercy continue to run the club. The Blue Nuns saw the core work of St Cecilia's as running the clinic, and they had absolutely no problem with that. They'd started Mothers' Meetings and sewing classes, and "recreation for grumbling old people", and were happy to help with anything else that was directly evangelistic or pastoral, but they drew the line at the Girls' Club. Mgr Ring argued to Mother Evangelist that the Blue Nuns really couldn't be expected to run it, because the girls were quite rough. The Mercies, who'd taught those girls from childhood and knew them well, should be able to handle them, and aftercare of girls after they'd left school was properly part of their charism.

Senrab Street School was conveniently close to St Cecilia's, but something of a trek there and back from the new Convent of Mercy. Mother Evangelist explained that over the past few months she'd been very frightened about having to leave the convent gates unlocked up to 10.30 at night, with

Communists and Fascists holding meetings in Hardinge Street just outside (constantly hurling abuse, and trying to pick fights with each other), while she waited for the Sisters to return from Senrab Street, and worried in case anything had happened to them. To the nuns, accustomed to early hours, anything after 10.00 pm was frighteningly late, and she really wanted them home by 9.00. She was only willing to consider letting her community continue to supervise the clubs if they could be moved to Johnson Street, so the Sisters could return to the convent using the short-cut past Our Lady's Hall, and be let in at the back door.

Unfortunately, because of the LCC involvement and the practicalities of running evening classes, Mgr Ring wasn't in a position to change the arrangements. Edith Ramsay was dragged into the dispute, and eventually Abp Hinsley intervened, and it was arranged for the nuns to be brought home each evening by taxi. The row blew over, and the following year Mgr Ring was full of praise for the Sisters of Mercy over the marvellous Passion Play put on by the St Cecilia's Girls' Club Drama Class, under their guidance. Edith Ramsay often used to pop into the presbytery late at night, after classes, to chat to Mgr Ring. She also sometimes attended Mass to hear the St Cecilia's choir, though on one occasion she was mortified to hear him reading out a letter she'd written to him, defending her own (Presbyterian) view of the Eucharist, in order to ridicule her arguments. Lady FitzAlan wrote to Mgr Ring on 20th April 1938, asked for the prayers of the nuns and children of the parish for Lord FitzAlan. She died two days later.

Catholic Action

The raising of the school leaving age to 15, and introduction of some form of secondary education for all children over 11, was due to come into force on 1st September 1939. Abp Hinsley launched a fundraising drive for a major building programme, and Mgr Ring, preaching at a special service at St Joseph's, Highgate, in support of the archbishop's initiative, rubbished objections to his appeal for £100,000 from the diocese as a whole. As he told the packed congregation, just *three* of the impoverished East End parishes – his own, and two others – had raised £80,000 for schools in the last 20 years.

The decrepit Westminster Catholic Federation was wound up and merged with a new organisation, Catholic Action, under Dr O'Donovan as National Lay President. Everyone was assured that it wasn't supposed to compete with, or supersede, existing groups, but co-ordinate and revitalise them, and help them work better. But it was very top-down, and in most parishes it just seemed to mean yet more meetings, for people who had lots of meetings to go to already. Mgr Ring stated, firmly and sensibly, that Catholic Action was basically what St Mary and St Michael's was already doing. But one new idea which was beginning to interest him, and other Westminster priests, was Cardijn's YCW.

The Communist Party was steadily gaining sympathy and support among the people of the East End, by identifying and taking up key issues. Under the leadership of Phil Piratin and Tubby Rosen, the Comrades gleefully organised tenants associations and launched rent strikes, and they got results: again and again, the landlords caved in. Piratin got onto Stepney Council in 1937, and as a major European war came to appear increasingly likely, the Communists took up the highly emotive issue of Air Raid Precautions (ARP), and hammered the Council for its failure to provide adequate shelters. Catholic leaders, who knew only too well how religious believers were treated in the Soviet Union, were worried sick by the Comrades' growing popularity. The YCW offered a means to counter-attack.

YCW branches were now flourishing all over Belgium and France, and in many other countries throughout the world, and the Pope had praised it as a legitimate model of Catholic Action. A group had been started in London in 1937 by Harry Tolfree. There was also one in Wigan, so Tolfree got in touch with them, and a third YCW section was started in Poplar. The scattered groups then joined up for a congress in Wigan, at which Tolfree was elected National President. Mgr Ring organised a big YCW rally at Limehouse Town Hall in December 1938. Author and publisher Frank Sheed gave a talk, emphasising the threat of the "Marxist Utopia" which was really a dystopia, suitable for supermen or insects but not for real human beings. Tolfree explained how big the YCW movement was on the continent, Ted Moriarty from Poplar gave an impassioned speech, and Fr Vincent Rochford, assistant priest at Poplar, spoke of the forthcoming pilgrimage to Rome in which 25,000 YCWs were going to take part, including a delegation from East London: it was planned for 5th September 1939.

As the 1930s wound to a close, Mgr Ring had two projects on hand. One was the conversion of the church's left-hand corner chapel into a shrine to the English Martyrs: by mid-1939 it had been beautifully furnished and decorated by Frank Lapthorne, the current organist. The other was, at long last, to get the church spire built…

Evacuation

Everyone's plans had to be put on hold when, on 1st September 1939, Hitler invaded Poland. Immediate air attacks were expected on Britain's largest population centres, so ever since April plans had been in place to organise the schoolchildren into "squads" of 50, with teachers and other adult helpers assigned, ready for evacuation to "reception areas" well outside London. St Bernard's Central School, and part of the Johnson Street Senior Schools, went to Egham near Windsor, where the teachers found Eton sixth formers waiting at the station to meet them and carry their luggage. The biggest single contingent from St Mary and St Michael's were taken on the East London Line from Shadwell to New Cross Gate, and put on a train for Brighton. Lewin Timms wrote home to Mgr Ring, describing the "lovely country" they'd seen during the train ride, and the rations of chocolate, biscuits, milk and 'bully beef' on arrival. The Sisters made sure the children were all billeted, then set off to find the Convent of Mercy where they received a warm welcome and, even though there were 13 of them, beds were found for everyone. Some mothers and younger children from the parish were also in Brighton, mostly billeted on local households, though some were lucky enough to get an empty house: the Hendersons and Penfolds shared one between them. At Mass on Sunday the children heard the priest announce that war had been declared, and as they left the church the sirens began to howl.

East End children being evacuated in September 1939

Many Catholic children had become separated from their schools and were billeted all over the countryside, often in traditionally anti-Catholic areas, and with no provision for their religious needs. Amigo, who was now an archbishop, declared that he'd rather the children were killed by the bombs than lose their souls, and Mgr Ring soon turned strongly against the whole policy of evacuation. It wasn't as if air raids were actually taking place, so why separate children from their families, and disrupt their education? However most of the Commercial Road schoolchildren weren't doing too badly. Fr Flannagan at St John the Baptist's, Brighton, agreed to share his parish school on a shift system: them in the morning, and the Brighton children in the afternoon. Billy Hayes and Joseph Hutchinson wrote to say they were very happy and being kindly treated, but hoped they could come home soon. Mary Riley, an older girl, explained that in the afternoons they met in a hall to do painting, needlework or singing, or else did some educational sightseeing, and Irene Dunne excitedly described their visit to the Pavilion – "the most beautiful building in Brighton". St Bernard's was allocated a beautiful house at Englefield Green in which to hold classes. All the London theatres had been closed, and to Mother Emmanuel's amazement Ninette de Valois, celebrated founder of the English National Ballet, came along to say that as there was nothing doing at Sadler's Wells, could she help out? She gave dancing lessons, devoting to each little girl as much care and attention as if she'd been a budding prima ballerina.

John Oldfield was keen to enlist, and when he was rejected for everything else he signed on as an ordinary seaman. Dr O'Donovan enlisted in the Royal Army Medical Corps. Fr James Coughlan and Fr Hinsley had both wanted to volunteer as chaplains to the forces, but they couldn't both go, so Hinsley was picked. With one priest down it was difficult to cover all the St Mary and St Michael's Masses (including the convent Masses), but Frs Bernard Schnitzler and Joseph Simml, from St Boniface's German Church, came to help. Usually when a confirmation was held at St Mary and St Michael's there were about 300 candidates, but when David Mathew, the new auxiliary bishop for Westminster, came in October 1939, there were only 40, mostly adult converts, and the Children of Mary formed the choir because the schoolboys had been evacuated. Bp Mathew recalled the temperance meetings his famous great-uncle had held on the church site, noted with approval that the parish was carrying on as usual, and said that when he'd been in Ireland a short while ago, he'd discovered that the name of Mgr Ring was just as famous there as in England. Although so many parishioners had been got out of London, the service was well attended.

Evacuated adults usually returned home very quickly. Returnees to Commercial Road confided to the Sisters of Mercy that the countryside was too quiet for them: they couldn't stand the "'orrible 'ush". Soon the children began returning as well, and as the months passed, the drift back to London swelled into a flood. Around the end of November most of the Sisters of Mercy returned to Hardinge Street, because so many of their children had already come home that there seemed no point in staying. St Bernard's pupils also drifted home, and the numbers at Englefield Green went down to about 150. As it was forbidden to reopen the schools in London, thousands of children were running around the streets, getting into trouble and creating havoc. Altogether, about 700 from Commercial Road's parish schools were back home. Six of them wrote to their MPs to ask for their schools to be reopened, while hundreds signed a petition to the President of the Board of Education. Mgr Ring, who had put them up to it, also wrote to the MPs, and issued a press statement pointing out that if there was an air raid, the children would be safer in school where their teachers could keep them under control and ensure they took shelter. Clem Attlee replied to Edward Davey and Mary Wood: "Dear Children, – Thank you for your letter. I have already been working to get the schools re-opened when possible. You may be sure I will do everything I possibly can in this matter." Jimmy Hall, who wasn't as busy and important as Attlee, wrote a longer and more personalised reply to his two young constituents, Marie McCarthy and Henry Wilcox, in which he referred to Mgr Ring's letter: "If you will forgive the use of a big word, as no other appears to be adequate, he has dealt with the matter trenchantly." All the MPs promised support, and so did Cardinal Hinsley.

Commercial Road was *not* allowed to celebrate Midnight Mass as usual that Christmas: all churches had to bring the service forward, to comply with blackout regulations. While the LCC did its best for the evacuees, allocating £50,000 for parties and presents, the non-evacuated didn't qualify. However Mgr Ring defiantly threw a party for his children in Our Lady's Hall. This was just before rationing kicked in, and although he had to make do with margarine because it becoming difficult to get butter, he managed to order large quantities of jam and sweets, and even 430 oranges! While the men teachers put up the decorations and did their best to "beautify" the blackout arrangements, the Sisters of Mercy and women teachers, along with William Brown and Mr Johnson (caretakers respectively of St Bernard's and the Junior School), organised the food. During the party Fr Coughlan and Mr Moffat, the St Bernard's sports master, provided musical entertainment.

The Sisters of Mercy and the other teachers did what they could, organising classes for small groups in the convent, or in the children's homes, but they couldn't do much beyond basic reading and arithmetic, and setting work for the children to do on their own. Joan Donovan was one of a group of nine from her class who attended lessons at the home of a Mrs Cain, the mother of one of them. Miss Watson, one of their teachers at Johnson Street, came to give the lessons, and in the afternoon she took them out to the park or the People's Palace. Eventually the government gave permission for the schools to reopen, and announced that compulsory attendance would reapply from 1st April. St Bernard's was reopened as an "Emergency School" for Catholic children over 11, and Joan and her friends went there for a while. Despite Jimmy Hall's strenuous efforts on the parish's behalf, the Board of Education refused to designate Lukin Street an official Emergency School, but in practice it was permitted to operate, and all the parish schools quickly filled up again – including the overflow classes in Our Lady's Hall. By March most men parishioners under 30, and St Bernard's old boys, were being called up, and lists of their names were published in *Rector's Realm.* The Vaughan Club began a Benevolent Society to provide assistance to its members serving in the forces: a collecting box stood in the clubroom, and fortnightly dances were held to raise money. Fr Hinsley was with the British Expeditionary Force in France. Letters came in from men overseas, saying that on Wednesday nights, wherever they were, they always joined in the Guild prayers.

St Mary and St Michael's held its annual mission as usual in the spring of 1940. There was double the usual attendance at Sunday Mass on the last Sunday of May, which had been declared a national Day of Prayer because France was collapsing, but a week later the usual outdoor procession was held – a great morale-booster, as everyone in the East End would have been disappointed if such a treasured tradition had to be cancelled. During the desperate rush for Dunkirk, a soldier whom Mgr Ring called "Casey" (which might not have been his real name) made a vow to the Blessed Virgin that if he got back safely, he would walk in the procession, "however footsore and weary he was." Arriving at Euston on Sunday 2nd June, he obtained permission to phone home, but in fact hopped on a bus, walked in the procession as promised (playing an instrument in the band), then got himself back to Aldershot before midnight and before his absence had been noticed, so nobody knew he'd been AWOL. A number of soldiers who were legitimately on leave also walked in the procession, in their khaki battledress. In the evening, when the priests went round to bless the shrines along the routes, they publicly thanked "all, whether Catholic, non-Catholic, or Jew, for the efforts they had made to make the Procession such a success."

Arthur McSorley had been taken off from Dunkirk in a boat that was then bombed and sunk; however he was picked up by an oil tanker and made it home. Fr Hinsley was still missing, so everyone was asked to pray for him. But he was with the Highlanders of the 51st Division who were cut off from Dunkirk, and trapped at St Valery-en-Caux where the steep cliffs made it impossible for boats to come in to take them off. After a ferocious stand (which deeply impressed General de Gaulle, future leader of the Free French), the survivors had to surrender. Fr Hinsley was to spend the rest of the war in a POW camp, but afterwards he was awarded the MBE. Gordon Grant and Edward McCready had also been taken prisoner, and Mgr Ring requested prayers for them. Lawrence Isaacs's plane had gone down in Belgium, and there was no news whether he'd survived, but Mgr Ring wrote:

"it is a great consolation to his mother to know that he was a good lad and that if death came he was prepared to meet it." James Coveney and William Marriott were in the army, Tom Aylward was in the navy. James Brown, formerly at the Port of London Authority, who'd earned two stripes for helping to bring troops off from Dunkirk, was picked for officer training at Sandhurst.

A German invasion was imminently expected, and the LCC launched yet another push to evacuate the children. A contingent of 893 Catholic youngsters from the East End was sent off in the general direction of Devon, including children from various parishes, but mostly St Mary and St Michael's. Mother Emmanuel set up her headquarters in Torquay, and spent the next six weeks getting all 893 into Catholic schools in Devon – by squeezing them into existing schools where possible, or else finding suitable premises in which to set up temporary schools, and then arranging for Catholic teachers and children to be transferred to billets nearby. Meanwhile Sr Philomena, and the remaining evacuees in Brighton, were moved inland, and most of them ended up in Byfleet, Surrey.

The small Devon town of Ashburton, to which Srs Ita Keane and Therese O'Connell, and a lot of the Commercial Road children, were despatched, was a "rather bigoted place". The Sisters found it very upsetting to watch people picking and choosing which children they'd take in: the well-dressed and good-looking ones were taken first, and the "poor shabby ones" were "rejected time after time". Hostility to the nuns themselves was such that no one wanted to take *them*, and "there was even a question of us being allowed to walk freely through the village". They had nowhere to set up school, and no equipment, so the children were fretting and unhappy: all the nuns could do was take them for country walks and encourage them to "explore nature". On Sundays the children's "foster parents" expected to take them along to their various Protestant services, which led to more friction. The nuns managed to set up a Sunday School, so they could offer to take the children while the services were on, but even so some of the children were forced to attend the non-Catholic churches.

Mussolini was convinced it could only be a matter of a few months, at most, before Britain surrendered, and as he wanted to be on the winning side, he brought Italy into the conflict in alliance with Germany. In Ashburton, as the Sisters of Mercy recalled, "The day that Italy joined the War was a bad one for us and children. The Pope was the cause of all the trouble and we were a bad lot." Over the next day or so, while newspapers published (wildly exaggerated) reports of ferocious riots in Soho, a few windows of Italian cafés in Poplar were broken, and in Cable Street a crowd of 200 local English waded into an Italian family row, resulting in London-born John Pioli being fined 10s (50p) for allegedly making anti-British remarks. Nevertheless it wasn't long before Churchill issued an order, and large numbers of London Italians were arrested and interned.

Eventually an old grammar school in Ashburton "where famous Devonians were educated" was cleaned up and given to the Catholics – though the villagers thought this "a desecration of a sacred spot". The Sisters recalled: "We had no tables or chairs, but we had pews, like monks' stalls round the side and a number of long forms for sitting. Our teaching methods were rather chaotic especially when the forms got unbalanced. However we managed and we were glad to have a roof over our heads." The small Catholic chapel was served by a priest from Buckfast, who came every morning to say Mass for the nuns, and gave them a key so they could go in and pray at any time. The monks were tremendously helpful, arranging sports days for the children at the Abbey, and giving them parties. 32 children made their First Communion that year, after which they were served a breakfast of honey, new-laid eggs and home-made jam, and had their photo taken with the Lord Abbot.

First Communions in Ashburton

Extra efforts were often put in to ensure that children who'd won places at selective schools, like St Bernard's, could be evacuated to the same reception areas as their schools, and also that such schools could continue to recruit fresh intakes at the beginning of each academic year. So St Bernard's continued to operate at Englefield Green throughout the war. Each summer they put on open air dramatic performances, and they even held old pupils' reunions there.

The 1940-41 Blitz

Looking after evacuated schoolchildren, and keeping them cheerful so they would stay evacuated, was very hard work for teachers. Sr Sylvester Gill recalled the "great strain and responsibility" of caring for the children in Ashburton who, as Sr Perpetua Anglim pointed out, "often felt sad and miserable because of separation from parents and friends." But the strain increased almost to breaking point from September 1940, when the Blitz got under way, because of each day's "fear of what we might hear from home". Any news, good or bad, was likely to be delayed: there was no telephone, and letters arrived infrequently. The East End was in the front line, with bombs raining down night after night as the Luftwaffe tried to knock out the docks. Another wave of evacuees left London, either with official help or under their own steam. A lot of Stepney bombed-outs went to Byfleet, where the billeting officers were particularly helpful, and more Sisters of Mercy went out to Byfleet to help look after the increasing number of evacuees there from Commercial Road. When Cardinal Hinsley came to visit the blitzed parishes, he was told that quite a high proportion of the Catholic families were already away hopping when it started. The Warrens were forced to leave their flat at Gosling House after the first night, because of an unexploded bomb, so the women of the family arranged to go to the hopfields. Once the hopping was over, many of these families managed to get themselves evacuated somewhere else, without returning to London.

Those Sisters of Mercy not needed to help with the evacuees refused to be evacuated for their own safety. They had their own shelter in the convent basement, where they slept on makeshift beds surrounded by sandbags, and were happy to share it with their neighbours, who loved to "join in the prayers with the Sisters feeling encouraged and strengthened beneath the convent roof." A great many rosaries were recited. On one particularly bad night, when incendiaries were dropping on nearby warehouses, and stables where horses were kept, Srs Rufina Malone and Felicity Hayes went up to the convent roof to inspect, and while they were there some incendiaries dropped on the roof. They raced down to fetch for buckets of sand and stirrup pumps, and managed to put them out. In due course a rota was organised for firewatching, and each Sister took duty once a week, staying awake all night to keep a lookout. The Sisters started making up urns of tea for the people sheltering under the railway arches in Hardinge and Johnson Streets. Supplies were sent by Stepney ARP Control, and every night the nuns brewed 10 gallons of tea, as strong and sweet as the ration would permit, and packed up 200 cakes and sandwiches, to be taken round by Fr John Leigh and some volunteers from the shelters. Shelterers were asked to pay ½d for each item, to cover costs, but they often insisted on paying more. Fr Leigh used to go round the shelters each night, and the people, regardless of what religion they were, never wanted to go to sleep till he'd been round and given his blessing.

Blitz-damaged East End

During one of the worst nights, 17th-18th September, a large bomb fell in the church grounds but didn't go off. The priests were asleep in the Junior School basement, and knew nothing about it till Fr Halvey saw the crater next morning. The priests had to vacate the premises while the bomb disposal squad was at work. Mgr Ring went to see Cardinal Hinsley, who agreed with him that the *Memorare* prayer was a very suitable response. The bomb was safely removed, but for a whole fortnight afterwards there was no gas or electricity supply anywhere in Stepney. The presbytery – like most private homes – had been dependent on a gas stove, but Mrs Guazzelli provided a midday meal at her café each day for the priests, and their "faithful domestic staff" managed somehow to rustle up their other meals, until the architect John Sterrett was able to fix them up with a coal-fired kitchen range. For lighting they "switched back to the days of tallow candles". Services in the church continued as usual, though with attendance halved, but as a small concession to the circumstances Mgr Ring agreed to move the Sunday evening service from 7.00 to 6.00. On 18th October a shell from an ack-ack gun came through the roof of Our Lady's Chapel, ricocheted off the wall, and went into the organ, smashing several pipes. The damage wasn't noticed till the following afternoon, whereupon the police got some engineers round to dig out the shell. Mgr Ring noted glumly that it would cost £140 to repair the organ.

The LCC asked him to allow the Junior School (his pride and joy) to be used as a rest centre. He agreed, but on condition that the Sisters of Mercy run it. Three of the Sisters who'd been caring for evacuees in Ashburton or Byfleet were therefore recalled to Hardinge Street. Sr Philomena was to be in charge, and assisting her would be Srs Cyril and Perpetua. So that the place would look like a home from home, rather than an institution, the Sisters busied themselves putting up bright curtains and installing easy chairs, and set out a children's room with gold-coloured tables, blue chairs, and plenty of toys. The St Mary and St Michael's Rest Centre opened shortly before Christmas, when teachers and students were available to come and help out as volunteers. LCC VIPs visited the Centre on Christmas Day. So did Mgr Ring: he had some of the Christmas pudding, but wouldn't tell anyone what he'd wished for.

Alerted by a parishioner named John Murphy to the plight of some of the frailest and oldest in the parish, Mgr Ring worked with the Warden of Toynbee Hall to try to get something done for the elderly, who were terribly distressed by the air raids. Eventually St Bernard's School was turned into a rest centre, with Mother Emmanuel in charge, and while doing a lot of general work, it specialised in the "aged and infirm". The ground floor was converted into an air raid shelter, bricked in against blast, and set up with trestle beds. There was a first aid post, mainly for new arrivals who needed cleaning up and plenty of TLC, and a clothing centre full of donated clothing. Students arriving to help care for the bombed-outs over the Christmas holidays were "amazed at the patience and cheerfulness of these old people, most of whom had lost everything. No word of complaint, but only gratitude to the nuns!" There were still children who hadn't been evacuated, so two teachers taught on the upper floor, each taking a large mixed-grade class. Bombed-outs, schoolchildren and workers were all provided with a delicious midday meal by Maggie, the cook, and a children's party was held on the day after Boxing Day 1940. There had been no bombing for about a fortnight, and it was widely assumed that some sort of Christmas truce had been arranged – though in fact there hadn't.

St Mary's Whitechapel blitzed and never rebuilt

The bombers returned with a massive raid on the night of 29th December, when the Thames was very low on water, so it was difficult to put out the fires. The firewatchers on the roof of the East End Methodist Mission watched the City burning, with the dome of St Paul's silhouetted against the flames. Although the East End was not the primary target, it came in for its share. St Mary's Whitechapel was gutted by incendiaries and left a roofless ruin, and English Martyrs, Tower Hill, rendered unusable by an unexploded bomb embedded in the floor. Wapping was ablaze, and the

"Dead End Kids", a bunch of intrepid teenage irregulars, were out as usual doing whatever they could to help: two of them, Ronnie Eyres and Bert Eden, were killed that night. A few hours before the raid, Ronnie had got engaged to Bruna Mentessi, daughter of an Italian café proprietor who'd been interned: the café was hit and burned down, leaving the family homeless. In the morning Nev Coates, a pacifist serving with the Friends Ambulance Unit, kindly borrowed a truck and took Bruna, accompanied by a priest and one of Ronnie's sisters, to the mortuary to say goodbye to her fiancé, then brought the whole family to Lukin Street, where the nuns could look after and comfort them. Sr Philomena later paid tribute to Bruna for the dignity and courage with which she coped with the tragedy, and how – after the first outpouring of grief – she concentrated on helping the other bombed-outs at the rest centre, and keeping up their spirits. Thirty-four old people could sleep at St Bernard's overnight while efforts were made to get them evacuated. No official evacuation scheme was in place for the elderly, so arrangements had to be made privately: Edith Ramsay helped with this, and offers of accommodation came through Cardinal Hinsley's Sword of the Spirit movement. The nuns rumbled one or two naughty old people who turned out to be Catholics, but hadn't been to Mass for years, and sorted them out. An 88-year-old lapsed Italian, who'd lived in England since boyhood, but whose excuse was that he'd never learned enough English to go to confession, was triumphantly delivered to St Peter's Italian Church.

Bombed-outs coming to Lukin Street had at first to sleep on mattresses on the floor, but as soon as possible they got beds, and the Sisters made patchwork quilts to go on them. The night of 19th-20th March was another one of terror for the East End, with 500 bombers starting nearly 2,000 fires. Sr Philomena recalled how the 120-odd bombed-out people in the rest centre sang and joked to keep their spirits up against "the constant scream of bombs and screech of fire-engines". Hundreds of incendiaries fell on nearby Cowley Gardens, but a group of about 30 men supervised by Warden Wally Wales rushed around extinguishing them. They were sheltering under a railway arch ready for the next wave when a 500kg high explosive bomb fell in the road, killing almost all of them, and blowing in most of the centre's windows and doors. "Flames from the adjacent burning houses began to lick through the centre's windows like hungry tongues, gripping the gay curtains and crackling up the window sashes" but the fire watchers, mostly teenage lads and OAPs, dealt with the fire. When the all-clear sounded

Stepney streets were utterly devastated. Mains were broken everywhere; there was no lighting; cables hung like snakes in the roadways; streams of people rushed here and there, crying out the names of loved ones who had vanished… Using a Valor paraffin

stove, the Sisters distributed hot tea among these poor people, and soothed them as best they could. How blessed was the first grey glimmer of morning light over the black skeletons of burned-out buildings in the east, even though it showed the whole terrible picture in unsoftened clearness.

Altogether 750 people had been killed that night. Joan Donovan was in Ashburton, but a bomb fell in Heckford Street and failed to go off, and her parents had to leave their home and rush to the shelter. In the morning the street was roped off, and nobody was allowed back. Her father went off to 11.00 Mass at St Mary and St Michael's while the rest of the family stood at the corner in Cable Street, waiting. A woman decided she had to go back for something from her house, so a policeman escorted her down, but the bomb went off and both of them were killed. Joan's parents had to spend six weeks at the Lukin Street rest centre. Frequent entertainments were staged in the school hall, the artistes sometimes being local amateurs, and sometimes professionals deployed by one of the official government-funded agencies: however the nuns insisted on using the highbrow CEMA rather than the more popular ENSA, because ENSA artistes had a reputation for making dirty jokes.

Although it wasn't immediately apparent, the main London Blitz was over – Hitler was moving his aircraft across to the other end of Europe in preparation for attacking the Soviet Union. Two East End Catholic churches, St Boniface's and Poplar, had been destroyed, and Bow Common very badly damaged, but English Martyrs was restored to use in April. Far more local Anglican and Methodist buildings suffered than Catholic ones, because there were so many more to start with, and it had already been decided that some of them – including Christ Church Watney Street, and St Thomas Arbour Square – would not be replaced. St Mary's Whitechapel was also never rebuilt: the site is now Aftab Ali Park. But St Mary and St Michael's remained unscathed. Celebrating a Mass of thanksgiving for the preservation of church, Mgr Ring urged parishioners to make the forthcoming annual mission one of thankgiving for their safety. And once the mission was over, of course the outdoor procession would go ahead as usual.

A little way along Commercial Road, the East London Mosque was opened in August 1941. It was a makeshift affair, just some old houses (Nos 446-8) adapted for communal worship. The London Muslims had been saving up for years, but they still didn't have quite enough, so the British Council helped with a grant. The government was trying to be supportive and helpful, because a high proportion of the men serving in the merchant navy, braving

East London Mosque Commercial Road

the German U-boats to bring food and war materials to Britain, were South Asian Muslims. Most were based in Asia, but some were East End residents: out of an official list of Stepney sailors reported killed during the winter of 1940-41, five names were Muslim. Other merchant seamen casualties were from the Limehouse Chinese community.

A heart of gold

Mother Emanuel had to resign as headmistress of St Bernard's, because she'd been appointed to another school. When she went to tell Mgr Ring he said, "Yes, and I too shall be handing in my resignation to the Master very soon." He was 83. That night he was taken into St John and St Elizabeth's Hospital, where he died on 8th August 1941. In the *Tablet* Bp Mathew wrote:

> *He was devoted to the Catholic Church and to his country. Short and robust, with his wide-set eyes and the small tufts of hair upon his cheeks, he was alive with merriment and understanding. He stood as strong and unbending as an Irish oak. He was shrewd and alert, and simple and direct in character. He had that strong religious faith which withstands martyrdom. His long life was given to Christ's poor.*

According to the *Daily Telegraph* "his complexion resembled a rugged Kerry mountainside. He had a pugnacious nose, a mouth that could snap like a rat-trap and a heart of gold." Over 2,000 people attended his funeral at St Mary and St Michael's. Cardinal Hinsley and several other bishops were present, along with an array of local politicians and dignitaries including Clem Attlee, who was shortly to become Churchill's deputy prime minister. Members of the Men's Guild bore the coffin to the boundary of the parish, with nearly a hundred cars and crowds of people following the cortege. Mgr Ring's will directed that the bulk of his substantial personal fortune of £8,947, derived primarily from the sale of the family farm in Co Cork inherited from his mother, go to St Bernard's School to support the education of boys between 14 and 16.

Thomas Fitzgerald was born in London, but always insisted he was Irish, and usually spent his summer holidays in Tipperary, where his family came from.

Thomas Canon Fitzgerald

As a child he'd been dared to steal an apple but was caught in the act – by a man who gave him a stern warning, but then kindly let him go. The man who'd caught him happened to be a Jew. For this reason, he always said, "Right to my dying day no one will be able to get away with anti-Semitism while I am about." When he decided to become a priest his father, a wealthy, self-made businessman, disinherited him on the grounds that rich priests were a nuisance. He deliberately avoided being sent to do his training in Rome, because he didn't want to be channelled into an academic career – though he *was* bright, and quite matter-of-fact about it: "If God gave you brains it's not for you to protest." Sitting out the First World War at St Sulpice in Paris, he acquired fluent French, and was quite capable of preaching in that language. After returning to England in 1918, aged 23, he was ordained, and tried his vocation briefly with the Oblates of St Charles in Bayswater. Leaving the Oblates he spent three years in Chelsea, but got fed up with the "constant round of dinner engagements", asked to be transferred to a parish where there was plenty of work to be done, and was sent to Sacred Heart, Holloway. In 1929 he was put in charge of Willesden Green (he wasn't actually made parish priest until 1934), and there he showed an amazing flair for fundraising: in just a few years he built a church and a presbytery, and enlarged the school. When asked how he managed it, he replied, "Raising money is easy. It's saving men's souls that is difficult."

He was rather taken aback to be asked to go to St Mary and St Michael's: he'd expected to live out his days at Willesden, and thought the responsibility of Commercial Road would be too much for him. Nevertheless, he accepted the assignment. Soon after he arrived, he set off for the West Country, to visit his parish children in the places they'd been evacuated to. Joan Donovan recalls him coming to Ashburton, but soon after that, having reached school leaving age, she herself returned to London. Her family had been given a nice flat in Regent House, and she got a job as a machinist at a war factory near Aldgate East Station, making sailors' and soldiers' uniforms. St Cecilia's Girls' Club was being re-started, so she joined: at first there were just eight of them, meeting in Whitehorse Road, but the numbers soon picked up again to about a hundred, and they moved to Johnson Street School. All sorts of sports and cultural activities were to be had for a subscription of 3d (1.25p) a week, which the girls tried hard to pay regularly, though sometimes they couldn't afford even 3d. St Cecilia's was run mainly by Eileen Harvey, while the Boy's Club, which came to adopt the name St John Bosco's, was run by Bob Leaper. Fr Raymund Tomalin, one of the assistant priests, supervised both.

St Mary and St Michael's School had reopened officially, for both Juniors and Infants, on 19th August 1941. Initially the children, aged 5-10, were divided into four classes under four teachers: Mr Kilcoyne and Mr Gallaher, Miss Zimmerman and Miss O'Byrne. But the number of children was still so low that after a few weeks, Mr Kilcoyne was withdrawn by the education authorities, and the number of classes went down to three. Things improved in October, when Srs Cyril and Perpetua were released from rest centre duties and allowed to resume teaching, and by April 1942, enough children were back in London for it to be necessary to reopen the Johnson Street building for the Infants.

Bombing incidents were now relatively infrequent, though always a possibility: two members of St Cecilia's – Monica Callaghan who was a committee member, and Ada Sweeney – were killed in air raids. But you had to get on with life. Joan Donovan used to go to dinners and dances at the Vaughan Club, often organised by the Knights of St Columba, and afterwards she would walk home through the blackout, holding her torch. Fr Coughlan ran the Vaughan, and signed members' tickets: a year's membership for a man was 3s, and for a woman 2s, and you were supposed to bring your ticket with you and show it if asked. Fr Coughlan also used to play the drums. During the summer, all sorts of open air entertainments and dances were provided in local parks: this was to cut down on unnecessary travel by enabling people to take a "holiday at home". Marie and Monica Henderson recall going to the railway arch during one air raid, but usually their family (like most Londoners) didn't go to the shelter but stayed in the house. If a raid was really bad, the family went to the basement under Carlile House, the Church Army lodging house in Johnson Street. Their mother and three older sisters worked as cleaners at St George's Hospital, in Wapping, and the family went off every summer to the country to help with the hop or fruit harvest, but any fruit they saw in London was likely to have come not from an English orchard, but from across the Atlantic. Big crates full of oranges or apples, or lard, arrived periodically at the schools and were distributed to the children. Those considered malnourished used to be given cod liver oil, or malt extract, but Marie and Monica's mother looked after them so well (despite having to buy everything on tick) that they never qualified. Monica, who was attending the Infant School in Johnson Street, did line up once for malt, and got away with it.

Martyrs of England, save our schools

No general elections were held during the war. If a bye-election was needed, the previous MP's party named a candidate, and the other parties did not contest the seat. When Jimmy Hall died in June 1942, the Labour Party shortlisted two candidates who were serving in the navy: John Oldfield and Walter Edwards. Oldfield, whose destroyer was in American waters, was promptly flown home but missed the Party Conference, so Edwards, a stoker on a minesweeper, was selected. A docker's son, born in Limehouse and brought up in Wapping, in St Patrick's Parish, he reckoned he'd made history: "It's not new for a workman to become an M.P., but for that to happen to a rating from the lower deck breaks fresh ground."

Collections were constantly being held for war charities. Lily Maynard, who went round regularly with a friend to collect for the Red Cross in Peabody Buildings, in the "Troxy" – the area behind the Troxy cinema – found lots of Catholics living there. The accommodation was extremely basic, with communal lavatories and washing facilities: each front door opened straight into the living room, and directly ahead there would usually be a chest of drawers with a beautiful cloth on, and above it a picture of the Pope. Lily noted that these families, who were obviously not all that well off, gave very generously. When the National Council of Christians and Jews was started in 1942, Cardinal Hinsley became one of the presidents, and Fr Fitzgerald was very involved, along with Bp Mathew and Frank Pakenham (the future Lord Longford). After the tragic Bethnal Green Tube Disaster in 1943, German propaganda broadcasts spread the rumour that the panic had been caused by the Jews: this led to a resurgence of anti-Semitism in London, and Fr Fitzgerald preached a strong message against it, at a civic service attended by the Mayor and Council.

A consensus was gaining ground that once the war was over, all the unsung heroes who'd kept up the fight against Hitler *must* have decent jobs, decent homes, proper health care and education for their kids: the Beveridge Report, outlining an all-out attack to be waged on the five giant evils of Want, Disease, Ignorance, Squalor and Idleness, immediately became a best seller. The country's swing to the left was given an added touch of spice by the fact that the Soviet Union was now an ally of Britain in the struggle, with Uncle Joe Stalin as everyone's hero – but this naturally raised alarm bells in many quarters. London's Catholic leaders recognised the urgency of developing an effective pastoral strategy for the postwar world, and Fr Fitzgerald was the sort of priest who would know how to engage with the issues: for example, he was the first national chaplain to the Catholic Association of Trade

Unionists. In October 1942 Cardinal Hinsley inaugurated a new youth association, in which Fr Fitzgerald was to be chairman, and Fr Charles Carr secretary. Though Hinsley died the following March, over 2,000 young Catholics gathered at the Stoll Theatre a few months later for the unveiling of a "Charter of Youth" that had been worked out in a series of consultations around the archdiocese. Fr Fitzgerald and Bob Leaper were among the speakers.

Under a revamped Education Act, drawn up by R A Butler, faith schools were offered the choice of handing over their buildings to the state system, thereby becoming fully funded but losing control over staff appointments and religious instruction, or retaining their denominational character but only being able to claim 50% funding for building repairs and alterations, and nothing at all for new buildings. On the face of it, this was a worse deal than the (unimplemented) 1936 Act. At their 1943 Low Week meeting, therefore, the Catholic hierarchy of England and Wales declared war on the British government over Butler's proposals. Once again, meetings were organised all over London, and a Catholic Parents' and Electors' Association was launched. Mary Sullivan, as hon secretary of the Commercial Road branch, shot off several strongly-argued letters to the *East London Advertiser.* "We pay our rates and taxes in the same way as other citizens," she wrote

> *yet they have their schools provided at the expense of the State, whilst we are to be penalised for conscience sake. Is this what our men and women are fighting for? We claim that equality of opportunity is a mockery and a sham if it is only offered on terms that we cannot in conscience accept,. To Catholics their greatest possession and treasure is their Catholic faith and we are determined that our children shall not be deprived of this priceless gift, and that they shall be brought up in the Faith of their Fathers.*

In August the Limehouse branch organised a meeting at the People's Palace, Mile End, with Jerry Long in the chair. Over 1,500 turned up, from all the East London parishes. Walter Edwards MP, John Oldfield LCC, and Jack Donovan from the TUC conference, spoke in support of the bishops, and the Catholic Women's League and Union of Catholic Mothers organised a big march of witness on a Sunday afternoon in October.

8,000 women turned out for it. No political slogans were allowed, only religious banners: the usual parish and sodality ones would be fine, but for any group making banners specially, the suggested inscription was "Martyrs of England, Save Our Schools". From Tower Hill Green, everyone marched past the Tower, past English Martyrs church, along Leman Street and into Commercial Road, praying the rosary as they walked along. No men were allowed in the procession except priests accompanying their parishioners, and Knights of St Columba who were acting as marshals: husbands, brothers and sons had to watch from the pavement. At St Mary's and St Michael's everyone crowded into the big church, filling it completely: they were crammed into the side chapels and standing in the aisles, with their banners stacked along the walls. Those who couldn't get into the church were directed into the school playground, where an open air altar had been erected. Auxiliary Bishop Edward Myers greeted them with the scripture text: "Well done, good and faithful servants", and told them they'd thrown "a spiritual spanner into the work of those who were seeking to destroy the Kingdom of Heaven on earth". Finally there was Benediction *again*, three times over, twice in the church and once at the altar in the playground.

Hitler's revenge

Ever since the War began, Adolf Hitler had been threatening to deploy mysterious "secret weapons". On the morning of 13th June 1944 the first flying bomb, a robotic, unmanned aircraft filled with explosive, landed in Grove Road, Mile End. Before long an average of a hundred flying bombs was coming over each day, heading for London. The official term was "V1", from the German "Vergeltungswaffe 1", meaning "Vengeance Weapon 1", but the public irreverently nicknamed them "doodlebugs". Wherever they hit, the newspapers could give the location only as "Southern England", so the Germans couldn't work out where they'd landed, and correct their range. They arrived at any time of the day or night, with no let-up: people were constantly in and out of the air raid shelters, and there was massive disruption to work and sleep. They made a dreadful racket –you could hear them all the way from Dagenham – and it was completely different from the sound made by bomber aircraft. As soon as people heard the noise, they tensed up, but so long as it kept going you were all right. It was when it cut out that you had to worry, because it meant the thing was about to drop. If the choirboys in the sacristy at St Mary and St Michael's heard a doodlebug and the sound stopped, they all got down on the floor: this was sensible, and could save your life. Sr Philomena, two or three years past her 60th birthday, had resigned as headteacher of St Mary and St Michael's School in January 1944, and Sr Cyril – who'd taught at the school since it was opened – was now acting headteacher. Her entry in the logbook for 16th June reads "Flying Bomb raids begin. Attendance drops immediately. Children and Teachers spend greater part of the day in shelters." From the beginning of July attendance dropped faster still, as evacuation measures began – though on hearing that three Junior County Scholarships had been won by Holly Groves, Margaret Lanigan and Eileen Dawler, Sr Cyril made haste to record the good news which, she wrote "somewhat relieves the general air of depression". The school reopened for the autumn term on 22nd August, but only 11% of the children turned up – and then the hop picking began, so numbers fell lower still!

Hop picking that summer attracted so few workers as to cause widespread concern: what would happen to British morale if there was a shortage of beer? V1s which didn't make it to London were likely to land in Kent, but it wasn't that people were avoiding Kent: the Hendersons were fruit picking in Wateringbury, where a doodlebug came over so low it shook the hut. Altogether 36 V1s had dropped on Stepney, including three inside the Tower of London. But now the Allied armies were sweeping through France, forcing the Germans to retreat into the Netherlands and abandon their launching sites. On 7th September a government spokesman triumphantly announced, "Except possibly for a few last shots, the Battle of London is over." Immediately, despite warnings to stay put, the evacuees began flooding back to London.

V2 Rocket

At 6.43 on the following afternoon, a supersonic rocket fell from the stratosphere: the V2 had arrived. Because there was no warning at all, many people found the V2s even more unnerving than the V1s, but others took the line that since there was nothing you could do about them, there was no point worrying. Each rocket was potentially more dangerous and destructive than anything that had gone before, but thankfully Hitler didn't have a huge supply. As with the doodlebugs, strict censorship was imposed so that the Germans wouldn't find out exactly where they were landing. A government expert reckoned they were aimed at Wapping, but a high proportion fell outside London, in sparsely populated parts of Essex.

By now it was obvious the Allies were going to win the war, and everyone hoped it would end by Christmas. But meanwhile, most people had to live in blast-damaged houses. Tarpaulins over the roof, doors smashed in, and windows without glass, made it rather difficult to exclude draughts, and fuel was hard to come by. People went out as much as they could, if only because sitting in public buildings was so much warmer than staying at home. Food was also scarce. Those who could grew their own vegetables, and every possible piece of vacant ground in East London was used for allotments. It was already accepted that not all those who'd been evacuated would return to

London after the war, but many people who did want to come back had nowhere to live. As a temporary stopgap, supposedly just for a few years, they were offered prefabricated wooden structures. Stepney, after some hesitation, decided to accept these "prefabs", and German and Italian POWs were brought in to help clear sites and put them up.

When the Hendersons returned to London from Waterbury, Monica was seven, so due to start at the Junior School in Lukin Street. When she arrived she could smell parsnips cooking. This was a new thing: facilities were being set up in all schools, offering midday meals five days a week. The Milk in Schools scheme had also been expanded, so that each child got a small bottle of milk each day. Kath Marriott had been evacuated to Chertsey for most of the war, but was now back at home and also attending Lukin Street. Among their many other ceremonial engagements, Walter Edwards and his wife made a visit to St Mary and St Michael's School one lunch hour, and Fr Fitzgerald and the Sisters gave him a warm welcome. The school meals, like the school, were run by the Sisters of Mercy, and usually over a hundred children stayed for lunch. Part of the school still had to be kept ready to be used as a rest centre, but during quiet periods when there was no one living there, just one nun stayed on duty. The chance of newly homeless families having to be admitted was fairly high: from October 1944 to March 1945, eight rockets fell on Stepney, nine on Poplar, and two on Bethnal Green. Not all the incidents were "major", but rockets which failed to kill anyone could wreck thousands of homes.

St Patrick's Day, 17th March 1945, fell on a Saturday, and the Sisters of Mercy working with the evacuees in Byfleet got permission to come in to Hardinge Street to visit the rest of the community. After an early lunch Srs Bonaventure Kelly and Pius Flynn went over to St Mary and St Michael's School in Lukin Street to visit Sr Cyril, who was currently in charge of the empty rest centre. Victor Guazzelli was being ordained that day, and it had been hoped that the ceremony could take place at St Mary and St Michael's – but it was impossible for him to return to Britain, so he was being ordained in faraway Lisbon. Instead of an ordination, there was a wedding on at the church, and the bride and bridegroom – Elizabeth Donovan and Harold Bullman – were just arriving. The three nuns were sitting chatting when suddenly the school collapsed on top of them. People close to the point of impact of a V2 never heard the bang. Kath Marriott had gone to Harding's Pie and Mash Shop, four or five doors down Jubilee Street from the Commercial Road end, to buy her lunch, and was there when it happened: there was a strange silence, and then everything was vibrating and the windows shattering. At the Henderson home, Monica was in the back room

Elizabeth (née Donovan) and Harold Bullman at Our Lady's Hall in the 60s

when the windows shattered: she ran out into the street and saw debris flying around. Maureen Warren, in Gosling House, was standing in front of the fire having a wash when suddenly all the soot came down the chimney.

Thankfully, because it was Saturday, no children were in the school. The visiting Sisters only had scratches on their hands, and were able to crawl out of the wreckage. Sr Cyril was rescued, but she had glass embedded in her chest, and eye injuries. The blast wrecked the presbytery, and Fr Fitzgerald had to be dug out, while Fr George Lee, who since he'd come to Commercial Road was known as "tall Fr Lee" to distinguish him from "little Fr Leigh", had been walking across the school playground only about 30 yards away when the rocket landed. These three were all rushed round to the London Hospital. At the church, the bride and groom and their guests were covered in dust, but not hurt. The fire brigade swept the debris from one of the aisles, and the wedding went ahead.

Parishioners came to salvage items from the church and take them over to the Convent of Mercy and Our Lady's Hall, after which the damaged building was roped off. Fr Fitzgerald was discharged from hospital quite quickly: he'd lost the sight in his left eye, but reckoned the V2 had cured the terrible headaches he used to have before then. The statue of St Patrick hadn't even been scratched, so, he said: "I told St Patrick I'd never burn a candle for him again." He joked afterwards that he was the 13th parish priest (going by the plaque in the porch) and that was what had brought down such catastrophic bad luck. Men parishioners set up an altar in the Hall, and got everything ready so that Mass could be said there the following day: it was made the temporary church, and officially registered for marriages.

The church itself was in a bad way: the walls were intact, but some of the roofs were off, and asbestos sheeting had to be put over to keep out the weather. The school was a write-off, and the assistant caretaker Thomas Detnon was eventually pulled out dead. Three other people were killed in nearby houses. Sr Cyril was in hospital for four weeks, with another month's convalescence, and her eyesight was left permanently impaired. Fr Lee had been in charge of the choir, and played the piano beautifully, but his left hand was so badly crushed that he was never able to play again – something he found a severe trial.

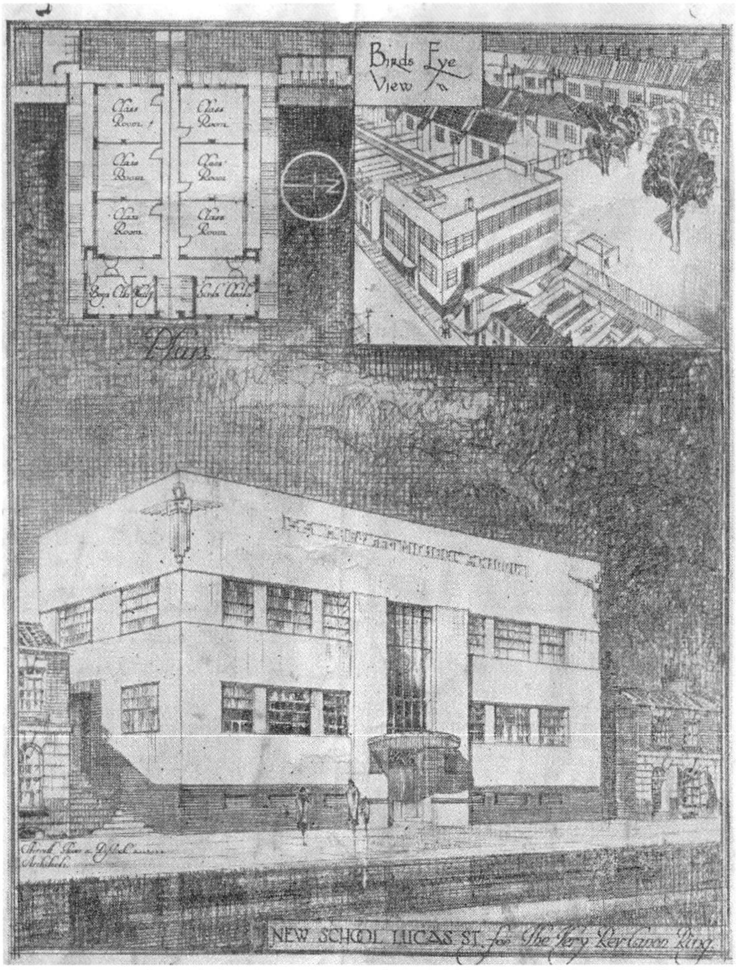

St Mary and St Michael's Primary School destroyed in the V2 blast

Just over a week later, on Sunday 25th March, Kath Marriott had a much narrower escape from a V2. Her family lived at No 11 Havering Street, opposite Arbour Square. A rocket fell at the Commercial Road end of the street, destroying Nos 1-5. The remaining houses were rendered uninhabitable, so the Marriotts had to move to Senrab Street, and live in a rest centre for six months. Stepney's last V2, which blasted Hughes

Mansions in Vallance Road on 27th March, was the worst of all: it killed over 130 people.

A bomb-damaged St Mary and St Michael's

Germany actually surrendered on Monday 7th May. That evening all the ships and boats along the Thames began sounding their hooters, and people started putting the flags out. Next day was the official VE (Victory in Europe) Day. Huge crowds gathered in Trafalgar Square, going crazy, while hawkers did a roaring trade in mini union jacks, victory rosettes, Churchill badges and party hats. Joan Donovan was there, and later on she lost her shoes in Villiers Street and had to walk home without them.

East End Victory Party

Marie and Monica Henderson, who were staying with their aunt in Byfleet, remember people dancing in the streets. In Cable Street and all round Shadwell and Wapping there were bonfires in the streets, and people dancing. On 9th May the King and Queen, together with the princesses, toured the East End. In Ashburton, where Srs Sylvester and Ita soldiered on until VE Day, the little evacuee Catholic community had come to be fully accepted by the local people. When the time did come to leave, the Sisters recalled: "We had a great send off, a very different one from our arrival, most of the village came to cheer us on our way and the Mayor, or Reeve, as he was called, made a farewell speech."

"If ever there was a place where it might succeed…"

St Mary and St Michael's School had to operate from March to June on the ground floor of St Bernard's – the part that had been adapted as an air raid shelter, so all the windows were bricked up, and there was no natural light or ventilation. Fr Fitzgerald and his curates, like so many other bombed-outs, were homeless for about two months, but then, with some help from the Borough Council, they were able to move into No 370 Commercial Road. With the ending of the war lots of people wanted to get married, so there were frequent weddings in Our Lady's Hall. Meanwhile a lot of hard work went into giving St Mary and St Michael's the basic, but essential, "first aid" treatment which would allow it to be used again: John Sterrett acted as surveyor, and John Bowman was contracted for the building work. The baptismal registers had been preserved, but sadly, many of the other old records were never recovered – though a copy of the old charity school minute books survived in Wapping, because during the 1920s Canon Joseph Reardon had sent a curate, Frederick Bentley, over to Commercial Road with a battered typewriter, and strict instructions not to come back till he'd made a full transcript.

A General Election was held at the beginning of July, but the count was delayed to allow time for the forces vote to be brought in. Meanwhile the new Archbishop of Westminster, Bernard Griffin, maintained his predecessor's focus on mobilising young people, attending a Festival of Youth at the People's Palace which, according to the *Universe*, put even the 1943 Youth Charter Rally well into the shade. A whole range of youth clubs and associations contributed, including the St John Bosco Club which gave a five-minute display of boxing, and the highlight was a Way of the Cross presentation by the Grail. At the end the archbishop got up on the stage, accompanied by Fr Fitzgerald and Walter Edwards MP, who was currently also Mayor of Stepney, to thank everyone and call on the young people to be apostles at home and at work.

On 26th July the election results were finally announced: Labour had won, and Clem Attlee, the MP for Limehouse, was the new Prime Minister. Walter Edwards won Whitechapel again, but Mile End returned Phil Piratin, England's first Communist MP. In November, the Communists captured ten seats on Stepney Borough Council, though Labour still retained a large majority. Joseph O'Connor, a porter at Bethnal Green Hospital who'd survived the Hughes Mansions disaster, and was now living in a prefab, was chosen as the new Mayor. Whereas Jerry Long, who'd been in the same class with O'Connor at English Martyrs School, and most of the Labour Catholics were rigidly hostile to the new Communist Councillors, O'Connor was quite laid back about them, treated them with kind good humour, and rather enjoyed having a proper opposition to liven up debates.

By a happy chance, St Mary and St Michael's church was ready to be reopened again just in time for O'Connor's mayoral Mass, and volunteers from the parish got stuck in and gave it a thorough clean. The walls struck them as terribly bleak and bare, because the oil paintings had gone missing and were never replaced, and a lot of the windows were boarded up, but at least the building was usable.

On the last Sunday in November, Fr Fitzgerald met the Mayor and Mayoress at the church door, and escorted them to the special prie dieus placed before the sanctuary, while the Borough Councillors and special guests were shown to their reserved places. Fr Leigh celebrated, and Fitzgerald preached. He started off, naturally enough, with a brief reference

to the joy of the parish in seeing their beautiful Church restored at last to Divine Worship. Much of its former splendour had, of course, disappeared. But substantial repairs had been effected on what – without such repairs – would have been a dangerous structure. Thus bit by bit they had pulled themselves out of their troubles.

Next he welcomed the Mayor and Councillors, extending

a special welcome to the Jewish Councillors present. If ever anti-Semitism should raise its foul head they would find in him, and he hoped and believed in all of his people, staunch opponents of the infamy. The Preacher expressed his satisfaction in seeing some of the Communist members in the Church. Relationships between Catholicism and Communism were, at present, about as bad as they could be, especially abroad. And it was not too much to say that the peace of the world depended on their ability to ease this tension and diminish this hostility. Could it be done? It would undoubtedly be difficult. But it was well worth attempting, and if ever there was a place where it might succeed it was here in the East End where so many Catholic priests and workers had proved by their lives of public service that they were in the vanguard of progressive thought and action. He, the preacher, would certainly make the attempt if he could get co-operation from anywhere. And if success attended the effort, the result would have repercussions far beyond Stepney.

And in conclusion, he called down God's blessing on the whole Borough Council, Communists and all.

The Years of Austerity

Every street had gaps in its terraces where houses had been bombed, and some – such as Lake Street, which ran between Hardinge and Devonport Streets – had been flattened completely. Yellow ragwort and pink rose-bay willow-herb blossomed on the bomb sites, and the children played there. Inevitably there were accidents: Matt Henderson fell and broke his arm, and his younger sister Marie had to accompany him to hospital. American soldiers were billeted in Bower Street, and the children used to hang around them crying "Got any gum, chum?" They quickly made friends with the Italian POWs who came to build prefabs, and who made them rings that turned their fingers green, and occasionally wangled them a tin mug of tea when the mobile canteen came round. When the concrete was laid for the path leading to the prefabs, the Italians made pretty designs in it. On St Patrick's Day 1946, the anniversary of the V2, Fr Fitzgerald made a special request that the schoolchildren sing the Mass in Latin. The girls, at least, had never done anything in Latin before, but Mrs O'Connell the music teacher, and Sr Joseph, the headteacher, practised them, and they sang it. They all stood on the right side of the church, near the Guild Chapel, because the other side was cluttered up with the remains of the organ, and there were pipes lying around all over the place. The Blue Nuns had finally left, and only the Sisters of Mercy remained. No fresh recruits had been admitted to the community during the war, and they were very short-handed. However: "in response to earnest prayer, and as a result of visits to Ireland, postulants began to appear and the outlook brightened considerably. But nevertheless those years were marked by struggle and frustration". The first new candidate to arrive, Sr Malachy Haugh, got a tremendous welcome. Sr Elizabeth O'Connor, who came in September 1946, spent her first few days in London going round with Sr Bernardine McMahon, who was trying to carry out a census.

People were still only gradually returning to Stepney, and it was essential to track down parishioners as they reappeared. Sr Josephine Browne, who came in June 1947, noted that visitation was given very high priority, as the Sisters strove to maintain contact with, and provide support to, the families (often large) who were

> *trying to eke out a living after the war, which had scattered them, and in some cases deprived them of their homes and livelihood. The Sisters had been through it all, with many of their school children, so there was a strong bond between Sisters and parishioners.*

Crushing Hitler had left Britain bankrupt, and rationing of food and clothing remained in place for years. Fuel was in desperately short supply, and the winter of 1946-47 was the coldest in the twentieth century. Hardly any houses in Stepney had had a bathroom or an inside toilet even before the war, so the bitter cold made life very tough for everyone. The priests suffered a lot because their temporary house only had outside toilets, and each morning they had to go to the freezing ice-cold church to say Mass. The convent had five bedrooms up on the roof, which was fine in summer but very cold in winter. All the Sisters had to carry water up from the basement each evening to wash, as that was the only source of hot water. They *did* have a bathroom, but the furnace to heat water for baths was only lit on Friday afternoons and Saturdays, so all baths had to be taken on a stringent half-hourly rota. The state of the tenements in which most of the parishioners were living was absolutely awful: they had no hot water, and in winter the pipes froze and there was no running water at all. Nevertheless, Sr Elizabeth noted that every day the children came to school in beautifully clean white shirts, and if you went inside the parishioners' homes, they were like a palace because they were so well looked after. The doorsteps were always clean: it was a matter of pride to keep your doorstep well scrubbed. Old people used to be put outside the front door in a chair, and everyone who passed by would say hello to them. The Sisters ran a Mothers' Needlework Guild, to help women keep their children clothed as inexpensively as possible, and it was very popular.

St Mary and St Michael's Junior School was allocated the top floor, and part of the ground floor, of the Christian Scott School in Cranford Street – also known as Heckford Street School – a typical London three-decker with a hall on each floor. The top floor had been damaged in air raids, which meant they couldn't move in until repairs had been made. Various temporary arrangements had to be made in the meantime, and it wasn't until 31st October 1945 that the whole school reassembled at Heckford Street. The roll at that date was 259. There was a Catholic playground and a Protestant playground, a Catholic entrance and a Protestant entrance, and the children respected the demarcation lines, but there was only one phone line, and the two headteachers, Sr Cyril and Miss Touching, had to share that. Sr Cyril was confirmed in post as headteacher in 1947. The building-share arrangement meant that St Mary and St Michael's initially had no dinner facilities, and children staying for meals had to be marched to another school, escorted there and back by two teachers: but then a small building which had previously been the woodwork centre was made into a dining hall for them. All the equipment had been destroyed by the V2 and the items couldn't easily be replaced; as late as 1949, an Inspector noted that they were still desperately short of reading books, and also of plimsolls – so the existing stock of plimsolls had to be shared. (School inspectors must also have been in short supply, as the next inspection didn't take place till 1962!) For concerts, which were so important for the fundraising efforts for a new school, the Mayor always ensured they were given free use of either St George's or Limehouse Town Hall, though they had to carry all the stuff over. Despite all the difficulties, the children took part regularly in music festivals, and both girls and boys won acclaim for their singing and dancing. Dancing was taken very seriously by the whole school, and they had an impressive repertoire. Sometimes they did Irish dancing, but at other times it was Welsh or Scottish, or even Italian gypsy dancing, and the boys favoured sailors' hornpipes.

St Bernard's returned to Damien Street, now as a mixed school under Mr McGann as sole headteacher. Once two Communists had got themselves onto the LCC, as representatives for Mile End, they caused a flurry by nominating a fellow-Communist, Jane Carver, as the new LCC manager for St Bernard's School. However the Comrades were determined to make a good impression and allay suspicions, so they were tremendously helpful. Most of the school's equipment had mysteriously gone missing, but they kicked up a fuss and got it returned in two days. Frank 'Bumpy' Greenan delivered an enthusiastic address to the East London Teachers' Association, which had elected him President for 1946-47, saying that teaching conditions in the East End must be made so attractive that the most promising young teachers would be fighting to come here. Sadly, he was unable to change the reality, which was that teachers only took jobs in East End schools as a stopgap, if they couldn't get anything better.

During the occupation years in France and Belgium the YCW had been deeply involved in the Resistance, and with liberation it bounced back. A gathering in July 1945 to mark the twentieth anniversary of its official founding brought together 12,000 Belgian leaders, and smaller delegations from France, America and Canada, and England. Pat Keegan from Wigan was there, still in his army uniform, and when an international bureau was set up he found himself on it: he became International President, and one of Cardijn's closest collaborators in the postwar years. Pope Pius XII was supportive of the movement, and his Under-Secretary, Giovanni Battista

Montini (later Pope Paul VI) even more so. Expansion of the YCW in England and Wales, which had been disrupted by the war, now went ahead with an eagerness to make up for lost time, and Cardinal Griffin came to Commercial Road in December 1946 to open a Westminster Archdiocesan YCW headquarters at the Fitzalan Trust houses. Fr Fitzgerald was naturally present, as was the Cardinal's young assistant secretary Fr Derek Worlock. Afterwards they all dropped in briefly on the St John Bosco Club in the same building.

There were sound historical reasons for locating a YCW office in the East End, which had arguably played such a crucial role in developing the Church's Social Teaching: Cardinal Manning's successful mediation in the Great Dock Strike, as we have seen, helped inspire *Rerum Novarum*, and the experiences of the 1912 strike had undoubtedly influenced the early years of the YCW. Also, Fr Fitzgerald was a key adviser to Cardinal on both youth and labour issues. Nevertheless, it's likely that the Commercial Road houses were selected mainly because the diocese happened to own them. There's no indication that St Mary and St Michael's had a thriving YCW section, if it had one at all, whereas the local sections which were to make most of the running were those in the parishes influenced by Fr Vincent Rochford: Poplar, and Millwall where he became parish priest after serving as an RAF chaplain during the war. Indeed, although Cardinal Griffin tried hard to promote the YCW, it never became particularly strong in Westminster – though it did better in Southwark, and in the North of England.

Fr Worlock became very involved with the YCW, but his contacts were with the South London office in Clapham Road, because that was where the real action was. The movement grew steadily, thought it never attracted a mass membership. It was quite demanding, and those who did join saw themselves (like the Communists) as a specially committed elite, dedicatedly working to bring about change for the good of everyone. Arguably, the YCW's main impact on the Catholic community at large would be in the ideas and new ways of thinking which its trained leaders communicated, through personal contact, to key members of the hierarchy, and to lay activists and decision-makers in a range of important areas of Church life.

The St Mary and St Michael's sodalities were now being run largely by the Sisters of Mercy, and the usual devotions had resumed on Monday, Wednesday and Friday nights. Sr Bernard was in charge of the Men's Guild. In parish processions the Guild of St Agnes girls carried palms. The Children of Mary marched as before in blue cloaks and white veils, only you couldn't get decent muslin, so they looked like the Ku Klux Klan – but they consoled themselves with the thought that none of the boys would be able to recognise them. The whole family would go round to the Vaughan Club on Saturday nights. There was a tea bar, run by Mr Stevens and Mrs Wells, and there was always a big rush for the sandwiches, and the plain Madeira cake which seemed like a tremendous treat. By this time the Vaughan had already acquired a licence to serve alcoholic drinks, so you *could* get a beer. Some very committed Catholics, like Bob Collins, refused to go to there after alcohol was permitted: he always maintained that that was never how Cardinal Bourne had envisaged it, and on principle he refused even to step inside the building. Nevertheless, the Vaughan remained primarily a social club with a healthy family atmosphere. The men played billiards, there was singing and dancing, and at the end everyone always sang God Save Our Pope. Even on Christmas Day, the Vaughan Club was the place to be. On weekday evenings, the young people in the parish made the most of the club activities at St Cecilia's and St John Bosco. St Cecilia's had netball, athletics and keep fit, tennis, ballroom and Irish dancing, choral singing, art and needlework. St John Bosco had boxing, football and cricket, and a band: when the parish band re-formed after the war, the instruments had survived, but there were only five musicians left out of a pre-war 20, so the leader Mr Billingsley decided to make it part of the St John Bosco Club, and invite volunteers from the Club to learn to play. Classes and practice sessions were held every Tuesday and Thursday, and after a few months they played in their first parade. The bandmaster was Jim Clark, a Council employee who'd learned to play while in the army before the First World War. From 1948, when St Cecilia's Club couldn't use the Johnson Street building any more, they moved to Bigland Street School. Once a week, on Tuesdays, the two clubs would mix for ballroom dancing. When St Cecilia's was hosting the dance, the girls in charge of the refreshments were told strictly that the biscuits must only be sold to the girls, because they were the girls' biscuits – issued for the girls under the rationing system – but in practice it was difficult to refuse the boys. Afterwards they used to wash up in a big tin bath. Another area where the St John Bosco and St Cecilia's Clubs used to collaborate was on drama productions: they produced Shakespeare plays, and Gilbert and Sullivan operettas. Both of the clubs used to organise rambles and camping holidays, and camping was so popular that the parish acquired its own campsite, at Havering-atte-Bower in Essex. When Bob Leaper moved on, Tom Brien took over the running of St John Bosco's.

The Legion of Mary had an adult praesidium and also a junior one, which Miss Knight was in charge of. Marie Henderson was persuaded to join shortly after the war, while she was still at school, and she was made treasurer. As with the adult Legion and the SVP, a secret bag collection was taken at meetings (so nobody knew how much each person put in). Marie was supposed to hold it, but most people used to put buttons in, so she got fed up and decided not to go any more, and handed the bag back to Miss Knight – who was shocked to see how little there was in it, and accused her of not returning all the money! Like before the war, all the parish groups were constantly fundraising, for the restoration of the church and to replace the schools. A lot of money was raised from a scheme selling "football tickets": after buying your ticket you opened it up and saw what your number was, and you might win a money prize. The raising of the school age, and transferring of all 11-year-olds to some kind of secondary school, went ahead despite the fact that even the government had no proper resources to implement the change, and if the Catholics wanted their own secondary schools, they were going to have to pay at least 25% towards the new buildings. Fr Fitzgerald advised all the Tower Hamlets Catholics to study the issue, so they could argue knowledgeably for more support: after all, he pointed out, if the Catholic schools closed down, the state would be put to even greater expense to accommodate all the children whose education was presently being subsidised by their parishes. Delegations of Catholics attended all the local electoral meetings to question candidates as to where they stood on the schools issue. At the same time there was a box at the back of the church for the Catholic Education Fund, and people used to have envelopes which they filled regularly and put in.

But for the grace of God…

The late 1940s weren't only a time of shortages and misery. The advent of the NHS, which came into effect at midnight on 4th July 1948, were a great boon to East Enders who in the past had often struggled to put up with ill-health, rather than seek medical treatment which they couldn't afford. Many Catholic leaders were chary of the state taking over what had traditionally been charitable responsibilities, and Fr Paul Crane, for example, fell out with the Catholic Social Guild, and started *Christian Order* to attack the new system. But Fr Fitzgerald cogently defended the benefits of the welfare state.

His own brief venture into juvenile delinquency had left him with a soft spot for petty criminals, and a general tendency to take the side of all actual or alleged wrongdoers. This was probably the logic behind his coming out with mind-boggling observations like "Nothing is better for a wife than a good beating from her husband" (as reported by Edith Ramsay). While at Holloway he did a lot of prison chaplaincy work, and never turned a hair at difficult customers who shouted obscenities at him: he simply pointed out that what they were telling him to do was physically impossible. He'd also developed a habit of using swear words very freely in public. Like Mgr Ring, he could be a bit of a tyrant at times, but in many respects he was a much more gentle and empathic soul. Men from the Church Army hostel who called at the door, claiming to be wounded ex-servicemen, were always given monetary assistance, though a lot of them were definitely frauds. People around Fr Fitzgerald eventually intervened when the situation got out of hand: one chap who'd got a fiver out of him by telling a pack of lies was prosecuted, and sent to prison.

True to his own principles, when a campaign was got up calling for action against the burgeoning Maltese-controlled vice trade in Cable Street, Fr Fitzgerald wouldn't get involved because he refused to condemn the brothel keepers. He also tried sincerely to co-operate with the Communists. Quite a lot of ordinary Catholics saw the Communists in overwhelmingly positive terms as friendly, constructive people who'd helped win the war, and who weren't afraid to take direct action on key local issues like housing. Fr Fitzgerald's view will have been far better informed, and among his interests in *Catholic Who's Who*, he listed "Dishing the Reds" – though by this, he probably meant beating them at their own game, by being more radically socialist than they were. But he always got on well with Piratin, and when two Communists were taken to court in Yorkshire for sedition, and had no money to pay a lawyer, Fr Fitzgerald subscribed to their defence fund on the grounds that no citizen should be defenceless for lack of money. His approach was somewhat at odds with that of most of the other local priests, and the Catholic Labour politicians, who were determined to do whatever it took to drive out both the Reds and the pimps, and gave no quarter. John Oldfield was very fiercely anti-Communist, and the Communists complained that at LCC elections in Whitechapel, priests and nuns stood outside the polling booths warning people to vote against them, and – because the Communist candidates were almost always Jewish – they repeatedly accused the Catholics of playing the race card. Walter Edwards, who was made a Civil Lord of the Admiralty under Attlee, always refused to speak on the same platform with any of the Communists.

At the ceremonial presentation when he was made a canon in 1948, Fitzgerald insisted that he was "not a big shot", and wasn't even capable of running the parish, as his four curates did that. Referring to an incident when little Fr Leigh and tall Fr Lee had both had to go to court as witnesses in the trial of a gang of casual labourers who'd broken into the church, and stolen four carpets and a purificator, he said that "But for the grace of God he might have been one of them". Notwithstanding the parish priest's modesty, the parish celebrated the honour in the grand old style. Sr Ita created a beautiful illuminated address, Frank Greenan made a speech on behalf of the school, Maurice Mahoney on behalf of the Men's Guild, and Patricia Murphy on behalf of the women. The Mayor of Stepney, currently Tom Aylward (Matt Aylward's son), also made a speech. The parishioners had subscribed about three-fifths of the money for his canon's robes, the convent had been very generous, the schools had collected, and the balance came from the Jewish community – particularly his fellow-managers at Park House, a Jewish approved school of which he had been a manager for many years.

All work on restoring the church had to be halted in 1948. No construction could go ahead without a government permit, and priority had to be given to rebuilding the country's housing stock. All over Tower Hamlets the Council and the LCC were finishing off what Hitler had started, by demolishing old streets of terraced cottages to make room for blocks of flats. A lot of the houses could have been restored, but that option was given less consideration than hindsight suggests it should have been, and houses that weren't demolished were neglected, and left to degenerate still further. Although most people would rather have had houses, the new estates did look very nice (for the first few years, anyway) and the indoor toilets and bathrooms seemed like a dream come true. In the short term, there was a very high demand for skilled builders in Stepney, while for the unskilled there were plenty of jobs in demolition. But a tragedy occurred in January 1950, while the ruined presbytery was being demolished. A Limehouse man named Thomas Long climbed up to the top to knock a wall down, missed his footing and fell, suffering a fractured skull, and died in the London Hospital two weeks later. There was a large fresh influx of Irish immigration into London – men to work in the building trade, and women to work as nurses in the burgeoning NHS: a few of these newcomers settled in the East End, but for the most part, if they stayed in London, they chose to live elsewhere. Meanwhile new towns were developed to encourage people to move out of London (or not come back from evacuation), and industries were being encouraged to move out: however the out-migration worked selectively, creaming off the more skilled workers from inner city areas like Stepney.

Sr Philomena, who was currently superior at Hardinge Street, was determined to establish a nursery school. As usual after a war there'd been a baby boom, and there were huge numbers of little children in the parish, but their mothers as well as their fathers were mostly having to go out to work, to make ends meet. So they needed child care. Sr Philomena therefore purchased a site in Thirza Street, and erected a temporary building (constructed from Nissen huts) big enough to take about 50 children aged 3-5. She then approached the LCC at County Hall to ask for staff. Approval was given for the building, and for the assignment of two teachers, on condition that space be added for a toy store, and the Rosary Nursery was opened in 1949. The first two teachers were Miss Sheila Mellish and Sr Angela Rossiter, and the assistants were Mrs Sheila O'Mahoney and Sr Felicity Hayes. When teaching religious of other congregations began to withdraw from neighbouring parishes, the Commercial Road Sisters of Mercy provided teachers for some of them as well. In 1950 Mr McGann retired as headmaster of St Bernard's, and was replaced by Joseph Kelly – a man with an unusual background for a headteacher, as he'd started off in a string of unskilled labouring jobs before switching to teaching.

Rebuilding

The population of Stepney was down to half what it was before the war, and continuing to fall. So it was only reasonable to merge the three pre-war parliamentary and LCC constituencies into a single Stepney constituency, with three LCC representatives and just one MP. In the 1949 local elections the Communists won none of the LCC seats, and they also lost one of their seats on Stepney Borough Council. In the General Election of February 1950, Clem Attlee modestly bowed out of Tower Hamlets, and moved to Walthamstow, leaving Walter Edwards to contest Stepney. Phil Piratin stood against Edwards, but Edwards romped home, streets ahead of all his rivals – and even the Conservative candidate got more votes than Piratin. The Comrades wailed about gerrymandering, but the truth was that Communism had never had a large following in Britain, and the special circumstances which had brought significant numbers of East Londoners flocking into the Party during the 1930s had disappeared. When the 1953 elections came along, the Communists couldn't even manage to keep their seats on the Borough Council.

Ration books

Rationing and building restrictions began to be relaxed, and real income for working-class people began to rise to unprecedented levels – though at first there wasn't much you were allowed to spend it on, because most of the consumer goods produced by British industry were strictly reserved for export. However St Mary and St Michael's parishioners had never been in a position to complain that they didn't know what to do with their money – and so, in 1952, Canon Fitzgerald began a thoroughgoing restoration of the church. Compensation for war damage was also available, and was very generous. Around the same time the Sisters of Mercy were able to acquire the freehold of their convent. Because they now had so many recruits that they were running out of space they purchased two houses adjoining the convent, and began planning to build an extension. While waiting for construction went ahead, they used one of the houses to accommodate the overflow. Something else that became possible, now that people had a bit of money to spare, was to organise parish pilgrimages to Lourdes for sizeable groups.

Fr Patrick Peyton
Family Rosary Crusade

The Irish-American Fr Patrick Peyton brought his Family Rosary Crusade team over to Great Britain, and a whole series of big rallies were held in places like Wembley Stadium. Canon Fitzgerald attended all the London events. The biggest was at Hyde Park, when the police estimated the number present at 100,000. East London had its own rally on a Tuesday evening in July 1952, at the dog racing track in Hackney Wick. Lots of parishioners from St Mary and St Michael's came, and not only the solidly devout core. Cardinal Griffin was there, and as the East End Mayors arrived (six of them) with their Mayoresses, each pair was played in by a recorded trumpet fanfare relayed through the stadium's amplification system. A lot of cockney humour was flying around, as Fitzgerald noted:

At one end of the ground, right across the Tote Board was a huge streamer bearing the slogan 'The family that prays together, stays together'. Was it mere accident, or was it some 'Cockney Wag' who arranged the Tote Board so that, immediately below the slogan, appeared the words, 'Odds-on?' In the arena itself, before the beautifully decorated platform and the graceful plinth supporting Our Lady's Statue stretched first a big group of Altar Servers arranged in the form of a cross, and behind them in blue cloaks and veils an imposing array of Children of Mary arranged in the form of a mighty 'M'. The stadium terraces were packed with people whose frequent and vociferous applause re-verberated from the covered roofs of the terraces and re-echoed in a majestic way that made it sound more wonderful than would have been the case in an open park… This was a really exciting rally.

For the coronation of Queen Elizabeth II, in 1953, the Borough Council

Troxy Cinema Commercial Road

organised treats for all the local schoolchildren. St Mary and St Michael's School went to the People's Palace, Mile End Road, for an entertainment on 5th June, and on 9th June they all went to the Troxy to see the film "A Queen is Crowned". Another coronation treat was a two-week holiday for 40 children, accompanied by two teachers, at St Mary's Bay Holiday Camp, Dymchurch.

During the postwar years the widespread perception that the Mayor of Stepney was "always" a Catholic became almost literally true, and it was reckoned that there were as many as 33 St Mary and St Michael's parishioners on the Borough Council. Joe McCarthy, who became Mayor in 1954, had been brought up in the parish, and was one of the founder members of the East London Catholic School of Social Study. He and his wife were very involved with the Vaughan Club, and he gave a lot of help to local youth clubs, especially the St John Bosco. All mayors, whatever their own religion, socialised with all the local communities: Joe joked that you had to be prepared to eat four dinners every evening, meet film stars at Rev Edwyn Young's garden parties at St Dunstan's, and be called "Yossel" by Rabbi Zeffert. When your time came to stand down, your main worry (given the rising cost of living) would be having to buy your own dinners in future.

The former Frost's site, on the west side of the church, was allocated to the parish for the new St Mary and St Michael's Junior and Infant Schools. The first tender for the old Lukin Street school had been received on St Patrick's Day, and then the school had been destroyed on another St Patrick's Day, so Canon Fitzgerald was delighted to pick St Patrick's Day 1954 to lay claim to the site. About a hundred parishioners gathered, all wearing something green (hardly anyone could get hold of real shamrock). A flagpole had been erected, Fitzgerald raised the Papal flag, and an 11-year-old boy led everyone in giving three cheers. On a Sunday afternoon in May 1955, Mayor McCarthy came to lay the foundation stone. In his speech he pointed out that his grandparents were the first caretakers of the original school in Lukin Street, and he himself had been a pupil there. The building was completed and opened in July 1956. Sr Cyril wrote in the logbook:

Today we began work in our new school. It is a truly magnificent building and we are fortunate to be in it. We have been rather chaotic today but I expect we shall soon be settled. Classes are very large as our roll is 355 for eight classes.

Around the same time, a former council school building in Christian Street was made available to house the new Catholic girls' secondary school, Bishop Challoner: the Commercial Road Sisters of Mercy were in charge, and it served the parishes of Commercial Road, Wapping and Tower Hill.

Bishop Challoner School, Christian Street

During Joe McCarthy's mayoral year, Auxiliary Bishop George Craven came to a fundraising dance in Our Lady's Hall, held by the St Mary and St Michael Social and Reconstruction Association. He presented the Noble Cup to the Vaughan Club, for coming top in the Southwark Catholic Diocesan Senior Men's Clubs' League for billiards, snooker, table tennis and darts; and also handed over two individual prizes, to Mr J Callahan for table tennis, and to Mr W Bryan for darts. Back again in December as guest of honour at the annual dinner and dance at Shoreditch Town Hall, Bp Craven acknowledged that he was only second best (the Apostolic Delegate had had to pull out at short notice) but said he was very pleased to be there, as he had a great admiration for the Vaughan Club:

I don't suppose there is a club in London that could present a gathering such as this… You men and women from Stepney are the best in the world. I have known the district for many years and know that there is a tradition here. I hope you will remember it.

He was introduced to the new Mayor and Mayoress of Stepney (Catholics again), and the MP Walter Edwards proposed a toast, saying they should all take their hats off to Joe McCarthy for the club's success.

The club is serving a very great purpose. No one here would be afraid to take their friends to the club and experience the atmosphere which pervades.

Canon Fitzgerald sometimes used to give radio talks, and so became quite well-known around the country. Two series of broadcasts that he made, in 1948 and 1955, were published in pamphlet form. He acted as official chaplain to Bill Sullivan when he was Mayor of Stepney, and his command of French came in handy when there was a twinning scheme with a French town. It was later reported in the newspapers that, thanks to his excellent relations with all the Labour Councillors, and the Communist ones as well, the replacement St Mary and St Michael's School was entirely paid for from public funds. However this may have been a journalistic exaggeration: the parishioners had been fundraising hard to meet their share, and the Sisters of Mercy had made a donation of £1,000 towards the total. However it was achieved, the £80,000 cost was met, and the school opened without debt. After the opening, the Sisters made further financial contributions to improve the internal décor – for example by putting down lino, as the floors were too slippery to be safe for small children.

Monica Henderson joined the adult praesidium of the Legion of Mary, along with Joan Donovan, Mary Avery, Mary Horan, Sheila Reed, Harry Fitzer, Charlie Harvey, Johnny Keefe and others. They met once a week to say the rosary, and went out in pairs to conduct the periodic parish census, and visit parishioners. There was a little prayer you had to say with your partner before you started out. The Legion held meetings at which both a priest and a layperson would give a talk on some topics, and then there'd be questions for discussion. They used to go on retreats, and you were supposed to be in silence during the day. St John Bosco and St Cecilia's Clubs went in for all sorts of competitions, and were constantly carrying off prizes: members used to win both group and individual awards. St Cecilia's usual opponents in netball matches were the Stepney Jewish Club, whose star player was Irene Luderman, but they also played Catholic clubs, and held the netball trophy for the Westminster Catholic Youth for many years. Maureen Warren won some individual certificates for singing: Cardinal Griffin presented her with one when she was 14. She and some of the other girls who had good voices used to sing in the choir. St John Bosco teams competed in a range of London Federation of Boys' Clubs sports events. In the boxing finals at the Albert Hall, they scored wins seven year running; they also staged boxing tournaments for good causes, and in 1952 raised £128 for the Crusade of Rescue. The Club took part in drama and music festivals, and had a discussion group which Canon Fitzgerald considered particularly important, so the boys could learn how to express themselves, and be able to participate in trade unions and community activities.

Ceilidhs used to be held in Our Lady's Hall, and a few St Mary and St Michael's parishioners also used to patronise the Irish dancing on Sunday nights at Guardian Angels – though the bulk of the patrons there weren't locals, but recent arrivals from Ireland, some lodging temporarily in Tower Hamlets to be near their work, and others coming in from a distance. For many years the Council kept up the wartime open air dancing (ballroom style) in Shadwell Park and Victoria Park, with proper bands: it was free, and everyone went – all as beautifully dressed up as they could manage. According to Wapping parishioner Patrick Hanshaw, the Sunday night dances at Our Lady's Hall remained popular with young people all through the 1950s: they'd come from all over Tower Hamlets, and from Stratford and Canning Town, and there would often be a couple of hundred there, dancing to a live band. He met his wife at one of these dances.

Fr Ron Aylward

The parish had its own scout and cub troops – the 8th Stepney. Miss Veronica Collins was Akela, and Mrs Hayes also used to help with the cubs. But in 1956 there was a terrible tragedy during a trip to Whipsnade Zoo. 10-year-old Tony Murphy climbed over the 5 ft outer safety barrier round the lion's cage, and the lion got him. His friend John Barry ran for help, and the priest who was accompanying the cubs, Fr Ron Aylward, jumped over, hit the lion with an iron bar, and dragged Tony away. He then wrapped his shirt round the boy, and took him to hospital where he was rushed into the operating theatre. Both arms had to be amputated, and he was put on an iron lung. Everyone at St Mary and St Michael's was praying for Tony, and the Pope sent his blessing, but he died a week later. He'd been an only child, and his parents were devastated. The church was packed for the funeral: all his schoolfriends were there, cubs and scouts from all over Stepney, while outside the traffic was jammed all the way to Aldgate. Canon Fitzgerald stated that he hoped safety precautions would be improved, so there wouldn't be another tragedy. At St Patrick's Cemetery, black-robed choirboys led the way as Tony's coffin, covered in the cub flag, was carried to the graveside, where two trumpeters from the Brompton Oratory Army Cadet Corps played the Last Post. The new Mayor and Mayoress, who happened this year not to be Catholics, sent a wreath, and prayers were said for Tony Murphy's family when the Borough Councillors attended the inaugural civic service at St Dunstan's the following Sunday evening.

Centenary of the church

In December 1956 there was a centenary service to commemorate the opening of St Mary and St Michael's Church, and Fr Tomalin gave a talk about the history. He said that in the walls, occasionally you can see a brick put in the wrong way (upright), and that's because while they were building it, every time they ran out of money the builders stopped work, but put a brick upright so they could see quickly where they needed to carry on. Fr Tomalin also explained that it had now become absolutely clear that the spire could never be built, because the foundations weren't strong enough to take the weight.

Over the seven years 1952-59 Canon Fitzgerald raised and spent £250,000 on the church. It was re-tiled and re-roofed, and all the structural damage made good. The front was nicely remodelled, and statues of Christ the King, Our Lady and St Michael placed in niches. A large new presbytery went up on the Lukin Street side where the old Junior School had been. The priests were naturally delighted, but Fr Fitzgerald commented that he was most pleased for the sake of the housekeeper, Mary Lord, because now she would have her own sitting room and wouldn't have to sit "among the pots and pans" when she had visitors. The house was deliberately built with double doors because it was expected to become an episcopal residence. At the time, it was thought that the London area would be subdivided into more than three dioceses, with East London having its own bishop, so that St Mary and St Michael's really would be "the cathedral of the East End". Of course, this never happened. Bill Sullivan,when Mayor, tried hard to get Canon Fitzgerald made a bishop, but to no avail.

Some of the pre-war fittings had survived: the pulpit and communion rails; the original Bolton and Swailes altar in the Guild Chapel; the 1929 Lady Altar; and the two Phyffers statues, which were returned to their traditional pedestals at the entrance to the sanctuary. The high altar was also salvaged, though the six niches in its reredos were reduced to four (it had to be shortened to fit), and the little statues were missing. The windows had all been smashed, though fragments survived in the tracery from the memorial windows to Fr Twomey and Mother De Sales in the Guild Chapel, including their tiny portraits. Four new stained glass windows were therefore commissioned from the John Hardman studios. The ones above the high altar, and in the Guild Chapel, replicated the iconographic themes of the pre-war windows which they replaced. The pre-war window in the Lady Chapel had been extremely elaborate, so much so that from a distance it looked like a blur, and the replacement design for this one was relatively simple, with the

Annunciation in the central panel, flanked by scenes of the Assumption and Coronation of Our Lady, and the appearances at Lourdes and Fatima. Another stained glass window was installed over the entrance (which had previously always had plain glass). This one shows the sacrificed Lamb of God, adored by the Church on earth – with the Tower and church spires of London in the background – and above is Christ the King glorified in heaven, surrounded by saints and angels.

At this point (around 1957) Canon Fitzgerald took lots of photos, and commissioned a beautiful set of monochrome postcards of the church and the school – though this can't have helped the finances, since thousands remained unsold. The new shrine to the English Martyrs wasn't completed till 1959. The window in this chapel is the fourth of those commissioned from Hardman's: it shows Our Lady Queen of Martyrs flanked by St John Fisher and St Thomas More, and below is Henry Webley. The altar, which was new, has a reredos with two panels depicting on one side the executions of the Stepney Martyrs, and on the other the Barque of Peter sailing along the Thames towards Tower Bridge. A plaque was placed on the wall, listing all the Martyrs who died within the then Borough of Stepney. Finally a new organ, commissioned from Slater of London, was installed on the opposite side of the church, in front of the Guild Chapel.

In January 1959 work began on the convent extension, and the Sisters spent the rest of that year (the centenary of their arrival in Commercial Road) "in a state of upheaval", since proper heating and a lift were being installed in the main convent at the same time. But it was well worth the temporary inconvenience. On Saturday 19th December the beautiful new chapel was blessed, and the official opening took place on the Feast of St Thomas the Apostle, 21st December, when Mass was celebrated by Canon Fitzgerald. Among the clergy present were two distinguished former pupils of the Sisters: Mgr Frederick Row, Master of Ceremonies at Westminster Cathedral, and Fr Victor Guazzelli. Afterwards the clergy and other visitors were entertained in the community room, while a reception was put on downstairs in the refectory for the construction workers – a "motley crowd" of English, Irish and West Indians, "but all honest, hard-working, respectful men". Only after the Sisters' guests had departed did they sit down to their own lunch.

Winds of change

By now, the Sisters reckoned, good times had come at last to the East End:

> *We no longer live in a depressed area. The slums, the squalor, the poverty and*

the over-crowding have almost completely disappeared. In this 'brave new world' of ours, the worker has come into his own, and our Dockers reap the benefits of social justice and equality. Modern flats, hygienically and tastefully furnished, replace the hovels of the poor. Parks and open spaces are much more plentiful and trees and gardens provide, in a small measure, the natural beauty of the countryside. Our people are prosperous and are gradually learning how to use their increased prosperity to the best advantage. Standards of education and living generally are higher and all, even the poorest, have the opportunity to qualify for the highest positions, at the expense of the State. The introduction of a National Health Service has been an inestimable boon to the poor, and has resulted in a vast improvement in the physical welfare of the nation at large.

There was a great deal of truth in this, and certainly it reflected common opinion in 1959, when everything seemed to be on the up and up. The issues which mainly now concerned the Sisters were the inevitable flip side of the new prosperity: the materialism and "worship of mammon", and "the growth of irreligion and a disregard for all the traditions of the ancient Church." However the positive note which they chose to round off their community's centenary report was to prove over-optimistic, in a number of key aspects.

People who stayed in Stepney, rather than moving out to the expanding suburbs and new towns, were often very attached to the district, and to the traditional lifestyle which involved extended families all living in the same locality, for mutual companionship and support. But it was also true that, by and large, the people who stayed were less successful in material terms than those who left, and less able to adapt to a rapidly changing world. Many were still appallingly poorly housed. While the Irish and Jewish communities gradually shrank, and London's Chinatown moved from Limehouse to Soho, the East End's black and South Asian communities (which also went back centuries but had up to then been very small) expanded, so that once again a high proportion of the local population were first-generation immigrants, struggling to become established. Most of the longstanding residents of Cable Street had moved out, and it was now said to be one of the most racially mixed areas in Britain. Social problems were growing: the vice trade could not be suppressed, and gutted and derelict houses attracted meths drinkers.

Key aspects of the old East End culture were either disappearing, or under imminent threat. Hopping came to an abrupt end when the harvesting process was mechanised. There was another blitz on eradicating slum housing in the inner city, with more new towns, and the replacement of streets by tower blocks. On 18th July 1962, St Mary and St Michael's School had the Mayor of Stepney, Ellen Aylward, to distribute prizes in the morning, and the children gave a concert. In the afternoon

> *we had the great privilege of seeing Her Majesty, the Queen. The children were lined up in Jamaica Street and had a wonderful view of Her Majesty as she visited the new seventeen storey flats.*

Tower blocks were seen as *the* model for the city of the future: hundreds went up all over London in just a few years, and it wasn't until after they were up that the drawbacks became apparent. Some of them were so badly designed that they became dangerous. The three in Jamaica Street, opened with such fanfare, had to be evacuated and demolished before the century was out. The LCC was replaced with the Greater London Council (GLC) and the Borough of Stepney subsumed into the larger Borough of Tower Hamlets. Meanwhile the winding down of the British Empire was leading to a drop in Commonwealth trade, toward which the old inner docks had been heavily geared. Although nobody as yet comprehended what was in store, the East India Docks would close in 1967, the St Katherine's and London in 1968, and all the other inner docks during the 1970s, with everything switched to the containerised system at Tilbury. But already, people were acutely anxious about the housing situation, and the plans and policies which were breaking up their neighbourhoods, and dispersing their kinship networks. As the local government bodies came to cover larger and larger areas, they inevitably seemed more remote and faceless, and the impression grew among the traditional East End communities that decisions were constantly being made, with far-reaching implications for their lives, by outside forces with no understanding of their heritage, and no respect for their values.

Meanwhile, as the new youth culture for teenagers came in, they gradually lost interest in the sporting and cultural activities at the parish clubs. St Cecilia's closed down. The John Bosco Club kept going, but in 1962 Nos 531-35 Commercial Road were acquired by the Council to extend the Marion Richardson School's playground, and alternative premises were provided in Whitehorse Road, at the corner of Salmons's Lane. A new mixed club for young adults was started: it began on the Feast of the Epiphany, so was called the Three Kings Club. It was originally started by Fr John Norton, and then taken over by Fr Austin Hart. Quite a lot of couples met at the Three Kings Club, and went on to get married – among them Bernadette Day and Dennis Taylor, Kevin Ashby and Carol Olley.

Fr Harry Hamill used to push a pram around the parish with a tape recorder inside, to bring the Mass to the housebound. When he wasn't pushing his pram, he zoomed round on a motor scooter. He not only knew everyone, he also knew who everyone was related to – which, in a parish like St Mary and St Michael's, was very vital information. Although the Mass was still in Latin, and would remain so for a number of years more, Fr Hamill started teaching the Children of Mary the Mass in English. Canon Fitzgerald was remarkably ecumenical, at a time before ecumenism as we known it had been invented: on the first Procession Sunday after Peter Clynick took over as Vicar of St Mary's Cable Street, Canon Fitzgerald took his arm so that they walked down Johnson Street together, and he always told him, "Because history has put a fence between us through no fault of our own there is no reason why we should not look over the fence and wish each other well."

During the 1950s, Mass attendance had still been about 2,000 (though unlike before the war, this figure now included the children), but in the 1960s it began to fall, and so did the level of the regular income which kept things going, so the parish began sliding into deficit. In 1963, in an effort to place the finances on a firmer footing, the outdoor collection was abolished in favour of planned giving envelopes, launched in an "Offertory Promise Campaign". That year the outdoor procession was held as usual. But problems were developing with the processions. A feeling was growing among the clergy and the Sisters that they were turning into a carnival, devoid of real spiritual meaning. In any case all the old streets were disappearing, and those that were left were filling up with non-Irish immigrants. Without the old thickly Catholic neighbourhoods and the house shrines, people had a sense of processing through "empty space". Canon Fitzgerald therefore decided that there would be no more processions. As the decision had to be made, he felt it best that it be made by him, not left to his successor.

He announced his retirement in April 1964. He'd been in too much pain for some time with terrible arthritis, and too drugged up with the heavy medication he had to take, to be able to do his work properly. Although the parishioners begged him to stay, he thought that was unfair both on the curates, and on the parish which needed a younger man. The Sunday before he left Stepney he went to St Mary's Cable Street to give a talk to the Anglican congregation there, and gave them a blessing in English. Retiring to Ireland, which he would have liked to do, was out of the question because the damp climate would have aggravated his arthritis, so he went to live at a retirement home on the seaside in Hampshire, run by Franciscan nuns. Later, when that closed, he moved to a home in Barnet.

The parishioners didn't forget him, and groups used often to go and visit him during his retirement. Around Christmastime 1967, he had to be taken into St John and Elizabeth's. Insofar as it was possible to have a celebration, he celebrated his Golden Jubilee there on 3rd February 1968, and three weeks later he died. A magnificent funeral was celebrated at St Mary and St Michael's, and the church was packed to capacity.

"It's different now at St Mary and St Michael's"

Fr Worlock had been promoted to first secretary of Cardinal Griffin in 1947, and remained in the post ever since; at the age of 29 he'd been given the rank of monsignor, and subsequently that of Domestic Prelate to the Pope. After Cardinal Griffin died in 1956, he stayed on as secretary to Cardinal Godfrey, accompanying him to the first session of the Second Vatican Council, October – December 1962. Cardinal Godfrey died in January 1963, and a new archbishop, Ilford-born John Carmel Heenan, was appointed in September. Again, Mgr Worlock stayed on as secretary, but only temporarily while handing over to a new appointee. He remained secretary of the Bishops' Conference of England and Wales, and was asked to serve as a peritus (expert adviser) during the Council's second session. For some years he'd been chaplain to a group of laymen known as "The Team", who were strongly committed to the lay apostolate both in Britain and internationally. The Team had grown out of the YCW, and the members included Pat Keegan, Romeo Maione (Keegan's successor as YCW president), Maurice Foley (another product of that first generation of the YCW), and a number of others. They met regularly at Archbishop's House in Westminster, to feed in their views both to Mgr Worlock and to Abp Heenan, and Keegan was a lay auditor at the Council. A number of radio broadcasts and television appearances had made Mgr Worlock quite famous, and everyone was astonished when he was chosen to succeed Canon Fitzgerald at Commercial Road. According to Mgr Worlock, Abp Heenan had intended to give him a West End parish, but he specifically requested St Mary and St Michael's.

As had happened previously when, in pursuance of a diocesan experiment, a prominent non-Irish parish priest was appointed, the whole clergy team was changed. Fr Tomalin, who was senior curate and had been there for 23 years, was given a full-scale leaving do in the hall of St Mary and St Michael's School, with speeches from the Mayor Ernest Hill, and from Walter Edwards MP, and a cheque from the parishioners. The new team, hand-picked by Mgr Worlock, comprised Fr Louis Marteau who'd been at seminary with him; Fr Jack O'Connell who was a great-great-grandson of Daniel O'Connell, and a late vocation with a background in banking; Fr Paul Mullins; and Fr Brian Nash.

On a Sunday morning in early May, 91 schoolchildren received their First

Communion from Mgr Worlock, and on the same day Abp Heenan came to preside at the evening Mass, and induct the new parish priest. The archbishop processed round from the new presbytery in Lukin Street, preceded by Michael O'Leary, head boy of St John Bosco's, and imparting his blessing en route to the 127 members of the Blessed Sacrament Guild, in their red sashes, who lined the route. At that time the Gelineau psalms were just coming in, and Sr Elizabeth was already beginning to play them for the children's Mass. Mgr Worlock was very involved with the Grail, which was popularising them, and keen to have them for his induction, but Frank Lapthorne absolutely refused to play them. He was a brilliant organist, but the simple Gelineau melodies weren't his idea of music. So Fr Marteau asked Sr Elizabeth to play. It was very short notice, and she had butterflies in her stomach about playing in front of the archbishop, but all went well.

Virtually everyone at St Mary and St Michael's still identified as Irish, though they'd all been born in Stepney, and many of them only had one Irish grandparent. On St Patrick's Day everyone wore something green, because the nuns pushed it, and everyone knew and joined in the Irish songs. Irishness meant different things to different people: many parish families were apolitical and even a bit naïve about politics, and didn't realise for a long time the extent to which some parishioners sympathised with the IRA. The Catholic population of the Archdiocese of Westminster had gone up by nearly half as many again since the end of the war, but the Catholic population of Stepney had stagnated: it was currently estimated at about 7,000 – 8,000. The old sodalities still existed, but they were in steady decline. Most marriages were mixed, and the lapsation rate was up to 80%. Mass attendance was down to 1,400. Stepney, as a district, was by now terribly run down. Mgr Worlock and his team saw themselves as parachuting into a disaster zone, which needed immediate first aid while foundations were laid for a different sort of future. According to George Scott:

> *'For three days Worlock and his curates stumped the streets with the message 'It's different now at St Mary and St Michael's – you can come back.' An old man said, 'It's all right, Father, you can go home.' 'What do you mean?' said Monsignor Worlock. 'It's all right, Father, we know the priest is back.'*

The last member of the new team to arrive was Fr Nash. After training in Rome (where he'd got to know Mgr Worlock, as he was sometimes called on to do some typing for him), he'd spent three years at St John's Wood. He arrived in Lukin Street on 1st August 1964. The presbytery walls were still bare plaster, but soon they were painted in bright colours, and comfortable modern furniture was put in. The laid-back atmosphere in the presbytery, with a lot of laughter, was very unusual for the time. The priests called themselves the Ovalteenies, because they always had Ovaltine in the evening, but when Fr Nash arrived coffee had to be added, since he didn't like Ovaltine. Mary Lord remained housekeeper. Mgr Worlock himself was still spending a lot of time in Rome. He sent home tapes, outlining his plans for the parish, and the priests used to sit round late at night, over their cups of Ovaltine (or coffee) listening to them: the recordings were punctuated by the chimes of the clock at the English College where Mgr Worlock was staying. They in turn reported to him on their work in the hospitals, schools and youth club, and what was being done to liven up the liturgy. The tapes were shared with the convent, and the nuns were delighted to be able to hear all about the Council discussions at first hand, and before anything was officially published.

The Worlock team *left to right:*
Fr P Mullins, Fr L Marteau, Fr B Nash,
Fr J O'Connell, Mgr D Worlock

The Sisters of Mercy gave their full support to the efforts of the clergy team, who very much appreciated it. Because the services were still in Latin, most people didn't really have a clue what was going on. So at every Mass, a second priest gave a commentary. On Sundays the whole team stood at the door after each Mass, to greet parishioners and get to know them. Some of the Mass times were changed to times which suited the dockers better, and at the 6.30 am weekday Mass, the handful who attended were invited to abandon the "perishing cold" church and come into the sacristy. The dockers used to gather in Tolaini's café, and Fr Mullins went down there after Mass to get to know them better. Regular visitation of parish homes was maintained (de-linked now from any financial collections): the streets designated for visitation each week were published in the newsletter, and as Fr Nash recalled:

woe betide a defaulting cleric. Mind you a volley of expletives from the back room when the Mrs of the house said who had called, though rare, was a reminder of past antagonisms as well as a certain source of amusement...

Fr Nash was amused by local Catholics' habit of introducing their wives to the clergy with the deprecating explanation "She's not one of our own, Father." In most places this would have meant she was a "Sozzo" (a Protestant – from the Irish "Sasanač", meaning an English person), but here it usually meant she came from another parish. Bernard Keniry's wife Nell was "not one of our own" because she was brought up in Limehouse.

The priests visited all three hospitals for which the parish had responsibility: the London, the Maternity Hospital on Commercial Road, and the London Jewish in Stepney Green. They organised an intensive programme to get to know all the schoolchildren who were coming up to leaving age, and visit their homes, in the hope of managing to keep in touch afterwards. Every Saturday night they joined the parishioners at the Vaughan Club from 9.30 to 11.00, but they didn't order drinks at the bar, because Mgr Worlock felt very strongly that they shouldn't be seen drinking in public. At his Silver Wedding celebration, to which Fr Nash was a specially invited guest, Bernard Keniry treated him to a Scotch, but discreetly brought it over in a teacup. After a year's hard work, it was claimed that Mass attendance had been jacked up to 2,200, but even if this was true, the increase was not sustainable.

Tony Murphy's parents had decided to take legal action against the zoo, even if it meant they had to sell their house to pay the costs. When Fr Marteau found out, he alerted Mgr Worlock who used his contacts to get in touch with the zoo's Board of Directors, and arrange for the case to be settled out of court. A difficult situation had developed with the St John Bosco Club, but it was resolved by installing a full-time paid youth worker, Frank Skerrett – a married man who lived with his wife in a flat in the basement of the club. There was a gym at the back, a snooker room and TV room, a tea and soft drinks bar and a jukebox. The St John Bosco at this period was tending to get the throw-outs from all the other clubs, but it was kept going, and Fr Nash – who was described as "incredibly good with the kids in the East End"

– felt it continued to have a positive impact. He was also chaplain to the Scouts, though he knew nothing about scouting, but fortunately the lay scout leaders organised everything. Frs Marteau and Mullins took over the Three Kings Club.

The five priests made a very strong team, and they worked hard at being a team. When Mgr Worlock was at home, they'd often spend a whole day together, planning their pastoral strategy. They also made a point of getting home by 10.00 pm for Night Prayer in the presbytery common room. This wasn't easy: it could mean that Fr Marteau had to cut short his night round at the London Hospital (during which he made a point of seeing patients due for an operation the following morning), and Fr Nash couldn't stay late at St John Bosco's. But they all agreed it was important: Mgr Worlock never forgot Fr Nash once hitting the table and yelling, "How can we really work together if we don't b****y pray together?" However problems developed over the fact that the parish priest was hardly ever there. Even when he wasn't in Rome for the Vatican Council, he usually spent every morning at his office in Archbishop's House, and in the afternoons and evenings he had a *very* full diary. When Fr Marteau started going through the parish accounts, he found them in a terrible muddle, so buttonholed him to say they needed to talk. Mgr Worlock looked in his diary and offered him an appointment three months down the line – whereupon Fr Marteau blew his top, went to his room and slammed the door. A bit later Mgr Worlock crept in and asked "Did you want to see me?" From then on the accounts were always published to the parishioners, but their response was "We're not interested in what you do with the money, Farver, just let us know how much you need." Unfortunately it wasn't as easy as that, and financial problems persisted.

A key element in the new pastoral strategy was the introduction of "Family Groups": they started by making up a group of about six couples, who would be asked to visit each other's houses for a couple of hours to discuss the teaching of the Gospel as it related to their day-to-day lives. Those involved in the Family Groups found them very helpful, and often an eye-opener. The initiative was connected with the Grail, and the newsletter was printed at Pinner. Talks by the down-to-earth Fr Rochford were particularly popular. Mgr Worlock encouraged the Family Groups to do something for the elderly in the parish, so they got 160 old people together and took them on an outing. It became a regular thing, and the parishioners involved with it were referred to as the Old Age Pensioners Group – though they were all young people. They'd visit, run dances and raise money – the men went on sponsored walks to Aylesford – and then they'd take the old people for a day out to the hop fields, and give them Christmas parties. Among those involved were a number of married couples with children, such as Tom and Betty Morgan, Jerry and Sheila Crawley, Terry and Eileen Mahoney, and George and Eileen Bidicant. Also there were Norry Davy, Beattie Hynes, Marie Henderson, Dannie Keefe (who were all single), and the widowed Kathleen Harvey.

The Legion of Mary, SVP and choir continued to flourish. So did the Children of Mary, which was being run by Sr Berchmans Flaherty – and the members still tended to call it "Children of Mary", although officially the old name had been dropped in favour of the more modern "Marian Association". Five or six of them decided to form a singing group, and they used to go around and sing at various events. Daphne Harvey was in it, Margaret Wright, Maria Gorni who was Fr Guazzelli's niece, and several others. As Fr Guazzelli was currently working at Westminster Cathedral, they often used to go down there to sing, especially for old people's parties. The Men's Guild continued to parade from time to time, and Mother Bernard could always get them together when they were needed: the red sashes were stored in a cupboard in the wall, near the confessionals. The Vaughan Club was still important, and as St Catherine's Bow, and Guardian Angels, also had parish clubs, they sometimes got together for an inter-parish social at the York Hall. To make up for there being no procession in the summer of 1964, a Rosary Rally was held behind the church. That year a "tame bishop" was found to do an open-air confirmation service for 136 children. It was preceded by a pageant on the "Seven Gifts of the Holy Spirit", with a script written by Mgr Worlock and read by three BBC commentators. Unfortunately, although it was late June, the day turned out cold and showery, but at least the rain held off until the ceremony was over. From then on a tradition was kept up of having an annual parish day on which something extra special would be organised: in 1965 Mgr Worlock found a candidate for ordination who was willing to have the ceremony performed at St Mary and St Michael's, arranged for Cardinal Heenan to come and do it, and mobilised the parishioners to organise a big celebration.

Among progressive-minded intellectuals it was quite fashionable at that time to live in the East End, and the upstairs flat at the St John Bosco Club was used by Maurice Foley and his wife Kitty, and their children. The couple were both close friends of Mgr Worlock, and took part in the Family Groups. Maurice Foley was now MP for Bromwich, and a junior minister in the Labour government with responsibility for immigration. Kenneth Kaunda, who led Northern Rhodesia to independence and became its President under the new name of Zambia, often used to come to stay. The Foleys' youngest child, Joseph, was in St Mary and St Michael's Infant School, and one day

Kaunda asked him, "Are there any black children in your class?" He didn't realise that very small children don't notice what colour anyone is. Joseph answered solemnly: "I don't know, tomorrow I will look."

Ecumenical contacts were initiated with Rev Young at St Dunstan's, Rev Ron Gibbons at the East End Methodist Mission, and with the Ebenezer Church under Rev John Pellow. One evening when Mgr Worlock and Rev Young were walking home together, Rev Young remarked that their respective parishioners were observing them from the windows of their homes, and it might be an idea to separate before it caused a row, but Mgr Worlock insisted that they walk together down the middle of the street. St Mary's Cable Street used to ring its bell at the time of the consecration at Mass in St Mary and St Michael's.

One night a lot of banging was to be heard in the closed church. Fr Marteau had taken a sledgehammer, and was demolishing the pulpit. The first most of the parishioners knew about it was when a builder's lorry called next morning to take away the rubble, and they were very upset. Fr Marteau next made an elegant wooden altar, for Mass facing the people. Another change was that the Phyffers statues were taken off their pedestals and moved to the side chapels. The Gelineau psalms were catching on: after a special Maundy Thursday afternoon Mass for the school, Fr Nash heard a boy running down Lukin Street, kicking an empty can in time to the antiphon for Ps 23 (The Lord's My Shepherd): "His goodness shall follow me always/ To the end of my days". Mgr Worlock did a BBC radio broadcast one afternoon from the church – featuring the psalm melodies, organ music and children playing flutes – and a listener phoned in from Greenland. But in the middle of it all, as Mgr Worlock was supervising from the sanctuary, the curates noticed a small boy come in at the back of the church with a rubber. There was a book there for people to sign when they attended the Forty Hours Prayer, and someone had written a rude word in it (fortunately in pencil). Srs Cyril and Sylvester had seen this, so sent a child from the Infant School, who couldn't yet read, to rub it out.

Because the parish priest was a monsignor, the dockers called him "the Mon". Mgr Worlock was always the sort of person that some people liked a lot, and other people definitely did not like. A lot of people blamed him for stopping the processions – since, although Canon Fitzgerald claimed to have made the decision, Mgr Worlock had taken over before the next one was due. He was also blamed for destroying the old sodalities, though he doesn't appear to have actually closed them down. But parishioners who didn't warm to the Family Groups, and chose not to take part, often felt excluded and resentful. Above all, Mgr Worlock was held responsible for the destruction of the pulpit. Later on, when he wrote a book about his Stepney experiences, that also upset some people. But he definitely had a following in the parish – and some of those who didn't particularly like him, acknowledged that he'd achieved some things that were very positive, especially for the old people. The Family Groups loved him, and some of the participants were to keep in touch with him for years afterwards.

In September 1965, Mgr Worlock was informed by the Cardinal that he was being appointed Bishop of Portsmouth. For the time being it had to be kept a secret, and when he flew off to Rome in October, for the final session of Vatican II, the parishioners still hadn't been told. The news was announced while he was away, and he returned to St Mary and St Michael's only to make the final arrangements for departure. The dockers gave him an oil painting of the Cure d'Ars, telling him, "Stay like him Father, and you'll be all right," and a docker's hook. Fr Marteau organised a whole lot of practical jokes around the presbytery, including a label on Mgr Worlock's dressing table drawer saying "Papal Briefs", but the bishop-elect studiously ignored them. On his last morning in the presbytery, Fr O'Connell returned the compliment by sitting stolidly eating his breakfast as if it was just another day. In the end Mgr Worlock asked, "Aren't you going to wish me luck?" and Fr O'Connell looked up, completely deadpan, and said, "Oh, have you got something important on?" But as Mgr Worlock actually left, the nuns got all the children from St Mary and St Michael's School to line up along the road to wave goodbye, and he was very touched. The curates all drove to Portsmouth in Fr Marteau's landrover to attend his consecration, and it was only afterwards that he told them the vehicle had faulty breaks.

Bishop Casey

Bishop Casey with Rosie Armstrong

Pat Casey was born in Stoke Newington in 1913, and ordained for Westminster in 1939. After serving as assistant priest at St James, Spanish Place, for 22 years, he was made parish priest of Hendon in 1961, but then in December 1963 he was made Vicar General. The following year he became a canon and a Domestic Prelate, and early in 1966 he was made an auxiliary bishop. Though he'd been warned not to give Bp Casey too much work, Heenan then decided to put him in to replace Mgr Worlock at St Mary and St Michael's. Since it was already clear that the assistant priests could run the parish in the absence of the parish priest, the assumption was that Casey could just be a figurehead. But he himself wasn't prepared to be a figurehead.

Soon after St Mary and St Michael's School reopened in January 1966, Bp Casey went round each class to introduce himself. He was consecrated by Cardinal Heenan on 2nd February, and a week later he gave "a grand party" to the whole school to celebrate: he himself attended in full episcopal robes, which must have delighted the kiddies. He made every possible effort to get round and visit his new parishioners. Those who were in when he called remember him as very gentle, and always well groomed – his shoes were well polished. He was very unassuming, and a lot of them didn't realise he was a bishop. Due to pressure of work, some of the visits were made quite late at night – which parishioners found rather startling.

But after only three or four months, Bp Casey resigned as parish priest, because it was impossible to cope with all the work. He left on Friday, and the new parish priest arrived the following week.

A prayerful and humble man

Cardinal Heenan had decided to try no more experiments, but trust instead to his old fashioned instincts, and chosen Charles Philip Carr, formerly parish priest of Homerton. "I'm not going to make you a bishop," he told him, and Carr replied "Thank God for that." He was delighted to find himself with a team of priests who got on so well with each other, and he made sure nobody was moved, so it stayed that way. He brought with him his own housekeeper, Sally, from Homerton, and Sally's brother Larry, who worked on the railway but lived in the presbytery, and helped her with the heavy work. This meant that Mary Lord, after many year's service, had to go, but she eventually found a new post at St John the Baptist's, Hackney, for herself and her cat. Fr Carr wasn't indifferent to her plight, and he set himself to get better conditions and legally binding contracts for priests' housekeepers, and persuaded the diocese to agree. Soon after coming to Commercial Road he was made a canon. He was also made Chairman of the Senate of Priests – a post formerly occupied by Cardinal Heenan himself. The Cardinal was very grateful for having this responsibility taking off his hands. It made Canon Carr a very key figure in the diocese.

Confirmations that June were done by Bp Worlock, and Sr Cyril recorded that "There was great rejoicing at his return to the Parish." But for the next few years, the most readily available bishop was usually Bp Casey. The Rosary Nursery in the Nissen huts had served the parish for over 16 years, but now it was closed and replaced by a new building in the grounds of St Mary and St Michael's School. Bp Casey performed the opening ceremony for that, and he came for confirmations in 1968. However he left Westminster in December 1969, on becoming Bishop of Brentwood.

Just outside St Mary and St Michael's School was a very dangerous crossroads. Patrick Mahoney, son of Terry and Eileen, about 10 or 11 and in his final year at St Mary and St Michael's School, went to cross over Commercial Road, hesitated and stepped backwards, fell and hit his head against the pavement, and suffered severe brain damage. At that time a new system of exercises was being introduced for brain-damaged people, which required four people (one on each arm, one on each leg) and had to be carried out for quite long periods each day. So the parish rallied round and people came in shifts, when one lot was finished, another would come and take over. All those who'd been involved in the Family Groups helped with the therapy, and various other people, including a Jewish man named Harry Jacobs. The parishioners also raised merry hell with the Council to get traffic lights installed opposite the school. When Bp Worlock heard, he was very concerned, and made a point of visiting the Mahoneys whenever he could. They were to remain great friends of his: years later, when as Archbishop of Liverpool he celebrated the Golden Jubilee of his ordination, they and the Wilcoxes travelled up to Liverpool to be there, and both families went again in 1996 for his funeral.

According to Fr Nash, Canon Carr was "A prayerful and humble man… with a fierce loyalty to his bishop." He got to grips with the parish finances, turned them round and resolved the growing deficit. A Parish Council was started, and it was at one of the meetings that Bernard Keniry made the suggestion of staring a parish savings scheme, whereby parishioners would entrust the cash they were keeping under their mattress (or wherever) to the parish, which would bank it and keep the interest, and the lenders could have their money back any time. This scheme proved quite popular, because there were a lot of people who never used banks, but felt their savings were safer with the parish. Football pools were also important, and during the summer months

Canon Carr got them to do the Australian matches, so they could keep it up all year. The Parish Council was quite lively for a while, though people who raised criticisms at meetings often did not feel capable of constructive engagement in the search for solutions. Eventually (as happened in most parishes) doubts began to surface about its relevance, and it ceased to meet regularly.

Charles Philip Canon Carr with Sister Josephine Cleary

Canon Carr was very keen on the strong scriptural emphasis which came out of Vatican II: he subscribed to an Irish publication called "Scripture in Church", with articles on the Bible and homily notes, and made sure every priest or deacon living in the house got a copy. At Homerton, he'd been quite strict about things like always wearing clerical dress, but at St Mary and St Michael's he started wearing an ordinary collar and tie. Fr O'Connell also eventually went over to wearing lay dress, mainly so as not to be bothered by the maudlin Irish drunks who haunted Aldgate, but his shirt was still black so they knew he was a priest anyway. He was greatly loved in the parish, as he always took a keen interest in everyone. Ever since he came, he'd been chaplain to St Mary and St Michael's Junior School, and he was very involved with both children and parents: he would notice things – such as if a child wasn't eating.

Under Canon Carr the organ was serviced twice a year, and there were always properly paid organists. For baptisms he would often play organ himself, with Fr Nash doing the baptism, and Harry Fitzer reading "the bits in between". Being a trained musician, Canon Carr wanted to start an operatic society: he applied to the Inner London Education Authority to be appointed a drama instructor, and this was agreed, so he was paid to put on productions in Our Lady's Hall. They never tackled high opera, but they did Gilbert and Sullivan pieces like the Pirates of Penzance; musicals like My Fair Lady, Oklahoma, Oliver, and The King and I; and pantomimes. The Children of Mary singing group all joined the operatic society, as did Harry Fitzer, "black-haired" Kathleen Donovan (as she was called to distinguish her from other parishioners with the same name), Carol Hurley, Joan Donovan, Charlie

Harvey, Teddy Sexton, and Esther O'Toole who later married Teddy. Maureen Warren had already married, but she was in it, and her husband Harry Hayward used to look after the kids when she came to rehearsals. Carol Thomas, a music teacher at Bishop Challoner, used to play for the operas, and the Sisters of Mercy served as prompters (keeping well out of sight). Canon Carr also got help from a professional actor, Charles Farrell, who didn't live locally but used to come on Monday and Thursday evenings to help with rehearsals. The productions were choreographed by Farrell's wife Babs, another show business professional who used to choreograph West End productions.

A bishop of our very own

When yet another new auxiliary bishop was needed for Westminster, there was the usual discreet consultation, and some of the laypeople said it would be good to have someone from the East End. So Victor Guazzelli was chosen, and he was consecrated in May 1970. Commercial Road's parish visitations in 1971 and 1974 were conducted by Bp Guazzelli. In 1976, when Cardinal Hume decided to create Pastoral Areas within the Archdiocese of Westminster, each to be served by an auxiliary bishop, Bp Guazzelli was put in charge of the Eastern Area – though he was never Bishop *of* East London (he was titular Bishop of Lindisfarne) and he didn't have a cathedral. He lived at Pope John House, in Poplar.

Bishop Victor Guazzelli

For a number of years a big annual service was held in St Dunstan's for Church Unity Week, bringing together delegations from churches all over Tower Hamlets. Bp Guazzelli usually took part, and the children from St Mary and St Michael's School were among the groups usually asked to give a presentation. In some years a large-scale and very impressive passion play was acted around the streets of Stepney, organised by St Dunstan's, though with actors from various local churches. It was a red letter day for East End ecumenism when Cardinal Hume visited St Dunstan's.

In June 1970, only a few weeks after Bishop Guazzelli's consecration, Fr

O'Connell died quite suddenly at Sunday lunchtime: he was only 54. The parish was plunged into grief: Sr Josephine recalls a West Indian woman coming into the school in tears, saying "Oh, he used to come and sit in my kitchen." The Men's Guild formed a guard of honour at the Requiem Mass in St Mary and St Michael's, for which the parish clergy used the new rite. Cardinal Heenan, who was presiding, was rather startled when they all appeared in white vestments, and in his homily pointed out that this was *not* a canonisation. Afterwards the body was taken back to Ireland to be buried in the O'Connell family vault under the Round Tower, in Glasnevin Cemetery, Dublin.

Legion of Mary outing 1970

In consultation with the Parish Council, Canon Carr had arranged for the Bene Merenti medal (a Papal honour) to be bestowed on several parishioners: Miss Pat Murphy, Mr Bob Collins, and Mr Phil Warendorf, for outstanding service to the Church, and Bp Guazzelli came to present the medals at a parish social in July. Miss Maud Edgley, who'd been a teacher in the Infant School from 1945 to 1970, and was now retiring, received a medal at a separate celebration a week later, arranged by the Parents' Association. For the canonisation of the 40 Martyrs of England and Wales, in October that year, there was an open air Mass at Tower Hill, and the parishioners were all urged to attend. It was outside the grounds of All Hallows Church. A special group picture of the Forty Martyrs was produced for the canonisation, and reproductions in various sizes made available, so a large one was acquired for the Martyrs' Chapel at St Mary and St Michael's. Matt Henderson, who was a carpenter, framed it for Canon Carr.

A Junior St John Bosco Club was being run for the under-12s (girls as well as boys), by Srs Lawrence Collins and Rosarii Ryan, and their helpers Mr and Mrs Greeno, a young couple in Johnson Street, who must have continued their involvement for over 20 years, with Brian Greeno keeping the football team going. Around 1970 the Three Kings Club died out, and Canon Carr decided to close the teenage St John Bosco Club, because it had outlived its relevance. The club building was sold off, and so was the campsite in Essex, which was no longer being used. But the Junior Club continued to thrive. From 1970, the annual parish day was turned into a garden fete: people worked hard at it, and over the years it became a very useful fundraiser. Canon Carr had taken charge of the Legion of Mary, and he used to take the members rambling: they had very nice outings. As the junior praesidium had long died the death, he asked the Sisters of Mercy to organise an intermediate one for younger parishioners: Srs Elizabeth and Joan Cecil agreed to run it, and George Clark, Seamus Power and Mary Short were among those who took part. As well as meeting weekly for prayer, the members took part in activities such as parish visiting, and made enjoyable trips out together with the senior praesidium.

Another change in the secondary school situation had gone through in 1964, whereby St Bernard's moved to Bethnal Green, and became an exclusively boys' school, under a Marist Brother as headteacher, while the girls from St Bernard's were transferred to Bishop Challoner, which became an all-girls comprehensive school. With a roll of less than 800, Bishop Challoner wasn't particularly large as London comprehensives went, but it was too big for the Christian Street premises, so it had to take over the old St Bernard's building as well, using it as an annexe to accommodate the older girls, and operating on a split site. Among the Sixth Formers being prepared for their GCEs by Sr Teresita Heenan, that first year after the merger, was Amelia Obertelli whom she'd taught in the first form at Christian Street: Amelia did well in her exams, took teaching training at Strawberry Hill, and went on to become a headmistress. Bishop Challoner had been under Sr Berchmans as head since Sr Joseph retired in 1968. She was very strict on discipline: the girls had to behave themselves and wear correct uniform (and they did), and the penalty for being late for school was to be made to pick up litter in the playground. In 1969 came the marvellous news that permission had been granted for the construction of a new school, on the west side of Lukin Street, but it wasn't until 1974 that it was possible to move into the building – and even then, there was only enough room for the Upper School. The Lukin Street premises were solemnly blessed and officially opened by Cardinal Heenan on 28th June 1975. But the Lower School had to remain at Christian Street, under Sr Teresita Heenan as deputy headteacher, and it would be many years before it was possible to unite the whole school at Lukin Street.

Sr Josephine took over as headteacher of the Infant School in 1973. Sr Cyril continued as head of the Junior School until her retirement in 1975, after 44 years in Stepney and 28 as headmistress. She was subsequently awarded the

MBE, and continued to serve as a school governor. She was also a governor of Bishop Challoner, as was Sr Perpetua. Sr Perpetua took a keen interest in any legislation likely to affect Catholic schools, and in her late 80s pursued a correspondence with the local MP, Peter Shore, insisting that he keep her informed of Commons debates on the topic. From 1975 Sr Elizabeth O'Connor was headmistresss of the Junior School.

Mgr Warren Wall

Canon Carr liked to have a full house, and often had visitors to stay. They came from all over the world, and many were, or had been, missionaries. Each year two deacons came from the North American College in Rome, for pastoral experience, and because they liked their beer cold, Carr hired a domestic appliance to keep a barrel at the temperature they liked, and obtained gas from Whitbreads. Some visitors came for nearly a year, while taking a course in London: one of these students, John Battersby from Australia, is now Archbishop of Brisbane. In the summer of 1975 Deacon Warren Wall came on a placement from the North American College. Now a Monsignor he has remained a very good friend of the parish and has returned on frequent visits. Gerry Brady, a Kiltegan Father who'd been working in Nigeria but was unable to return there, had been a lodger with Bp Guazzelli in Pope John House, and then moved into Lukin Street and stayed for many years: he was Head of RE at Canon Palmer School in Ilford, but helped out in St Mary and St Michael's at weekends.

Fr Frank Greenan

When Frank 'Bumpy' Greenan's wife developed cancer, he nursed her devotedly till she died, then offered himself for the priesthood. Westminster wasn't interested, but Bp Beck was only too happy to accept him for Brentwood Diocese. He trained at the Beda, then gave 15 years' service in Essex parishes – many of his parishioners there being people he'd known (and often taught) in Commercial Road – before retiring in 1973, at the age of 86. Canon Carr then invited him to come and live in the presbytery in Lukin Street. He brought with him his cat, Boffin, which used to sit on his lap while he heard confessions. Canon Carr urged Fr Greenan to write a history of St Mary and St Michael's, and he happily got started on the research. He went to Trinity House to find out more about the Virginia Street Chapel site, and at first they were very helpful, but suddenly there was a change of line and they really shut down on him. It seems they'd got mixed up and thought the chapel was Anglican, and that it might be possible for the Church of England to claim mediaeval rights in the land. Fr Greenan was very taken aback, and it rather put him off. Although he got quite a lot of material together, he hadn't got beyond the research stage when he died, on Boxing Day 1976. At the funeral Edith Ramsay, who was still living in Stepney, and had become over the years a close friend of Sr Cyril, sat among the nuns.

For many years priests based at St Mary and St Michaels provided a very high quality chaplaincy service to the London Hospital, and to the other two hospitals until they closed down. (The Maternity Hospital became Steel's Lane Heath Centre, and the London Jewish was demolished to make room for a private hospital.) Fr Marteau, and in later years Frs Cedric Stanley and Paul McGinn, were a tower of strength not only to the patients, but also to the nurses. From the late 1970s the Commercial Road clergy also provided chaplaincy services to several local care homes for old people: Braybrooke House, Fitzgerald Lodge (which was named after Canon Fitzgerald), and Sidney House. The Vaughan Club during the 1970s and 1980s used to do a lot of good work fundraising for St Joseph's Hospice. As well as a Sunday evening Mass, an "anticipated" one on Saturday evenings, had been introduced, and because there were still five Sunday morning Masses (at 7.00, 8.00, 9.15, 10.30 and 12.00), the parish had seven Sunday Masses altogether. The downside of evening Masses was that they tended to crowd out non-liturgical evening services like Benediction, but Fr Brady packed the large chapel at the Convent of Mercy each month for his Sunday evening Holy Hour, followed by tea and cakes in the Community Room. For several years this was a valued spiritual and social experience for many parishioners, and occasionally – such as around Christmas – there would be a renderings of "Danny Boy", and other old favourites, before the gathering dispersed.

However a crisis was developing in the Catholic Church, with priests and nuns leaving, and new recruitment tailing off. Paul Mullins served two stints in South America, but then left the priesthood and got married. He and his wife Daphne, with their two children, came one day to the presbytery on a visit. Noticing that the kids were at a bit of a loose end, Canon Carr went out and bought some toys ready for their next visit. By the mid-1970s, the Legion of Mary in the parish was dying out, and Canon Carr decided to close the praesidium. Around this time catechists came to introduce the Neocatechumenate, and some of the former Legion members were among those who went along to the talks. A community was formed, and some years down the line a small second community. However there was some dissension in the parish about it, and eventually Bp Guazzelli intervened, and arranged for the two communities to be transferred to Guardian Angels.

When the Golden Jubilee of Canon Carr's ordination was approaching, the curates held collections around the parish, using envelopes, and although they didn't expect to be able to keep it a secret, he didn't catch on. The Midlands Bank at that time was offering fancy cheques for presentations, so Fr Nash put the money into Barclays Bank to get interest, but then switched it to the Midlands just before the event, to get the fancy cheque. It was handed over at a reception in the Vaughan Club, after the celebratory Mass. At the time of his Jubilee, Canon Carr was the same weight as he'd been in the seminary. As Fr Nash put it, "He knew he looked sort of miserable and joked about it. In fact he had a fantastic sense of humour…" However he needed to have an operation on his eyes, and this seems to have triggered the onset of Alzheimers. At first he had some awareness of what was happening, and asked Fr Nash "Why am I going barmy?" He became unable to celebrate Mass alone, though he continued to concelebrate with other priests. The process of deterioration took its time, but was unstoppable, and in 1980 Fr Nash had to take charge of the parish. The 7.00 am Sunday Mass was then dropped, making the 8.00 the Mass of choice for communicants, because afterwards they could go round to Golding's, the Jewish bakers near the corner of Jubilee Street, and buy warm fresh bread for breakfast. Canon Carr continued to live in the presbytery, and the other priests – Fr Nash, Fr Steve Delaney, Fr Paul McGinn and, later on, Fr John Cunningham – were together able to care for him until, eventually, he had to be transferred to Nazareth House. He died in St John and Elizabeth's on 7th November 1985.

Fr Cunningham is fondly remembered by the Sisters for his practical skills (for example in carpentry) and for his "constant and generous readiness to 'come to the rescue' in all sorts of situations." Throughout the 1980s and into the 1990s, a handful of young people, including Dennis Mentessi, John Morgan, Billy Nash, Michelle Morris, Caroline and Carmel Bohan, collaborated in maintaining their Confirmation commitment to help the work of the Church. Sr Maureen Hill was initially involved with them in their prayer and discussion groups, and later Sr Alma Coogan worked with them. They engaged in fundraising; provided minibus transport to take the elderly parishioners out for social occasions, pilgrimages and seaside outings; and helped organise Christmas bazaars, summer fetes and jumble sales. For several years they provided a Christmas dinner, in early January, for the local homeless men and women: they saved up to buy a whole good quality dinner service, and with the aid of their parents would cook and serve a three-course meal for the homeless in Our Lady's Hall. All of them have now moved on and out of the area.

In the 1980s, when Our Lady's Hall was falling into disrepair, the Junior St John Bosco Club moved into St Mary and St Michael's School hall. Sister Lawrence, her helpers and the children were regularly involved in fundraisingand other activities: they did sponsored walks, went carol singing at the railway stations in the lead-up to Christmas, and raised money for Rehab and Providence Row, and for the local homeless and people in need. They were also taken for annual holiday camps at Bognor Regis and Minehead, Barry Island, Isle of Wight and Cornwall. The McGuire O'Shea School of Irish Dancing came under the umbrella of the St John Bosco Club, and held weekly sessions under the tutorship of Kathleen McGuire. A local Councillor – Charlie Mudd – was very supportive, and he helped make it possible to hold a dancing class on Monday evenings in the St Mary and St Michael's School hall, with a teacher of Modern Dance called Pam Rhodes, who has since become well-known as the presenter of the BBC's Songs of Praise. This modern dance class was very popular also with the older girls from the Bishop Challoner Sixth Form, and continued for seven years. Charlie Mudd obtained flood lighting for the school's five-a-side pitch, so it could be used during winter evenings.

Pam Rhodes

The character of the East End was changing radically. The East Pakistanis who had come to live in Tower Hamlets up to the end of the 1960s were almost all men, working hard to send money to their families back home, where they intended eventually to return. In 1971 civil war broke out in their homeland, resulting in its becoming independent as Bangladesh. But from around this time their plans changed: they brought their families over to join them, and a permanently settled Bangladeshi community grew up. The original East London Mosque in Commercial Road was compulsorily purchased by the Council in 1983, but an alternative site was provided in Whitechapel Road for a much more ambitious structure.

By 1991 nearly a quarter of Tower Hamlets residents were Bangladeshi, and by the end of the century the proportion would be over one-third. Islam was becoming the dominant religion in the borough, and the Bangladeshi community was achieving the same kind of salience in local politics as Irish Catholics in bygone years. At the same time, many parts of Tower Hamlets underwent extensive redevelopment to accommodate a completely new kind of migratory influx, of "Yuppy" (young upwardly mobile) individuals and couples.

Approach of a new Millennium

Fr Nash's role had never been formalised (and he didn't want it to be), so St Mary and St Michael's had been technically without a parish priest for a number of years when Fr John Murphy, formerly in charge of Barnet, was appointed in January 1987. He decided to engage a full-time paid parish catechist, and appointed Sr Helen of the Holy Cross congregation: she took charge of all the preparation of children for First Communion and Confirmation, and also worked with their parents. The RCIA (Rite of Christian Initiation for Adults) was introduced, and Fr Murphy got a team of parishioners, including married couples, to help him with this. During his pastorate the interior of the church was refurbished – it hadn't been touched since the restoration over 30 years previously. The old Guild Chapel was now simply the Sacred Heart Chapel (the demise of the Guilds having removed the rationale for its rather unusual dual purpose). Henry Webley, the layman commemorated in the stained glass window in the Martyrs' Chapel, was among the 85 English and Welsh Martyrs beatified in November 1987. In 1992, after a very thorough consultation among the parishioners, the sanctuary was re-ordered: the architect was Martin Goalen, and the contractors were Peak of Harlow.

After the retirements of Sr Josephine as Infant headmistress in 1989, and Sr Elizabeth as Junior headmistress in 1991, St Mary and St Michael's School was taken over by lay headteachers, and subsequently the Infants and Juniors were combined under a single head. In preparation for Sr Berchmans' retirement as head of Bishop Challoner, the trusteeship was transferred from the Sisters of Mercy to the Archdiocese in late 1991. Meanwhile, however, the school was involved in a lawsuit. Two Bangladeshi girls – one Muslim and the other Hindu – had applied for places; when they were turned down, their parents appealed; and when the appeals committee again turned them down, the case went to court. Contrary to some press reports, it was not the case that the school was trying to "ban" non-Christians. But the strict discipline at Bishop Challoner made it very popular with parents, so it was heavily oversubscribed, and when not all applicants could receive places, the admission policy gave preference first to Catholics, and then to Christians of other denominations. In August 1991 a High Court judge ruled that the policy was unlawful, but this judgment was overturned by the Court of Appeal. The case then went to the House of Lords, and Bishop Challoner secured a landmark legal decision in June 1992, when the Law Lords affirmed the right of a Catholic voluntary aided school, if oversubscribed, to prioritise admissions according to religious criteria. The Governors expressed gratitude to Cardinal Hume, Bishop Guazzelli and the Westminster Education Service for their support and help, and stressed that the admissions policy was purely to do with religion, not race: Bishop Guazzelli stated, "We do not operate a colour bar. When we have places to spare and provided the parents accept our Catholic ethos we will admit them."

In the extraordinary circumstances of Tower Hamlets, with such an extremely large Muslim minority population, the issue of faith schools' admission policies was inevitably going to raise concern, because they tended to result in a de facto racial segregation of schools. Almost all the girls at Bishop Challoner at the time were white, though they certainly weren't a privileged elite, as they mostly came from quite rough backgrounds. However the Catholic community does feel very strongly that the right to base admission policies on religious criteria is essential to maintaining a school's faith identity – and also that it is possible to find better, and much more constructive, ways to resolve issues of social cohesion. A month after the Lords' decision, at the end of the summer term Sr Berchmans retired, and Cardinal Hume arranged for her to be awarded the Pro Ecclesia et Pontifice medal. She was succeeded by Catherine Myers. The withdrawal of the Sisters of Mercy from teaching enabled them to devote more time and energy to pastoral work.

Churches Together in Stepney and Wapping (CTSW) was then very lively, and Fr Murphy took part in joint activities with all the local Anglican churches, and the East End Methodist Mission. He worked particularly closely with the Dutch-born United Reformed Church Minister at Stepney Meeting House, Rev Tertius M C (Taco) Bos, on behalf of homeless people. Later, in Fr Van Son's time, the St Mary's and St Michael's School children took part in a series of learning experiences around the local scientific pioneer William Henry Perkin: these included a play acted in St Mary's Cable Street, where Perkin married his first wife.

As the end of the century approached, the parishioners raised money for another stained glass window, in a side wall of the nave. Fr Francis Van Son obtained an estimate, and as the money in hand was only enough for part of the window, the parishioners agreed they would all give a certain amount

The Jubilee window

extra. So a beautifully bright stained glass window, depicting Our Lady and St Michael, was installed to mark the 2000 Millennium Jubilee. As the morning sun streams through from the east this window looks quite stunning and adds to the atmosphere of worship at the morning Masses. Around the same time another splendid new, or rather not so new, acquisition came into the possession of the parish. The original monstrance used in Viginia St Chapel was spotted for sale in a jeweller's shop near Westminster Abbey. Hasty negotiatons took place and the monstrance was purchased, reacquired for St Mary and St Michael's, and takes pride of place on special occasions.

The Virginia St Chapel Monstrance

As the number of priests on the staff fell, the Sunday evening Mass had to be dropped, and then the 12.00 also had to go. By the turn of the century, sadly, the Vaughan Club, like many parish clubs in the London area, was turning more and more into a drinking club, losing its Catholic character, and no longer appropriate for the purposes for which it was established. It was closed, the premises in Johnson Street (which of course included Our Lady's Hall) sold, and the proceeds used to fund the building of a new Our Lady's Parish Community Hall just to the rear of the church. The new parish hall, a functional rather than impressive building, was opened in 2003 and supplies much appreciated facilities for the parish including use by St Mary and St Michael's Primary School and for the St John Bosco youth club.

Troubled Days

We have seen in the history of St Mary and St Michael's parish each century begin with a massive row: the nineteenth century with a row over the liturgy in Virginia Street Chapel and the twentieth century with a row which ended with Fr Magrath of the parish suing the *Catholic Herald.* True to form the twenty-first century continued this tradition with a dispute which ended up in the High Court of Justice.

The background to this dispute was a decision to close the Blessed John Roche Boys' Secondary School in Poplar, which had a diminishing roll and had failed two OFSTED (Office for Standards in Education) inspections – the second failure after the school had been put into special measures. Accordingly there was a need to provide a replacement school within the area. A number of alternative options to accommodate a new school were investigated but no suitable sites were identified which would accommodate:

- A four form entry (11-16 years) Boys' School (600 pupils)
- A five form entry (11-16 years) Girls' School (750 pupils)
- A co-educational 6th form (16-18 years) (350 pupils)

A proposal for the redevelopment of Bishop Challoner Girls' School for this purpose was first articulated by Archbishop Bishop Vincent Nicols, then auxiliary bishop in Westminster. Plans went ahead on this proposal and in November 2002 a 'Statement in Principle' was signed by parties involved – including the Parish Priest of St Mary and St Michael's, Fr Francis Van Son. So far so good. Thereafter, however, something went wrong. By early 2004 the parish newsletter was making it clear that there was opposition to the plans for the school as the development would encroach on parish grounds. Part of the new school building would be sited across Lukin Street on a piece of land formerly used as a playground for St Mary and St Michael's Primary

School. The land had now been disused for some time and was not required for the primary school needs. Parishioners were exhorted in the parish newsletter to make their feelings known, and quite a number wrote to the diocese, via Fr Francis, to complain. Some parishioners, however, it must be said, wrote to express their support for the Bishop Challoner plans. A Parish Advisory Committee was formed and lobbying against the proposal developed.

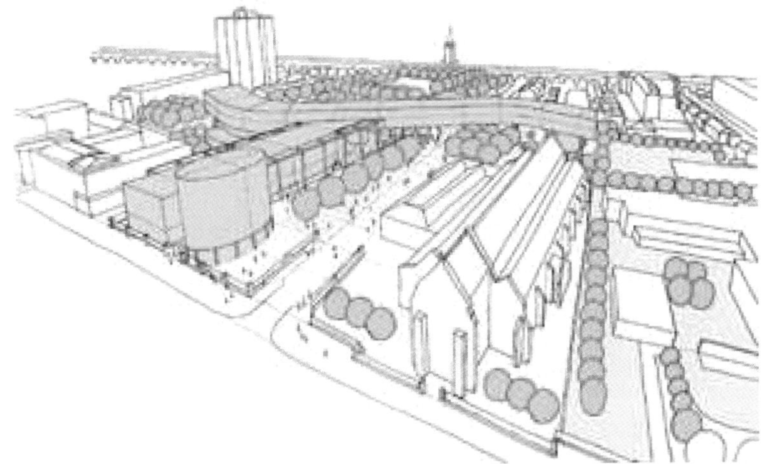

Drawing of the proposed Bishop Challoner Catholic Collegiate School

On 30th March 2004 Cardinal Cormac Murphy O'Connor and diocesan officers met the Parish Advisory Committee to start discussing the difficulties that had arisen. The Cardinal in fact came to the parish on 3rd July, celebrated Mass, and afterwards met parishioners about their concerns. Also present at this meeting was Mr John Gibbs the diocesan financial secretary. Another meeting with parishioners then took place at Bishop Challoner School on 19th July at which were present Bishop George Stack, Mrs Catherine Myers the Bishop Challoner Headteacher and the Dean of Tower Hamlets, Fr Digby Samuels. Despite this, and a further meeting with the Cardinal in September, opposition to the Bishop Challoner plan continued in the parish and it was announced in the parish newsletter that the services of a canon lawyer had been engaged and that an appeal would be made to Rome.

The matter did indeed proceed to Rome when, in August 2004, Fr Van Son appealed to the Vatican's Congregation for Clergy requesting that the Archdiocese be prevented from going ahead with this project. The Holy See has a number of 'dicasteries', or departments that exercise the jurisdiction of the Holy See in various areas. The Congregation for Clergy is the competent dicastery for matters relating to ecclesiastical goods (property) in instances such as this. The Congregation considered the matter and on 17th March 2005 the Secretary of the Congregation, Bishop Csaba Ternyák, wrote to Fr Van Son to communicate that, after reviewing the situation, the Congregation's decision was that, "it would seem that the Archdiocese has just cause to go ahead with the Bishop Challoner project as planned. Therefore this Dicastery must encourage you to cooperate fully with him (the Cardinal) in this project for the good of the parish and the educational needs of the diocese". For reasons not entirely clear Fr Van Son did not accept the competence of Bishop Ternyák to communicate this judgment and, as a result of a further approach to the Congregation by Fr Van Son, the Prefect of the Congregation, His Eminence Dario Cardinal Castrillón, wrote to reiterate the Congregation's decision in a letter dated 30th June 2005.

That would normally be that, but feelings were inflamed in the parish and, when soon after this work began on the project, Fr Francis Van Son was arrested, briefly detained, and released without charge after he attempted to prevent the construction workers gaining access to the part of the site containing the disputed land. This caused quite a stir with, for example, front page articles in the *Catholic Hearld* and reporting of the issue in the national press. The project was then halted for the excavation of the graves on this plot of land – the cemetery that had been in use from 1843 until 1854. The cemetery here seems to have been generally forgotten. Certainly there was no mention of it in the protest letters written in 2004, nor was it mentioned at any of the meetings held in 2004 to discuss parishioners' concerns. At first glance this may seem strange, but it must be borne in mind that, apparently, no burial records have survived and that the land had been tarmaced over and used as a children's football ground. The Department of the Environment had the human remains removed and remains of 820 persons were found - mostly those of children. (At the time of this book going to print it is planned that, after the Department of the Environment realease the remains, a special burial ceremony will be held in St Patrick's Cemetery, Leytonstone where the remains will be reinterred.)

In November 2005 Fr Van Son was transferred from the parish and Fr Martin Hayes was sent in as Administrator. He was assisted by Fr Chris Vipers, the Diocesan Vocations Director, and both priests did sterling work in a situation tense, to say the least.

Meanwhile the St Mary and St Michael Advisory Committee transmogrified itself into an incorporated company, The St Mary and St Michael Advisory

Company Ltd, and in the spring of 2006 took the matter to the High Court. Their claim was that trusts established in 1851 governed the use of part of the land to be used for the proposed development and the diocesan plan was breaching the terms of these trusts in that, *inter alia*,

> 'The 1851 trusts are trusts for charitable purposes (religious and educational) within and for the benefit of what became the Roman Catholic Parish of St Mary and St Michael and for the people and their families who treat the Church of St Mary and St Michael as the centre or focus of their Catholic lives and religious observance. The trusts were intended to operate for the benefit of the Parish, and not simply for any purposes which may be advantageous to the Diocese.'

The case, which turned out to be a lengthy and costly action in the Royal Courts of Justice in the Strand, was heard before Mr Justice Lawrence Collins who delivered judgement on 6th April 2006. His judgement firmly supported the right of the Archdiocese to develop the Bishop Challoner project, salient points being:

> 'In my judgment, there is nothing in the point that the project is outside the trust that any School or Schools standing on any part of the land were "to be always used as and for the purpose of bringing up and educating of poor children according to and in the doctrines and tenets of the Roman Catholic Church."'

And:

> 'The claimant contends in effect that the trusts of the disputed land are for Parish purposes only, "within and for the sole benefit of the Catholic Parish of St Mary and St Michael within the Diocese of Westminster and of its parishioners." The trustee defendants contend that the disputed land can properly be used for any Catholic religious or educational purposes which can in fact be furthered by such use.
>
> I am satisfied that the trustee defendants are right. The habendum of the 1851 Trust Deed expressly states that the conveyance of the land is "upon the trusts and to and for the intents and purposes hereinafter expressed". There are no words in the 1851 Trust Deed capable of bearing a meaning which imposes the suggested limitation on the permitted objects and purposes.

The formulation put forward by the claimant is impossible to reconcile with the position in 1851. There was no parish in 1851 when the Trust Deed was executed (nor in 1843 when the land was bought, nor in 1856 when the church was completed).'

Catherine Myers Headteacher Bishop Challoner
(Photo Graham Turner: *The Guardian*)

After the High Court judgement work immediately went ahead on the Bishop Challoner project. It was projected for the construction to take place for three years with the students moving into new classrooms as they became available. The construction company Haymills, who had had to stand by during the disinterring of the remains from the cemetery and while the court case unfolded, was the principal contractor on the project.

The scheme was given a terrific shot in the arm when in the 2006 GCSE results – the first of the intake after the closing of Blessed John Roche – the boys' school achieved 86% five A*-C. These were in effect the same boys who had been achieving 13% A*-C in the failing school! Even better was achieved in the 2007 GCSEs when the boys scored 93% A*-C.

In June 2007 Bishop Challoner Catholic Collegiate School gained further kudos when it received an award from the Lithuanian government in recognition of its work with Lithuanians living in East London. A significant percentage of the new intake of the school has been from the recent Eastern Eupopean immigration to the East End.

New Horizons

In April 2006 Cardinal Cormac Murphy-O'Connor appointed Fr Jim Mulligan in charge of St Mary and St Michael's. Fr Mulligan, a late vocation to the priesthood, had been ordained in St Patrick's, Wapping in July 2005. The parish was now heavily in debt, and a number of the parishioners had been left embittered by the High Court decision. His immediate concern therefore was reconciliation, and he quickly organised two Sunday sessions of prayer and reconciliation in the church, led by the Franciscan Friars of the Renewal. Both were well-attended and successful, and in October 2006 they were followed up by a four-day session of prayer, healing and reconciliation led by a priest who has for many years specialised in the area of reconciliation, Fr Jimmy Collins from Liverpool. A saintly-looking octogenarian, he got a very positive reception, and many felt that they benefited enormously from his personalised approach to healing prayer.

Fr Jimmy also delighted many with his tales of his life and priesthood in Liverpool. One story he told was of how, when he was curate in St Joseph the Worker Parish in Kirby in the Sixties, the parish commissioned the mercurial Liverpool sculptor, Arthur Dooley, to sculpt a statue of St Joseph and the Child Jesus. Fr Jimmy asked Arthur Dooley how much his fee would be, and Dooley asked for £5,000. "We just can't afford that sort of money," replied Fr Jimmy. "Okay," said Arthur Dooley in the next breath, "Make it £500." Fr Jimmy also told of how, in the same parish, around 1960, the youngsters in his youth club kept asking him to hire this great new group for their Sunday evening dances. He hired the group, and they played many Sunday evenings for a fee of around £6.00 a night. The group was The Beatles. So Fr Jimmy had got to know John Lennon, Paul McCartney and George Harrison (Ringo Starr had not yet joined the group) before their days of fame. In fact, Lennon and McCartney used to play some of their latest compositions to Fr Jimmy for his opinion.

8th December 2006 would mark 150 years since the opening of St Mary and St Michael's church but, regrettably, there of course had been too much else going on to prepare a proper celebration. So it was decided, rather than organising a one-off event, to have a special Mass on that day with Bishop Bernard Longley to launch a whole anniversary year. As it happened, the Sisters of Mercy were celebrating the 175th anniversary of the founding of their congregation a few weeks later. There was Mass at Westminster

Cathedral, for Sisters from all over the UK, and Sr Elizabeth from Commercial Road carried a banner depicting "Education"; afterwards the Hardinge Street community and their guests all went for a celebration meal at Wetherspoons in Tower Hill.

Sisters of Mercy 175th Anniversay Year celebrated at Westminster Cathedral

The parish then decided to hold *another* celebration for the Sisters of Mercy anniversary, on Saturday 16th December, specially for their own convent and the parish. The two schools in the parish – St Mary and St Michael's Junior School, and Bishop Challoner – offered to involve both children and staff, and the kitchen staff at Bishop Challoner volunteered to give up their Saturday morning to decorate the Parish Centre, and prepare the buffet. Other staff, clergy and parishioners prepared the church and the liturgy. There was an excellent turnout for the Mass, at which music was provided by the combined choirs of both schools, and the Bishop Challoner orchestra. The buffet afterwards was superb, and there was also a magnificent cake. On 16th March 2007 St Mary and St Michael's Primary School took a special part in the anniversary celebrations, attending a Mass celebrated in the church by Bishop Bernard Longley, commemorating the history of the school and in thanksgiving for its achievements.

Soon after arriving in parish Fr Jim Mulligan told the congregations that one of his spiritual heroes was Saint Francis of Assisi, and that St Francis, despite his love and embrace of poverty, always made certain that the church, the House of God, was always as well-kept and as aesthetically pleasing as resources would allow. So church and presbytery were given a proper spring clean, the restored crucifix from the bombed Calvary was re-hung, and a prayer room established. The confessionals, one of which had accumulated over thirty years of junk, were cleared out, repainted and restored to use. (Fr Jim told his congregations that confessionals should be used to get rid of junk, not store it!) The brass and wrought iron altar rail gates, which had been removed in the 1970s, were found amid the junk stored in one confessional, and were restored and re-hung. Languishing in the presbytery courtyard was the crumbling-away statue of the Madonna and Child that had for so many years graced the wall of Our Lady's Hall in Johnson St. A Lithuanian visitor to the parish, Vitoldas Preibyes, offered to restore it free of charge. In August 2007 the restored Madonna and Child took its place on a newly built plinth outside Our Lady's Parish Community Hall.

Fr Jim also raised money from outside sources to erect a candle shrine to St Francis, provide new votive candle-stands, a chrome holy water dispenser, a sanctuary holy water vessel, a new high altar crucifix, and a set of altar cloths and lectern banners. In due course the sacristy was repainted, and hung with new and restored paintings. A new painting of the Sacred Heart was provided for the Sacred Heart Chapel and, near the chapel entrance, a beautifully framed large reproduction of Rembrandt's painting *The Return of the Prodigal Son* was hung. A careful restoration was carried out of eighteen of the remaining old pews (individually sponsored in the name of deceased parishioners). The side door to the church, and the confessional doors were also restored to their original state – something much appreciated and commented on by parishioners and visitors.

The new oak frame noticeboard

Another welcome improvement was the erection of a glass-fronted oak frame notice board at the church entrance. Haymills, the construction firm engaged on the Bishop Challoner project, and in particular the construction project manager, Phil Welsman, were exceptionally generous: they donated several thousand pounds, plus free service of tradesmen, to the restoration projects. Bishop Challoner Head, Catherine Myers, was also very helpful and supportive towards the restoration work.

The parish debt that Fr Mulligan inherited was a constant headache for him as one way and another it continued to grow. A considerable sum had still to be paid for the completion of the new Our Lady's Parish Community Hall plus, regrettably, almost £10,000 spent on replacement of the heating system in the hall. Several thousand was spent on repairs to the church roof and, surprisingly considering how recent the construction had been, on repairs to the roof of the new hall. But most of all the debt was building because of the offertory collections and other income not meeting day to day running costs – a situation which had existed for a number of years. It does seem money problems have always been synomyous with St Mary and St Michael's! Fr Jim carried out protracted negotiatons with the Archdiocese over the debt and in June 2007 he was informed by the Cardinal that the existing debt would be cleared through a very generous grant from the Trinity Fund. Fr Jim at this point initiated plans for a renewed planned giving campaign in the parish. This campaign took place in October 2007. The perilous state of the finances was laid transparently before parishioners. One parishioner, Michael Smith, (formerly a funeral director with the local untertakers who have served generations in the parish, A&C Tadman) made an impassioned plea that this historic parish and its church, the 'Cathedral of the East End', would not go under. Thankfully the offertory collection improved substantially – but that's a long way from saying that money troubles and St Mary and St Michael's are a thing of the past.

Congregation of Jacob Synagogue Commercial Road

Life never stands still for long in the East End and the inexorable changes are all too evident around the area of the parish. Along Commercial Road the East End Methodist Mission has closed down, and so have most of the synagogues – but not the Congregation of Jacob, which has been nicely refurbished. St Dunstan's and St Mary's Cable Street are still with us. Travelling in to Shadwell on the Docklands Light Railway, you can't miss the impressive sight of St George's in the East, with its distinctive lantern. The building was in fact gutted by incendiary bombs in May 1941, and part of it has been converted into flats, but a small modern church still functions inside the shell. Several old buildings have been adapted to serve as mosques – there is one in Damien Street, and another tucked under a railway arch. The George Tavern, alongside its boast of having been there, refreshing travellers, since 1654, offers you free internet access with your beer or cappuccino, and St George's Town Hall has acquired a new role as a centre for training courses and community projects. Although so much has changed, a great deal of the past is still around. Interest in local history has made a dramatic comeback in recent years, boosted particularly by the fascination of so many ordinary people around the country in researching their own family trees. At a Consultation Workshop organised in June 2007 to consider the future of the Local History and Archives in Tower Hamlets, very strong local support emerged for better resourcing, so that the present good-quality, professional services can be maintained, the facilities substantially improved, and outreach initiatives developed to make our unique heritage more accessible by the wider community. The need to address the issue of under-recorded areas, such as black and ethnic minority groups, and the Catholic community, was particularly noted.

The congregation of St Mary and St Michael's today includes people of a wide range of ethnic origins and backgrounds (as it probably always did), but the overwhelming majority of the parishioners are still Londoners of Irish extraction. There are now only three Sunday Masses: one on Saturday evening, and two on Sunday morning, but Mass attendance remains the highest of any of the parishes in Tower Hamlets Deanery except for St Anne's, Underwood Road, which currently serves the Brazilian community coming from all over London. The Junior St John Bosco Club, and the Irish Dancing, continue to thrive. Another group of people who certainly deserve to be "mentioned in despatches" are the church cleaners, some of whom have provided this loving service continually for over 50 years. They include Peggy Collins, Rosie Armstrong, Iris Mockford, Winnie Cupit, Vanda Reilly, Annie Long, Maria Holland and Tess Doran. Toward the close of 2007 parishioners were invited to hand in memorabilia so that an exhibition, organised by Patricia McCarthy and John Keefe, could be put together on past times, in tandem with the the publication of *A HISTORY OF ST MARY and ST MICHAEL'S PARISH.* Cardinal Murphy-O'Connor agreed to preside at the closing Mass of the anniversary year on 9th December with all the contactable priests and Sisters of Mercy religious who had served the parish invited. Fr Jim, at the time of publication of this book, is working on raising the money to have the church completely repainted, and also working on the possibility of the purchase of a reproduction of Michelangelo's *Pieta* – as would befit the 'Cathedral of the East End'.

At the start of the second 150 years of St Mary and St Michael's parish the future looks promising.

Priests in charge of St Mary and St Michael's Parish

In pre-Reformation times the area of Tower Hamlets was served by St Dunstan's, Stepney. Its last Roman Catholic rector, Fr Tristam Swadell, was 'deprived' in 1562. Virginia St Chapel resumed Catholic pastoral work in the area in 1758 and was replaced by St Mary and St Michael's Church in 1856.

Virginia St Chapel

Fr James Webb 1758-1771
Fr Michael Coen 1771-1810
Fr James Delaney 1810-1814
Fr Thomas Dobson 1814-1835
Fr Richard Horrabin 1815-1839
Fr James Foley 1839-1841
Fr Richard Horrabin 1841-1853

St Mary and St Michael's, Commercial Road

Fr William Kelly 1853-1874

Fr Joseph Cahill 1875

Fr Patrick O'Callaghan 1876-1896

Fr George Canon Akers 1896-1899

Fr Peter Amigo 1899-1901

Fr Thomas Dunphy 1901-1902

Fr Andrew Dooley 1902-1904

Fr Timothy Canon Ring 1904-1941

Fr Thomas Canon Fitzgerald 1941-1964

Mgr Derek Worlock 1964-1965

Bishop Patrick Casey 1966

Fr Charles Canon Carr 1966-1980

Fr Brian Nash 1980-1987

Fr John Murphy 1987-1993

Fr Patrick Egan **1993-1994**

Fr Francis Van Son **1995-2005**

Fr Martin Hayes **2005-2006**

Fr James Mulligan **2006-**

Superiors of the Convent of Mercy, Commercial Road and Hardinge Street

Angela Joseph Gilsenan	1859-1868
Patrick Gray	1868-1871
Evangelist Daly	1871-1874
Joseph Macken	1874-1880
Scholastica McDonald	1880-1883
Alphonsus Gilson	1883-1892
Bernard Alwell	1892-1895
Alphonsus Gilson	1895-1907

The Convent transferred to 88 Hardinge Sreet in 1906

Aloysius Sheridan	1907-1910
Alphonsus Gilson	1910-1919
Bridget Leahy	1919-1930
Mary Evangelist Seaborne	1930-1939
Gerard O'Connell	1939-1942
Clare Roberts	1942-1945
Philomena Conway	1945-1951
Perpetua Anglim	1951-1957
Bernardine McMahon	1957-1963
Perpetua Anglim	1963-1969
Bernardine McMahon	1969-1975
Cyril O'Sullivan	1975-1981
Sylvester Gill	1981-1984
Mary O'Malley	1984-1990
Elizabeth O'Connor	1990-1993
Josephine Browne	1993-1999
Anna Moloney	2000-2006
Majella Sheridan	2006-

Priests in charge of St Patrick Parish, Wapping

The area covered by St Patrick's parish was served from 1758 by Virginia St Chapel and then, from 1856, by St Mary and St Michael's Church, Commercial Road until St Patrick's Church in Wapping was opened in 1871.

1871	-		Fr David Hickey
1871	-	1877	Fr Angelo Lucas
1877	-	1882	Fr Francis Beckley
1882	-	1908	Fr William Donelan
1908	-	1911	Fr Charles Sims
1911	-	1921	Fr Joseph Reardon
1921	-	1936	Fr Andrew Reardon
1936	-	1956	Fr Samuel Steer
1956	-	1964	Fr Charles Lowe
1964	-	1968	Fr Desmond O'Neill
1968	-	1974	Fr John Kearsey
1974	-	1978	Fr John Edwards SJ
1978	-	1983	Fr Manus Keane SJ
1983	-	1999	Fr Austin Hart
1999	-		Fr Digby Canon Samuels

APPENDICES

Currency

¼d	farthing	
½d	halfpenny	(pronounced ha'penny)
1d	penny	
6d	sixpence	(slang term: tanner)
1s	shilling	(slang term: bob)
2s 6d	half-a-crown	
£1	pound	(sovereign)
£1 1s	guinea	

The abbreviation "d" for the old penny stood for the Latin "denarius": there were 12 pennies to the shilling, and 20 shillings to the pound. Pennies, and fractions of pennies, were copper coins. Sixpences, shillings and half-a-crowns were silver coins. The pound was a gold coin (sovereign) in the nineteenth century (when a presentations to a priest literally involved handing over a "purse of gold", often in a specially hand-sewn purse) but it later became a paper note. The guinea was not really a currency unit, but a prestigious way of expressing an amount of money (for a professional fee, purchase price of a luxury item, or donation) – which would then be paid over in pound notes and shilling coins.

Transcripts of letters in the Westminster Archdiocesan Archives (WAA)

WAA: A53 III L 31 (Douglass): To Bp Douglass from the priests at Virginia Street Chapel, 17th Feb 1809

Your Lordship's letter addressed to the Rev Mr Coen equally regarding us all, we in common beg leave to request Your Lordship's attention to the following reflections, which we have made on the subject of it.

We beg leave to represent to Your Lordship in the first place that it was with no small degree of surprise and with no little regret that we learnt for the first time from Your Lordship's letter, that a memorial, of which we had not received the slightest intimation had been presented to Your Lordship praying for the adoption of measures, by which we are personally most seriously affected. We feel indignant at the insinuation which the conduct of the petitioners in the present instance seems to hold forth – that we are less zealous, than themselves, for the Glory of God, less solicitous for their spiritual good, and less willing to promote both those objects by all the means, which our abilities afford – and on these heads we appeal humbly, but with confidence to Your Lordship's knowledge of our conduct since we have been employed in the sacred ministry.

We beg leave further to remark that, whatever degree of respectability may be supposed to attach to the individuals, by whom the said memorial is signed, we presume that, from the situation which we hold, we are better acquainted than they can be, with the spiritual necessities of the flock committed to our charge, and are more competent to judge the means most conducive to their spiritual advantage: at the same time we are confident that Your Lordship will give us credit when we assert that; knowing as we do the practice adopted in other chapels in London at this time, we should have been the first to adopt it in our own had we judged it necessary, or greatly beneficial to our flock, compatible with our other more weighty obligations.

We are willing to believe that signing the memorial in question some of the subscribers were activated by motives of religion and of piety, though, we presume, of a piety not according to knowledge, as an enlightened piety would feel the solemn performance of the Divine Worship, and the public preaching of the word of God are instituted for the general edification and instruction of congregations, not for the gratification of some few individuals. However we are compelled to say, that we cannot believe this much of all the petitioners. For we know them well: we are acquainted with their characters and dispositions, and we deem it expedient to make Your Lordship acquainted with them, as the present may not be the only occasion, on which they may be induced to address Your Lordship.

Several among them, whatever they may be in the eyes of the world, are far from being respectable in the eyes of the Church, to which in spite of frequent private admonitions, and of the public sermons, they remain habitual rebels, and therefore to be classed with heathens and publicans. Others of them are mere giddy apprentice boys, or lads still under their parents tuition. Others, and these are they, perhaps, whose names seem to bear the greatest weight, we are firmly persuaded, signed the petition to Your Lordship not because they seriously desire what the memorial prays for, but, as they would sign any other indifferent address, to comply with the request of the one or two promoters and instigators of the present business. What their motives are we are well aware: certainly they are not the Glory of God and their own sanctification.

We observe that the memorialists pray for Complin with Benediction and a discourse as is done in all the other chapels in town where the Divine Office is sung. We need to inform Your Lordship that what may be highly proper and expedient in one chapel, may on account of circumstances be not so in another. It is, we presume, from a consideration of such circumstances that in the chapel in St George's Fields, where the Divine Office is sung, and which is frequented by a congregation, if not more numerous certainly more respectable on every account than the one committed to our charge, they have no Complin, nor Benediction, nor discourse – on any evening in Lent. We further remark that those chapels, where Complin is sung etc, the Divine Office is sung on all festivals of obligation. Whereas in our Chapel the office is sung on the Sundays only and the most antient and most venerable festivals of the church are passed over without such solemnity, not through want of zeal on our part for the most solemn celebration of them, not for the sake of our personal convenience, but partly and indeed principally through the refusal of most of those, who have subscribed the petition, to afford us their assistance.

We also beg leave to state to Your Lordship that experience proves that these devotions of Lent are but little attended in this Metropolis: and we have reason to believe that in another Chapel where the practice in question was lately introduced, and where from situation and other circumstances it was expected that the greatest success would result, they are already convinced of its inutility, regret its introduction, and would wish to discontinue it, if it were the same thing to lay aside a custom already adopted, as to prevent its adoption.

Such being the case even in congregations, where from local situation and circumstances of the faithful, it might be naturally expected that these devotions would be respectably and numerously attended to, we are most firmly persuaded from the situation of our chapel at the extremity of the Metropolis, and from the circumstances of our people, who with the exception of [two? – *corner of page missing*] or three consist entirely of labouring people, or of people daily occupied [in?] business, that it would be deceiving ourselves to expect their attendance on working days,. Of this we are most fully convinced through the consideration, that notwithstanding our repeated public and private admonitions, reproofs and exhortations, we cannot induce them (not even those who signed the memorial) to assist at the instructions given in the afternoon on Sundays.- so that we have the mortification to remark that, with the exception of the children of the two charity schools and some other children, a few dozens only of persons attend, even on days when nothing but the want of good will can prevent their attendance. We think it proper also to state to Your Lordship, that the vicinity of our chapel is almost daily infested in the evenings by disorderly persons of both sexes, from which circumstances the most disagreeable as well as most serious consequences must be apprehended.

We must likewise humbly beg leave to request Your Lordship will please to consider that the Congregation committed to our charge is the most numerous and most widely extended of all the congregations in this Metropolis: and consequently that our duties are heavy and multiplied, particularly with regard to the sick, and at the present season of the year: that therefore to prepare additional sermons during the Lent wo'd be a burden severely felt by us, were we even possessed of the gifts of eloquence, and facility of composition, which are bestowed but on few, and which we are far from arrogating to our selves:- but under our present circumstances it would be a task, which we feel ourselves inadequate to perform.

From these considerations, which we have thought it our duty humbly to lay before Your Lordship, we beg leave to state to Your Lordship that it is our decided opinion that to grant the prayer of the beforementioned petition would be unnecessary and unbeneficial, and therefore inexpedient.

We have the honor to be with the sincerest respect Your Lordship's most obedient and most [?] servts

M Coen, James Delaney, Jn Serjeant

A SELECTION OF THE FATHER WILLAM KELLY LETTERS

WAA: W2/3/5/3: To Bp Wiseman from Fr William Kelly, 45 Wellclose Square, 18th January 1848

My Lord,

Having called on your Lordship before Christmas at the request and in the company of the Revd Mr Moore to solicit your Lordship to preach for his Schools, it has occurred to me since that I did so unthinkingly as I might be the cause at least partly of making your Lordship think there was no necessity of looking into the matter. I have been thinking over this matter for a few weeks as to the duty of writing to your Lordship or the more comfortable prudence of remaining silent. Your Lordships coming to preach on next Sunday has decided my hesitation. I am certain I shall be delighted in hearing your Lordship preach, but unfortunately for my own quiet and notwithstanding the displeasure of my highly esteemed friend Mr Moore, I feel it my duty to tell your Lordship how his new buildings stand. He has three day Schools of his own getting up, for which he really deserves very great credit and has I believe lately opened a fourth one. These will require any monies, your Lordship's sermon may produce. In the new Schools of which I am about to speak, he has I believe expended a great deal of anxiety and labour and no one can doubt the goodness of his intentions but unfortunately the Law of the land takes no account of these, should one come into collision with it. In [---?], that I can only speak of the Revd Mr Moore as of an excellently good and zealous Priest, I know his Esteem for your Lordship and I feel confident it is reciprocal. It is to save his health, perhaps his life that I write to your Lordship; for unless he give up the present undertaking or that your Lordship is prepared to come forward with a large sum of money to assist him, I feel confident he will get into sad troubles and most likely have to pass through the Bankruptcy Court. I have tried on several occasions, in the manner that appeared to me least hurtful to his feelings, to show him the difficulty in which he is placed, but I don't think I have succeeded. I shall here detail the facts for your Lordship as far as I have been able to ascertain them. I have not seen any documents.

A few years ago he took from the Gas Company a small plot of ground on a Lease of 64 years annual Rent £30. From the date of leasing to the Revd Mr Moore the Gas Company held of the Mercers Company the aforesaid ground for sixty four years only.

The condition of the lease was that the Buildings should be Roofed in on the first of last September or November. This condition has not been complied with. A contract was entered into with a Builder to erect the aforesaid buildings a portion of the walls of which now stand on the ground for a sum somewhere above £2,000 not including Architects fees nor Extra depth of foundations. This Extra alone amounts to nearly £300. The payment was to be spread over four years. One condition of the contract was that the Building was to be covered in on last September or November as specified in the Lease, but it appears the Builder incurs neither forfeiture nor fine by not complying with this condition which he has not done up to the present day.

Thus stands the matter at present Mr Moore's Lease is no good, he still continues in possession and paying the Rent, But it does not appear the Builder has forfeited his contract. Should he become Bankrupt of course the Creditors will step into his shoes. The Architect has been paid forty or fifty pounds the Builder £300 or £200.

Now this is not the only difficulty, at all times – and under the best of circumstances it is difficult to get money from the people for these charitable purposes but in this case the difficulty will be exceedingly great. Every man having a little bit of a shop – every tradesman or clerk in this Commercial Country understands the Exact value of money in Building. For instance a tradesman having saved a little money and building on a lease of 99 years always calculates in order to be repaid for the cost of his Capital and Interest thereon at least 7 per cent applying this to the present Building which I feel confident will never be finished under £3,000 if for this sum as the Lease is only for 64 years and now not so much then were the Lease valid a Builder would expect at least 9 per cent ie 270? per annum adding £30 ground Rent. These Schools if ever finished will be at an expense of about £300 yearly. Your Lordship will be surprised to find on experience how few Priests of this district understand these matters but a very large number of people in every parish understand them well; hence the great difficulty. As I have already observed under the best of circumstances it is difficult to get money for these purposes, but under circumstances like the present it becomes almost an impossibility. First of all a persons judgment and prudence is called in question in the place where he exercises his ministry; those best able to give do it grudgingly and sparingly and in many cases not at all. An undercurrent springs up and spreads to other localities frustrating one's exertions.

Besides the above difficulties Mr Moore has in this district another Piece of leasehold ground on the same terms, I do not know the Rental. Should he be taken Ill he has no means of meeting these annual Rentals and I feel confident no other Priest would undertake them. Neither will he with the best of health except aided largely by your Lordship be ever able to finish them and supposing them finished, there are no permanent funds to pay the Rentals much less teachers. Other Priests coming after him will not easily take the responsibility of these Rentals.

As to his new society I am confident from my local knowledge it will after a short time damage rather than assist his collections. I have endeavoured to hint this to him but he has given me no opportunity of clearly expressing my opinion.

I have certainly advised him to give up the new buildings altogether if he could and request your Lordships permission to build schools on the new cemetery ground, two capital Schools could be built there for £800 or £1000. This being a reasonable amount and no Rent, the congregation after a time would more easily and much more generally subscribe to it.

In conclusion I beg to assure your Lordship that I have written the above with no motive except that of the kindest feeling towards the Revd Mr Moor and the good of religion. If Mr Moore saw the necessity of explaining this matter to your Lordship I feel sure he would do so, but in this money matter of pounds shillings and pence he appears to me hoping against every principle by which men judge of these things.

Were your Lordship to Sanction from the pulpit these Buildings situated as they are, I feel confident a very large body of the people would conclude he deceived your Lordship. It is neither my wish nor inclination to interfere further in this matter. The eight first years of my ministry were spent I may say amid bricks and mortar. It was on a small scale to be sure but still not the less laborious. During that time I did not read, I believe, even one book for my own amusement recreation or improvement. I had scarcely time to read those works that enabled me to preach and catechise and notwithstanding a most laborious college life I find myself now deficient of three fourths of the Knowledge I acquired with so much labour. This statement I make to show your Lordship that I have neither wish not inclination to supplant my Revd friend Mr Moore, the more so as I find it absolutely necessary at least for a few years on account of my health and nervous system to abstain from these material works of the ministry.

Your Lordships ob serv
William Kelly

WAA: W2/3/5/11: To Cardinal Wiseman from Fr William Kelly, 22 Colet Place, Commercial Road East, 6th July 1854

My Lord Cardinal,

At a meeting held at the Poor School Committee yesterday various resolutions were discussed which were afterwards to be submitted to your Eminence and the other Bishops for approval or rejection. One of these resolutions had reference, I believe to a more accurate knowledge of the real numbers of Catholics and Catholic children we educate. I write this note to say that I purpose, in going my rounds collecting for the New Chapel, to take a Census of the entire District.

The guesses as to the number of Catholics in this one district are various and conflicting. My impression is, the number is between eighteen and twenty thousand. Others say 25 and others say thirty thousand. The general outline of the Census I will adhere to, will be; names of Father and Mother, Place of abode, number of Children, Age, how many Confirmed, how many have made their first Communion, how many going to School, and what School and how many made their Paschal Communion.

Should your Eminence have any suggestion to make on this subject I shall be happy to attend to it. I have introduced Class Rolls and Register books into the Schools and hope in Seven or Eight months time, to be able to submit to your Eminence more accurate data, than I can now do. I have found it a matter of very great difficulty indeed to make the Teachers attend to this matter. There is now a fortnights vacation and I am assured, they will attend to it regularly at the opening of the schools.

The repugnance of the Christian Brothers almost amounted to a refusal; as matters now stand I believe they have not yet moved in the matter. In preparing the children for the late Confirmation and first Communion I had also some difficulty in overcoming the repugnance of the Teachers and my fellow Priests, who thought it was too much work for one year. Again the Christian Brothers showed more repugnance than the other Teachers. Two of the Priests when they saw me resolved to carry out the work, joined me most cordially. One remained sulky to the end, did not I believe catechise a single child and only admitted twenty nine to the Confirmations and a still less number to the first Communion.

I shall not now mention any names, as I besought him on Sunday to cooperate with me more cordially in future otherwise I would lay the matter before your Eminence.

I have one thing more to say in reference to our poor or Working Classes. I had no opportunity of stating it yesterday. I have frequently mentioned it in private conversation. It appears to me a fact of great importance yet always overlooked in all our Catholic discussions. It is usual to refer to the Methodists or some other Sect and state that very large sums of money are annually collected amongst them. In the next place it is assumed that the Catholic body is as numerous and wealthy as the Methodists for instance, and consequently it has become a great puzzle why the Catholics are so much behind hand in this matter.

In the first place I have to observe, that there are some six millions of money raised annually in this Country for the support of the Poor. This is a bank upon which the Working Classes fall back in cases of distress arising from sackings and other causes. But owing to the intense bigotry in this Country, the Catholic Working Classes do not get their fair share out of this Bank; when they apply for any portion of this money contributed by Catholics as well as Protestants. They are generally told in the most insulting way to go to their Priests. They seldom meet with sympathy from any member of he various boards of Guardians; the Relieving Officer is frequently a ribald bully and the Parish Doctor, when they can get one, ridicules the faith of the Catholic mother during the throes of childbirth. The threat of being sent back to Ireland, even where they have legal rights to relief but no friend to vindicate it for them, sends the poor applicant back broken hearted among his or her friends. The consequence of all this is that the Catholic Working Classes, have a heavy burden thrown upon them in relieving their poorer brethren, whilst this duty is taken off the shoulders of the Protestant Working Classes, by falling back in cases of distress, upon the rates levied on Catholics and Protestants alike.

In the second place the Methodists and other sects, collect and <u>actually get money</u> from a vast number of every protestant sect in the land. Whereas for Catholic purposes, Catholics alone subscribe.

Hence I conclude that unless the object be local and of absorbing interest to the Poor, any calculations made on the supposition of getting large sums from the Working Classes will be falsified by the event.

Probably your Eminence understands all this a great deal better than I. But as it is the result of fifteen years experience I thought it better to mention it.

Your Eminences most Obedient Servant

William Kelly

WAA: W2/3/5/13: To Cardinal Wiseman from Fr William Kelly, 22 Colet Place, Commercial Road East, 9th July 1855

My Lord Cardinal,

Two weeks ago the Christian Brothers without previously communicating with me gave vacation to their School, which threw the other Schools of the District into great confusion. Though I could hardly spare the time, I felt compelled to communicate with their Superior (a matter I had long in contemplation) and bring under his notice the absolute necessity of a change in that School. I described to him in I believe a kindly and friendly spirit I may say confiding (as I kept no copy of the letter) that whilst making the Census I became aware of the distressing fact that of the children educated by the Brothers, many of them gave up their religion altogether, and that the great body of them never went to Mass and were the greatest blackguards in the Parish. I wished him therefore to infuse a new spirit into this school by sending me two Brothers from Ireland in place of those now here. I enclose the Superiors answer. As I have had much trouble with the Brothers since I came here, I mean the ones that hold command, I wrote the Superior a second letter as follows.

June 29th 1855

My Dear Sir,

Your letter of the 27th instant reached me yesterday. Writing hastily I fear I have expressed in my former letter, one or two points at variance with my conviction. Against two of the Brothers I can have no reasonable complaint, as I believe they are bound to obey the orders of the third – Brother Corbett. Secondly in asking for their removal, it might seem as if I wished it done instantly and without previous notice. I did not attribute the whole of the blame to the Brothers, I believe Father Horrabin will have much to answer for, in not looking more after this School, not to make the Brothers violate their Rules but to see that they acted up to the spirit of them, and report when necessary to their Superior as I am doing. I do not allow any of the other clergy to interfere in the affairs of this School but I shall not lose sight of it or the children educated therein. You assign many causes for the failure of this school in producing its proper fruit. These causes are more or less everywhere and they are inadequate in the present case. For more than twenty years, the Brothers have had unlimited, undisturbed possession and unchecked control of this School, yet the failure as described in my former note has been complete. It is clear this state of things cannot be allowed to continue. I want you therefore to appoint as Superior here a man who whilst he remains a faithful Christian Brother, will be capable of understanding, that the School he teaches, is not one sixth part of all the children receiving education in this parish, and that whiles he observes the spirit of his own Rules he is to accommodate himself as much as possible to the views of the Parish Priest who is responsible Coram Deo for all the children. Brother Corbett is I believe a very good man but seems incapable of accommodating himself to the peculiar circumstances of this mission. Brother Andrew seems much superior in common sense. It is therefore absolutely necessary either to subordinate Brother Corbett to Brother Andrew or send Brother Corbett elsewhere.

Yours etc

Mr Michael Paul Riordan (PS An early answer will much oblige)

To this note I have received no answer and have written him the following letter

22 Colet Place etc etc
July 9 1855
Dear Sir

To my note of June 29th 1855 I have not though I requested an early reply, received yet an answer.

This however is now of no consequence, the matter if finally settled. For nearly two years the Boys School conducted by the Brothers, has been to me a matter of deepest concern. I will not now speak of minor points which by dint of perseverance, I overcame, nor go at length into the melancholy results of this school, laid open to my view whilst making the census. It now turns out I had hoped against hope, I had a strong impression that by endeavouring to establish a friendly intercourse with the Brothers and writing to you their Superior in the same bona fide spirit, I should be able to harmonise this School with the other Schools of the Parish. With this view I wrote to you last year requesting you to fix the Brothers vacation at a fortnight in summer instead of a month. To this you consented. This rule was observed last summer. As I cannot at the present moment lay my hand upon the note I wrote you, I shall here freshly detail the evils to this parish, arising from the long vacations the Brothers took for themselves. In the first place when the Brothers who are not teaching one sixth of the children receiving education in this parish gave their long vacation, they threw about two hundred children out of school. These children drew away large bodies of children from the other Schools in actual operation and thus resistance to parental authority and demobilisation of the children, ensued and loud and bitter complaints from the parents, many of whom sent their children to Protestant schools in the interim and then kept them there. In the Second place, one of the main sources of support for the Schools – the pence of the children, was dried up during all this confusion. This summer as you have been informed in my first note of June last, the Brothers without even the Courtesy of telling me of their intention, gave vacation to the boys of their school and immediately followed the two consequences enumerated above – the children were drawn away from the other Schools and the School funds suspended from the loss of the weekly pence. On the following Thursday I gave vacation to the other Schools, but as the Brothers fortnights vacation, as fixed last year, ended last Saturday, I determined to avoid all confusion and harmonise the other Schools with theirs and to the credit of the other Teachers be it told they grumbled not though they had lost ten days of rest. The following announcement was read aloud last Sunday at each Mass yesterday. "Parents are particularly requested to take notice that the vacation ended last Saturday and that all the Schools of the Parish will reopen tomorrow (Monday) at ¼ to 9 oclock". Going my rounds this morning I found the Brothers School locked and several boys waiting in the passage. Those amongst them who were at Mass yesterday, told me that after the 9 oclock Mass Brother Corbett told them not to go to School today nor during the week. Well! Here is a man calling himself a Christian Brother and infusing into the minds of the children rebellion against the authority of the Church. This spirit unlocks the secret of the failure of this School. Now as I have failed and give up all hopes of harmonising this one School with the others and am firmly persuaded the action of the Brothers here is productive of evil instead of good, I hereby give you notice that I shall make them no payments after next quarter day and at that date I shall give possession of the School where they teach to another Master and shall give notice to quit to the Landlord of the House, where they now reside.

Your humble and u servant
William Kelly
Mr Michael Paul Riordan

I am sorry My Lord Cardinal to have troubled you with this long affair but as it is likely the Christian Brother's Superior will write to you, it seemed to me advisable to put Your Eminence in possession of the facts of the case as soon as possible.

Your Emin most Ob Serv
William Kelly

WAA: W2/3/5/14: Fr William Kelly's 1855 Census Report

A Summary of the Results of the Census of the Virginia Street District addressed to His Eminence, the Cardinal Archbishop of Westminster, by his devoted Servant in Christ, William Kelly, the 24 of August 1855, with explanatory observations.

This Census was commenced on the 8th of July 1854 and continued to the 22nd of December 1854, with the exception of three weeks spent in preparing children for their first Communion & hearing the Confessions at the indulgences, of the Communicant children of the Schools. Three weeks in 1855 brought the Census to a close. The time daily employed in making the Census ranged from 4½ to 9 hours, but as I did not go out every Saturday, being obliged to see to the preparation of the Collectors Books for the Sunday it may be stated, free from exaggeration, that for six days out of seven every week, five hours daily during a period of five months and fourteen days, were spent in this work of Census making, going personally from house to house & penetrating from cellar to garret. Number of persons, children included, contained in the Census Books, 15,566, discovered by Collectors about 200 more, say 234 more from various causes escaped our notice, total 16,000. No of children from 1 day to 4 years inclusively 2030, from 4 to 6 years inclusively 912 from 6 to 7 exclusively 86, total number of children under 7 years of age 3028. From 7 to 11 inclusively 1963 from 11 to 14 inclusively 257, total from 7 to 14 inclusively 2220, total number of children from 1 day to 14 years inclusively 5,248. At Catholic Schools 1060. At Protestant Schools 93. No of Protestant wives 38 Do of Husbands 70. No of Baptisms from July 2 1854 to July 2 1855 1,153.

Observations

The baptisms represent a larger population than 16,000, but the excess either lives not here, or is brought up protestant. Firstly we baptise children of Tramps and foreigners. Secondly bastards including those of prostitutes, these are almost invariably brought up in the Workhouse religion. 3rdly children belonging to parents of no religion brought by Catholics to the chapel sometimes because they seem to be dying and sometimes because the parents have a preference in that way and say the child may be a Catholic. 4thly Children of mixed marriages where we lose largely, many of those after public (and sometimes before) baptism in the Protestant Church are baptised and registered in our books. 5thly Children of persons descended either immediately or remotely of parents, sometimes one only and sometimes both Catholic, but either Protestant or of no religion, are brought by Catholic relatives to be baptised. 6thly there is always a certain amount of emigration from this parish. 7thly Every year especially years of unusual sickness, large numbers of our children are taken into the workhouse and brought up Protestants. This fact is notorious. These children are not kept in any of the workhouses of our District.

Two examples will illustrate this matter. Last year a girl of about 15 years of age came to me and was prepared for her first Communion. Not long before she was placed in the situation she then held, by the workhouse authorities. At ten years of age she was taken into the workhouse and though she knew the Catholic prayers, she was compelled to learn the Protestant and live so in all respects. About the age of 13, she was confirmed in the Protestant Church of St Georges in the East with many others from the workhouse about fifty others as far as she could recollect like herself, were of Catholic parents, but she did not know of any of them who returned to the Catholic Church when free from the authority of the workhouse. Whilst at Portsea several young men connected mainly with the Army or Navy came to me for their Baptismal Certificates, some of them descended of mixed marriages and some of parents both Catholic. These were almost invariably ignorant of the Catholic faith, having been brought up at some government establishment or at some local Protestant School or having entered their situations as lads and compelled always to attend Protestant service. I offered to teach them the Catholic faith, for which some seemed grateful, but none of them ever came. In most cases, I should say, such persons always mixing with Protestants, marry Protestant wives and the children are brought up in the sect to which the mother belongs.

I have come to this conclusion that baptisms however good as a test in reference to the population of a Protestant or Catholic country is fallacious in reference to the Catholic population of this country.

The next point is in reference to the children and the number of them at our Schools.

I regretted very much my inability to reckon the number of children prevented from attending school owing to the physical necessities of their parents. To make it a truthful test required an amount of investigation, for which I had not time. But it is a fact that hundreds of the children of this district are like the birds of the air, depending on each days labour for their sustenance, from the age of seven years and upwards labouring after one fashion or another from early morn, to late at nights. No system can educate this class of children unless schools that could feed and clothe them. I must observe that I do not count our school children as they are sometimes counted elsewhere (in great simplicity and I believe good faith) viz by adding the night to the day school, it being overlooked that generally five sixths of the children at the night school, are the same as those previously numbered at the day school. By holding out rewards or giving feasts I could make it appear I was educating some three thousand children but all this would end in deceiving myself and alternately disappointing others. The Census gives as nearly as possible the number (as known from other sources) of children receiving a Catholic education in this district at the time it was made. The children going to Protestant Schools represent four or five classes of parents. Those of weak faith and those who according to their own estimate of themselves lacking strong faith. Those where the father is Protestant and those who are too proud to send their children to a Charity School and lastly those who send them through fashion. I ought to have observed that, before the harvest the number of children at our schools was about 1,300 daily, it is not quite so large at present. There are more Protestant husbands than 70, but as their wives have no religious liberty and their children where there are any, are brought up Protestants, I have taken no account of them.

William Kelly

22 Colet Place Commercial Road East August 24 1855

PS Children going to our schools after 11 years of age are very few indeed.

WAA: W2/3/5/45: To Cardinal Wiseman from Fr William Kelly, 22 Colet Place, Commercial Road East, 31st August 1855

My Lord Cardinal,

Having received an invitation from the Clerk to the Board of Guardians of this parish, I, accompanied by the Revd Mr Foley, reached Plashet yesterday about 12¼ o'clock. We received from the Clerk who is a very respectable solicitor a pressing invitation to dine with the Guardians and officers at 4 o'clock PM. My energies both of body and mind have been so long on the strain that I felt unequal to the occasion – the more so as toasts and sentiments were due to be proposed in the presence of half a dozen parsons, which my impaired energy would almost certainly fail to make harmonise with the good cause. We therefore left at 4 o'clock, and walked to Stratford – the distance of about one mile, and took the Railway for Shadwell.

In going to Plashet I had in view to ascertain the number of Catholic children in that institution. Total number of children in the School at present 400 boys and girls. It struck me, nearly half these were Catholic. Mr Foley knew that a Mrs Conway with her four or five children, one or two of whom he brought to their first communion, was there. These two children we saw examined by the Parson as specified in the enclosed paper.

At 2½ o'clock a Class of about 23 boys under examination were requested to write their names and hand round the Slates for inspection. Five of these slates passed through my hands – bearing the following names Driscoll, Regan, Seuet, Gidney and Mills – the three first are manifestly irish names, Souet being generally pronounced by the poor Irish Seuet. Gidney very likely should be Gibney.

At three o'clock a Class of 24 Boys were examined and again five slates passed through my hands, bearing the names of Sullivan and Harrington and three other foreign names which I cannot remember, many eyes being upon me, I did not think it prudent to take notes. Poor Foley was nearly sick seeing So many of our children brought up protestant. About fourteen specimens of the Girls writing were handed round – Six of them bearing Irish names and among them the two girls Conway, whose father was an upholsterer, but having abandoned his family and gone to Australia, the mother was obliged to go into the House and (Institution?).

The Whitechapel and Spitalfields Union has another institution about a mile from Stratford, called the Forest Gate industrial Schools.

A Mrs Conway held at 12 guineas a year the office of needlewoman in that institution but as she was recently ordered to prepare the children for the Sacrament, a large portion of whom she knew to be Catholic, she has resigned her situation on the plea of ill health. I have seen her character from that establishment.

Mr Marshall the inspector of our Catholic Schools once or twice mentioned in my presence that before he was a Catholic he was at Norwood where he saw about 700 Workhouse Boys and that one of the Authorities told him they were all with hardly an exception the children of Catholic parents.

To meet this state of things I would most respectfully suggest the appointment, when it can be done of one or more priests with no other duties except to look after the various industrial and other Schools supported by public money in every part of the diocese. This would frustrate the ruse of the authorities in sending the children from a place where there is an active priest to places where there is not.

Your Eminences most obt.

William Kelly

WAA: W2/3/5/34: To Cardinal Wiseman from Fr William Kelly, 22 Colet Place, Commercial Road East, 5th April 1856

My Lord Cardinal,

I have ordered the benches for the New Church. The expence including architects fees £502. The benefactor who is giving the High Altar & pays me also £10 a month, will pay half the Amt. for the cost of the benches. He will also pay half the cost of the Sanctuary Rail.

A Mr Young of Market Raisen called here and Thursday during my absence, and left his address and taken one of the Patterns, he wishes to do something for the New Church in the way of an Altar or benches, or something of that kind. I hope it is not a hoax; I have however written to him and suggested an Altar & Tabernacle & gates and Railing for the Chapel of the Blessed Sacrament, and said I would write to the Architect, which I have done, that I might be able to let him know the probable expence. I am now under Mr Hartings advice in search of a Layman to guarantee the interest of the mortgage, the Trustees giving him a bond of indemnity.

As to the financial arrangements of the church, very considerable latitude must be allowed me, as I shall have to not only accommodate a numerous people but also raise a large revenue to meet the heavy demands permanent and transitory upon such an establishment. Your Eminence suggested yesterday there should be no altar on the east isle & it is certainly my wish, there should be none in the west isle. At the

South end of the former I would put a statue of the Immaculate Conception and in the latter one of St Patrick. But whether putting up these statues in such a place be your task or not your Eminence must decide. The High Altar and that of the Most Holy Sacrament will be sufficient for us.

My present views as to the price of admissions are these: There will be free space at each mass for three or four hundred. I purpose therefore charging for admission to the benches and chairs at the 7, 8, 9, 10 oclock masses one penny. The school children of course are free and will fill half the church at the 9 oclock mass. At the 11 oclock High mass 2d each person. At these masses the people would be admitted indiscriminately to every part of the church. First come, first served. For great benefactors I would of course, feel it my duty to reserve chairs.

At 7 oclock Vespers and Benediction, each person 1d. I purpose having a service for the Children at 3 oclock PM. Catechism, Catechestical instruction, Vespers and Benediction. At 7 oclock PM, I would not allow any children into the church except accompanied by their parents and paid for.

From the preceding your Eminence will see that I do not purpose letting seats by the quarter half year or year. I should not wish this to be made public at present as it might add to my difficulties.

There is another point on which I must now touch, and I do so with great reluctance; I have always endeavoured however feebly to confine myself to the work set before me and though holding opinions on passing events and the occurrences of the day, as strong probably as any man, not to allow them to interfere with the honest views, convictions and duties of others. In the present case I have no alternative. The Rev Mr Kyne, I feel confident, wishes to come to this mission, and I hope your Eminence will not allow it. We are and have always been good friends as far as I know, but we never did or could agree in our view of things missionary or parochial. In a word, I was as long as he would allow it, good friends with Mr Hodgson though I looked upon him as three parts cracked and Kyne I do not consider much better on many points.

your Eminence's obed
William Kelly

WAA: W2/1/7/8: To Cardinal Wiseman from Fr William Kelly, St Mary and St Michael's, Commercial Road, 23rd January 1857

I am happy to have to tell your Eminence that we are going on gloriously. I enclose the prospectus of what we are doing. I have also engaged a permanent catechist for the new church, a middle-aged woman at the rate of 10/ per week. I have long wished to be able to do this, as there was a certain class of children and Adults, that were outside the pale of instruction altogether. Here a large number of the children go to service when they get the chance, at 8 or 9 years of age, or go on the street to sell water cresses etc and Sunday is their best day. Again the same children will return to some of the schools for a short time, but off they are again as soon as anything turns up, by which they can earn a crust. On a rough calculation, I should say that half of the children that pass through our schools never learn to read.

As a fact I know, many of the parents are so pressed by physical want and misery that they send their children to the schools by starts hoping they may be brought to communion and be confirmed before, as they express it, they are tossed on the wide world. A large number of these children leave the schools, before they are brought to the sacraments. And as they cannot read, the difficulty of bringing them to the sacraments is very great. Night schools won't do, as that is sometimes the best market time, and if they are in service, they will not be allowed out. I have tried some experiments on night schools worthy of notice. Before Mr Phillips left John Street several persons in the parish, urged him to open night schools and they would find the money, which however they forgot to do. He opened the schools and had to find the money. I succeeded to the legacy.

I closely inspected the day and night schools and it seemed to me, the same children I saw at night, were also at school during the day. I mentioned my impressions to the teachers who by no means concurred in my opinion. I ordered the teachers to send the children to their seats and then said aloud all the children now present who were at the day school today turn out and stand around the school. This done there remained out of 60 boys 9 or ten in the seats and there was the same result in reference to the girls. This at once threw light on another matter. I previously observed a great number of the children came to the day school at 11 o'clock instead of 9. These were for the most part the very children that attended both day and night school. It was manifest both times were too much for children of their tender age. The worst part however was that the boys who attended the night schools only were for the most part regular toughs. The moment the schools were broken up and they got the girls in the dark, the scene became shocking, frightful. I came accidentally one night on one of these scenes and had not the Lord restrained my arm, I think I would have felled to the ground both male and female teachers. Those villainous boys and not unlikely some of the girls as bad, prevented egress from the stairs, boys and girls became huddled together – the boys kissing the girls and pulling their clothes about, shouts and screams intermingled with laughter formed a picture not to be equalled outside a brothel. Since that, there has been no night school in this rectory. By my catechist, who is to devote the whole time to this matter and suit her time to the class of persons alone alluded to, I hope on this head great good will have been done, without any admixture of evil. She attends during the confession hours and already I have sent her several boys and girls. I have requested the clergy to do the same, more especially when they attend the sick to make enquiries about the children that cannot go to school and have not gone to the sacraments.

This splendid church has in the eyes of our protestant neighbours raised this poor congregation at least fifty years in social position and consideration. And under God's blessing will in time do quietly yet really mighty things not only for the present congregation but for many outside it at present.

The wooden hoarding is still up, and it is wretchedly dirty and muddy going into the Church, the last few weeks, yet I have got each Sunday four or five pounds more than I would have got at Virginia Street and John Streets taken together, and as the tariff is lower than in the old buildings, surely this is proof positive that a much larger number attend now than formerly.

The children are free, no small congregation in themselves. They have half the pews at the 9 o'clock Mass. The girls in the Nave and the boys in the Isles – the whole of the Pews for the purpose of catechism classes at 3 o'clock. We are not yet moulded into shape, but shall be soon. Before Benediction, I give them a short discourse, and our attendance fourfold what it used to be. When they sing in tune with the organ, the effect is very fine. To be even with the soupers the children are not marched in [ladies?] to the church nor from it, so they will have some difficulty in finding out their whereabouts in order to torture them. The teachers of each school have to be in the church to look after their respective children and the regular catechist after those, who do not attend the day schools.

I have requested Mr Wardle to go to Moorfields and see the Archiepiscopal throne, and to give Mr Bird the drawing of one, which can be safely put up and taken down in St Mary and St Michaels, as I was sure your Eminence would pay us a visit, and many of them as soon as we were in a condition properly to receive you. The presbytery is far advanced the two upper floors are boarded, but this damp weather everything is in a great mess. I hope that Propagation will have the charity to send something to St Mary and St Michael's this year. I am going on with my weekly collections as usual. Any time after Easter would suit us very well for the confirmation. The Redemptorist Fathers will begin their mission here on the second Saturday of Lent. Would it be convenient for your Eminence to be present at the closing of it, which I suppose will be on a Sunday evening it is to continue three weeks. As their regular catechist will not be here I shall have to prepare the children for their first communion.

WAA: W2/1/7/9: To Cardinal Wiseman from Fr William Kelly, St Mary and St Michael's, Commercial Road, 14th December 1860

My Lord Cardinal,

The Vicar General Dr Hearn wrote to me a few days ago, telling me your Eminence's attention was now especially turned towards the East of London, with great anxiety and hopefulness. Since that I saw Dr Hearn twice, and it has struck me, I ought to put in a permanent form the substance of our conversation containing my own views about this mission – so that your Eminence might reflect, modify or adapt them as seemed fit to you. Your predecessors as far as I can see did little or nothing for this mission. It may seem that at one time the Vicar gave fifteen hundred pounds towards the purchase of the ground here in the Commercial Road, but from the accounts in my hands, it appears this amount was the results of collections made here for a long series of years and lodged in the hands of the Vicar. But of course it is far from my intention to cast any blame on them. No doubt they did everything according to the best of their judgement.

To begin with the church, here are its present liabilities. Messrs Bird 5,446:2:3. Messrs Hardman £803. Wardell £130. Mortgage 3,000. Total £9,379:2:3. interest on the above at five per cent £468:19 – more two life policies for £3,000 = 95:4:0 annually – total interest to pay £564:3:0.

In order to induce Mr Bird to go on with the New Church I had to obtain from your Eminence an undertaking that, this mission, should not be divided for ten years. About four years of this time remain yet. But if any charitable person would pay off Mr Bird, that undertaking would at once cease. Now taking the number of my congregation that do or can attend Mass on Sundays, I believe this Church with its various services, is capable of accommodating a much larger congregation. But suppose this fact admitted, it by no means follows, that for the general interest and progress of religion, this congregation ought not to be divided. But what I submit is this that the school question, if possible ought first of all, before clashing interest come into the way, to be permanently settled. I suppose Father Glenie told your Eminence of my interview with him in reference to religious teachers, and its failure. We have at present in the mission ample school accommodation and all the buildings are in the right place, a few infant schools here and there as circumstances may permit, would complete the whole matter. The buildings are as follows – Red Lion Street Wapping now nearly finished consists of three large schoolrooms, four classrooms, three sets of closets and a lavatory for the Girls. This building is freehold and capable of accommodating seven hundred children.

Pell Street close to Rosemary Lane, this was a Methodist chapel which as subtenant I took on a lease of 45 years, the longest term that could be granted. I had in view as circumstances might permit to buy out the ground landlord. The rent is £32 a year. I formed this building into two schools. At right angles but abutting onto this building were two ragged schools belonging to Lord Shaftesburys Society. About two years ago, I gook a letter for a lease for 25 years of these two rooms and opened them into the other schools rent £18 a year that is £50 for the entire building as it now stands. This building is now under substantial repair and is capable of accommodating seven hundred children.

John Street Commercial Road. The led in the windows, is no longer capable of holding glass so under the architects Wilson and Nicholls, and with the sanction of Canon ONeal I have entered into a contract to have all the tracery in the windows, except the central mullion, cut away and solid glass substituted, also what was the kitchen formed into a classroom etc. This building when finished will be capable of accommodating about seven hundred children. The rent is £30 yearly but the tenure is not good as the Mercers Company do not sell the ground, and indeed there is only as yet the promise of a lease as Messrs Harting have not moved in the matter as far as I know since I placed the papers in their hands. The convent private school will accommodate about one hundred children.

The whole of the schools when finished I shall owe I conceal nothing as nearly as possible five hundred pounds that is I shall want that amount as follows – on the convent school and fitting up the convent £300 on all the rest of the schools two hundred pounds.

Having now faithfully stated all the liabilities of the mission, I shall conclude my remarks in reference to the school question. Suppose the liability on the church lightened, the next step ought to be to build a convent for the Nuns on freehold ground, with ample space for extension. Thus a sufficient number of Nuns could be got for the schools and sick and other purposes even Poplar schools might be attended by the Nuns. Install a body of religious teachers in the Nuns present convent, they might take in Poplar schools. When all this was effected then let a church be built on freehold ground in or near the Minories to which a district might be assigned Pell Street schools being in the district. Then another Church in Wapping including the schools there also. Another might also be back at a remote corner of this district which we call the 'Worlds end' where several districts meet – this, Spicer Street, Hackney Stratford and Poplar.

Your Eminence's most obedt

William Kelly

WAA: W2/3/5/59: To the Vicar General, Dr Hearn, from Fr William Kelly, St Mary and St Michael's, Commercial Road, 20th June 1862

Dear Dr Hearn,

It has been reported to me that you are about sanctioning the opening of a Church in this District. In justice to myself and the creditors of this Church I beg most respectfully to object to the opening of said Church, and in doing so I am only putting in writing what I have so often already expressed to you "viva voce".

Since my incumbency, no works of any kind have been commenced or undertaken here without the proper ecclesiastical sanction. This is a very important principle in reference to the creditors. Allow me to say that before I undertook the continuation of the buildings in this mission I was fully under the impression that the Hierarchy amongst other things, meant parishes with parochial boundaries which could not be invaded during the life of the incumbent, without his consent.

When arrived here and finding out my mistake I made up my mind to resign unless I got an undertaking from the Cardinal that this mission was not to be divided for ten years. That undertaking I have now in my possession and Dr Errington said I was to keep it safely as it was a document binding on the present bishop and to be respected by his successor. Hence when you first spoke to me about dividing this mission, I wrote to the Cardinal reminding him of the aforesaid document. When Canon ONeal was consulted about purchasing the building in Union St Whitechapel, I sent him a respectful protest against opening that building as a church till a marked portion of the debt was paid off by this Church, and requested him to bring my protest before His Eminence the Cardinal.

The opening of the church in Union St Whitechapel will diminish the revenue with which I have to support this church and its clergy and to meet the just debts of its creditors and such opening is in substance a material infringement of the agreement above referred to, the pith of which was and is to prevent the abstraction of revenue or its sources during the number of years so specified. The mortgager and Mr Bird are aware of all I have written in this communication and they were influenced by those considerations in allowing this Church to be opened.

Yours obediently

William Kelly PS I have of course kept a copy of this note for my own justification and also sent a copy to Very Revd Canon ONeal.

WAA: W2/3/5/62: To Cardinal Wiseman from Fr William Kelly, St Mary and St Michael's, Commercial Road, 17th March 1863

Red Lion St Schools

My Lord Cardinal,

As Fathers Padbury and Bourke were present at the catechetical examination of the children of the above schools by the Revd Mr McMullin and they were not satisfied I spoke to the Master Mr Guilmartin. In fairness to Guilmartin, I think the Revd Mr McMullin ought to have recorded a fact of very considerable importance namely that the examination took place on a Friday, as it is well known all over London, the schools are nearly one third less in numbers than on any other day of the week. The oldest and best instructed of the children being kept at home by their parents, to prepare for Sunday. Between employers and employed, I am obliged to take this circumstance into account. Yet I am not quite satisfied with Guilmartin. But in the present entanglement with the Committee of Council in reference to Masters and Pupil Teachers and Inspectors it is not so easy to discharge a master as it used to be. Unfortunately I have had some experience in this matter. Some years ago a mistress at Red Lion St grossly neglected her duty, indeed as a married woman having children yearly she could not attend to the school and her children. I spoke to her privately and as she admitted the facts, I advised her to send me a letter resigning the situation and if she did so no one should know from me that her resignation was compulsory. She agreed. But the next time I went to the school, she became very impudent to me before the children. I then gave her written notice to quit after the Inspectors examination as I did not think it fair she should be deprived of her years pay from the Committee of Council. But lo and behold before I knew where I was standing I was in an embroilment. My notice to her to quit was taken or sent by one of the Priests here to one of the Vicars General, he took it or sent it to Marshall and thus was I put upon my defence. It was a fatal mistake to give Marshall the idea he had any thing to do with the retaining or dismissal of teachers. About the time of the examination I sent Marshall the usual invitation to dinner, which he never answered. Understanding the cause, I sent him a tolerably peremptory note to call at my house before going to the schools. I had it in my power to get him cashiered for the reason for which he ultimately lost his situation namely neglect of his duty and consequent false reports. This matter caused me no small loss of time and no little annoyance. Afterwards I took on his recommendation "the three first teachers in Europe" from St Leonards. With the exception of morality there never was a more perfect breakdown. His own reports disclose this, but he threw all the fault on the buildings. Then came from the Committee of Council peremptory orders about the Buildings that all Grants would be withheld unless they were put in order. It was this set of circumstances that led me to seek for nuns some three or four years sooner than intended. And thus by throwing so many things into a few years, I became financially embarrassed. To add to the confusion four or five Nuns I sent to St Leonards were refused their certificates of merit on the charge of copying. Marshall from being a worshipper of nuns became their enemy because his demigod McMullin hated them owing to some row he had at Chelsea. I believe from what I heard from Sandford head of the Pupil teachers department of the Council office, it was through Marshalls report from St Leonards my Nuns got into trouble.

The second case was this: a master whom I found here Fahy by name, was reported to me as having recently married another mans wife. I spoke to him on the subject he denied it. I said to him my authority for the statement was good and if I got some further facts to substantiate the charge I would be obliged to discharge him. In two or three days he resigned and bought an action against me for seventy pounds sterling for services rendered to the collection for the New Church. The second master Scott now in Australia would if Fahy succeeded have done the same thing and likely enough some of the collectors would have followed suit. At that time Guilmartin recently appointed to Red Lion St rendered me most important service and hence I feel some consideration is due to him. But the Schools will be all right. The Nuns are now free from the embarrassment of the Committee of Council and have no excuse for not giving first rate religious instruction. But it has hitherto been quite different with the masters and mistresses and I don't know that the New Code will relieve them much. To begin at the beginning and without blame to any one at the initiation of a new system, the appointment of the two first Catholic Inspectors was a great mistake. Their appointment seemed to have divested them of all common sense. Not content with the standard of education laid down by the Committee of council which is now admitted on all hands to have been too high, they had a higher standard of their own and unless the teachers whipped up the children to this standard, they had to fear loss of character and salary. The consequences to the great body of the children were most unjust. I found it out in this way. I had at one time 3 certificated masters and 3 certificated mistresses and 27 Pupil teachers. Yet I never found so many complaints amongst the parents of the children. I was puzzled. I visited the schools and examined class after class and soon found the complaints were well grounded. In order to please the Inspector, the teacher had to devote the whole of his or her time to the first class. The character of the teacher depended on this class. The masters wished me to represent the whole matter to the Committee of Council, but if I did, Marshall would have been cashiered. Hence I refused. But since Morell has been appointed I told him plainly I would not tolerate such a system in future. To return to Father McMulllin and his ecclesiastical reports of which I know nothing except in reference to Red Lion St I believe he has been completely duped. One year he had a set number of questions for every school. After he examined the first school in the Dioces, the questions were known the next day all over London and of course were very satisfactorily answered in all the schools except the first; which he said afterwards was the worst in the Dioces except his own Nuns School. I dare say he sent in some good reports now and again from the Schools of this mission but he was deceived by the flash class as Marshall wished to be deceived. It is to be hoped that under the New Code the certificated teachers will be able to get their salaries and also to teach the Catechism as it ought to be taught.

Certainly here it must be done. I have already proclaimed public examinations at each school before or after the summer examinations at which all the clergy and the parents of the children are to attend. Hence when I discharge a teacher the parents will see he ought to be discharged.

I am sorry this communication should be so lengthy but the questions has so many ins and outs it cannot be briefly stated. The last point however refers to numbers, I cannot state if Father McMullins 200 be correct or not but if so there are more causes than the high payments which under the circumstances could not be helped. The block of buildings in Pell St near Rosemary Lane is capable of containing at least six hundred children, this is to all intents and purposes a free school, is taught by the Nuns and a certificated master it is never sufficiently filled. It is a ragged school though frequented by children able to pay in the other schools. Some two or three years ago on the representation of my masters who threatened to resign unless the Spicer St Fathers were restrained from receiving such large numbers of their Scholars drawn away by all sorts of inducements, I made a representation to your Eminence, as the Masters said they could neither prepare the children for the secular or ecclesiastical Inspectors. At that time there were about 400 four hundred children little weeds thrown on the bosom of the Thames floating between Spicer St Schools and Commercial Road Schools. I don't know at present how the matter stands but I shall enquire. I see Mr Purcell says he has three hundred children in his schools. Those scholars are partly drawn from our Schools and from those of this mission that went to Spicer St. Our Schools are capable of accommodating every child in this mission but constant disturbing causes throw all calculations overboard; and prevent consolidation. The last eighteen months two private schools in addition to two others already existing were opened in this mission charging on the average more than is charged in any of the parochial schools. These have drawn away several children. It is illegal to denounce them from the altar and the ignorant people who send their children drawn from our schools would rebel. It is to no purpose hitherto we use all private efforts to extinguish them. They are the sources of fearful immorality, boys and Girls corrupting each other and then bring the plague into our schools.

Your Eminences most obd servt
William Kelly

Sources and acknowledgements

Archival Material:

- Archives of the Convent of Mercy, Hardinge Street
- Westminster Archdiocesan Archives: A53 III L 31 (letter of Virginia Street priests to Bp Douglass), AAW: W2/1/7/6; AAW: W2/1/7/8; AAW: W2/1/7/9; AAW: W2/1/7/10; AAW: W2/3/5/3; AAW: W2/3/5/8; AAW: W2/3/5/11; AAW: W2/3/5/13; AAW: W2/3/5/14; AAW: W2/3/5/34; AAW: W2/3/5/45; AAW: W2/3/5/48; AAW: W2/3/5/53; AAW: W2/3/5/59; AAW: W2/3/5/62 (correspondence of Fr Kelly with Cardinal Wiseman); AAW: W3/36/74 (letter from Fr Santry); SMSM box (Minute book of Virginia Street Auxiliary Catholic Institute, Canon Ring's diary for 1923, typescript accounts of Rosary Crusade by Canon Fitzgerald, etc)
- Brentwood Diocesan Archives: Correspondence and other material concerning Fr John Moore
- Charles Booth Archive, c/o London School of Economics: B209, B221, B387
- Arundel Castle Archives: Correspondence of the 15th Duke of Norfolk, CH/3/54, CH/3/ 55, CH/6/108 (letters from Fr Gorman)
- City of London, London Metropolitan Archives: MR/R/H/1/10 (registration of St Mary and St Michael's, 1791)

Periodicals:

Catholic Miscellany, Truthteller, Orthodox Journal, Tablet, Weekly Register, Universe, Catholic Times, Catholic Herald, Monitor, Monitor and New Era, Catholic Standard and Ransomer, East London Observer, East London Advertiser, Jewish Chronicle, Rector's Realm/ Messenger of the Sacred Heart 1906-40 (c/o Westminster Diocesan Archives)

Select bibliography of published works:

- Memoirs of Missionary Priests, Bishop Challoner, 1741
- London Labour and the London Poor, Henry Mayhew, 1851-52
- Ragged London, John Hollingshead, 1861
- Bibliographical Dictionary of the English Catholics Vol III, Joseph Gillow, 1887
- The Story of the Dock Strike, H Llewellyn Smith and Vaughan Nash, 1889
- Father Mathew, Frank J Mathew, 1890
- Catholic London Missions, Johanna Harting, 1903
- Personal Reminiscences of Fifty Years, Rev E Pennington, 1905
- Catholic London a Century Ago, Bernard Ward, 1905
- Biographies of English Catholics, John Kirk, 1909
- The Life and Times of Bishop Challoner Vol II, Edwin H Burton, 1909
- The Dawn of the Catholic Revival in England, Bernard Ward, 1909

- The Eve of Catholic Emancipation, Bernard Ward, 1911-12
- The Sequel to Catholic Emancipation, Bernard Ward, 1915
- Random Recollections of Homerton Mission, Langton George Vere, 1912
- Settlement Work, Lady Edmund Talbot, 1913
- Rescue Work, Lady Edmund Talbot, 1914
- Three Historical Sermons, Canon Burton, June 1920
- Henry Edward Manning, Shane Leslie, 1921
- Father Bernard Vaughan, C C Martindale, 1924
- London Catholic Churches, Alexander Rottmann, 1926
- Francis Cardinal Bourne, Ernest Oldmeadow, 1940
- Letters of Herbert Cardinal Vaughan to Lady Herbert of Lea, ed Shane Leslie, 1942
- The Young Christian Workers, Vincent Rochford, 1943
- Cockney Campaign, Frank Lewey, 1944
- Fenian Memories, Mark Ryan, 1946
- These My Brethren, R G Burnett, 1946
- Our Flag Stays Red, Phil Piratin, 1948
- The East End of London, Millicent Rose, 1951
- Mother Mary Potter, Patrick Dougherty, 1961
- Cardinal Manning, Vincent Alan McClelland, 1962
- The R.C.s, George Scott, 1967
- Stepney Churches, Gordon Barnes, 1967
- Shepherd of the Second Spring, Jude Mead, 1968
- The Roman Catholic Mission to the Irish in London, Sheridan Gilley, in Recusant History Vol 10, 1969
- Roman Catholics in London, K G T McDonnell, in: Studies in London History, ed Hollaender and Kellaway, 1969
- The Story of Catholic Wapping, Vincent Worley, 1971
- The Garibaldi Riots of 1862, Sheridan Gilley, in: the Historical Journal, Dec 1973
- One Hundred Years of the Catohlic Church in Southend-on-Sea and its Neighbourhood, Canon Fr Dobson, in: Essex Recusant Vol 15, 1973
- Cardijn, Marguerite Fievez and Jacques Meert, 1974
- Point of Arrival, Chaim Bermant, 1975
- The Christian Brothers in England 1825-1880, William Liguori Gillespie, 1975
- The New Poor Law in the Nineteenth Century, ed Derek Fraser, 1976
- Exiles of Erin, Lynn Hollen Lees, 1979
- A History of Tower Hamlets, Colm Kerrigan,1982
- Charles Lowder and the Ritualist Movement, L E Ellsworth, 1982
- Nicholas Wiseman, Richard Schiefen, 1984
- Westminster, Whitehall and the Vatican, Thomas Moloney, 1985
- The Red Cliffs of Stepney, J E Connor & B J Critchley, 1986

- Amigo Friend of the Poor, Michael Clifton, 1987
- Edith and Stepney, Bertha Sokoloff, 1987
- Gloucestershire Catholic Martyrs, P & M Gethen, Gloucestershire and North Avon Catholic History Society, 1987
- The Great Dock Strike 1889, Terry McCarthy, 1988
- Reapers of the Harvest, John Sharp, 1989
- Returns of Papists Vol II, ed E S Worrall, Catholic Record Society, 1989
- London Jewry and London Politics, Geoffrey Alderman, 1989
- A Survey of the Irish in England, Hugh Heinrick, ed Alan O'Day, 1990
- Catholic Poor Schools in Tower Hamlets 1765-1856 Part 1: Wapping and Commercial Road, Michael Murphy, 1991
- English and Welsh Priests 1801-1914, Charles Fitzgerald- Lombard, 1993
- Cardinal Herbert Vaughan, Robert O'Neil, 1995
- London Jews and British Communism, Henry Felix Srebrnik, 1995
- The Tower Hamlets Connection, Harold Finch, 1996
- East London for Mosley, Thomas P Linehan, 1996
- All My Yesterdays, Patrick Hanshaw, 1996
- Clem Attlee, Francis Beckett, 1997
- Archbishop Derek Worlock, John Furnival and Ann Knowles, 1998
- Catholic Churches of London, Denis Evinson, 1998
- Charity and the London Hospitals, Keir Waddington, 2000
- The Worlock Archive, Clifford Longley, 2000
- Catholic Charitable Endeavours in London 1810-1840, Brian Carter, in: Recusant History Vol 25, 2001
- The Rise and Fall of the YCW in England, Sylvia Collins and Michael P Hornsby-Smith, in: Journal of Contemporary Religion, Vol 17, No 1, 2002
- Fortress Church, Kester Aspden, 2002
- Bringing Science to Life, Davie E Leaback, in: Science and Public Affairs, Feb 2002
- East End Past, Richard Tames, 2004
- Blitz, M J Gaskin, 2005
- The Diaries of Bishop William Poynter, ed Canon Peter Phillips, Catholic Record Society, 2006
- The New East End, Dench Gavron & Young, 2006

Oral history informants:

Frs Brian Nash, Steve Delany and Bryan Jones, Srs Josephine Browne, Elizabeth O'Connor and Teresita Heenan, Joan Donovan (RIP), Kath Donovan (née Marriott) Marie and Monica Henderson, Maureen Hayward (née Warren), Rosie Armstrong, Margaret Wright, Lily Stone (née Maynard), Natasha Bolter (née Ahmed)

Miscellaneous sources:
Catherine Myer photo on page 322 courtesy of *The Guardian*
Laity/ Catholic Directory; London Post Office Directory; Census Returns; maps; photographs

Grateful thanks to Westminster archdiocesan archivists Miss Poyser, Fr Ian Dickie and Fr Nicholas Schofield; Brentwood diocesan archivist Fr Stewart Foster; Joan Bond of the National Catholic Library; Malcolm Barr-Hamilton, Tower Hamlets Archivist, and Chris Lloyd, Tower Hamlets Local History Librarian; staff of the British Newspaper Library, Colindale; London School of Economics Library; and London Metropolitan Archives; Rosemary Clerkin, Chigwell Convent; the Sisters of Mercy, Hardinge Street (especially archivists Srs Anna Moloney and Josephine Browne, and Sr Elizabeth O'Connor); Sr M Raphael Butler, Little Company of Mary Archivist; Sr Joan Conroy, Sisters of Charity of St Vincent de Paul Provincial Archivist; and Fr Peter Harris for all their assistance in tracking down material.

Grateful thanks also to City of London, London Metropolitan Archives for permission to publish image of 1791 registration of St Mary and St Michael's (MR/R/H/1/10); and to the editors of the *Universe* and *East London Advertiser* for permission to use photographs.